STOCK TRADER'S ALMANAC 2027

Jeffrey A. Hirsch & Christopher Mistal

WILEY

www.stocktradersalmanac.com

Published by John Wiley & Sons, Inc., Hoboken, New Jersey.

Editor-in-Chief	Jeffrey A. Hirsch
Director of Research	Christopher Mistal
Graphic Design	Darlene Dion Design
Publisher 1966–2000 & Editor 1966–2003	Yale Hirsch (1923–2021)

ISBN: 9781394441815 (paper)
ISBN: 9781394441839 (ePDF)
ISBN: 9781394441822 (ePub)
SKY10160496_071626

THE 2027 STOCK TRADER'S ALMANAC

CONTENTS

DIRECTORY OF TRADING PATTERNS AND DATABANK

STRATEGY PLANNING AND RECORD SECTION

INTRODUCTION TO THE 60TH ANNIVERSARY EDITION

We are honored to present the 60th anniversary annual edition of the *Stock Trader's Almanac*. The *Almanac* provides you with the necessary tools and data to invest and trade successfully in the twenty-first century.

In 1966, Yale Hirsch founded the *Stock Trader's Almanac* on the conviction that humans and their institutions are creatures of habit, and they move their money and assets in well-defined, repetitive patterns. That conviction is still the heart of this book.

Six decades on, in an era when artificial intelligence can summarize the past in seconds, identifying market cycles matters more, not less. AI retrieves history. It does not understand it. Machines can read every market report ever written in an afternoon. They still can't tell you why October bottoms, why Januarys forecast, or why presidents matter to price. Pattern recognition without context is just noise compression. Sixty years of pattern recognition is the asset that compounds when everything else gets commoditized.

Santayana warned that those who fail to remember the past are condemned to repeat it. We've always believed: "Those who understand history are bound to profit from it."

J.P. Morgan's classic retort "Stocks will fluctuate" is often quoted with a wink-of-the-eye implication that the only prediction one can make about the stock market is that it will go up, down, or sideways. Many investors and traders agree that no one ever really knows which way the market will move. Nothing could be further from the truth.

We discovered many years ago that while stocks do indeed fluctuate, they do so in well-defined, often predictable patterns. These patterns recur too frequently to be the result of chance or coincidence. How else do we explain that since 1950 the Dow has gained 7.2% on average during November through April compared to just 1.1% May through October? (See page 54.)

The *Almanac* is a practical investment tool. It alerts you to those little-known market patterns and tendencies on which shrewd professionals enhance profit potential. You will be able to forecast market trends with accuracy and confidence when you use the *Almanac* to help you understand:

- How our presidential elections affect the economy and the stock market—just as the moon affects the tides. Many investors have made fortunes following the political-cycle. You can be sure that money managers who control billions of dollars are also political-cycle watchers. Astute people do not ignore a pattern that has been working effectively throughout most of our economic history.

- How the passage of the Twentieth Amendment to the Constitution fathered the January Barometer. This barometer has an outstanding record for predicting the general course of the stock market each year with only 12 major errors since 1950 for an 84.2% accuracy ratio. (See page 18.)

- Why there is a significant market bias at certain times of the day, week, month and year.

Even if you are an investor who pays scant attention to cycles, indicators, and patterns, your investment survival could hinge on your interpretation of one of the recurring patterns found within these pages. One of the most intriguing and important patterns is the symbiotic relationship between Washington and Wall Street. Aside from the potential profitability in seasonal patterns, there's the pure joy of seeing the market very often do just what you expected.

The *Stock Trader's Almanac* is also an organizer. Its wealth of information is presented on a calendar basis. The *Almanac* puts investing in a business framework and makes it easier because it:

- Updates investment knowledge and informs you of new techniques and tools.
- Is a monthly reminder and refresher course.
- Alerts you to both seasonal opportunities and dangers.
- Furnishes a historical viewpoint by providing pertinent statistics on past market performance.
- Supplies forms necessary for portfolio planning, record keeping, and tax preparation.

The WITCH icon signifies THIRD FRIDAY OF THE MONTH on calendar pages and alerts you to extraordinary volatility due to expiration of monthly equity options, index options, and index futures contracts. "Triple-Witching" days appear during March, June, September, and December (see page 108).

The BULL icon on calendar pages signifies favorable trading days based on the S&P 500 rising 60% or more of the time on a particular trading day during the 21-year period January 2005 to December 2025.

A BEAR icon on calendar pages signifies unfavorable trading days based on the S&P falling 60% or more of the time for the same 21-year period.

Clusters of two or more BULLs or BEARs can be especially helpful in identifying periods of strength or weakness throughout the year. Clusters can also be three out of four days or three out of five days. An example of four BEARs in five days can be observed on pages 91 and 93 from September 21 to 27. One of the most bullish weeks of the year is illustrated by a streak of five BULLs in a row during the first week of November on page 103.

On pages 123–130 you will find complete Market Probability Calendars for both the long term and the recent 21-year period for the Dow, S&P and NASDAQ, as well as for the Russell 1000 and Russell 2000 indices. To give you even greater perspective, we have listed on the weekly planner pages next to the date every day that the market is open, the market probability numbers for the same 21-year period for the Dow (D), S&P 500 (S) and NASDAQ (N). You will see a "D," "S" and "N" followed by a number signifying the actual market probability number for that trading day based on the recent 21-year period.

Other seasonalities near the ends, beginnings, and middles of months; options expirations, around holidays and other times are noted for *Almanac* investors' convenience on the weekly planner pages. All other important economic releases are provided in the Strategy Calendar every month in our digital newsletter, *Almanac Investor*, available at our website *www.stocktradersalmanac.com*. Please see a special offer for new subscribers between pages 66 and 67.

One-year seasonal pattern charts for Dow, S&P 500, NASDAQ, Russell 1000, and Russell 2000 appear on pages 42 and 44. There is one chart of the Dow that spans our entire database starting in 1901, one each for the Dow and S&P 500 back to 1950 and one each for the younger indices. As 2027 is a pre-election year, each chart contains typical pre-election-year performance compared to all years.

The Russell 2000 is an excellent proxy for small- and mid-caps, and the Russell 1000 provides a broader view of large caps. Annual highs and lows for all five indices covered in the *Almanac* appear on pages 151–155. Top "10 Best & Worst" days, weeks, months, quarters, and years for all five indices are listed on pages 174–183.

We have converted many of the paper forms in our Record Keeping section into spreadsheets for our own internal use. As a service to our faithful readers, we are making these forms available at our website *www.stocktradersalmanac.com*. Look for a link titled "Forms" at the bottom of the home page.

You can find all the market charts of pre-election years from 1943 to 2023 on page 26. "Pre-Presidential Election Years: Only One Loser In 88 Years" on page 28 showcases the amazing streak and impressive gains in the pre-election year. "Why A 50% Move in the Dow Is Possible From Its 2026 Low to Its 2027 High" is detailed on page 30.

"Welcome to the Sweet Spot of the 4-Year Cycle" on page 34 explains the usual weakness that occurs during Q2 and Q3 of the midterm, setting up the "Sweet Spot" of the 4-Year Cycle from Q4 in the midterm year through Q2 pre-election year and beyond. On page 86, our "Best Investment Books of the Year" features half a dozen hand-picked recently published off-the-radar titles that help frame the future of the AI Super Boom and a few savvy practical market navigation manuals.

"Bulls Win When Market Hits the January Trifecta" on page 20 shows a new indicator we built in 2013 that combines our Santa Claus Rally (page 118) and January Barometer (page 18) with the First Five Days (page 16), creating a more powerful indicator. On page 104 is a new trading strategy, "Traders Feast on Small Stocks Thanksgiving through Santa Claus Rally."

"How to Trade Best Months Switching Strategies" appears on page 38. "Summer Market Volume Doldrums Drives Worst Six Months" is updated on page 50. Revised sector seasonalities including several consistent shorting opportunities, appear on pages 94–98.

Our 2027 Outlook on pages 10–11 forecasts a classic pre-election year. This is the strongest year of the Four-Year Presidential Election Cycle, averaging 17.2% since 1949 and up 17 of the last 19. After volatility early in Q1 and through

NASDAQ's notorious Worst Four Months July–October, the 4-Year Cycle "Sweet Spot" favors strengthening conditions and a move to new highs into year-end.

On page 46 we reflect on our "60 Years on the Street: Market Cycles That Still Work" and on page 100 we project our outlook for the future with "NASDAQ 74,000: Welcome to the AI Super Boom."

After 60 years, the *Almanac* stands on the shoulders of many. My father Yale Hirsch imagined it in 1966. Sam Coslow lit the fire under him to do it in 1961. And my mother, Davida — six months pregnant with me when Yale went out on his own — ran the business at his side for decades until I was ready to take over. To Chris Mistal, my co-author and partner in the work, and Darlene Dion, our designer — thank you.

Special thanks to those whose work has helped shaped ours: Larry Williams, Sam Stovall, Art Cashin, Marty Zweig, Ned Davis, Ralph Acampora, John Bollinger, Victor Niederhoffer, Larry McMillan, Tom McClellan, Pamela van Giessen, Joe Childrey, John Person, Craig Johnson, Barry Ritholtz, Helene Meisler, Ryan Detrick, JC Parets, Danny Riley, Adrian Zdunczyk, Kim Githler, Judd Brown, Bob Cardwell, and George Brooks.

And to our readers, who have carried this work forward through every cycle since 1966 — thank you.

We are constantly searching for new insights and nuances about the stock market and welcome any suggestions from our readers.

To the next 60 years and beyond!

2027 OUTLOOK

We came into 2026 with a firmly bullish outlook. Our discovery of the Trump Presidency Seasonal Cycle on March 23 helped us call the crisis bottom and anticipate the sharp rebound, keeping newsletter subscribers on the right side of the market. Our base case for 2026 of 8-12% full-year gains remains on track. The ongoing war in Iran and the rising probability of a stalemate will likely keep energy prices, inflation, and interest rates elevated and a lid on equities during the Worst Six Months (May–October) and 4-Year Cycle Weak Spot (midterm Q2–Q3).

In a perfect world, the S&P 500 closes the April ceasefire gap in the 6600–6700 zone sometime in August or September — setting up a textbook launching pad for the sweet spot of the 4-year cycle and a prototypical pre-election year bull run in 2027. Now that the Trump Presidency Seasonal Cycle is widely recognized, the market is desensitized to the pattern of threats and reversals that drove the tape in 2025 and 2026. We suspect seasonal patterns and 4-year cycle forces will be more impactful for the remainder of 2026 and the market's overall trend for 2027.

Pre-election years are the strongest year of the Four-Year Presidential Election

Cycle, averaging 17.2% since 1949 – up 17 of the last 19. Trump's first term pre-election year, 2019, finished with the S&P 500 up 28.9%, against a backdrop that rhymes with the current. Like 2019, 2027's setup features ongoing tariff and trade issues, a market dealing with a midterm crisis, and a Fed in transition. Though today's Fed is confronted with an inflation problem and a deeper, more regime-oriented post-pandemic transition than the 2019 pivot away from an overly restrictive policy posture.

We expect 2027 to follow a classic pre-election-year pattern, with a predominantly upward bias. Periods of volatility, pullback, and consolidation are most likely to occur early in Q1 and during NASDAQ's notorious Worst Four Months July-October. From there, the 4-year cycle favors strengthening conditions and a move to new highs into year-end. This is the Sweet Spot of the 4-Year Cycle and the move from the midterm low to the pre-election year high has averaged a gain of nearly 50% (page 30). A 50% advance from the March 30, 2026, low of 6343.72 projects to roughly 9515 on the S&P 500.

The chart here of the S&P 500 Seasonal Patterns from 1949-2025 depicts three rather bullish scenarios — All Pre-Election Years, the STA Aggregate Cycle, and All Years — and one shakier outlook in the 7th Year of a Presidency. The 7th Year of the Presidency, or the second pre-election year, is a smaller dataset of six and is heavily influenced by the 1987 crash. As 1987 is also the 7th year of the decade and a pre-election year you can also see its effect on All Pre-Election Years and our STA Aggregate Cycle. Save a black swan geopolitical or systemic market event in 2027, which we do not anticipate, our outlook is for base case gains of 12-16% for full-year 2027.

Beyond 2027, the Super Boom thesis we laid out a decade and a half ago has been validated and is still in play. The pre-election year sweet spot is the next leg — see "NASDAQ 74000: Welcome to the AI Super Boom" on page 100.

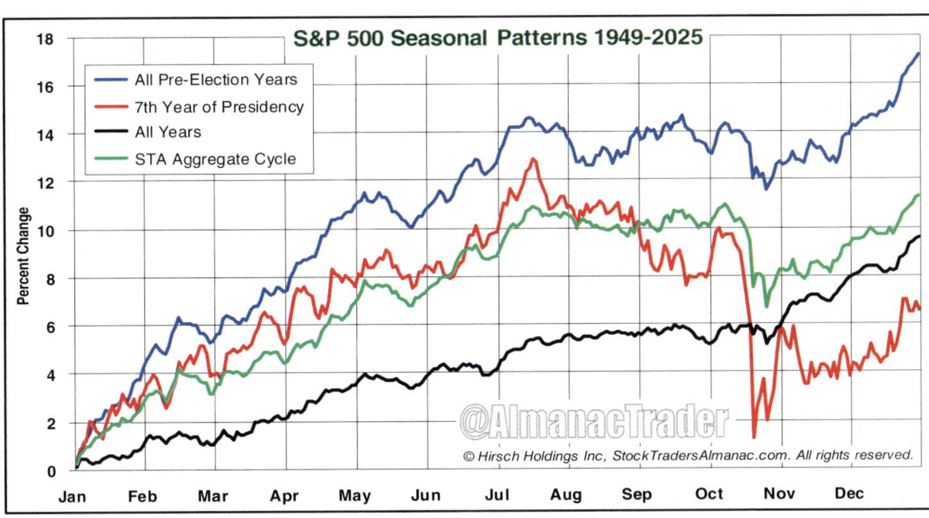

Jeffrey A. Hirsch, May 26, 2026

2027 STRATEGY CALENDAR

(Option expiration dates circled)

	MONDAY	TUESDAY	WEDNESDAY	THURSDAY	FRIDAY	SATURDAY	SUNDAY
	28	29	30	31	1 JANUARY New Year's Day	2	3
	4	5	6	7	8	9	10
JANUARY	11	12	13	14	15	16	17
	18 Martin Luther King Jr. Day	19	20	21	22	23	24
	25	26	27	28	29	30	31
	1 FEBRUARY	2	3	4	5	6	7
FEBRUARY	8	9	10 Ash Wednesday	11	12	13	14 ♥
	15 Presidents' Day	16	17	18	19	20	21
	22	23	24	25	26	27	28
	1 MARCH	2	3	4	5	6	7
	8	9	10	11	12	13	14 Daylight Saving Time Begins
MARCH	15	16	17 ♣ St. Patrick's Day	18	19	20	21
	22	23	24	25	26 Good Friday	27	28 Easter
	29	30	31	1 APRIL	2	3	4
	5	6	7	8	9	10	11
APRIL	12	13	14	15 Tax Deadline	16	17	18
	19	20	21	22 Passover	23	24	25
	26	27	28	29	30	1 MAY	2
	3	4	5	6	7	8	9 Mother's Day
	10	11	12	13	14	15	16
MAY	17	18	19	20	21	22	23
	24	25	26	27	28	29	30
	31 Memorial Day	1 JUNE	2	3	4	5	6
	7	8	9	10	11	12	13
JUNE	14	15	16	17	18	19 Juneteenth	20 Father's Day
	21	22	23	24	25	26	27
	28	29	30	1 JULY	2	3	4 Independence Day

Market closed on shaded weekdays; closes early when half-shaded.

2027 STRATEGY CALENDAR

(Option expiration dates circled)

MONDAY	TUESDAY	WEDNESDAY	THURSDAY	FRIDAY	SATURDAY	SUNDAY	
5	6	7	8	9	10	11	JULY
12	13	14	15	(16)	17	18	
19	20	21	22	23	24	25	
26	27	28	29	30	31	1 AUGUST	
2	3	4	5	6	7	8	AUGUST
9	10	11	12	13	14	15	
16	17	18	19	(20)	21	22	
23	24	25	26	27	28	29	
30	31	1 SEPTEMBER	2	3	4	5	SEPTEMBER
6 Labor Day	7	8	9	10	11	12	
13	14	15	16	(17)	18	19	
20	21	22	23	24	25	26	
27	28	29	30	1 OCTOBER	2 Rosh Hashanah	3	
4	5	6	7	8	9	10	OCTOBER
11 Yom Kippur Columbus Day	12	13	14	(15)	16	17	
18	19	20	21	22	23	24	
25	26	27	28	29	30	31	
1 NOVEMBER	2 Election Day	3	4	5	6	7 Daylight Saving Time Ends	NOVEMBER
8	9	10	11 Veterans' Day	12	13	14	
15	16	17	18	(19)	20	21	
22	23	24	25 Thanksgiving Day	26	27	28	
29	30	1 DECEMBER	2	3	4	5	DECEMBER
6	7	8	9	10	11	12	
13	14	15	16	(17)	18	19	
20	21	22	23	24	25 Chanukah Christmas	26	
27	28	29	30	31	1 JANUARY New Year's Day	2	

JANUARY ALMANAC

JANUARY						
S	M	T	W	T	F	S
				1	2	3
4	5	6	7	8	9	10
11	12	13	14	15	16	17
18	19	20	21	22	23	24
25	26	27	28	29	30	31

FEBRUARY						
S	M	T	W	T	F	S
1	2	3	4	5	6	7
8	9	10	11	12	13	14
15	16	17	18	19	20	21
22	23	24	25	26	27	28

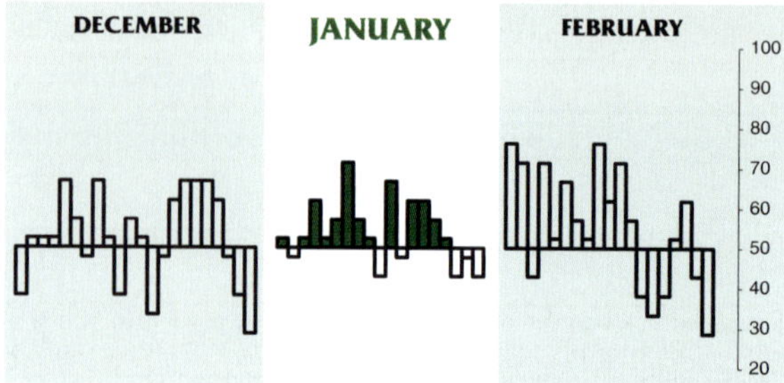

Market Probability Chart above is a graphic representation of the S&P 500 Recent Market Probability Calendar on page 126.

◆ January Barometer predicts year's course with .737 batting average (page 18) ◆ 17 of last 19 pre-election years followed January's direction ◆ Every down January on the S&P since 1950, *without exception*, preceded a new or extended bear market, a flat market, or a 10% correction (page 22) ◆ S&P gains January's first five days preceded full-year gains 83.7% of the time, 14 of last 19 pre-election years followed first five day's direction (page 16) ◆ November, December, and January constitute the year's best three-month span, a 4.3% S&P gain (pages 52 & 149) ◆ January NASDAQ powerful 2.6% since 1971 (pages 60 & 150) ◆ January Effect now starts in mid-December and favors small-cap stocks (pages 112 & 114) ◆ 2009 has the dubious honor of the worst S&P 500 January on record ◆ Dow gained more than 1000 points in 2018 & 2019 ◆ See January Indicator Trifecta (page 20)

January Vital Statistics

	DJIA		S&P 500		NASDAQ		Russell 1K		Russell 2K	
Rank		5		5		1		5		3
Up		49		47		38		30		37
Down		28		30		18		18		21
Average % Change		1.0		1.1		2.6		1.1		1.5
Pre-Election Yr Avg % Chg		3.8		4.2		7.1		3.7		4.4
Best & Worst January										
	% Change		% Change		% Change		% Change		% Change	
Best	1976	14.4	1987	13.2	1975	16.6	1987	12.7	1985	13.1
Worst	2009	–8.8	2009	–8.6	2008	–9.9	2009	–8.3	2009	–11.2
Best & Worst January Weeks										
Best	1/9/76	6.1	1/2/09	6.8	1/12/01	9.1	1/2/09	6.8	1/9/87	7.0
Worst	1/8/16	–6.2	1/8/16	–6.0	1/28/00	–8.2	1/8/16	–6.0	1/21/22	–8.1
Best & Worst January Days										
Best	1/17/91	4.6	1/3/01	5.0	1/3/01	14.2	1/3/01	5.3	1/21/09	5.3
Worst	1/8/88	–6.9	1/8/88	–6.8	1/2/01	–7.2	1/8/88	–6.1	1/20/09	–7.0
First Trading Day of Monthly Options Expiration Week: 1980–2026										
Record (#Up–#Down)		29–18		26–21		24–23		24–23		24–23
Current streak		U2		U2		U1		U2		U2
Avg % Change		0.03		0.02		0.08		–0.004		–0.05
Monthly Options Expiration Day: 1980–2026										
Record (#Up–#Down)		27–20		27–20		28–19		27–20		29–18
Current streak		D1		D1		D1		D1		U4
Avg % Change		0.05		0.09		0.08		0.08		0.25
Monthly Options Expiration Week: 1980–2026										
Record (#Up–#Down)		26–21		22–25		28–19		22–25		26–21
Current streak		D1		D1		D1		D1		U2
Avg % Change		–0.06		0.05		0.36		0.05		0.25
Week After Monthly Options Expiration: 1980–2026										
Record (#Up–#Down)		27–20		29–18		28–19		29–18		31–16
Current streak		D1		D1		D1		D1		D1
Avg % Change		0.12		0.27		0.25		0.25		0.16
First Trading Day Performance										
% of Time Up		59.7		49.4		53.6		45.8		47.9
Avg % Change		0.24		0.14		0.16		0.12		0.05
Last Trading Day Performance										
% of Time Up		53.2		58.4		60.7		54.2		66.7
Avg % Change		0.14		0.2		0.24		0.23		0.18

Dow & S&P 1950–May 1, 2026; NASDAQ 1971–May 1, 2026; Russell 1K & 2K 1979–May 1, 2026.

20th Amendment made "lame ducks" disappear.
Now, "as January goes, so goes the year."

DECEMBER 2026/JANUARY 2027

MONDAY
D 71.4
S 61.9
N 57.1
28

Three passions, simple but overwhelmingly strong, have governed my life: the longing for love, the search for knowledge, and unbearable pity for the suffering of mankind.
— Bertrand Russell (British mathematician and philosopher, 1872-1970)

TUESDAY
D 42.9
S 47.6
N 38.1
29

I really do inhabit a system in which words are capable of shaking the entire structure of government, where words can prove mightier than ten military divisions.
— Vaclav Havel (Czech dramatist, essayist, political leader, and president, b. 1936)

WEDNESDAY
D 42.9
S 38.1
N 33.3
30

The problem with the world is that the intelligent people are full of doubts, while the stupid ones are full of confidence.
— Charles Bukowski (American poet, novelist & writer, *Barfly*, 1920-1994)

Last Trading Day of the Year, NASDAQ Down 20 of last 26
NASDAQ Was Up 29 Years in a Row 1971-1999

THURSDAY
D 33.3
S 28.6
N 28.6
31

We always live in an uncertain world. What is certain is that the United States will go forward over time.
— Warren Buffett (CEO Berkshire Hathaway, investor & philanthropist, CNBC 9/22/2010, b. 1930)

New Years Day *(Market Closed)*

FRIDAY
1

You don't owe anybody anything and nobody owes you nothing. Life is short and everyday is only what you make of it. Nothing more and nothing less.
— Phil Pearlman (Founder, Pearl Institute, b. 1967)

SATURDAY
2

January Almanac Investor Sector Seasonalities: See Pages 94, 96, and 98

SUNDAY
3

JANUARY'S FIRST FIVE DAYS: AN EARLY WARNING SYSTEM

The last 49 up First Five Days were followed by full-year gains 41 times for an 83.7% accuracy ratio and a 14.2% average gain in all 49 years. The eight exceptions include flat years 1994, 2011, 2015, four related to war, and 2018. Vietnam military spending delayed start of 1966 bear market. Ceasefire imminence early in 1973 raised stocks temporarily. Saddam Hussein turned 1990 into a bear. The war on terrorism, instability in the Mideast and corporate malfeasance shaped 2002 into one of the worst years on record. In 2018, a partially inverted yield curve and trade tensions triggered a fourth-quarter selloff. The 27 down First Five Days were followed by 15 up years and 12 down (44.4% accurate) and an average gain of 1.1%.

In pre-election years this indicator has a good record. In the last 19 pre-election years 14 full years followed the direction of the First Five Days. See January Indicator Trifecta (page 20).

THE FIRST-FIVE-DAYS-IN-JANUARY INDICATOR

Chronological Data

	Previous Year's Close	January 5th Day	5-Day Change	Year Change
1950	16.76	17.09	2.0%	21.8%
1951	20.41	20.88	2.3	16.5
1952	23.77	23.91	0.6	11.8
1953	26.57	26.33	−0.9	−6.6
1954	24.81	24.93	0.5	45.0
1955	35.98	35.33	−1.8	26.4
1956	45.48	44.51	−2.1	2.6
1957	46.67	46.25	−0.9	−14.3
1958	39.99	40.99	2.5	38.1
1959	55.21	55.40	0.3	8.5
1960	59.89	59.50	−0.7	−3.0
1961	58.11	58.81	1.2	23.1
1962	71.55	69.12	−3.4	−11.8
1963	63.10	64.74	2.6	18.9
1964	75.02	76.00	1.3	13.0
1965	84.75	85.37	0.7	9.1
1966	92.43	93.14	0.8	−13.1
1967	80.33	82.81	3.1	20.1
1968	96.47	96.62	0.2	7.7
1969	103.86	100.80	−2.9	−11.4
1970	92.06	92.68	0.7	0.1
1971	92.15	92.19	0.04	10.8
1972	102.09	103.47	1.4	15.6
1973	118.05	119.85	1.5	−17.4
1974	97.55	96.12	−1.5	−29.7
1975	68.56	70.04	2.2	31.5
1976	90.19	94.58	4.9	19.1
1977	107.46	105.01	−2.3	−11.5
1978	95.10	90.64	−4.7	1.1
1979	96.11	98.80	2.8	12.3
1980	107.94	108.95	0.9	25.8
1981	135.76	133.06	−2.0	−9.7
1982	122.55	119.55	−2.4	14.8
1983	140.64	145.23	3.3	17.3
1984	164.93	168.90	2.4	1.4
1985	167.24	163.99	−1.9	26.3
1986	211.28	207.97	−1.6	14.6
1987	242.17	257.28	6.2	2.0
1988	247.08	243.40	−1.5	12.4
1989	277.72	280.98	1.2	27.3
1990	353.40	353.79	0.1	−6.6
1991	330.22	314.90	−4.6	26.3
1992	417.09	418.10	0.2	4.5
1993	435.71	429.05	−1.5	7.1
1994	466.45	469.90	0.7	−1.5
1995	459.27	460.83	0.3	34.1
1996	615.93	618.46	0.4	20.3
1997	740.74	748.41	1.0	31.0
1998	970.43	956.04	−1.5	26.7
1999	1229.23	1275.09	3.7	19.5
2000	1469.25	1441.46	−1.9	−10.1
2001	1320.28	1295.86	−1.8	−13.0
2002	1148.08	1160.71	1.1	−23.4
2003	879.82	909.93	3.4	26.4
2004	1111.92	1131.91	1.8	9.0
2005	1211.92	1186.19	−2.1	3.0
2006	1248.29	1290.15	3.4	13.6
2007	1418.30	1412.11	−0.4	3.5
2008	1468.36	1390.19	−5.3	−38.5
2009	903.25	909.73	0.7	23.5
2010	1115.10	1144.98	2.7	12.8
2011	1257.64	1271.50	1.1	−0.003
2012	1257.60	1280.70	1.8	13.4
2013	1426.19	1457.15	2.2	29.6
2014	1848.36	1837.49	−0.6	11.4
2015	2058.90	2062.14	0.2	−0.7
2016	2043.94	1922.03	−6.0	9.5
2017	2238.83	2268.90	1.3	19.4
2018	2673.61	2747.71	2.8	−6.2
2019	2506.85	2574.41	2.7	28.9
2020	3230.78	3253.05	0.7	16.3
2021	3756.07	3824.68	1.8	26.9
2022	4766.18	4677.03	−1.9	−19.4
2023	3839.50	3892.09	1.4	24.2
2024	4769.83	4763.54	−0.1	23.3
2025	5881.63	5918.25	0.6	16.4
2026	6845.50	6921.46	1.1	??

Ranked by Performance

Rank		5-Day Change	Year Change
1	1987	6.2%	2.0%
2	1976	4.9	19.1
3	1999	3.7	19.5
4	2003	3.4	26.4
5	2006	3.4	13.6
6	1983	3.3	17.3
7	1967	3.1	20.1
8	1979	2.8	12.3
9	2018	2.8	−6.2
10	2019	2.7	28.9
11	2010	2.7	12.8
12	1963	2.6	18.9
13	1958	2.5	38.1
14	1984	2.4	1.4
15	1951	2.3	16.5
16	2013	2.2	29.6
17	1975	2.2	31.5
18	1950	2.0	21.8
19	2012	1.8	13.4
20	2021	1.8	26.9
21	2004	1.8	9.0
22	1973	1.5	−17.4
23	2023	1.4	24.2
24	1972	1.4	15.6
25	1964	1.3	13.0
26	2017	1.3	19.4
27	1961	1.2	23.1
28	1989	1.2	27.3
29	2026	1.1	??
30	2011	1.1	−0.003
31	2002	1.1	−23.4
32	1997	1.0	31.0
33	1980	0.9	25.8
34	1966	0.8	−13.1
35	1994	0.7	−1.5
36	1965	0.7	9.1
37	2009	0.7	23.5
38	2020	0.7	16.3
39	1970	0.7	0.1
40	2025	0.6	16.4
41	1952	0.6	11.8
42	1954	0.5	45.0
43	1996	0.4	20.3
44	1959	0.3	8.5
45	1995	0.3	34.1
46	1992	0.2	4.5
47	1968	0.2	7.7
48	2015	0.2	−0.7
49	1990	0.1	−6.6
50	1971	0.04	10.8
51	2024	−0.1	23.3
52	2007	−0.4	3.5
53	2014	−0.7	11.4
54	1960	−0.9	−3.0
55	1957	−0.9	−14.3
56	1953	−1.5	−6.6
57	1974	−1.5	−29.7
58	1998	−1.5	26.7
59	1988	−1.5	12.4
60	1993	−1.5	7.1
61	1986	−1.6	14.6
62	2001	−1.8	−13.0
63	1955	−1.8	26.4
64	2022	−1.9	−19.4
65	2000	−1.9	−10.1
66	1985	−1.9	26.3
67	1981	−2.0	−9.7
68	1956	−2.1	2.6
69	2005	−2.1	3.0
70	1977	−2.3	−11.5
71	1982	−2.4	14.8
72	1969	−2.9	−11.4
73	1962	−3.4	−11.8
74	1991	−4.6	26.3
75	1978	−4.7	1.1
76	2008	−5.3	−38.5
77	2016	−6.0	9.5

Based on S&P 500

JANUARY 2027

First Trading Day of Year NASDAQ Up 18 of Last 29

MONDAY

D 66.7
S 52.4
N 57.1

4

Another factor contributing to productivity is technology, particularly the rapid introduction of new microcomputers based on single-chip circuits.… The results over the next decade will be a second industrial revolution.
— Yale Hirsch (Creator of *Stock Trader's Almanac, Smart Money Newsletter* 9/22/1976, 1923-2021)

Second Trading Day of the Year, Dow Up 23 of Last 33
Santa Claus Rally Ends (Page 118)
***Almanac Investor* Subscribers Emailed Results (Learn More Page 67)**

TUESDAY

D 61.9
S 47.6
N 38.1

5

Don't compete. Create. Find out what everyone else is doing and then don't do it.
— Joel Weldon

January Ends "Best Three-Month Span" (Pages 52, 60, 149, and 150)

WEDNESDAY

D 47.6
S 52.4
N 47.6

6

A good general [or trader] plans in two ways: for an absolute victory and for absolute defeat. The one enables him to squeeze the last ounce of success out of a triumph; the other keeps a failure from turning into a catastrophe.
— Frederick Schiller Faust (AKA Max Brand, American author, *Way of the Lawless*, 1892-1944)

THURSDAY

D 61.9
S 61.9
N 57.1

7

It is totally unproductive to think the world has been unfair to you. Every tough stretch is an opportunity.
— Charlie Munger (Vice-Chairman Berkshire Hathaway, 2007 Wesco Annual Meeting, 1924-2023)

January's First Five Days Act as an "Early Warning" (Page 16)
***Almanac Investor* Subscribers Emailed Results (Learn More Page 67)**

FRIDAY

D 42.9
S 52.4
N 66.7

8

There is a habitual nature to society and human activity. People's behavior and what they do with their money and time bears upon economics and the stock market.
— Jeffrey A. Hirsch (Editor, *Stock Trader's Almanac*, b. 1966)

SATURDAY

9

SUNDAY

10

THE INCREDIBLE JANUARY BAROMETER (DEVISED 1972): ONLY 12 SIGNIFICANT ERRORS IN 76 YEARS

Devised by Yale Hirsch in 1972, our January Barometer states that as the S&P 500 goes in January, so goes the year. The indicator has registered **12 major errors since 1950 for an 84.2% accuracy ratio**. Vietnam affected 1966 and 1968; major bull market started in August 1982; two January rate cuts and 9/11 affected 2001; anticipation of military action in Iraq held stocks down in January 2003; new bull market began in 2009; the Fed saved 2010 with QE2; QE3 likely staved off declines in 2014; global growth fears sparked selling in January 2016; a partially inverted yield curve and trade tensions fueled Q4 selling in 2018; and Covid-19 disrupted 2020 and 2021. (*Almanac Investor* subscribers receive full analysis of each reading.)

Including the eight flat-year errors (less than +/- 5%) yields a 73.7% accuracy ratio. A full comparison of all monthly barometers for the Dow, S&P and NASDAQ can be seen at *www.stocktradersalmanac.com* in the January 15, 2026 issue. Full years followed January's direction in 17 of the last 19 pre-election years. See pages 20 and 22 for more.

AS JANUARY GOES, SO GOES THE YEAR

Market Performance in January

	Prev Yr Cls	Jan Cls	Jan Chg	Yr Chg	
1950	16.76	17.05	1.7%	21.8%	
1951	20.41	21.66	6.1	16.5	
1952	23.77	24.14	1.6	11.8	
1953	26.57	26.38	−0.7	−6.6	
1954	24.81	26.08	5.1	45.0	
1955	35.98	36.63	1.8	26.4	
1956	45.48	43.82	−3.6	2.6	flat
1957	46.67	44.72	−4.2	−14.3	
1958	39.99	41.70	4.3	38.1	
1959	55.21	55.42	0.4	8.5	
1960	59.89	55.61	−7.1	−3.0	flat
1961	58.11	61.78	6.3	23.1	
1962	71.55	68.84	−3.8	−11.8	
1963	63.10	66.20	4.9	18.9	
1964	75.02	77.04	2.7	13.0	
1965	84.75	87.56	3.3	9.1	
1966	92.43	92.88	0.5	−13.1	X
1967	80.33	86.61	7.8	20.1	
1968	96.47	92.24	−4.4	7.7	X
1969	103.86	103.01	−0.8	−11.4	
1970	92.06	85.02	−7.6	0.1	flat
1971	92.15	95.88	4.0	10.8	
1972	102.09	103.94	1.8	15.6	
1973	118.05	116.03	−1.7	−17.4	
1974	97.55	96.57	−1.0	−29.7	
1975	68.56	76.98	12.3	31.5	
1976	90.19	100.86	11.8	19.1	
1977	107.46	102.03	−5.1	−11.5	
1978	95.10	89.25	−6.2	1.1	flat
1979	96.11	99.93	4.0	12.3	
1980	107.94	114.16	5.8	25.8	
1981	135.76	129.55	−4.6	−9.7	
1982	122.55	120.40	−1.8	14.8	X
1983	140.64	145.30	3.3	17.3	
1984	164.93	163.41	−0.9	1.4	flat
1985	167.24	179.63	7.4	26.3	
1986	211.28	211.78	0.2	14.6	
1987	242.17	274.08	13.2	2.0	flat
1988	247.08	257.07	4.0	12.4	
1989	277.72	297.47	7.1	27.3	
1990	353.40	329.08	−6.9	−6.6	
1991	330.22	343.93	4.2	26.3	
1992	417.09	408.79	−2.0	4.5	flat
1993	435.71	438.78	0.7	7.1	
1994	466.45	481.61	3.3	−1.5	flat
1995	459.27	470.42	2.4	34.1	
1996	615.93	636.02	3.3	20.3	
1997	740.74	786.16	6.1	31.0	
1998	970.43	980.28	1.0	26.7	
1999	1229.23	1279.64	4.1	19.5	
2000	1469.25	1394.46	−5.1	−10.1	
2001	1320.28	1366.01	3.5	−13.0	X
2002	1148.08	1130.20	−1.6	−23.4	
2003	879.82	855.70	−2.7	26.4	X
2004	1111.92	1131.13	1.7	9.0	
2005	1211.92	1181.27	−2.5	3.0	flat
2006	1248.29	1280.08	2.5	13.6	
2007	1418.30	1438.24	1.4	3.5	flat
2008	1468.36	1378.55	−6.1	−38.5	
2009	903.25	825.88	−8.6	23.5	X
2010	1115.10	1073.87	−3.7	12.8	X
2011	1257.64	1286.12	2.3	−0.003	flat
2012	1257.60	1312.41	4.4	13.4	
2013	1426.19	1498.11	5.0	29.6	
2014	1848.36	1782.59	−3.6	11.4	X
2015	2058.90	1994.99	−3.1	−0.7	flat
2016	2043.94	1940.24	−5.1	9.5	X
2017	2238.83	2278.87	1.8	19.4	
2018	2673.61	2823.81	5.6	−6.2	X
2019	2506.85	2704.10	7.9	28.9	
2020	3230.78	3225.52	−0.2	16.3	X
2021	3756.07	3714.24	−1.1	26.9	X
2022	4766.18	4515.55	−5.3	−19.4	
2023	3839.50	4076.60	6.2	24.2	
2024	4769.83	4845.65	1.6	23.3	
2025	5881.63	6040.53	2.7	16.4	
2026	6845.50	6939.03	1.4	??	

January Performance by Rank

Rank		Jan Chg	Yr Chg	
1	1987	13.2%	2.0%	flat
2	1975	12.3	31.5	
3	1976	11.8	19.1	
4	2019	7.9	28.9	
5	1967	7.8	20.1	
6	1985	7.4	26.3	
7	1989	7.1	27.3	
8	1961	6.3	23.1	
9	2023	6.2	24.2	
10	1997	6.1	31.0	
11	1951	6.1	16.5	
12	1980	5.8	25.8	
13	2018	5.6	−6.2	X
14	1954	5.1	45.0	
15	2013	5.0	29.6	
16	1963	4.9	18.9	
17	2012	4.4	13.4	
18	1958	4.3	38.1	
19	1991	4.2	26.3	
20	1999	4.1	19.5	
21	1971	4.0	10.8	
22	1988	4.0	12.4	
23	1979	4.0	12.3	
24	2001	3.5	−13.0	X
25	1965	3.3	9.1	
26	1983	3.3	17.3	
27	1996	3.3	20.3	
28	1994	3.3	−1.5	flat
29	2025	2.7	16.4	
30	1964	2.7	13.0	
31	2006	2.5	13.6	
32	1995	2.4	34.1	
33	2011	2.3	−0.003	flat
34	1972	1.8	15.6	
35	1955	1.8	26.4	
36	2017	1.8	19.4	
37	1950	1.7	21.8	
38	2004	1.7	9.0	
39	2024	1.6	23.3	
40	1952	1.6	11.8	
41	2007	1.4	3.5	flat
42	2026	1.4	??	
43	1998	1.0	26.7	
44	1993	0.7	7.1	
45	1966	0.5	−13.1	X
46	1959	0.4	8.5	
47	1986	0.2	14.6	
48	2020	−0.2	16.3	X
49	1953	−0.7	−6.6	
50	1969	−0.8	−11.4	
51	1984	−0.9	1.4	flat
52	1974	−1.0	−29.7	
53	2021	−1.1	26.9	X
54	2002	−1.6	−23.4	
55	1973	−1.7	−17.4	
56	1982	−1.8	14.8	X
57	1992	−2.0	4.5	flat
58	2005	−2.5	3.0	flat
59	2003	−2.7	26.4	X
60	2015	−3.1	−0.7	flat
61	2014	−3.6	11.4	X
62	1956	−3.6	2.6	flat
63	2010	−3.7	12.8	X
64	1962	−3.8	−11.8	
65	1957	−4.2	−14.3	
66	1968	−4.4	7.7	X
67	1981	−4.6	−9.7	
68	1977	−5.1	−11.5	
69	2000	−5.1	−10.1	
70	2016	−5.1	9.5	X
71	2022	−5.3	−19.4	
72	2008	−6.1	−38.5	
73	1978	−6.2	1.1	flat
74	1990	−6.9	−6.6	
75	1960	−7.1	−3.0	flat
76	1970	−7.6	0.1	flat
77	2009	−8.6	23.5	X

X = major error Based on S&P 500

JANUARY 2027

First Trading Day of January Monthly Expiration Week, Dow Up 21 of Last 34, But Down 8 of Last 13

MONDAY
D 52.4
S 57.1
N 66.7
11

Tell me and I'll forget; show me and I may remember; involve me and I'll understand.
— Confucius (Chinese philosopher, 551-478 B.C.)

TUESDAY
D 61.9
S 71.4
N 66.7
12

The thing you do obsessively between age 13 and 18, that's the thing you have the most chance of being world-class at.
— William H. Gates (Microsoft founder, "Charlie Rose" interview 2/22/2016, b. 1955)

January Monthly Expiration Week, Dow Up 11 of Last 16

WEDNESDAY
D 57.1
S 57.1
N 61.9
13

The only person who never makes a mistake is someone who does nothing.
— Albert Einstein (German-American physicist, 1921 Nobel Prize, 1879-1955)

THURSDAY
D 47.6
S 52.4
N 47.6
14

Thieves of private property pass their lives in chains; thieves of public property in riches and luxury.
— Marcus Porcius Cato (Roman soldier, senator, historian, Cato the Elder, 234-149 B.C.)

January Monthly Expiration Day Improving Since 2011, Dow Up 13 of Last 16
Day Before Martin Luther King Jr. Day, NASDAQ Up 9 of Last 12

FRIDAY
D 38.1
S 42.9
N 42.9
15

Individualism, private property, the law of accumulation of wealth and the law of competition... are the highest result of human experience, the soil in which, so far, has produced the best fruit.
— Andrew Carnegie (Scottish-born U.S. industrialist, philanthropist, *The Gospel Of Wealth*, 1835-1919)

SATURDAY
16

SUNDAY
17

BULLS WIN WHEN MARKET HITS THE JANUARY TRIFECTA

We invented our January Indicator Trifecta in 2013 by combining our Santa Claus Rally (page 118) and January Barometer (page 18), both invented by our late founder Yale Hirsch in 1972 published in the *1973 Almanac*, with the age-old First Five Days Early Warning System (page 16).

The predicative power of the three is considerably greater than any of them alone; we have been rather impressed by its forecasting prowess. When the market hits this trifecta, the bulls win. Since 1950 when our January Barometer, Santa Claus Rally and First Five Days indicators are all positive for the S&P 500 the odds of the rest of the year—and the year as a whole—being up increase dramatically.

When all three are up, the S&P 500 has been up 90.6% of the time, 29 of 32 years, with an average gain of 17.7%, and the next 11 months are up 87.5 % of the time, 28 of 32 years, with an average gain of 12.5%. When any of them are down the year's results are reduced with S&P up 61.4% of the time, 27 of 44 years, with an average gain of 3.7%. When all three are down the S&P was down 3 of 8 years with an average loss of –3.6% with bear markets in 1969 (–11.4%), 2000 (–10.1%) and 2008 (–38.5%), flat years in 1956 (2.6%), 1978 (1.1%), and 2005 (3.0%). Down Trifecta's were followed by gains in 1982 (14.8%) and 2016 (9.5%).

When the January Indicator Trifecta was preceded by a bear market in the year prior the results were even more striking. Next-11-months and full-year performance were always positive, up 14-0, with average gains of 16.8% and 22.2%, respectively. S&P 500 did not hit this trifecta in 2026, the Santa Claus Rally was negative. *Almanac Investor* newsletter subscribers receive our full analysis (see special offer between pages 66 and 67).

S&P 500 JANUARY INDICATOR TRIFECTA — THREE POSITIVE

Year	SC Rally	FFD	JB	Feb	Feb-Dec	Full Year
1950	1.3%	2.0%	1.7%	1.0%	19.7%	21.8
1951	3.1	2.3	6.1	0.6	9.7	16.5
1952	1.4	0.6	1.6	−3.6	10.1	11.8
1954	1.7	0.5	5.1	0.3	38.0	45.0
1958	3.5	2.5	4.3	−2.1	32.4	38.1
1959	3.6	0.3	0.4	−0.02	8.1	8.5
1961	1.7	1.2	6.3	2.7	15.8	23.1
1963	1.7	2.6	4.9	−2.9	13.3	18.9
1964	2.3	1.3	2.7	1.0	10.0	13.0
1965	0.6	0.7	3.3	−0.1	5.6	9.1
1966	0.1	0.8	0.5	−1.8	−13.5	−13.1
1971	1.9	0.04	4.0	0.9	6.5	10.8
1972	1.3	1.4	1.8	2.5	13.6	15.6
1975	7.2	2.2	12.3	6.0	17.2	31.5
1976	4.3	4.9	11.8	−1.1	6.5	19.1
1979	3.3	2.8	4.0	−3.7	8.0	12.3
1983	1.2	3.2	3.3	1.9	13.5	17.3
1987	2.4	6.2	13.2	3.7	−9.9	2.0
1989	0.9	1.2	7.1	−2.9	18.8	27.3
1995	0.2	0.3	2.4	3.6	30.9	34.1
1996	1.8	0.4	3.3	0.7	16.5	20.3
1997	0.1	1.0	6.1	0.6	23.4	31.0
1999	1.3	3.7	4.1	−3.2	14.8	19.5
2004	2.4	1.8	1.7	1.2	7.1	9.0
2006	0.4	3.4	2.5	0.05	10.8	13.6
2011	1.1	1.1	2.3	3.2	−2.2	−0.003
2012	1.9	1.8	4.2	4.1	8.7	13.4
2013	2.0	2.2	4.8	1.1	23.4	29.6
2017	0.4	1.3	1.8	3.7	17.3	19.4
2018	1.1	2.8	5.6	−3.9	−11.2	−6.2
2019	1.3	2.7	7.9	3.0	19.5	28.9
2023	0.8	1.4	6.2	−2.6	17.0	24.2
			Average	**0.4%**	**12.5%**	**17.7%**
			# Up	**20**	**28**	**29**
			#Down	**12**	**4**	**3**

Martin Luther King Jr. Day *(Market Closed)*

MONDAY
18

I have a dream that my four little children will one day live in a nation where they will not be judged by the color of their skin but by the content of their character.
— Martin Luther King Jr. (Civil rights leader, 1964 Nobel Peace Prize, 1929-1968)

Day After Martin Luther King Jr. Day, NASDAQ Down 8 of Last 11

TUESDAY
19
D 57.1
S 66.7
N 66.7

If buying equities seem the most hazardous and foolish thing you could possibly do, then you are near the bottom that will end the bear market.
— Joseph E. Granville

WEDNESDAY
20
D 47.6
S 47.6
N 47.6

Man's mind, once stretched by a new idea, never regains its original dimensions.
— Oliver Wendell Holmes (American author, poet and physician, 1809-1894)

THURSDAY
21
D 52.4
S 61.9
N 52.4

Experience is helpful, but it is judgment that matters.
— General Colin Powell (Chairman Joint Chiefs 1989-93, Secretary of State 2001-05, *NY Times* 10/22/2008, b. 1937)

FRIDAY
22
D 47.6
S 61.9
N 57.1

The most important lesson in investing is humility.
— Sir John Templeton (Founder Templeton Funds, philanthropist, 1912-2008)

SATURDAY
23

SUNDAY
24

DOWN JANUARYS: A REMARKABLE RECORD

In the first third of the 20th century, there was no correlation between January markets and the year as a whole. Then in 1972 Yale Hirsch discovered that the 1933 "Lame Duck" Amendment to the Constitution changed the political calendar and the January Barometer was born—its record has been quite accurate (page 18).

Down Januarys are harbingers of trouble ahead, in the economic, political, or military arenas. Eisenhower's heart attack in 1955 cast doubt on whether he could run in 1956—a flat year. Two other election years with down Januarys were also flat (1984 & 1992). Sixteen bear markets began and 10 continued into second years with poor Januarys. 1968 started down as we were mired in Vietnam, but Johnson's "bombing halt" changed the climate. Imminent military action in Iraq held January 2003 down before the market triple-bottomed in March. After Baghdad fell, pre-election and recovery forces fueled 2003 into a banner year. 2005 was flat, registering the narrowest Dow trading range on record. 2008 was the worst January on record and preceded the worst bear market since the Great Depression. A negative reading in 2015 and 2016 preceded an official Dow bear market declaration in February 2016. In 2020 the shortest bear market in history began after the close on February 19. ZIRP and QE fueled a banner 2021 however, NASDAQ did correct 10.5% during February and March. Aggressive interest rate hikes triggered a bear in 2022.

Unfortunately, bull and bear markets do not start conveniently at the beginnings and ends of months or years. Though some years ended higher, **every down January since 1950 was followed by a new or continuing bear market, a 10% correction or a flat year. Down Januarys were followed by substantial declines averaging *minus* 13.3%**, providing excellent buying opportunities later in most years.

FROM DOWN JANUARY S&P CLOSES TO LOW NEXT 11 MONTHS

Year	January Close	% Change	11-Month Low	Date of Low	Jan Close to Low %	% Feb to Dec	Year % Change	
1953	26.38	−0.7%	22.71	14-Sep	−13.9%	−6.0%	−6.6%	bear
1956	43.82	−3.6	43.42	14-Feb	−0.9	6.5	2.6	bear/FLAT
1957	44.72	−4.2	38.98	22-Oct	−12.8	−10.6	−14.3	Cont. bear
1960	55.61	−7.1	52.30	25-Oct	−6.0	4.5	−3.0	bear
1962	68.84	−3.8	52.32	26-Jun	−24.0	−8.3	−11.8	bear
1968	92.24	−4.4	87.72	5-Mar	−4.9	12.6	7.7	−10%/bear
1969	103.01	−0.8	89.20	17-Dec	−13.4	−10.6	−11.4	Cont. bear
1970	85.02	−7.6	69.20	26-May	−18.6	8.4	0.1	Cont. bear
1973	116.03	−1.7	92.16	5-Dec	−20.6	−15.9	−17.4	bear
1974	96.57	−1.0	62.28	3-Oct	−35.5	−29.0	−29.7	Cont. bear
1977	102.03	−5.1	90.71	2-Nov	−11.1	−6.8	−11.5	bear
1978	89.25	−6.2	86.90	6-Mar	−2.6	7.7	1.1	Cont. bear/bear
1981	129.55	−4.6	112.77	25-Sep	−13.0	−5.4	−9.7	bear
1982	120.40	−1.8	102.42	12-Aug	−14.9	16.8	14.8	Cont. bear
1984	163.42	−0.9	147.82	24-Jul	−9.5	2.3	1.4	Cont. bear/FLAT
1990	329.07	−6.9	295.46	11-Oct	−10.2	0.4	−6.6	bear
1992	408.79	−2.0	394.50	8-Apr	−3.5	6.6	4.5	FLAT
2000	1394.46	−5.1	1264.74	20-Dec	−9.3	−5.3	−10.1	bear
2002	1130.20	−1.6	776.76	9-Oct	−31.3	−22.2	−23.4	bear
2003	855.70	−2.7	800.73	11-Mar	−6.4	29.9	26.4	Cont. bear
2005	1181.27	−2.5	1137.50	20-Apr	−3.7	5.7	3.0	FLAT
2008	1378.55	−6.1	752.44	20-Nov	−45.4	−34.5	−38.5	bear
2009	825.88	−8.6	676.53	9-Mar	−18.1	35.0	23.5	Cont. bear
2010	1073.87	−3.7	1022.58	2-Jul	−4.8	17.1	12.8	−10%/no bear
2014	1782.59	−3.6	1741.89	3-Feb	−2.3	15.5	11.4	−10% intraday
2015	1994.99	−3.1	1867.61	25-Aug	−6.4	2.5	−0.7	bear
2016	1940.24	−5.1	1829.08	11-Feb	−5.7	15.4	9.5	Cont. bear
2020	3225.52	−0.2	2237.40	23-Mar	−30.6	16.4	16.3	bear
2021	3714.24	−1.1	3768.47	4-Mar	1.5	28.3	26.9	−10% NAS
2022	4515.55	−5.3	3577.03	12-Oct	−20.8	15.0	−19.4	bear
				Totals	**−398.7%**	**92.0%**	**−52.2%**	
				Average	**−13.3%**	**3.1%**	**−1.7%**	

MONDAY
D 57.1
S 57.1
N 52.4
25

Benjamin Graham was correct in suggesting that while the stock market in the short run may be a voting mechanism, in the long run it is a weighing mechanism. True value will win out in the end.
— Burton G. Malkiel (Economist, April 2003 Princeton Paper, *A Random Walk Down Wall Street*, b. 1932)

FOMC Meeting (2 Days)

TUESDAY
D 61.9
S 52.4
N 66.7
26

There is a vitality, a life force, an energy, a quickening, that is translated through you into action, and because there is only one of you in all time, this expression is unique. And if you block it, it will never exist through any other medium and will be lost.
— Martha Graham (American choreographer, dancer, teacher)

WEDNESDAY
D 52.4
S 42.9
N 57.1
27

Two signposts on the road to wisdom: 1. Nothing is the end of the world and, 2. Nobody gives a hoot what you think.
— Phil Pearlman (Founder, Pearl Institute, b. 1967)

THURSDAY
D 47.6
S 47.6
N 47.6
28

If you bet on a horse, that's gambling. If you bet you can make three spades, that's entertainment. If you bet cotton will go up three points, that's business. See the difference?
— Blackie Sherrod (Sportswriter, 1919-2016)

"January Barometer" 84.2% Accurate *(Page 18)*
***Almanac Investor* Subscribers Emailed Results** **(Learn More Page 67)**

FRIDAY
D 38.1
S 42.9
N 52.4
29

Prosperity is a great teacher; adversity a greater.
— William Hazlitt (English essayist, 1778-1830)

SATURDAY
30

February Almanac Investor Sector Seasonalities: *See Pages 94, 96, and 98*

SUNDAY
31

FEBRUARY ALMANAC

FEBRUARY						
S	M	T	W	T	F	S
	1	2	3	4	5	6
7	8	9	10	11	12	13
14	15	16	17	18	19	20
21	22	23	24	25	26	27
28						

MARCH						
S	M	T	W	T	F	S
	1	2	3	4	5	6
7	8	9	10	11	12	13
14	15	16	17	18	19	20
21	22	23	24	25	26	27
28	29	30	31			

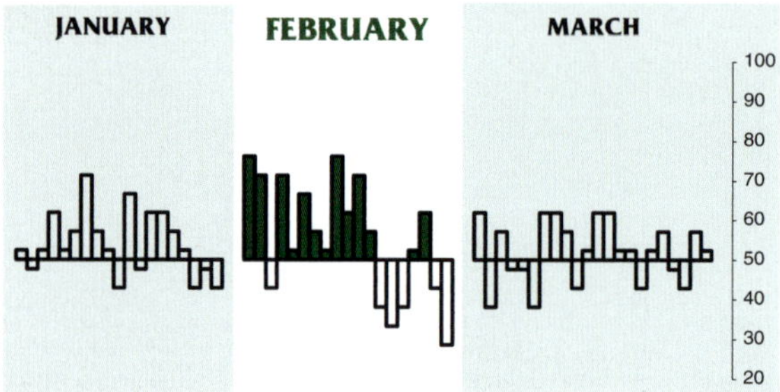

Market Probability Chart above is a graphic representation of the S&P 500 Recent Market Probability Calendar on page 126.

◆ February is the weak link in "Best Six Months" (pages 52, 54, & 149) ◆ RECENT RECORD: S&P up 8, down 7, average change +0.6% last 15 years ◆ #6 NASDAQ month in pre-election years average gain 2.5%, up 10 down 4 (page 166), #7 Dow, up 12 down 7 and #7 S&P, up 12, down 7 (pages 156 & 162) ◆ Day before Presidents' Day weekend S&P down 21 of 35, 11 straight 1992–2002, day after mixed up 19 down 16 (see page 80 & 135) ◆ Many technicians modify market predictions based on January's market in February

February Vital Statistics

	DJIA		S&P 500		NASDAQ		Russell 1K		Russell 2K	
Rank		8		11		10		11		6
Up		45		41		29		27		28
Down		32		36		27		21		20
Average % Change		0.1		–0.03		0.4		0.2		1.0
Pre-Election Yr Avg % Chg		1.1		1.0		2.5		1.3		2.4
Best & Worst February										
	% Change		% Change		% Change		% Change		% Change	
Best	1986	8.8	1986	7.1	2000	19.2	1986	7.2	2000	16.4
Worst	2009	–11.7	2009	–11.0	2001	–22.4	2009	–10.7	2009	–12.3
Best & Worst February Weeks										
Best	2/1/08	4.4	2/6/09	5.2	2/4/00	9.2	2/6/09	5.3	2/5/21	7.7
Worst	2/28/20	–12.4	2/28/20	–11.5	2/28/20	–10.5	2/28/20	–11.6	2/28/20	–12.0
Best & Worst February Days										
Best	2/24/09	3.3	2/24/09	4.0	2/11/99	4.2	2/24/09	4.1	2/24/09	4.5
Worst	2/10/09	–4.6	2/10/09	–4.9	2/16/01	–5.0	2/10/09	–4.8	2/10/09	–4.7
First Trading Day of Monthly Options Expiration Week: 1980–2026										
Record (#Up–#Down)		29-18		32-15		28-19		32-15		28-19
Current streak		U4		U2		U2		U2		D1
Avg % Change		0.29		0.26		0.14		0.24		0.19
Monthly Options Expiration Day: 1980–2026										
Record (#Up–#Down)		24-23		19-28		19-28		20-27		22-25
Current streak		U1		U1		U1		U1		D3
Avg % Change		–0.06		–0.15		–0.30		–0.15		–0.10
Monthly Options Expiration Week: 1980–2026										
Record (#Up–#Down)		27-20		24-23		25-22		24-23		30-17
Current streak		U1		U1		U1		U1		U1
Avg % Change		0.38		0.23		0.14		0.23		0.37
Week After Monthly Options Expiration: 1980–2026										
Record (#Up–#Down)		22-25		22-25		26-21		22-25		23-24
Current streak		D1		D2		D2		D2		D4
Avg % Change		–0.51		–0.44		–0.51		–0.42		–0.42
First Trading Day Performance										
% of Time Up		64.9		63.6		71.4		68.8		68.8
Avg % Change		0.18		0.20		0.40		0.27		0.42
Last Trading Day Performance										
% of Time Up		45.5		50.6		50.0		47.9		54.2
Avg % Change		–0.07		–0.04		–0.05		–0.09		–0.03

Dow & S&P 1950–May 1, 2026; NASDAQ 1971–May 1, 2026; Russell 1K & 2K 1979–May 1, 2026.

Either go short or stay away the day before Presidents' Day.

FEBRUARY 2027

First Trading Day in February, Dow Up 20 of Last 24

MONDAY
D 81.0
S 76.2
N 81.0
1

Become more humble as the market goes your way.
— Bernard Baruch (Financier, speculator, statesman, presidential adviser, 1870-1965)

TUESDAY
D 57.1
S 71.4
N 66.7
2

I would rather be positioned as a petrified bull rather than a penniless bear.
— John L. Person (Professional trader, author, speaker, *Commodity Trader's Almanac,* personsplanet.com, 11/3/2010, b. 1961)

WEDNESDAY
D 52.4
S 42.9
N 38.1
3

No other country can substitute for the U.S. The U.S. is still No. 1 in military, No. 1 in economy, No. 1 in promoting human rights and No. 1 in idealism. Only the U.S. can lead the world. No other country can.
— Senior Korean official (to Thomas L. Friedman *NY Times* Foreign Affairs columnist, 2/25/2009)

THURSDAY
D 61.9
S 71.4
N 61.9
4

The bigger a man's head gets, the easier it is to fill his shoes.
— Anonymous

FRIDAY
D 57.1
S 52.4
N 52.4
5

Those that forget the past are condemned to repeat its mistakes, and those that mis-state the past should be condemned.
— Eugene D. Cohen (Letter to the Editor *Financial Times* 10/30/06)

SATURDAY
6

SUNDAY
7

MARKET CHARTS OF PRE-PRESIDENTIAL ELECTION YEARS

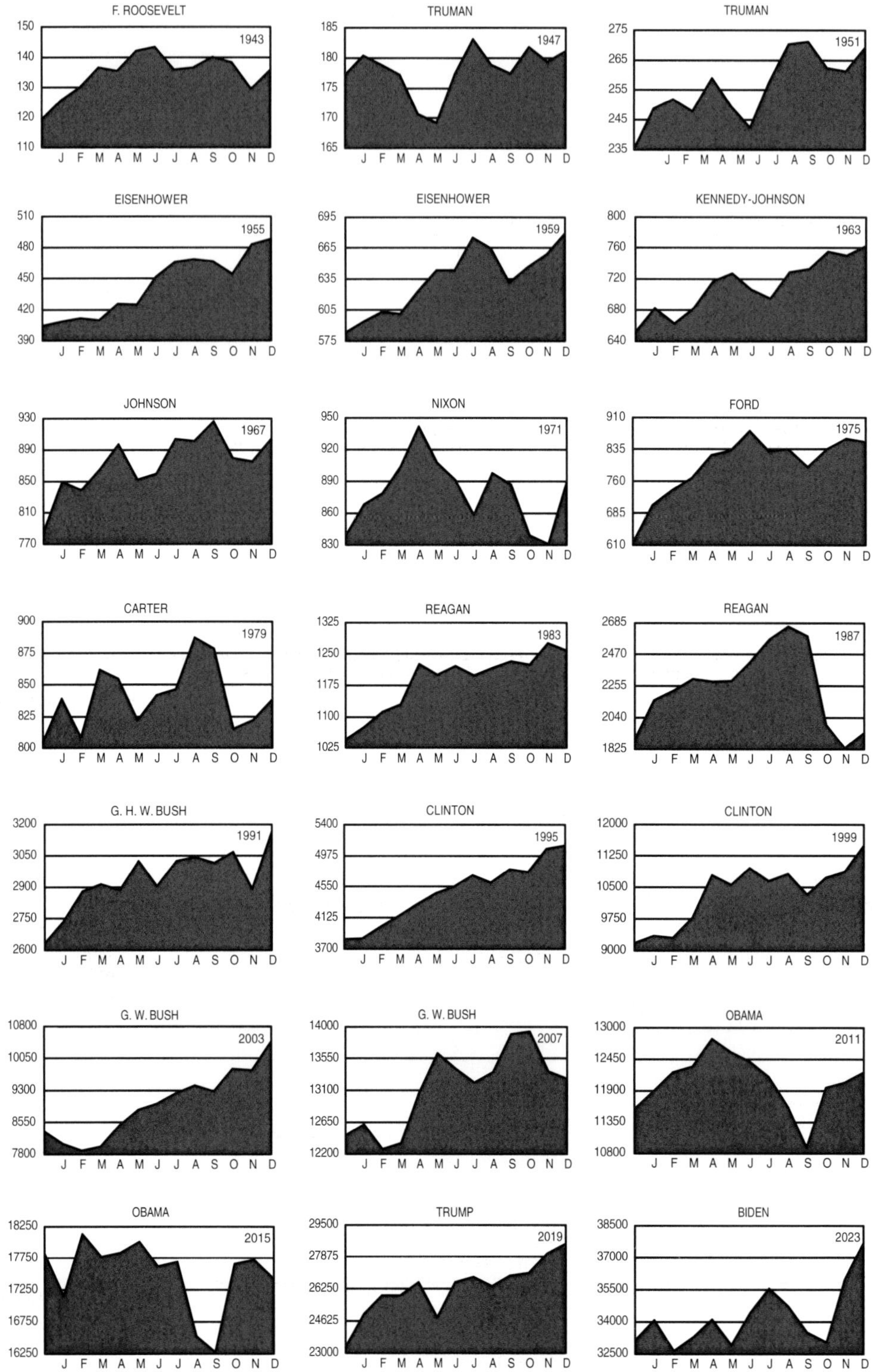

Based on Dow Jones Industial Average monthly closing prices

FEBRUARY 2027

MONDAY
D 52.4
S 66.7
N 66.7
8

Complexity is the enemy of execution.
— Anthony Robbins (American author, coach, speaker, and philanthropist, b. 1960)

Week Before February Monthly Expiration Week, NASDAQ Up 11 of Last 17

TUESDAY
D 52.4
S 57.1
N 57.1
9

People won't have time for you if you're always angry or complaining.
— Professsor Stephen Hawking (English theoretical physicist, cosmologist, and author, 1942-2018)

Ash Wednesday

WEDNESDAY
D 57.1
S 52.4
N 57.1
10

Any human anywhere will blossom in a hundred unexpected talents and capacities simply by being given the opportunity to do so.
— Doris Lessing (Iranian-born British writer, 2007 Nobel Prize in Literature, 1919-2013)

THURSDAY
D 61.9
S 76.2
N 76.2
11

Laws are like sausages. It's better not to see them being made.
— Otto von Bismarck (German-Prussian politician, 1st Chancellor of Germany, 1815-1898)

Day Before Presidents' Day Weekend, S&P Up 11 of Last 16

FRIDAY
D 47.6
S 61.9
N 85.7
12

All great truths begin as blasphemies.
— George Bernard Shaw (Irish dramatist, 1856-1950)

SATURDAY
13

Valentine's Day ♥

SUNDAY
14

PRE-PRESIDENTIAL ELECTION YEARS: ONLY ONE LOSER IN 88 YEARS

Investors should feel somewhat secure going into 2027. There has only been one down year in the third year of a presidential term since war-torn 1939, Dow off 2.9%. That one loss occurred in 2015, Dow off 2.2%. The only severe loss in a pre-presidential election year going back 100 years occurred in 1931 during the Depression.

Electing a president every four years has set in motion a 4-year political stock market cycle. Most bear markets take place in the first or second years after elections (see pages 133-134). Then, the market improves. Typically each administration does everything in its power to juice up the economy so that voters are in a positive mood at election time.

Quite an impressive record. Chances are the winning streak will continue and that the market, in pre-presidential election year 2027 will gain ground.

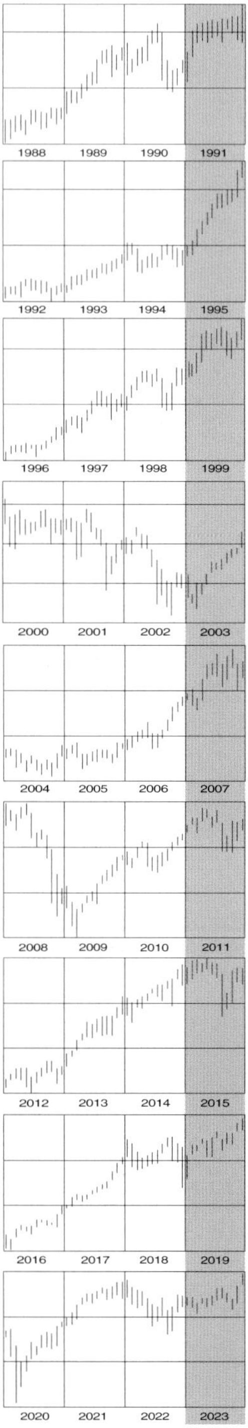

THE RECORD SINCE 1915

1915	Wilson (D)	World War I in Europe, but Dow up 81.7%.
1919	Wilson (D)	Post-Armistice 45.5% gain through Nov. 3rd top. Dow +30.5%.
1923	Harding/Coolidge (R)	Teapot Dome scandal a depressant. Dow loses 3.3%.
1927	Coolidge (R)	Bull market rolls on, up 28.8%.
1931	Hoover (R)	Depression, stocks slashed in half. Dow –52.7%, S&P –47.1%.
1935	Roosevelt (D)	Almost straight up year, S&P 500 up 41.2%, Dow 38.5%.
1939	Roosevelt (D)	War clouds, Dow –2.9% but 23.7% Apr.–Dec. gain. S&P –5.5%.
1943	Roosevelt (D)	U.S. at war, prospects brighter, S&P +19.4%, Dow +13.8%.
1947	Truman (D)	S&P unchanged, Dow up 2.2%.
1951	Truman (D)	Dow +14.4%, S&P +16.5%.
1955	Eisenhower (R)	Dow +20.8%, S&P +26.4%.
1959	Eisenhower (R)	Dow +16.4%, S&P +8.5%.
1963	Kennedy/Johnson (D)	Dow +17.0%, S&P +18.9%.
1967	Johnson (D)	Dow +15.2%, S&P +20.1%.
1971	Nixon (R)	Dow +6.1%, S&P +10.8%, NASDAQ +27.4%.
1975	Ford (R)	Dow +38.3%, S&P +31.5%, NASDAQ +29.8%.
1979	Carter (D)	Dow +4.2%, S&P +12.3%, NASDAQ +28.1%.
1983	Reagan (R)	Dow +20.3%, S&P +17.3%, NASDAQ +19.9%.
1987	Reagan (R)	Dow +2.3%, S&P +2.0% despite Oct. meltdown. NAS –5.4%.
1991	G.H.W. Bush (R)	Dow +20.3%, S&P +26.3%, NASDAQ +56.8%.
1995	Clinton (D)	Dow +33.5%, S&P +34.1%, NASDAQ +39.9%.
1999	Clinton (D)	Millennial fever crescendo: Dow +25.2%, S&P +19.5%, NASDAQ +85.6%.
2003	G.W. Bush (R)	Straight up after fall of Saddam: Dow +25.3% S&P +26.4%, NASDAQ +50.0%
2007	G.W. Bush (R)	Credit bubble fuels all-time market highs before bear starts & Great Recession: Dow: +6.4% S&P: +3.5% NASDAQ: 9.8%.
2011	Obama (D)	Debt Ceiling Debacle and U.S. credit rating downgrade: Dow +5.5%, S&P –0.003%, NASDAQ: –1.8%
2015	Obama (D)	Tepid growth: mild bear market ending February 2016: Dow –2.2%, S&P –0.7%, NASDAQ +5.7%
2019	Trump (R)	Dow +22.3%, S&P +26.9%, NASDAQ +35.2%
2023	Biden (D)	Dow +13.7%, S&P +24.2%, NASDAQ +43.4%

Graph shows Pre-Presidential years screened
Based on Dow Jones industial average monthly ranges

FEBRUARY 2027

Presidents' Day *(Market Closed)*

MONDAY
15

If I had eight hours to chop down a tree, I'd spend six sharpening my axe.
— Abraham Lincoln (16th U.S. President, 1809-1865)

Day After Presidents Day, NASDAQ Down 19 of Last 32, But Up 9 of Last 14
First Trading Day of February Monthly Expiration Week Dow Up 23 of Last 33

TUESDAY
16
D 71.4
S 71.4
N 71.4

The riskiest moment is when you are right. That's when you're in the most trouble, because you tend to overstay the good decisions.
— Peter L. Bernstein (Economist, *Money Magazine* 10/15/2004, 1919-2009)

WEDNESDAY
17
D 66.7
S 57.1
N 47.6

I was absolutely unemotional about numbers. Losses did not have an effect on me because I viewed them as purely probability-driven, which meant sometimes you came up with a loss. Bad days, bad weeks, bad months never impacted the way I approached markets the next day.
— James Leitner (Trader, hedge fund manager, Falcon Management Corp, b. 1953)

THURSDAY
18
D 42.9
S 38.1
N 38.1

Successful innovation is not a feat of intellect, but of will.
— Joseph A. Schumpeter (Austrian-American economist, *Theory of Economic Development*, 1883-1950)

February Monthly Expiration Day, NASDAQ Down 15 of Last 23

FRIDAY
19
D 38.1
S 33.3
N 33.3

Whoso would be a man, must be a non-conformist...Nothing is at last sacred but the integrity of your own mind.
— Ralph Waldo Emerson (American author, poet and philosopher, *Self-Reliance*, 1803-1882)

SATURDAY
20

SUNDAY
21

WHY A 50% GAIN IN THE DOW IS POSSIBLE FROM ITS 2026 LOW TO ITS 2027 HIGH

Normally, major corrections occur sometime in the first or second years following presidential elections. In the last 16 midterm election years, bear markets began or were in progress 10 times—we experienced bull years in 1986, 2006, 2010, and 2014, while 1994 was flat. A correction in 2018 ended on Christmas Eve day.

The puniest midterm advance, 14.5% from the 1946 low, was during the industrial contraction after World War II. The next five smallest advances were: 2014 (tepid global growth) 19.1%, 1978 (OPEC–Iran) 21.0%, 1930 (economic collapse) 23.4%, 1966 (Vietnam) 26.7%, and 2022 (Fed interest rate tightening) 31.3%.

Since 1914 the Dow has gained 46.3% on average from its midterm election year low to its subsequent high in the following pre-election year. A swing of such magnitude is equivalent to a move from Dow 50000 to nearly 75000.

POST-ELECTION HIGH TO MIDTERM LOW: –20.2%

Conversely, since 1913 the Dow has dropped –20.2% on average from its post-election-year high to its subsequent low in the following midterm year. Dow's 2025 post-election-year high was 48731.16. A 20.2% decline could put the Dow back around 38887 at the 2026 midterm bottom. At press time, the Iran war and the resulting surge in energy prices could make a decline to this level possible. Whatever the level, the rally off the 2026 midterm low could be another great buying opportunity.

Pretty impressive seasonality! There is no reason to think the quadrennial Presidential Election/Stock Market Cycle will not continue. Page 132 shows how effectively most presidents "managed" to have much stronger economies in the third and fourth years of their terms than in their first two.

% CHANGE IN DOW JONES INDUSTRIALS BETWEEN THE MIDTERM YEAR LOW AND THE HIGH IN THE FOLLOWING YEAR

	Midterm Year Low				Pre-Election Year High				
	Date of Low			Dow	Date of High			Dow	% Gain
1	Jul	30	1914*	52.32	Dec	27	1915	99.21	89.6%
2	Jan	15	1918**	73.38	Nov	3	1919	119.62	63.0
3	Jan	10	1922**	78.59	Mar	20	1923	105.38	34.1
4	Mar	30	1926*	135.20	Dec	31	1927	202.40	49.7
5	Dec	16	1930*	157.51	Feb	24	1931	194.36	23.4
6	Jul	26	1934*	85.51	Nov	19	1935	148.44	73.6
7	Mar	31	1938*	98.95	Sep	12	1939	155.92	57.6
8	Apr	28	1942*	92.92	Jul	14	1943	145.82	56.9
9	Oct	9	1946	163.12	Jul	24	1947	186.85	14.5
10	Jan	13	1950**	196.81	Sep	13	1951	276.37	40.4
11	Jan	11	1954**	279.87	Dec	30	1955	488.40	74.5
12	Feb	25	1958**	436.89	Dec	31	1959	679.36	55.5
13	Jun	26	1962*	535.74	Dec	18	1963	767.21	43.2
14	Oct	7	1966*	744.32	Sep	25	1967	943.08	26.7
15	May	26	1970*	631.16	Apr	28	1971	950.82	50.6
16	Dec	6	1974*	577.60	Jul	16	1975	881.81	52.7
17	Feb	28	1978*	742.12	Oct	5	1979	897.61	21.0
18	Aug	12	1982*	776.92	Nov	29	1983	1287.20	65.7
19	Jan	22	1986	1502.29	Aug	25	1987	2722.42	81.2
20	Oct	11	1990*	2365.10	Dec	31	1991	3168.84	34.0
21	Apr	4	1994	3593.35	Dec	13	1995	5216.47	45.2
22	Aug	31	1998*	7539.07	Dec	31	1999	11497.12	52.5
23	Oct	9	2002*	7286.27	Dec	31	2003	10453.92	43.5
24	Jan	20	2006	10667.39	Oct	9	2007	14164.53	32.8
25	Jul	2	2010**	9686.48	Apr	29	2011	12810.54	32.3
26	Feb	3	2014	15372.80	May	19	2015	18312.39	19.1
27	Dec	24	2018	21792.20	Dec	27	2019	28645.26	31.4
28	Sep	30	2022*	28725.51	Dec	28	2023	37710.10	31.3
29	Mar	27	2026	45166.64	*As of May 22, 2026*				
								Average	**46.3%**

** Bear Market ended ** Bear previous year*

End of February Miserable in Recent Years (Page 24 and 135)

MONDAY
D 52.4
S 38.1
N 42.9
22

It isn't the incompetent who destroy an organization. It is those who have achieved something and want to rest upon their achievements who are forever clogging things up.
— Charles E. Sorenson (Danish-American engineer, officer, director of Ford Motor Co. 1907-1950, helped develop first auto assembly line, 1881-1968)

Week After February Monthly Expiration Week, Dow Down 16 of Last 28, But Up 9 of Last 15, 2020 Down 12.4% 5th Worst Week Since 1950

TUESDAY
D 52.4
S 52.4
N 42.9
23

Thank God for recording. It's the best thing that's happened to us since writing.
— Keith Richards (Rolling Stones, *Life*, b. 1943)

WEDNESDAY
D 52.4
S 61.9
N 76.2
24

Your organization will never get better unless you are willing to admit that there is something wrong with it.
— General Norman Schwartzkof (Ret. Commander of Allied Forces in 1990-1991 Gulf War)

THURSDAY
D 42.9
S 42.9
N 57.1
25

Over time, you weed out luck.
— Billy Beane (American baseball player and general manager, b. 1962)

FRIDAY
D 28.6
S 28.6
N 38.1
26

If a political party does not have its foundation in the determination to advance a cause that is right and that is moral, then it is not a political party; it is merely a conspiracy to seize power.
— Dwight D. Eisenhower (34th U.S. President, 1890-1969)

SATURDAY
27

March Almanac Investor Sector Seasonalities: See Pages 94, 96, and 98

SUNDAY
28

MARCH ALMANAC

MARCH						
S	M	T	W	T	F	S
	1	2	3	4	5	6
7	8	9	10	11	12	13
14	15	16	17	18	19	20
21	22	23	24	25	26	27
28	29	30	31			

APRIL						
S	M	T	W	T	F	S
				1	2	3
4	5	6	7	8	9	10
11	12	13	14	15	16	17
18	19	20	21	22	23	24
25	26	27	28	29	30	

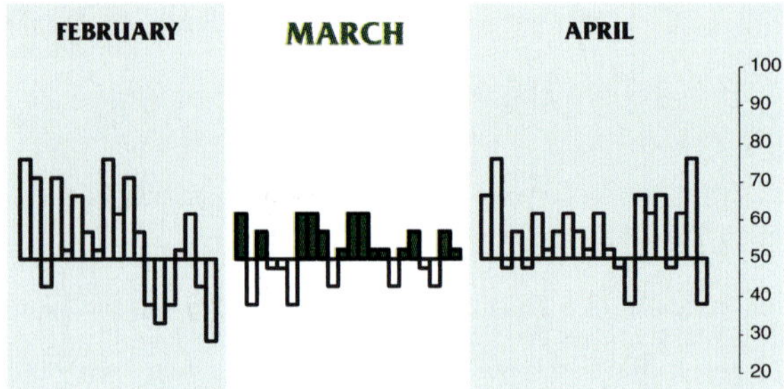

Market Probability Chart above is a graphic representation of the S&P 500 Recent Market Probability Calendar on page 126.

◆ Mid-month strength and late-month choppiness are most evident above ◆ RECENT RECORD: S&P 13 up, 8 down, average gain 0.9%, fifth best ◆ Rather turbulent in recent years with wild fluctuations and large gains and losses ◆ March 2020 Dow declined 13.7%, worst March loss since 1938 ◆ March has been taking some end-of-quarter hits (page 136), down 1469 Dow points March 9-22, 2001 ◆ Last three or four days Dow a net loser 23 out of last 37 years ◆ NASDAQ hard hit in 2001, down 14.5% after 22.4% drop in February ◆ #3 NASDAQ month during pre-election years average gain 3.3%, up 12, down 2 ◆ Third Dow month to gain more than 1000 points in 2016

March Vital Statistics

	DJIA		S&P 500		NASDAQ		Russell 1K		Russell 2K	
Rank		6		6		9		8		8
Up		49		49		35		31		32
Down		28		28		21		17		16
Average % Change		0.8		1.0		0.6		0.7		0.4
Pre-Election Yr Avg % Chg		1.8		1.9		3.3		2.1		1.9
Best & Worst March										
	% Change		% Change		% Change		% Change		% Change	
Best	2000	7.8	2000	9.7	2009	10.9	2000	8.9	1979	9.7
Worst	2020	–13.7	2020	–12.5	1980	–17.1	2020	–13.4	2020	–21.9
Best & Worst March Weeks										
Best	3/27/20	12.8	3/13/09	10.7	3/13/09	10.6	3/13/09	10.7	3/13/09	12.0
Worst	3/20/20	–17.3	3/20/20	–15.0	3/20/20	–12.6	3/20/20	–15.3	3/13/20	–16.5
Best & Worst March Days										
Best	3/24/20	11.4	3/24/20	9.4	3/13/20	9.4	3/24/20	9.5	3/24/20	9.4
Worst	3/16/20	–12.9	3/16/20	–12.0	3/16/20	–12.3	3/16/20	–12.2	3/16/20	–14.3
First Trading Day of Monthly Options Expiration Week: 1980–2026										
Record (#Up–#Down)		31-16		29-18		25-22		27-20		25-22
Current streak		U3		U2		U2		U2		U2
Avg % Change		–0.07		–0.14		–0.40		–0.19		–0.54
Monthly Options Expiration Day: 1980–2026										
Record (#Up–#Down)		24-23		26-21		24-23		25-22		23-23
Current streak		D1		D1		D1		D1		D2
Avg % Change		–0.06		–0.10		–0.10		–0.10		–0.14
Monthly Options Expiration Week: 1980–2026										
Record (#Up–#Down)		30-16		30-17		28-19		29-18		25-22
Current streak		D1		D1		D1		D1		D1
Avg % Change		0.46		0.45		0.07		0.40		–0.14
Week After Monthly Options Expiration: 1980–2026										
Record (#Up–#Down)		21-26		17-30		22-25		17-30		21-26
Current streak		D2		D2		D2		D2		U1
Avg % Change		–0.05		–0.02		0.01		–0.02		–0.10
First Trading Day Performance										
% of Time Up		66.2		63.6		62.5		60.4		66.7
Avg % Change		0.20		0.22		0.31		0.23		0.30
Last Trading Day Performance										
% of Time Up		44.2		44.2		62.5		52.1		79.2
Avg % Change		–0.05		0.05		0.26		0.15		0.45

Dow & S&P 1950–May 1, 2026; NASDAQ 1971–May 1, 2026; Russell 1K & 2K 1979–May 1, 2026.

March has Ides and St. Patrick's Day;
Begins bullishly, then fades away.

MARCH 2027

First Trading Day in March, S&P Up 18 of Last 27

MONDAY

1

D 61.9
S 61.9
N 57.1

I'm a trader that uses whatever he can find to get a leg up in a short-legged game. Sure, I use technical analysis, but much of it is mumbo jumbo, redundant, lacks a logical premise or does not hold up in testing. Fundamentals and technicals are both important and merge.
— Larry Williams (Legendary trader, author, politician, b. 1942)

TUESDAY

2

D 33.3
S 38.1
N 42.9

We may face more inflation pressure than currently shows up in formal data.
— William Poole (Economist, president Federal Reserve Bank St. Louis 1998-2008, June 2006 speech, b. 1937)

WEDNESDAY

3

D 52.4
S 57.1
N 52.4

The death of contrarians has been greatly exaggerated. The reason is that the crowd is the market for most of any cycle. You cannot be contrarian all the time, otherwise you end up simply fighting the tape the whole way up (or down), therefore being wildly wrong.
— Barry L. Ritholtz (Founder/CIO Ritholtz Wealth Management, *Bailout Nation*, The Big Picture blog, Bloomberg View 12/20/2013, b. 1961)

March Historically Strong Early in the Month *(Pages 32 and 136)*

THURSDAY

4

D 47.6
S 47.6
N 33.3

Price is a fact. Earnings are an estimate.
— Ralph Acampora (Godfather of Technical Analysis, co-founder CMT Association, Altaira Wealth Management, b. 1941)

FRIDAY

5

D 47.6
S 47.6
N 38.1

The key to long-term profits on Wall Street is not making big killings, it's not getting killed.
— Daniel Turov (*Turov on Timing*, b. 1947)

SATURDAY

6

SUNDAY

7

WELCOME TO THE SWEET SPOT OF THE 4-YEAR CYCLE: Q4 MIDTERM YEAR TO Q2 PRE-ELECTION YEAR

"Fourth-Quarter Market Magic" is detailed on page 82 and the "50% Gain in the Dow" from the midterm year low to the pre-election year high is highlighted on page 30. The intersection of the annual seasonal pattern and the 4-Year Cycle produces the quadrennial Sweet Spot. We created the charts here to highlight this critical juncture of 4-Year Cycle.

The second and third quarters of the midterm year have been the weakest period of the entire 4-year pattern averaging losses over the 2-quarter period of -2.0% for the Dow, -2.5% for the S&P 500 and -6.6% for the NASDAQ Composite Index. But thankfully, this sets up the even more important Sweet Spot of the cycle where the Dow gains 19.3%, S&P 500 increases 20.2% and NASDAQ jumps 29.4% over the three-quarter span from midterm year Q4 to pre-election year Q2.

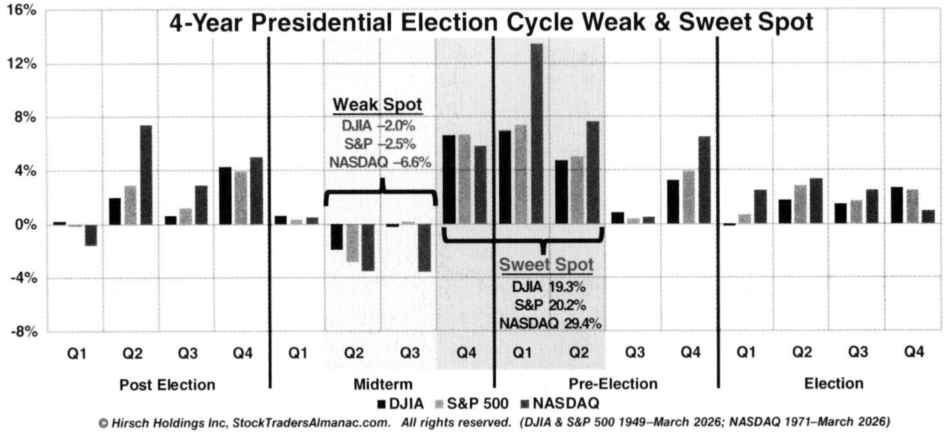

It is for this reason that we call midterm election years a "Bottom Picker's Paradise." From the midterm low to the pre-election year high DJIA gains 46.3% since 1914 and NASDAQ gains a whopping 66.6% since 1974! Be on the lookout for a late Q3 or early Q4 low in the August to October period of 2026. Then be prepared for the rally off that low into the Sweet Spot and beyond to new highs.

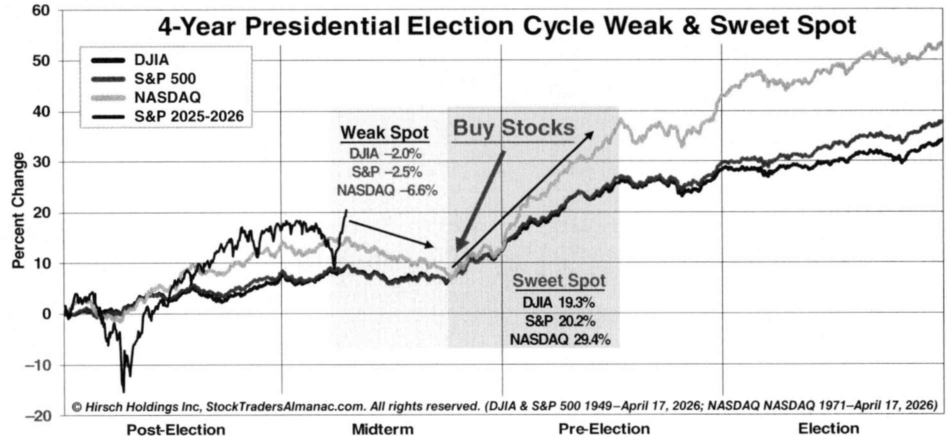

MARCH 2027

MONDAY
D 38.1
S 38.1
N 42.9
8

A bank is a place where they lend you an umbrella in fair weather and ask for it back again when it begins to rain.
— Robert Frost (American poet, 1874-1963)

Dow Down 1469 Points March 9-22 in 2001

TUESDAY
D 66.7
S 61.9
N 57.1
9

My dad always said that you don't live in the world you were born into, and that's not going to change. The rate of change is only going to accelerate.
— Mark Cuban (American billionaire entrepreneur, b. 1958)

WEDNESDAY
D 47.6
S 61.9
N 47.6
10

How a minority, Reaching majority, Seizing authority, Hates a minority.
— Leonard H. Robbins (Newspaper columnist, 1877-1947)

THURSDAY
D 52.4
S 57.1
N 61.9
11

When you get to the end of your rope, tie a knot and hang on.
— Franklin D. Roosevelt (32nd U.S. President, 1882-1945)

FRIDAY
D 66.7
S 42.9
N 47.6
12

The single best predictor of overall excellence is a company's ability to attract, motivate, and retain talented people.
— Bruce Pfau (Vice chair human resources KPMG, *Fortune* 1998)

SATURDAY
13

Daylight Saving Time Begins

SUNDAY
14

THE DECEMBER LOW INDICATOR: A USEFUL PROGNOSTICATING TOOL

When the Dow closes below its December closing low in the first quarter, it is frequently an excellent warning sign. Jeffrey Saut brought this to our attention years ago. The December Low Indicator was originated by Lucien Hooper, a *Forbes* columnist and Wall Street analyst back in the 1970s. Hooper dismissed the importance of January and January's first week as reliable indicators. He noted that the trend could be random or even manipulated during a holiday-shortened week. Instead, said Hooper, "Pay much more attention to the December low. If that low is violated during the first quarter of the New Year, watch out!"

Twenty-three of the 39 occurrences were followed by gains for the rest of the year—and 21 full-year gains—after the low for the year was reached. For perspective we've included the January Barometer readings for the selected years. Hooper's "Watch Out" warning was absolutely correct, though. All but two of the instances since 1952 experienced further declines, as the Dow fell an additional 10.7% on average when December's low was breached in Q1. At press time, Dow was rebounding after closing below its December closing low and suffering a modest 3.2% additional decline triggered by the Iran War.

Only three significant drops occurred (not shown) when December's low was not breached in Q1 (1974, 1981, and 1987). If the December low is not crossed, turn to our January Barometer (page 18) and January Indicator Trifecta (page 20) for guidance.

YEARS DOW FELL BELOW DECEMBER LOW IN FIRST QUARTER

Year	Previous Dec Low	Date Crossed	Crossing Price	Subseq. Low	% Change Cross-Low	Rest of Year % Change	Full Year % Change	Jan Bar
1952	262.29	2/19/52	261.37	256.35	–1.9%	11.7%	8.4%	1.6%[2]
1953	281.63	2/11/53	281.57	255.49	–9.3	–0.2	–3.8	–0.7[3]
1956	480.72	1/9/56	479.74	462.35	–3.6	4.1	2.3	–3.6[1, 2, 3]
1957	480.61	1/18/57	477.46	419.79	–12.1	–8.7	–12.8	–4.2
1960	661.29	1/12/60	660.43	566.05	–14.3	–6.7	–9.3	–7.1
1962	720.10	1/5/62	714.84	535.76	–25.1	–8.8	–10.8	–3.8
1966	939.53	3/1/66	938.19	744.32	–20.7	–16.3	–18.9	0.5[1]
1968	879.16	1/22/68	871.71	825.13	–5.3	8.3	4.3	–4.4[1, 2, 3]
1969	943.75	1/6/69	936.66	769.93	–17.8	–14.6	–15.2	–0.8
1970	769.93	1/26/70	768.88	631.16	–17.9	9.1	4.8	–7.6[2, 3]
1973	1000.00	1/29/73	996.46	788.31	–20.9	–14.6	–16.6	–1.7
1977	946.64	2/7/77	946.31	800.85	–15.4	–12.2	–17.3	–5.1
1978	806.22	1/5/78	804.92	742.12	–7.8	0.01	–3.1	–6.2[3]
1980	819.62	3/10/80	818.94	759.13	–7.3	17.7	14.9	5.8[2]
1982	868.25	1/5/82	865.30	776.92	–10.2	20.9	19.6	–1.8[1, 2]
1984	1236.79	1/25/84	1231.89	1086.57	–11.8	–1.6	–3.7	–0.9[3]
1990	2687.93	1/15/90	2669.37	2365.10	–11.4	–1.3	–4.3	–6.9[3]
1991	2565.59	1/7/91	2522.77	2470.30	–2.1	25.6	20.3	4.2[2]
1993	3255.18	1/8/93	3251.67	3241.95	–0.3	15.5	13.7	0.7[2]
1994	3697.08	3/30/94	3626.75	3593.35	–0.9	5.7	2.1	3.3[2, 3]
1996	5059.32	1/10/96	5032.94	5032.94	NC	28.1	26.0	3.3[2]
1998	7660.13	1/9/98	7580.42	7539.07	–0.5	21.1	16.1	1.0[2]
2000	10998.39	1/4/00	10997.93	9796.03	–10.9	–1.9	–6.2	–5.1
2001	10318.93	3/12/01	10208.25	8235.81	–19.3	–1.8	–7.1	3.5[1]
2002	9763.96	1/16/02	9712.27	7286.27	–25.0	–14.1	–16.8	–1.6
2003	8303.78	1/24/03	8131.01	7524.06	–7.5	28.6	25.3	–2.7[1, 2]
2005	10440.58	1/21/05	10392.99	10012.36	–3.7	3.1	–0.6	–2.5[3]
2006	10717.50	1/20/06	10667.39	10667.39	NC	16.8	16.3	2.5[2]
2007	12194.13	3/2/07	12114.10	12050.41	–0.5	9.5	6.4	1.4[2]
2008	13167.20	1/2/08	13043.96	7552.29	–42.1	–32.7	–33.8	–6.1
2009	8149.09	1/20/09	7949.09	6547.05	–17.6	31.2	18.8	–8.6[1, 2]
2010	10285.97	1/22/10	10172.98	9686.48	–4.8	13.8	11.0	–3.7[1, 2]
2014	15739.43	1/29/14	15738.79	15372.80	–2.3	13.2	7.5	–3.6[1, 2]
2016	17128.55	1/6/16	16906.51	15660.18	–7.4	16.9	13.4	–5.1[1, 2]
2018	24140.91	2/8/18	23860.46	21792.20	–8.7	–2.2	–5.6	5.6[1]
2020	27502.81	2/25/20	27081.36	18591.93	–31.3	13.0	7.2	–0.2[1, 2]
2022	34022.04	2/22/22	33596.61	28725.51	–14.5	–1.3	–8.8	–5.3
2023	32757.54	2/28/23	32656.70	31819.14	–2.6	15.4	13.7	6.2[2]
2025	42326.87	1/10/2025	41938.45	37645.59	–10.2	14.6	13.0	2.7[2]
2026	48063.29	3/12/2026	46677.85	45166.64	–3.2	*As of April 21, 2026*		1.4
				Average Drop	**–10.7%**			

[1]*January Barometer wrong.* [2]*December Low Indicator wrong.* [3]*Year Flat.*

MARCH 2027

Monday Before March Triple Witching, Dow Up 28 of Last 39

MONDAY
D 66.7
S 52.4
N 52.4
15

We are all born originals; why is it so many die copies?
— Edward Young (English poet, 1683-1765)

FOMC Meeting (2 Days)

TUESDAY
D 57.1
S 61.9
N 66.7
16

When I stand before God at the end of my life, I would hope that I would not have a single bit of talent left, and could say, 'I used everything you gave me.'
— Erma Bombeck (American humorist, columnist & writer, 1927-1996)

St. Patrick's Day ♣

WEDNESDAY
D 61.9
S 61.9
N 71.4
17

If more of us valued food and cheer and song above hoarded gold, it would be a merrier world.
— J. R. R. Tolkien (English writer, poet, philologist, and academic, *The Hobbit*, 1892-1973)

Dow Lost 4012 Points (17.3%) on the Week Ending 3/20/2020
Worst Dow Weekly Point Loss and 2nd Worst Percent Loss Overall

THURSDAY
D 61.9
S 52.4
N 76.2
18

Bear markets don't act like a medicine ball rolling down a smooth hill. Instead, they behave like a basketball bouncing down a rock-strewn mountainside; there's lots of movement up and sideways before the bottom is reached.
— Daniel Turov (*Turov on Timing, Barron's* May 21, 2001, b. 1947)

March Triple-Witching Day Mixed Last 30 Years,
But NASDAQ Up 8 of Last 12

FRIDAY
D 52.4
S 52.4
N 61.9
19

Stock market seasonality is a powerful force. When it fails to materialize in any given year, it is an indication that other more powerful forces are at work and when the seasonal period ends those forces often have a more intense impact.
— Jeffrey A. Hirsch (Editor, *Stock Trader's Almanac*, b. 1966)

SATURDAY
20

SUNDAY
21

HOW TO TRADE BEST MONTHS SWITCHING STRATEGIES

Our Best Months Switching Strategies found on pages 54, 56, 62, and 64 are simple and reliable, with a proven 76-year track record. Thus far we have failed to find a similar trading strategy that even comes close over the past six decades. And to top it off, the strategy has only been improving since we first discovered it in 1986.

Exogenous factors and cultural shifts must be considered. "Backward" tests that go back to 1925 or even 1896 and conclude that the pattern does not work are best ignored. They do not take into account these factors. Farming made August the best month from 1900–1951. Since 1988 it is the second worst month of the year for Dow and S&P. Panic caused by financial crisis in 2007–08 caused every asset class aside from U.S. Treasuries to decline substantially. But the bulk of the major decline in equities in the worst months of 2008 was sidestepped using these strategies. Much of the 2022 bear market and 2023's August through October correction were also avoided.

Our Best Months Switching Strategy will not make you an instant millionaire as other strategies claim they can do. What it will do is steadily build wealth over time with possibly less risk of a "buy and hold" approach and the strategy can be applied to any portion of your portfolio.

A sampling of tradable funds for the Best and Worst Months appears in the table below. These are just a starting point and only skim the surface of possible trading vehicles currently available to take advantage of these strategies. Your specific situation and risk tolerance will dictate a suitable choice. If you are trading in a tax-advantaged account such as a company sponsored 401(k) or Individual Retirement Account (IRA), your investment options may be limited to what has been selected by your employer or IRA administrator. But if you are a self-directed trader with a brokerage account, then you likely have unlimited choices (perhaps too many).

TRADABLE BEST AND WORST MONTHS SWITCHING STRATEGY FUNDS

Best Months		Worst Months	
Exchange Traded Funds (ETF)		**Exchange Traded Funds (ETF)**	
Symbol	**Name**	**Symbol**	**Name**
DIA	SPDR Dow Jones Industrial Average	SGOV	iShares 0-3 Month Treasury Bond
SPY	SPDR S&P 500	SHV	iShares Short Treasury Bond
QQQ	Invesco QQQ	AGG	iShares Core U.S. Aggregate Bond
IWM	iShares Russell 2000	TLT	iShares 20+ Year Treasury Bond
Mutual Funds		**Mutual Funds**	
Symbol	**Name**	**Symbol**	**Name**
VWNDX	Vanguard Windsor Fund	VFSTX	Vanguard Short-Term Investment-Grade Bond Fund
FMAGX	Fidelity Magellan Fund	FBNDX	Fidelity Investment Grade Bond Fund
AMCPX	American Funds AMCAP Fund	ABNDX	American Funds Bond Fund of America
FCGAX	Franklin Growth Fund	FKFSX	Franklin U.S. Government Securities Fund

Generally speaking, during the Best Months you want to be invested in equities that offer similar exposure to the companies that constitute Dow, S&P 500, and NASDAQ indices. These would typically be large-cap growth and value stocks as well as technology concerns. Reviewing the holdings of a particular ETF or mutual fund and comparing them to the index members is an excellent way to correlate.

During the Worst Months switch into Treasury bonds, money market funds or a bear/short fund. **Leuthold Grizzly Short** (GRZZX) and **AdvisorShares Ranger Equity Bear** (HDGE) are two possible choices. Money market funds will be the safest, but are likely to offer the smallest return, while bear/short funds offer potentially greater returns, but more risk. If the market moves sideways or higher during the Worst Months, a bear/short fund is likely to lose money. Treasuries can offer a combination of reasonable returns with limited risk.

Additional Worst Month possibilities include precious metals and the companies that mine them. **SPDR Gold Shares** (GLD), **VanEck Gold Miners** (GDX) and **Abrdn Physical Gold** (SGOL) are a few well recognized names available from the ETF universe.

BECOME AN ALMANAC INVESTOR

Almanac Investor subscribers receive specific buy and sell trade ideas based upon the Best Months Switching Strategies online and via email. Sector Index Seasonalities, found on page 94, are also put into action throughout the year with corresponding ETF trades. Buy limits, stop losses, and auto-sell price points for the majority of seasonal trades are delivered directly to your inbox. Visit *www.stocktradersalmanac.com* or see a special offer for new subscribers between pages 66 and 67.

Week After Triple Witching, Dow Down 24 of Last 39, 2000 Up 4.9%, 2009 Up 6.8%, 2020 Up 12.8% Best Week Since 1938

MONDAY
D 47.6
S 42.9
N 47.6
22

You try to be greedy when others are fearful, and fearful when others are greedy.
— Warren Buffett (CEO Berkshire Hathaway, investor and philanthropist, b. 1930)

March Historically Weak Later in the Month (Pages 32 and 136)

TUESDAY
D 47.6
S 52.4
N 52.4
23

The only function of economic forecasting is to make astrology look respectable.
— John Kenneth Galbraith (Canadian/American economist and diplomat, 1908-2006)

WEDNESDAY
D 61.9
S 57.1
N 66.7
24

A day will come when all nations on our continent will form a European brotherhood…A day will come when we shall see… the United States of Europe…reaching out for each other across the seas.
— Victor Hugo (French novelist, playwright, *Hunchback of Notre Dame* and *Les Misérables*, 1802-1885)

NASDAQ Up 22 of Last 26 Days Before Good Friday

THURSDAY
D 47.6
S 47.6
N 38.1
25

The CROWD is always wrong at market turning points but often times right once a trend sets in. The reason many market fighters go broke is they believe the CROWD is always wrong. There is nothing further from the truth. Unless volatility is extremely low or very high one should think twice before betting against the CROWD.
— Shawn Andrew (Trader, Ricercar Fund, 12/21/01)

Good Friday *(Market Closed)*

FRIDAY
26

I learned that courage was not the absence of fear, but the triumph over it. The brave man is not he who does not feel afraid, but he who conquers that fear.
— Nelson Mandela (1st President of South Africa, 1918-2013)

SATURDAY
27

Easter
April Almanac Investor Sector Seasonalities: See Pages 94, 96, and 98

SUNDAY
28

APRIL ALMANAC

APRIL						
S	M	T	W	T	F	S
			1	2	3	4
5	6	7	8	9	10	11
12	13	14	15	16	17	18
19	20	21	22	23	24	25
26	27	28	29	30		

MAY						
S	M	T	W	T	F	S
					1	2
3	4	5	6	7	8	9
10	11	12	13	14	15	16
17	18	19	20	21	22	23
24	25	26	27	28	29	30
31						

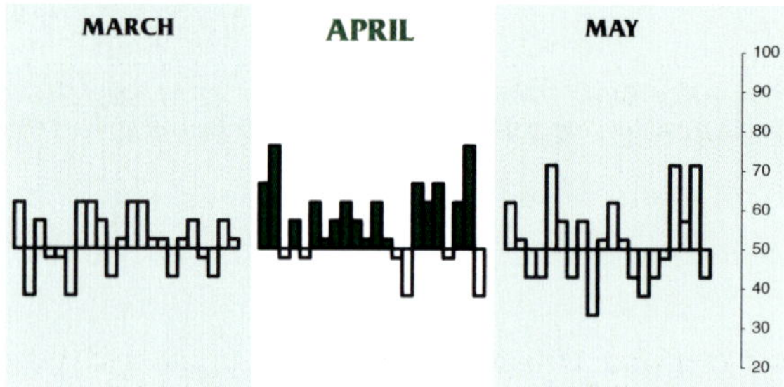

Market Probability Chart above is a graphic representation of the S&P 500 Recent Market Probability Calendar on page 126.

◆ April is the #2 Dow month (average 1.8%) since 1950 (page 52) ◆ April 1999 first month ever to gain 1000 Dow points, 856 in 2001, knocked off its high horse in 2002 down 458, 2003 up 488 ◆ Up 16 straight, 2006 to 2021 ◆ April 2020 Dow +11.1%, best April since 1938 ◆ Exhibits strength after tax deadline recent years ◆ Stocks anticipate great first quarter earnings by rising sharply before earnings are reported, rather than after ◆ Rarely a dangerous month, recent exceptions are 2002, 2004, 2005, 2022, 2024, and 2025 ◆ "Best Six Months" of the year end with April (page 54) ◆ Pre-election year Aprils since 1950, Dow 3.9%, S&P 3.4%, NASDAQ 3.3% ◆ End of April NASDAQ strength fading (pages 127 & 128)

April Vital Statistics

	DJIA		S&P 500		NASDAQ		Russell 1K		Russell 2K	
Rank		2		2		3		2		4
Up		52		54		37		33		29
Down		25		23		19		15		19
Average % Change		1.8		1.6		1.6		1.7		1.4
Pre-Election Yr Avg % Chg		3.9		3.4		3.3		2.7		2.5
Best & Worst April										
	% Change		% Change		% Change		% Change		% Change	
Best	2020	11.1	2020	12.7	2020	15.4	2020	13.1	2009	15.3
Worst	1970	–6.3	1970	–9.0	2000	–15.6	2022	–9.0	2022	–10.0
Best & Worst April Weeks										
Best	4/9/20	12.7	4/9/20	12.1	4/12/01	14.0	4/9/20	12.6	4/9/20	18.5
Worst	4/4/25	–7.9	4/14/00	–10.5	4/14/00	–25.3	4/14/00	–11.2	4/14/00	–16.4
Best & Worst April Days										
Best	4/9/25	7.9	4/9/25	9.5	4/9/25	12.2	4/9/25	9.6	4/9/25	8.7
Worst	4/14/00	–5.7	4/4/25	–6.0	4/14/00	–9.7	4/14/00	–6.0	4/14/00	–7.3
First Trading Day of Monthly Options Expiration Week: 1980–2026										
Record (#Up–#Down)		27-20		25-22		25-22		25-22		21-26
Current streak		U2		U2		U2		U2		U2
Avg % Change		0.14		0.08		0.07		0.07		–0.02
Monthly Options Expiration Day: 1980–2026										
Record (#Up–#Down)		30-17		30-17		26-21		30-17		30-17
Current streak		U1		U2		U1		U2		U4
Avg % Change		0.22		0.16		–0.08		0.16		0.28
Monthly Options Expiration Week: 1980–2026										
Record (#Up–#Down)		36-11		31-16		30-17		29-18		34-13
Current streak		U1		U1		U1		U1		U2
Avg % Change		0.94		0.76		0.82		0.75		0.77
Week After Monthly Options Expiration: 1980–2026										
Record (#Up–#Down)		29-18		31-16		32-15		31-16		32-15
Current streak		D1		U4		U4		U4		U3
Avg % Change		0.36		0.49		0.82		0.49		0.80
First Trading Day Performance										
% of Time Up		58.4		32.3		50.0		60.4		50.0
Avg % Change		0.11		0.09		–0.11		0.08		–0.19
Last Trading Day Performance										
% of Time Up		49.4		53.2		57.1		52.1		56.3
Avg % Change		0.02		–0.01		–0.03		–0.08		–0.15

Dow & S&P 1950–May 1, 2026; NASDAQ 1971–May 1, 2026; Russell 1K & 2K 1979–May 1, 2026.

April "Second Best Month" for Dow since 1950;
Market gains across the board are nifty.

Start Looking for Dow and S&P MACD SELL Signal on April 1 (Pages 56 & 64)
***Almanac Investor* Subscribers Emailed When It Triggers (Learn More Page 67)**

MONDAY
D 42.9
S 42.9
N 42.9
29

I want the whole of Europe to have one currency; it will make trading much easier.
— Napoleon Bonaparte (Emperor of France 1804-1815, 1769-1821)

TUESDAY
D 61.9
S 57.1
N 66.7
30

But how do we know when irrational exuberance has unduly escalated asset values, which then become subject to unexpected and prolonged contractions as they have in Japan over the past decade?
— Alan Greenspan (Fed Chairman 1987-2006, 12/5/96 speech to American Enterprise Institute, b. 1926)

Last Day of March, Dow Down 21 of Last 37, Russell 2000 Up 27 of Last 37

WEDNESDAY
D 52.4
S 52.4
N 52.4
31

The Stone Age didn't end for lack of stone, and the oil age will end long before the world runs out of oil.
— Sheik Ahmed Zaki Yamani (Saudi oil minister 1962-1986, 1930-2021)

First Trading Day in April, S&P Up 23 of Last 32

THURSDAY
D 61.9
S 66.7
N 61.9
1

What we call our future is the shadow that our past projects in front of us.
— Marcel Proust (French novelist, essayist and literary critic, *In Search of Lost Time,* 1871-1922)

FRIDAY
D 71.4
S 76.2
N 71.4
2

Buy a stock the way you would buy a house. Understand and like it such that you'd be content to own it in the absence of any market.
— Warren Buffett (CEO Berkshire Hathaway, investor and philanthropist, b. 1930)

SATURDAY
3

SUNDAY
4

DOW JONES INDUSTRIALS & S&P 500 ONE-YEAR SEASONAL PATTERN CHARTS SINCE 1901 & 1950

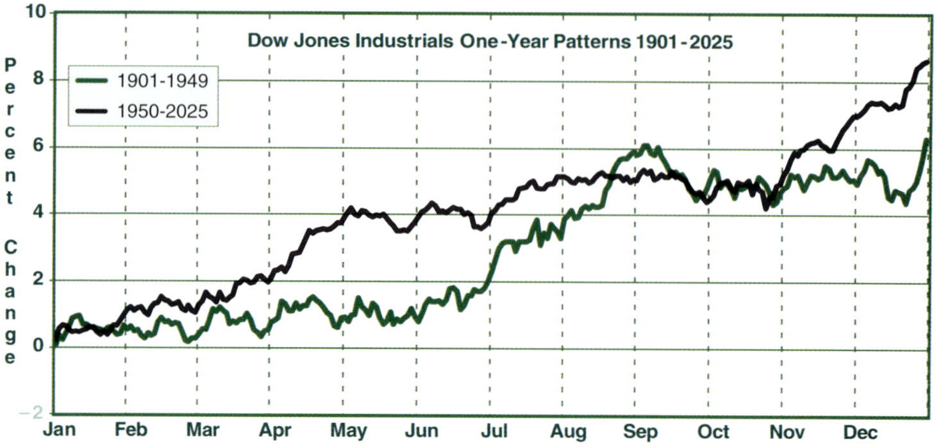

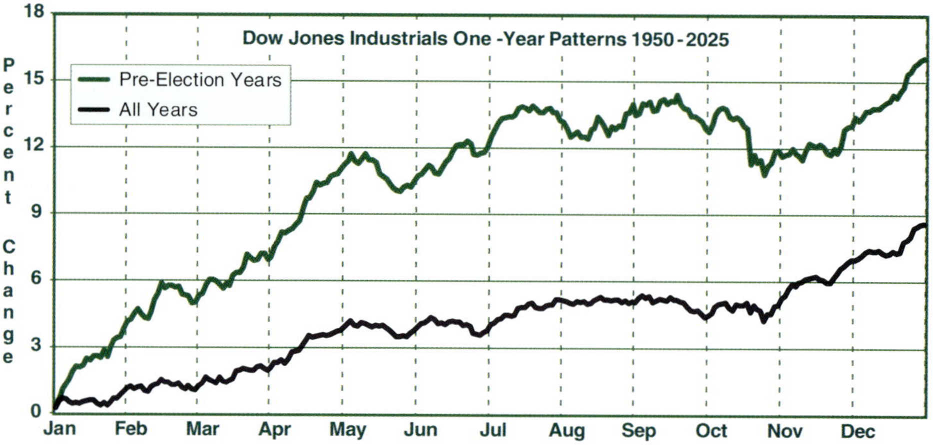

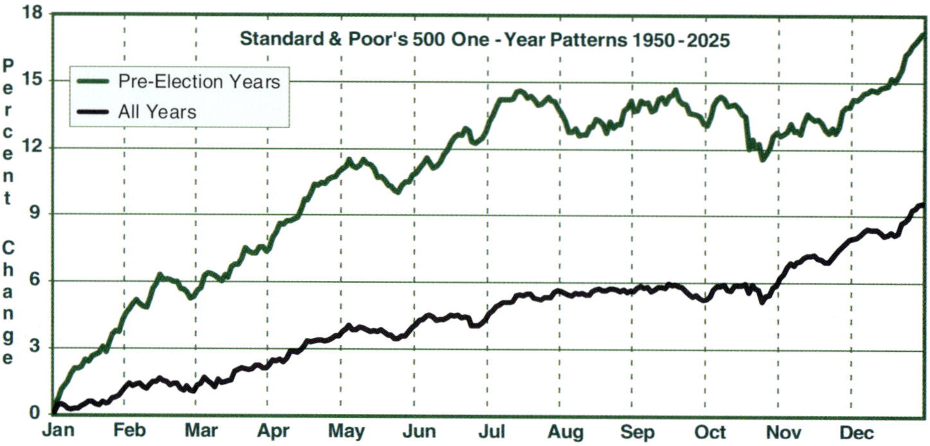

APRIL 2027

MONDAY 5

Day After Easter, Second Worst Post-Holiday (Page 80)

D 42.9
S 47.6
N 52.4

Of the S&P 500 companies in 1957, only 74 were still on the list in 1998 and only 12 outperformed the index itself over that period. By 2020, more than 375 companies in the S&P 500 will consist of companies we don't know today.
— Richard Foster and Sarah Kaplan (*Creative Destruction*)

TUESDAY 6

April Is the Second Best Month for the Dow, Average 1.8% Gain Since 1950

D 52.4
S 57.1
N 52.4

We spend $500 million a year just in training our people. We've developed some technology that lets us do simulations. Think of Flight Simulation. What we've found is that the retention rate from simulation is about 75%, opposed to 25% from classroom work.
— Joe Forehand (CEO, Accenture, *Forbes*, 7/7/03)

WEDNESDAY 7

April 1999 First Month Ever to Gain 1000 Dow Points

D 47.6
S 47.6
N 38.1

It wasn't raining when Noah built the ark.
— Howard Ruff (Financial advisor and author, *The Ruff Times*, 1930-2016)

THURSDAY 8

D 66.7
S 61.9
N 61.9

America, this brash and noble container of dreams, this muse to artists and inventors and entrepreneurs, this beacon of optimism, this dynamo of energy, this trumpet blare of liberty.
— Peter Jennings (Canadian-born anchor *ABC World News Tonight*, July 2003 after gaining U.S. citizenship in May, 1938-2005)

FRIDAY 9

April Is 2nd Best Month for S&P, 3th Best for NASDAQ (Since 1971)

D 47.6
S 52.4
N 47.6

Banking establishments are more dangerous than standing armies; and that the principle of spending money to be paid by posterity, under the name of funding, is but swindling futurity on a large scale.
— Thomas Jefferson (3rd U.S. President, 1743-7/4/1826, 1816 letter to John Taylor of Caroline)

SATURDAY 10

SUNDAY 11

NASDAQ, RUSSELL 1000 & 2000 ONE-YEAR SEASONAL PATTERN CHARTS SINCE 1971 & 1979

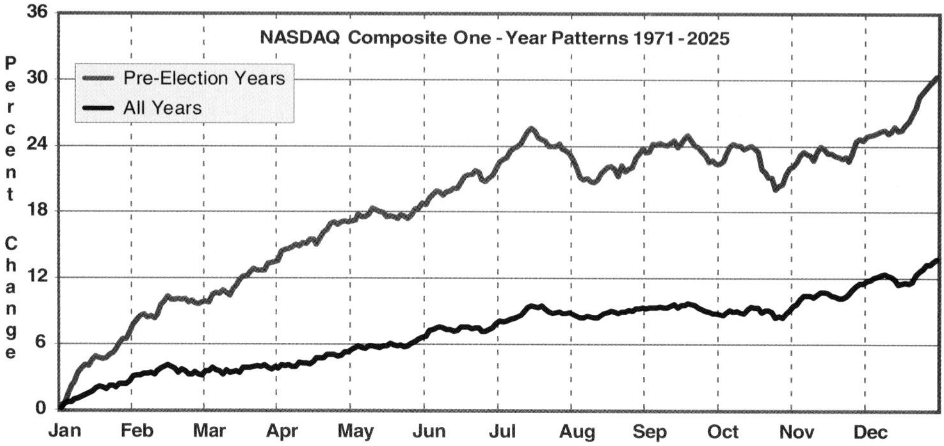

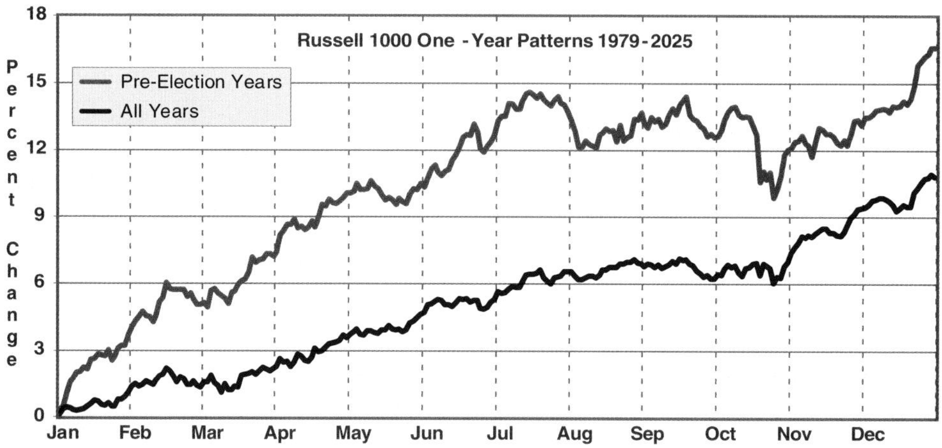

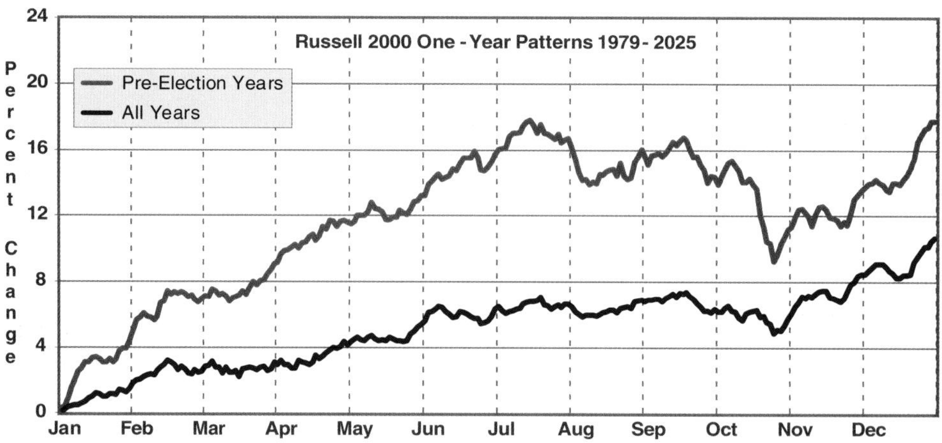

APRIL 2027

Monday Before April Monthly Expiration, Dow Up 23 of Last 38

MONDAY
12
D 47.6
S 57.1
N 61.9

In politics as in chess, or in the military or in business, when you have the advantage you must press it quickly -- or lose it. For the first time in history, we are in a position to checkmate tyranny. Momentum is largely on the side of democracy.
— Garry Kasparov (World Chess Champion 1985-2000)

TUESDAY
13
D 57.1
S 61.9
N 52.4

Doubt is the father of invention.
— Galileo Galilei (Italian physicist and astronomer, 1564-1642)

WEDNESDAY
14
D 61.9
S 57.1
N 47.6

The only thing I do know is that from chaos comes opportunity.
— Daniel S. Loeb (American investor, hedge fund manager & philanthropist, founder CEO CIO Third Point, b. 1961)

Income Tax Deadline
April Exhibits Strength After Tax Deadline Recent Years (Pages 40 and 136)

THURSDAY
15
D 47.6
S 52.4
N 42.9

Taxes are what we pay for civilized society.
— Oliver Wendell Holmes Jr. (U.S. Supreme Court Justice 1902-1932, "The Great Dissenter," inscribed above IRS HQ entrance, 1841-1935)

April Monthly Expiration Day Dow Up 20 of Last 30

FRIDAY
16
D 61.9
S 61.9
N 61.9

I invest in people, not ideas; I want to see fire in the belly and intellect.
— Arthur Rock (First venture capitalist)

SATURDAY
17

SUNDAY
18

60 YEARS ON THE STREET: MARKET CYCLES THAT STILL WORK

Six decades. Eleven presidents. Two secular bear markets. Two Super Booms. Three bubbles, three crashes, one pandemic. Through all of it, most of our seasonal patterns and cycles kept working — guiding readers to better trades and better results. Others now live in what our founder dubbed "the indicator graveyard." But these are the big ones — the top five seasonal patterns, cycles, and indicators most consistent in both frequency and magnitude.

Best Six Months Switching Strategy, *Yale Hirsch, 1986.* "Buy in October and get your portfolio sober." Our answer to Sell in May. The strategy isn't to sell — it's to reposition. Buy October 31, sell April 30: Since 1950, the Dow has gained 7.2% in the November–April window versus 1.1% May–October. $10,000 in the Best Six since 1950 grew to nearly $1.5 million; the same money in the Worst Six grew to $6,700. A simple MACD timing overlay nearly triples the results. Seasonal capital flows, year-end positioning, tax-loss dynamics, and the October 31 mutual fund accounting deadline don't change with the news cycle. *Pages 54 and 56.*

January Barometer & January Indicator Trifecta, *Yale Hirsch, 1972 / Jeffrey Hirsch & Christopher Mistal, 2013.* Yale invented the January Barometer in 1972: as goes January, so goes the year. Since 1950, an up January has been followed by an up year 41 of 46 times — 89.1% accuracy, average S&P gain 16.9%. When January is up, the next 11 months average +11.8%; when January is down, just +1.2%. No other month comes close. Why? The 1933 Twentieth "Lame Duck" Amendment concentrates new Congresses, inaugurations, policy and budget priorities, institutional forecasting and fund flows in January. We built the January Indicator Trifecta pairing the JB with Yale's Santa Claus Rally (1972, page 118) and the First Five Days (page 16). When all three are positive, the S&P is up 90.6% of the time, average gain 17.7%. *Pages 18 and 20.*

October: Bear-Killer & Bargain Month, *Yale Hirsch, 1969 Almanac.* Yale named October the bear-killer 57 years ago and coined the term "Octoberphobia." Crashes in 1929, 1987, 1997, 2008. October has turned the tide in 13 post-WWII bear markets — 1946, 1957, 1960, 1962, 1966, 1974, 1987, 1990, 1998, 2001, 2002, 2011, and the textbook October 2022 midterm low, the Dow's biggest point-gain month ever (+4,000 points, +14.0%). The October 31 mutual fund deadline forces portfolio managers by law (40 Act) to reconcile accounting for December 31 distribution, concentrating forced selling at the end of the worst six months and clearing the deck for the year-end rally. October is the most volatile month and the best month to buy stocks. *Page 88.*

Four-Year Presidential Election Cycle: Weak Spot, Sweet Spot, Bottom Picker's Paradise, *Yale Hirsch, 1967.* From the first edition 60 years ago, Yale put the four-year cycle on Wall Street's map. Since 1833, the last two years of the 48 presidential terms produced a net gain of 798.6%, dwarfing the 349.5% of the first two. Midterm Q2-Q3 Weak Spot — Dow –2.0%, S&P –2.5%, NASDAQ –6.6%. Sweet Spot: midterm Q4 to pre-election Q2 — Dow +19.3%, S&P +20.2%, NASDAQ +29.4% — three quarters account for the bulk of the cycle's gains. Bottom Picker's Paradise: 10 of 19 bear markets since 1961 bottomed in the midterm year, including October 2022. Dow has averaged +46.3% from midterm low to pre-election high since 1914. Pre-election years are nearly bulletproof — only one Dow loss since 1939 (2015, –2.2%). Incumbent administrations manipulate the economy to keep their party in power: least savory policy initiatives in the first two years, prime the pump in the next two. *Pages 26, 28, 30, 34, and 132.*

Hirsch Super Boom Cycle, *Yale Hirsch, 1976 / Jeffrey Hirsch, 2010.* Two secular bears, two Super Boom forecasts, two bullseyes — across two generations. Yale discovered the pattern in 1976: war drives government spending, spending generates inflation, inflation stimulates economic activity, and culturally enabling, paradigm-shifting technology ignites equities. The Dow moved +504% after WWI and +523% following WWII. Yale forecast a third 500% move and Dow 3,420 by 1990 which hit it in 1991. We applied the same framework off the 2000–2009 secular bear in 2010 and laid it out in *Super Boom* (Wiley, 2011) — Dow 38,820 by 2025. The Dow hit 38,820 in early 2024, a year early. Inflation arrived later than projected, surging in 2021–2022 on the heels of 2020–2021 COVID war-like spending — but the Super Boom is still in play. With a bit of hindsight, we now believe the current secular bull began in October 2011. A 500% move off the October 4, 2011, intraday low of 10,405 takes the Dow to 62,430. See NASDAQ 74,000: Welcome to the AI Super Boom. *Page 100.*

MONDAY
D 47.6
S 52.4
N 33.3
19

Losses loom larger than gains. The aggravation that one experiences in losing a sum of money appears to be greater than the pleasure associated with gaining the same amount.
— Daniel Kahneman (Israeli-American psychologist and economist, "Prospect Theory: An Analysis of Decision under Risk," *Econometrica*, March 1979, 2002 Nobel Prize, 1934-2024)

TUESDAY
D 61.9
S 47.6
N 52.4
20

New indicator: *CFO Magazine gave Excellence awards to WorldCom's Scott Sullivan (1998), Enron's Andrew Fastow (1999), and to Tyco's Mark Swartz (2000). All were subsequently indicted.*
— Roger Lowenstein (Financial journalist and author, *Origins Of The Crash*, b. 1954)

End of "Best Six Months" of the Year (Pages 54, 56, 64, and 149)

WEDNESDAY
D 57.1
S 38.1
N 61.9
21

I've never been poor, only broke. Being poor is a frame of mind. Being broke is only a temporary situation.
— Mike Todd (Movie producer, 1903-1958)

Passover

THURSDAY
D 61.9
S 66.7
N 61.9
22

Change is the law of life. And those who look only to the past or present are certain to miss the future.
— John F. Kennedy (35th U.S. President, 1917-1963)

FRIDAY
D 66.7
S 61.9
N 52.4
23

A good trader has to have three things: a chronic inability to accept things at face value, to feel continuously unsettled, and to have humility.
— Michael Steinhardt (Financier, philanthropist, political activist, chairman WisdomTree Investments, b. 1940)

SATURDAY
24

May Almanac Investor Sector Seasonalities: See Pages 94, 96, and 98

SUNDAY
25

MAY ALMANAC

MAY						
S	M	T	W	T	F	S
						1
2	3	4	5	6	7	8
9	10	11	12	13	14	15
16	17	18	19	20	21	22
23	24	25	26	27	28	29
30	31					

JUNE						
S	M	T	W	T	F	S
		1	2	3	4	5
6	7	8	9	10	11	12
13	14	15	16	17	18	19
20	21	22	23	24	25	26
27	28	29	30			

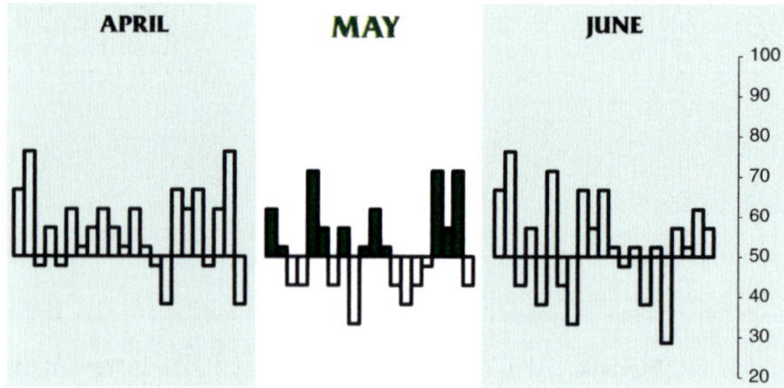

Market Probability Chart above is a graphic representation of the S&P 500 Recent Market Probability Calendar on page 126.

◆ "May/June disaster area" between 1965 and 1984 with S&P down 15 out of 20 Mays ◆ Between 1985 and 1997 May was the best month with 13 straight gains, gaining 3.3% per year on average, up 19, down 9 since ◆ Worst six months of the year begin with May (page 54) ◆ A $10,000 investment compounded to $1,375,007 gain for November-April in 76 years compared to a $6,676 gain for May-October ◆ Dow Memorial Day week record: up 12 years in a row (1984–1995), down 17 of the last 30 years ◆ Since 1950 pre-election year Mays rank, #11 Dow, #11 S&P, and #8 NASDAQ

May Vital Statistics

	DJIA	S&P 500	NASDAQ	Russell 1K	Russell 2K
Rank	9	8	5	6	5
Up	42	47	34	33	30
Down	34	29	21	14	17
Average % Change	0.03	0.4	1.3	1.1	1.3
Pre-Election Yr Avg % Chg	–0.5	–0.1	1.5	0.5	1.5
Best & Worst May					
	% Change	% Change	% Change	% Change	% Change
Best	1990 8.3	1990 9.2	1997 11.1	1990 8.9	1997 11.0
Worst	2010 –7.9	1962 –8.6	2000 –11.9	2010 –8.1	2019 –7.9
Best & Worst May Weeks					
Best	5/27/22 6.2	5/27/22 6.6	5/17/02 8.8	5/27/22 6.6	5/22/20 7.8
Worst	5/25/62 –6.0	5/25/62 –6.8	5/7/10 –8.0	5/7/10 –6.6	5/7/10 –8.9
Best & Worst May Days					
Best	5/27/70 5.1	5/27/70 5.0	5/30/00 7.9	5/10/10 4.4	5/18/20 6.1
Worst	5/28/62 –5.7	5/28/62 –6.7	5/23/00 –5.9	5/18/22 –4.0	5/20/10 –5.1
First Trading Day of Monthly Expiration Week: 1980–2026					
Record (#Up–#Down)	28-18	29-17	26-20	27-19	24-22
Current streak	U1	U1	U3	U1	U3
Avg % Change	0.16	0.17	0.17	0.14	0.04
Monthly Options Expiration Day: 1980–2026					
Record (#Up–#Down)	25-21	26-20	21-25	26-20	23-23
Current streak	U2	U2	U1	U2	U1
Avg % Change	–0.03	–0.05	–0.08	–0.04	0.05
Monthly Options Expiration Week: 1980–2026					
Record (#Up–#Down)	22-24	22-24	24-22	21-25	24-22
Current streak	U3	U3	U3	U3	U3
Avg % Change	–0.01	0.05	0.27	0.06	–0.12
Week After Monthly Options Expiration: 1980–2026					
Record (#Up–#Down)	25-21	30-16	32-14	29-17	32-14
Current streak	D3	D1	D1	D2	D3
Avg % Change	0.13	0.34	0.52	0.36	0.56
First Trading Day Performance					
% of Time Up	55.8	58.4	60.7	58.3	64.6
Avg % Change	0.15	0.19	0.29	0.18	0.20
Last Trading Day Performance					
% of Time Up	56.6	57.9	60.0	53.2	55.3
Avg % Change	0.13	0.20	0.13	0.12	0.15

Dow & S&P 1950–May 1, 2026; NASDAQ 1971–May 1, 2026; Russell 1K & 2K 1979–May 1, 2026.

Better to reposition in May
Than to sell in May and go away.

APRIL/MAY 2027

MONDAY
D 57.1
S 66.7
N 66.7
26

In bull markets promises trade at a premium, but in bear markets reality trades at a discount.
— Jim Chanos (Short seller, Founder Kynikos Associates, b. 1957)

FOMC Meeting (2 Days)

TUESDAY
D 52.4
S 47.6
N 38.1
27

I'm not better than the next trader, just quicker at admitting my mistakes and moving on to the next opportunity.
— George Soros (Financier, philanthropist, political activist, author and philosopher, b. 1930)

WEDNESDAY
D 71.4
S 61.9
N 52.4
28

When I talk to a company that tells me the last analyst showed up three years ago, I can hardly contain my enthusiasm.
— Peter Lynch (Fidelity Investments, One *Up On Wall Street*, b. 1944)

THURSDAY
D 76.2
S 76.2
N 85.7
29

If the models are telling you to sell, sell, sell, but if there are nothing but buyers are out there, don't be a jerk. Buy!
— William Silber, Ph.D. (New York University, *Newsweek*, 1986)

FRIDAY
D 33.3
S 38.1
N 28.6
30

A fundamental analyst goes into each store and studies the products to decide whether to buy or not.
A technical analyst sits on a bench watching people go into stores. Disregarding the intrinsic value,
the technical analyst's decision is based on the patterns or activity of people.
— Investopedia.com on Technical Analysis (Hat tip to JC Parets of All Star Charts via Ari Wald of Oppenheimer)

SATURDAY
1

SUNDAY
2

SUMMER MARKET VOLUME DOLDRUMS DRIVE WORST SIX MONTHS

Memorial Day weekend has become the unofficial start of summer. Not long afterwards, trading activity typically begins to slowly decline (barring any external event triggers) towards a later summer low. We refer to this summertime slowdown in trading as the doldrums due to the anemic volume and uninspired trading on Wall Street. The individual trader, if they are looking to sell a stock, is generally met with disinterest from The Street. It becomes difficult to sell a stock at a good price. That is also why many summer rallies tend to be short lived and are quickly followed by a pullback or correction.

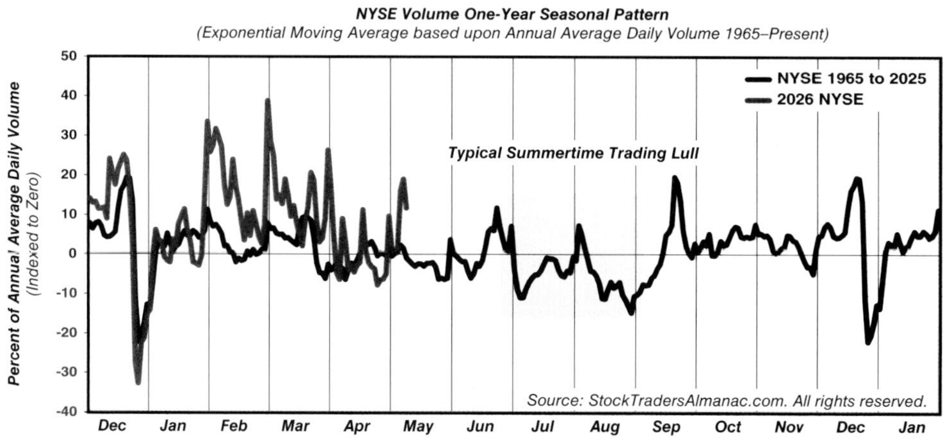

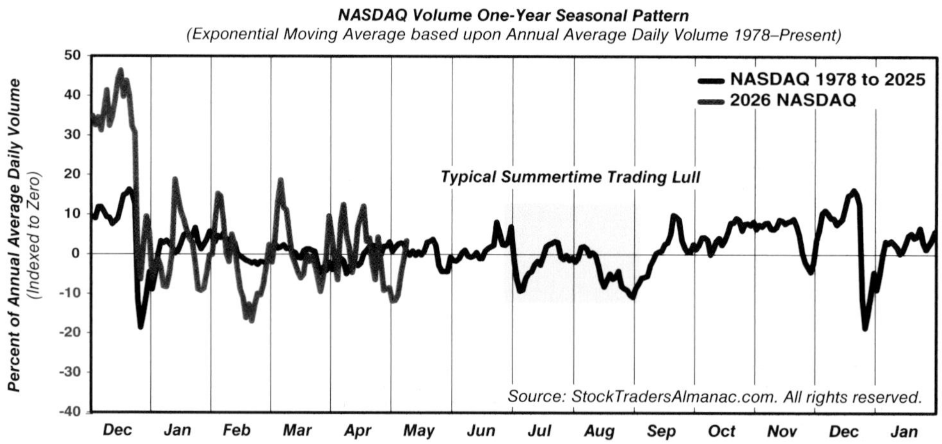

Above are plotted the one-year seasonal volume patterns since 1965 for the NYSE and since 1978 for NASDAQ against the annual average daily volume moving average for 2026 as of the close on May 8, 2026. The typical summer lull is highlighted in green. A prolonged surge in volume during the typically quiet summer months, especially when accompanied by gains, can be an encouraging sign that the bull market will continue. However, should traders lose their conviction and participate in the annual summer exodus from The Street, a market pullback or correction could quickly unfold.

MAY 2027

First Trading Day in May, S&P Up 20 of Last 29

MONDAY
D 57.1
S 61.9
N 61.9
3

To me, the "tape" is the final arbiter of any investment decision. I have a cardinal rule: Never fight the tape!
— Martin Zweig (Fund manager, *Winning on Wall Street*, 1943-2013)

TUESDAY
D 66.7
S 52.4
N 57.1
4

We are nowhere near a capitulation point because it's at that point where it's despair, not hope, that reigns supreme, and there was scant evidence of any despair at any of the meetings I gave.
— David Rosenberg (Economist, Merrill Lynch, *Barron's* 4/21/2008)

WEDNESDAY
D 52.4
S 42.9
N 38.1
5

Being uneducated is sometimes beneficial. Then you don't know what can't be done.
— Michael Ott (Venture capitalist)

THURSDAY
D 38.1
S 42.9
N 47.6
6

The more feted by the media, the worse a pundit's accuracy.
— Sharon Begley (Senior editor *Newsweek*, 2/23/2009, referencing Philip E. Tetlock's 2005 Expert *Political Judgment*)

Friday Before Mother's Day, Dow Up 21 of Last 32

FRIDAY
D 71.4
S 71.4
N 61.9
7

Securities pricing is, in every sense a psychological phenomenon that arises from the interaction of human beings with fear. Why not greed and fear as the equation is usually stated? Because greed is simply fear of not having enough.
— John Bollinger, CMT, CFA (American author, technical/financial analyst, developer of Bollinger Bands, Bollinger Capital Management, *Capital Growth Letter, Bollinger on Bollinger Bands*, b. 1950)

SATURDAY
8

Mother's Day

SUNDAY
9

TOP-PERFORMING MONTHS: STANDARD & POOR'S 500 AND DOW JONES INDUSTRIALS

Monthly performance of the S&P and the Dow are ranked over the past 76 1/3 years. NASDAQ monthly performance is shown on page 60.

April, November, and December still hold the top three positions in both the Dow and S&P. Disastrous Januarys in 2008, 2009, 2016, and 2022 knocked January into fifth. This, in part, led to our discovery in 1986 of the market's most consistent seasonal pattern. You can divide the year into two sections and have practically all the gains in one six-month section and very little in the other. September is the worst month on both lists. (See "Best Six Months" on page 54.)

MONTHLY % CHANGES (JANUARY 1950–APRIL 2026)

	Standard & Poor's 500					Dow Jones Industrials			
Month	Total % Change	Avg. % Change	# Up	# Down	Month	Total % Change	Avg. % Change	# Up	# Down
Jan	83.4%	1.1%	47	30	Jan	75.3%	1.0%	49	28
Feb	–2.7	–0.03	41	36	Feb	4.5	0.1	45	32
Mar	73.5	1.0	49	28	Mar	62.9	0.8	49	28
Apr	119.9	1.6	54	23	Apr	142.0	1.8	52	25
May	27.5	0.4	47	29	May	2.1	0.03	42	34
Jun	16.4	0.2	43	33	Jun	–8.0	–0.1	37	39
Jul	98.2	1.3	46	30	Jul	105.1	1.4	51	25
Aug	3.3	0.04	42	34	Aug	–4.1	–0.1	43	33
Sep*	–47.7	–0.6	34	41	Sep	–59.9	–0.8	31	45
Oct	68.9	0.9	45	31	Oct	57.1	0.8	45	31
Nov	140.5	1.8	53	23	Nov	144.1	1.9	53	23
Dec	107.2	1.4	55	21	Dec	110.6	1.5	53	23
% Rank					**% Rank**				
Nov	140.5%	1.8%	53	23	Nov	144.1%	1.9%	53	23
Apr	119.9	1.6	54	23	Apr	142.0	1.8	52	25
Dec	107.2	1.4	55	21	Dec	110.6	1.5	53	23
Jul	98.2	1.3	46	30	Jul	105.1	1.4	51	25
Jan	83.4	1.1	47	30	Jan	75.3	1.0	49	28
Mar	73.5	1.0	49	28	Mar	62.9	0.8	49	28
Oct	68.9	0.9	45	31	Oct	57.1	0.8	45	31
May	27.5	0.4	47	29	Feb	4.5	0.1	45	32
Jun	16.4	0.2	43	33	May	2.1	0.03	42	34
Aug	3.3	0.04	42	34	Aug	–4.1	–0.1	43	33
Feb	–2.7	–0.03	41	36	Jun	–8.0	–0.1	37	39
Sep*	–47.7	–0.6	34	41	Sep	–59.9	–0.8	31	45
Totals	**688.4%**	**9.1%**			**Totals**	**631.7%**	**8.3%**		
Average		**0.76%**			**Average**		**0.69%**		

**No change 1979*

Anticipators, shifts in cultural behavior and faster information flow have altered seasonality in recent years. Here is how the months ranked over the past 15 1/3 years (185 months) using total percentage gains on the S&P 500: November 46.7, July 38.3, October 30.5, April 26.8, January 20.5, June 19.1, February 12.0, May 12.0, March 2.3, December 2.3, August 0.0, and September –19.5.

January has declined in 13 of the last 27 years. Sizeable turnarounds in "bear killing" October were a common occurrence from 1999 to 2007 and 2022. Recent big Dow losses in the period were: September 2001 (9/11 attack), off 11.1%; September 2002 (Iraq war drums), off 12.4%; June 2008, off 10.2%; October 2008, off 14.1%; February 2009, off 11.7% (financial crisis); and March 2020 (Covid-19 shutdown), off 13.7%.

Monday After Mother's Day, Dow Up 20 of Last 32

MONDAY
D 71.4
S 57.1
N 71.4
10

A national debt, if it is not excessive, will be to us a national blessing.
— Alexander Hamilton (U.S. Treasury Secretary 1789-1795, The Federalist 1788, in April 30, 1781 letter to Robert Morris)

TUESDAY
D 33.3
S 42.9
N 52.4
11

During healthy bull markets you see breakdowns failing all the time. During the bear markets it's the breakouts that fail quite often.
— J. C. Parets, CMT (Founder All Star Charts, Stock Market Media and TrendLabs, b. 1982)

WEDNESDAY
D 57.1
S 57.1
N 47.6
12

Life is an illusion. You are what you think you are.
— Yale Hirsch (Creator of *Stock Trader's Almanac*, 1923-2021)

THURSDAY
D 28.6
S 33.3
N 52.4
13

Never bet on the end of the world, because it only happens once, and even if it does, who are you going to settle the trade with?
— Arthur D. Cashin, Jr. (Legendary NYSE floor trader, director of floor operations UBS Financial Services, 1941-2024)

FRIDAY
D 52.4
S 52.4
N 61.9
14

Based on my own personal experience—both as an investor in recent years and an expert witness in years past—rarely do more than three or four variables really count. Everything else is noise.
— Martin J. Whitman (Founder Third Avenue Funds, 1924-2018)

SATURDAY
15

SUNDAY
16

BEST SIX MONTHS: STILL AN EYE-POPPING STRATEGY

Our Best Six Months Switching Strategy consistently delivers. Investing in the Dow Jones Industrial Average between November 1st and April 30th each year and then switching into fixed income for the other six months has produced reliable returns with reduced risk since 1950.

The chart on page 149 shows November, December, January, March, and April to be the top months since 1950. Add February, and an excellent strategy is born! These six consecutive months gained 32007.77 Dow points in 76 years, while the remaining May through October months gained 17430.04 points. The S&P gained 7.0% in the same best six months versus 2.0% in the worst six.

Percentage changes are shown along with a compounding $10,000 investment. The November–April $1,375,007 gain overshadows May–October's $6,676 gain. (S&P results were $1,209,664 to $22,663.) Just four November–April losses were double-digit: April 1970 (Cambodian invasion), 1973 (OPEC oil embargo), 2008 (financial crisis), and 2019 (Covid-19 shutdown). Similarly, Iraq muted the Best Six and inflated the Worst Six in 2003. When we discovered this strategy in 1986, November–April outperformed May–October by $88,163 to minus $1,522. Results improved substantially these past 40 years, $1,286,844 to $8,198. A simple timing indicator nearly triples results (page 56).

SIX-MONTH SWITCHING STRATEGY

	DJIA % Change May 1–Oct 31	Investing $10,000	DJIA % Change Nov 1–Apr 30	Investing $10,000
1950	5.0%	$10,500	15.2%	$11,520
1951	1.2	10,626	−1.8	11,313
1952	4.5	11,104	2.1	11,551
1953	0.4	11,148	15.8	13,376
1954	10.3	12,296	20.9	16,172
1955	6.9	13,144	13.5	18,355
1956	−7.0	12,224	3.0	18,906
1957	−10.8	10,904	3.4	19,549
1958	19.2	12,998	14.8	22,442
1959	3.7	13,479	−6.9	20,894
1960	−3.5	13,007	16.9	24,425
1961	3.7	13,488	−5.5	23,082
1962	−11.4	11,950	21.7	28,091
1963	5.2	12,571	7.4	30,170
1964	7.7	13,539	5.6	31,860
1965	4.2	14,108	−2.8	30,968
1966	−13.6	12,189	11.1	34,405
1967	−1.9	11,957	3.7	35,678
1968	4.4	12,483	−0.2	35,607
1969	−9.9	11,247	−14.0	30,622
1970	2.7	11,551	24.6	38,155
1971	−10.9	10,292	13.7	43,382
1972	0.1	10,302	−3.6	41,820
1973	3.8	10,693	12.5	36,593
1974	−20.5	8,501	23.4	45,156
1975	1.8	8,654	19.2	53,826
1976	−3.2	8,377	−3.9	51,727
1977	−11.7	7,397	2.3	52,917
1978	−5.4	6,998	7.9	57,097
1979	−4.6	6,676	0.2	57,211
1980	13.1	7,551	7.9	61,731
1981	−14.6	6,449	−0.5	61,422
1982	16.9	7,539	23.6	75,918
1983	−0.1	7,531	−4.4	72,578
1984	3.1	7,764	4.2	75,626
1985	9.2	8,478	29.8	98,163
1986	5.3	8,927	21.8	119,563
1987	−12.8	7,784	1.9	121,835
1988	5.7	8,228	12.6	137,186
1989	9.4	9,001	0.4	137,735
1990	−8.1	8,272	18.2	162,803
1991	6.3	8,793	9.4	178,106
1992	−4.0	8,441	6.2	189,149
1993	7.4	9,066	0.03	189,206
1994	6.2	9,628	10.6	209,262
1995	10.0	10,591	17.1	245,046
1996	8.3	11,470	16.2	284,743
1997	6.2	12,181	21.8	346,817
1998	−5.2	11,548	25.6	435,602
1999	−0.5	11,490	0.04	435,776
2000	2.2	11,743	−2.2	426,189
2001	−15.5	9,923	9.6	467,103
2002	−15.6	8,375	1.0	471,774
2003	15.6	9,682	4.3	492,060
2004	−1.9	9,498	1.6	499,933
2005	2.4	9,726	8.9	544,427
2006	6.3	10,339	8.1	588,526
2007	6.6	11,021	−8.0	541,444
2008	−27.3	8,012	−12.4	474,305
2009	18.9	9,526	13.3	537,388
2010	1.0	9,621	15.2	619,071
2011	−6.7	8,976	10.5	684,073
2012	−0.9	8,895	13.3	775,055
2013	4.8	9,322	6.7	826,984
2014	4.9	9,779	2.6	848,486
2015	−1.0	9,681	0.6	853,577
2016	2.1	9,884	15.4	985,223
2017	11.6	11,031	3.4	1,018,721
2018	3.9	11,461	5.9	1,078,826
2019	1.7	11,656	−10.0	970,943
2020	8.9	12,693	27.8	1,240,865
2021	5.7	13,417	−7.9	1,142,837
2022	−0.7	13,323	4.2	1,190,836
2023	−3.1	12,910	14.4	1,362,316
2024	10.4	14,253	−2.6	1,326,635
2025	17.0	16,676	4.4	1,385,007
Average/Gain	**1.1%**	**$6.676**	**7.2%**	**$1,375,007**
# Up/Down	**47/29**		**59/17**	

Monday Before May Monthly Expiration, Dow Up 28 of Last 39

MONDAY
D 71.4
S 61.9
N 47.6
17

Take care of your employees and they'll take care of your customers.
— John W. Marriott (Founder Marriott International, 1900-1985)

TUESDAY
D 47.6
S 52.4
N 57.1
18

Only buy stocks when the market declines 10% from that date a year ago, which happens once or twice a decade.
— Eugene D. Brody (Oppenheimer Capital)

WEDNESDAY
D 42.9
S 42.9
N 38.1
19

History is a collection of agreed-upon lies.
— Voltaire (French philosopher, 1694-1778)

THURSDAY
D 38.1
S 38.1
N 42.9
20

People somehow think you must buy at the bottom and sell at the top. That's nonsense. The idea is to buy when the probability is greatest that the market is going to advance.
— Martin Zweig (Fund manager, *Winning on Wall Street*, 1943-2013)

May Monthly Expiration Day, Dow Up 17 of Last 25

FRIDAY
D 42.9
S 42.9
N 47.6
21

If you could kick the person in the pants responsible for most of your trouble, you wouldn't sit for a month.
— Theodore Roosevelt (26th U.S. President, 1858-1919)

SATURDAY
22

SUNDAY
23

MACD-TIMING TRIPLES BEST-SIX-MONTHS RESULTS

Using the simple MACD (Moving Average Convergence Divergence) indicator developed by our friend Gerald Appel to better time entries and exits into and out of the Best Six Months (page 54) period nearly triples the results. Sy Harding enhanced our Best-Six-Months Switching Strategy with MACD triggers, dubbing it the "best mechanical system ever." In 2006 we improved results with just four trades every four years (page 64).

Our *Almanac Investor* (see page 67) implements this system with quite a degree of success. Starting on the first trading day of October we look to catch the market's first hint of an uptrend after the summer doldrums, and beginning on the first trading day of April we prepare to exit these seasonal positions as soon as the market falters.

In up-trending markets, MACD signals get you in earlier and keep you in longer. But if the market is trending down, entries are delayed until the market turns up and exit points can come a month earlier.

The results are astounding applying the simple MACD signals. Instead of $10,000 gaining $1,375,007 over the 76 recent years when invested only during the Best Six Months (page 54), the gain nearly tripled to $3,983,414. The $6,676 gain during the worst six months became a loss of $4,161.

Impressive results for being invested during only 6.3 months of the year on average! For the rest of the year consider money markets, bonds, puts, bear funds, covered calls or credit call spreads.

Updated signals are emailed to our *Almanac Investor* subscribers as soon as they are triggered. Visit *www.stocktradersalmanac.com* or see a special offer for new subscribers between pages 66 and 67.

BEST SIX-MONTH SWITCHING STRATEGY+TIMING

	DJIA % Change May 1–Oct 31*	Investing $10,000	DJIA % Change Nov 1–Apr 30*	Investing $10,000
1950	7.3%	$10,730	13.3%	$11,330
1951	0.1	10,741	1.9	11,545
1952	1.4	10,891	2.1	11,787
1953	0.2	10,913	17.1	13,803
1954	13.5	12,386	16.3	16,053
1955	7.7	13,340	13.1	18,156
1956	−6.8	12,433	2.8	18,664
1957	−12.3	10,904	4.9	19,579
1958	17.3	12,790	16.7	22,849
1959	1.6	12,995	−3.1	22,141
1960	−4.9	12,358	16.9	25,883
1961	2.9	12,716	−1.5	25,495
1962	−15.3	10,770	22.4	31,206
1963	4.3	11,233	9.6	34,202
1964	6.7	11,986	6.2	36,323
1965	2.6	12,298	−2.5	35,415
1966	−16.4	10,281	14.3	40,479
1967	−2.1	10,065	5.5	42,705
1968	3.4	10,407	0.2	42,790
1969	−11.9	9,169	−6.7	39,923
1970	−1.4	9,041	20.8	48,227
1971	−11.0	8,046	15.4	55,654
1972	−0.6	7,998	−1.4	54,875
1973	−11.0	7,118	0.1	54,930
1974	−22.4	5,524	28.2	70,420
1975	0.1	5,530	18.5	83,448
1976	−3.4	5,342	−3.0	80,945
1977	−11.4	4,733	0.5	81,350
1978	−4.5	4,520	9.3	88,916
1979	−5.3	4,280	7.0	95,140
1980	9.3	4,678	4.7	99,612
1981	−14.6	3,995	0.4	100,010
1982	15.5	4,614	23.5	123,512
1983	2.5	4,729	−7.3	114,496
1984	3.3	4,885	3.9	118,961
1985	7.0	5,227	38.1	164,285
1986	−2.8	5,081	28.2	210,613
1987	−14.9	4,324	3.0	216,931
1988	6.1	4,588	11.8	242,529
1989	9.8	5,038	3.3	250,532
1990	−6.7	4,700	15.8	290,116
1991	4.8	4,926	11.3	322,899
1992	−6.2	4,621	6.6	344,210
1993	5.5	4,875	5.6	363,486
1994	3.7	5,055	13.1	411,103
1995	7.2	5,419	16.7	479,757
1996	9.2	5,918	21.9	584,824
1997	3.6	6,131	18.5	693,016
1998	−12.4	5,371	39.9	969,529
1999	−6.4	5,027	5.1	1,018,975
2000	−6.0	4,725	5.4	1,074,000
2001	−17.3	3,908	15.8	1,243,692
2002	−25.2	2,923	6.0	1,318,314
2003	16.4	3,402	7.8	1,421,142
2004	−0.9	3,371	1.8	1,446,723
2005	−0.5	3,354	7.7	1,558,121
2006	4.7	3,512	14.4	1,782,490
2007	5.6	3,709	−12.7	1,556,114
2008	−24.7	2,793	−14.0	1,338,258
2009	23.8	3,458	10.8	1,482,790
2010	4.6	3,617	7.3	1,591,034
2011	−9.4	3,277	18.7	1,888,557
2012	0.3	3,287	10.0	2,077,413
2013	4.1	3,422	7.1	2,224,909
2014	2.3	3,501	7.4	2,389,552
2015	−6.0	3,291	4.9	2,506,640
2016	3.5	3,406	13.1	2,835,010
2017	15.7	3,941	0.4	2,846,350
2018	5.0	4,138	5.2	2,994,360
2019	1.5	4,200	−13.3	2,596,110
2020	22.1	5,128	19.1	3,091,967
2021	2.8	5,272	−0.5	3,076,507
2022	−12.3	4,624	10.6	3,402,617
2023	0.2	4,633	16.6	3,967,451
2024	9.4	5,069	−5.4	3,753,209
2025	15.2	5,839	6.4	3,993,414
Average	**−0.2%**		**8.7%**	
# Up	**44**		**64**	
# Down	**32**		**12**	
76-Year Gain (Loss)		**($4,161)**		**$3,983,414**

**MACD generated entry and exit points (earlier or later) can lengthen or shorten six-month periods.*

MONDAY
D 47.6
S 47.6
N 42.9
24

Let me end my talk by abusing slightly my status as an official representative of the Federal Reserve. I would like to say to Milton [Friedman]: regarding the Great Depression, you're right; we did it. We're very sorry. But thanks to you, we won't do it again.
— Ben Bernanke (Fed Chairman 2006-2014, 11/8/02 speech as Fed Govenor, b. 1953)

TUESDAY
D 57.1
S 71.4
N 71.4
25

Make money and the whole nation will conspire to call you a gentleman.
— George Bernard Shaw (Irish dramatist, 1856-1950)

Start Looking for NASDAQ MACD Sell Signal on June 1 (Page 62)
Almanac Investor **Subscribers Emailed When It Triggers (Learn More Page 67)**

WEDNESDAY
D 52.4
S 57.1
N 61.9
26

People's spending habits depend more on how wealthy they feel than with the actual amount of their current income.
— A.C. Pigou (English economist, *The Theory of Unemployment*, 1877-1959)

THURSDAY
D 66.7
S 71.4
N 66.7
27

Welch's genius was the capacity to energize and inspire hundreds of thousands of people across a range of businesses and countries.
— Warren G. Bennis (USC Business professor, *Business Week*, 9/10/2001, referring to retiring CEO Jack Welch of GE)

Friday Before Memorial Day Tends to Be Lackluster with Light Trading, Dow Mixed, Up 13 Down 13, Average –0.05%

FRIDAY
D 33.3
S 42.9
N 38.1
28

We all want progress, but if you're on the wrong road, progress means doing an about-turn and walking back to the right road; in that case, the man who turns back soonest is the most progressive.
— C. S. Lewis (Irish novelist, poet, academic, 1898-1963)

SATURDAY
29

June Almanac Investor Sector Seasonalities: See Pages 94, 96, and 98

SUNDAY
30

JUNE ALMANAC

JUNE						
S	M	T	W	T	F	S
		1	2	3	4	5
6	7	8	9	10	11	12
13	14	15	16	17	18	19
20	21	22	23	24	25	26
27	28	29	30			

JULY						
S	M	T	W	T	F	S
				1	2	3
4	5	6	7	8	9	10
11	12	13	14	15	16	17
18	19	20	21	22	23	24
25	26	27	28	29	30	31

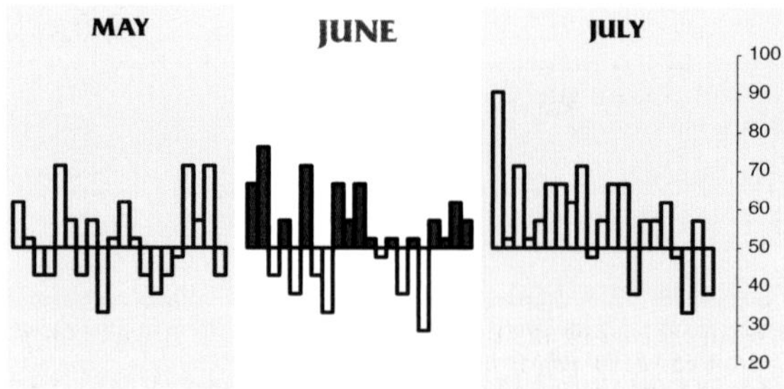

Market Probability Chart above is a graphic representation of the S&P 500 Recent Market Probability Calendar on page 126.

◆ The "summer rally" in most years is the weakest rally of all four seasons (page 76) ◆ Week after June Triple-Witching Day Dow down 29 of last 36 (page 108) ◆ RECENT RECORD: S&P up 13, down 8, average gain 0.2%, ranks eighth ◆ Summer doldrums can begin in late June (page 50) ◆ Watch out for end-of-quarter "portfolio pumping" on last day of June, Dow down 19 of last 35, NASDAQ up 11 of last 15 ◆ Pre-election year Junes: #5 S&P, #5 Dow, #5 NASDAQ ◆ June ends NASDAQ's Best Eight Months (page 62)

June Vital Statistics

	DJIA		S&P 500		NASDAQ		Russell 1K		Russell 2K	
Rank		11		9		6		9		7
Up		37		43		32		30		30
Down		39		33		23		17		17
Average % Change		–0.1		0.2		1.1		0.5		0.9
Pre-Election Yr Avg % Chg		1.3		1.7		2.7		2.0		2.4
Best & Worst June										
	% Change		% Change		% Change		% Change		% Change	
Best	2019	7.2	1955	8.2	2000	16.6	2019	6.9	2000	8.6
Worst	2008	–10.2	2008	–8.6	2002	–9.4	2022	–8.5	2022	–8.4
Best & Worst June Weeks										
Best	6/5/20	6.8	6/2/00	7.2	6/2/00	19.0	6/2/00	8.0	6/2/00	12.2
Worst	6/30/50	–6.8	6/30/50	–7.6	6/15/01	–8.4	6/17/22	–5.9	6/12/20	–7.9
Best & Worst June Days										
Best	6/28/62	3.8	6/28/62	3.4	6/2/00	6.4	6/24/22	3.1	6/2/00	4.2
Worst	6/11/20	–6.9	6/11/20	–5.9	6/11/20	–5.3	6/11/20	–5.9	6/11/20	–7.6
First Trading Day of Monthly Options Expiration Week: 1980–2026										
Record (#Up–#Down)		25-21		28-18		23-23		26-20		20-25
Current streak		U3		U3		U3		U3		U3
Avg % Change		–0.05		–0.09		–0.17		–0.11		–0.28
Monthly Options Expiration Day: 1980–2026										
Record (#Up–#Down)		25-21		25-21		22-24		25-21		23-23
Current streak		U2		D3		D3		D3		D1
Avg % Change		–0.11		–0.04		–0.06		–0.06		–0.07
Monthly Options Expiration Week: 1980–2026										
Record (#Up–#Down)		27-19		25-21		22-24		23-23		23-23
Current streak		U3		D1		U3		D1		U3
Avg % Change		–0.12		–0.10		–0.14		–0.14		–0.35
Week After Monthly Options Expiration: 1980–2026										
Record (#Up–#Down)		15-31		21-25		26-20		21-25		25-21
Current streak		U1		U1		U2		U1		U2
Avg % Change		–0.27		0.002		0.33		0.03		0.14
First Trading Day Performance										
% of Time Up		57.9		55.3		60.0		61.7		66.0
Avg % Change		0.14		0.13		0.15		0.11		0.21
Last Trading Day Performance										
% of Time Up		56.6		53.9		67.3		57.4		68.1
Avg % Change		0.09		0.13		0.32		0.10		0.41

Dow & S&P 1950–May 1, 2026; NASDAQ 1971–May 1, 2026; Russell 1K & 2K 1979–May 1, 2026.

Week after June Triple Witch gets nixed,
Dow down 29 of 36!

Memorial Day *(Market Closed)*

MONDAY
31

I have but one lamp by which my feet [or "investments"] are guided, and that is the lamp of experience. I know of no way of judging the future but by the past.
— Patrick Henry (U.S. Founding Father, twice Governor of VA, 1736-1799, March 23, 1775 speech)

First Trading Day in June, Dow Up 29 of Last 38, Down 4 of 5 2008-2012
Day After Memorial Day, Dow Up 24 of Last 40, But Down 8 of Last 11

TUESDAY
D 71.4
S 66.7
N 61.9
1

Great things are not accomplished by those who yield to trends and fads and popular opinion.
— Jack Kerouac (Beat Generation novelist and poet, *On the Road*, 1922-1969)

Memorial Day Week Dow Down 17 of Last 30, Up 12 Straight 1984-1995

WEDNESDAY
D 66.7
S 76.2
N 76.2
2

Markets are constantly in a state of uncertainty and flux and money is made by discounting the obvious and betting on the unexpected.
— George Soros (Financier, philanthropist, political activist, author and philosopher, b. 1930)

June Ends NASDAQ's "Best Eight Months" (Pages 60, 62, and 150)

THURSDAY
D 33.3
S 42.9
N 47.6
3

Whenever a well-known bearish analyst is interviewed [Cover story] in the financial press, it usually coincides with an important near-term market bottom.
— Clif Droke (Clifdroke.com, 11/15/04)

FRIDAY
D 66.7
S 57.1
N 57.1
4

The incestuous relationship between government and big business thrives in the dark.
— Jack Anderson (Washington journalist and author, *Peace, War and Politics*, 1922-2005)

SATURDAY
5

SUNDAY
6

TOP-PERFORMING NASDAQ MONTHS

NASDAQ stocks continue to run away during three consecutive months, November, December, and January, with an average gain of 6.2% despite the slaughter of November 2000, down 22.9%; December 2000, –4.9%; December 2002, –9.7%; November 2007, –6.9%; January 2008, –9.9%; November 2008, –10.8%; January 2009, –6.4%; January 2010, –5.4%; January 2016, –7.9%; December 2018, –9.5%; January 2022, –9.0%; and December 2022 –8.7%. Solid gains in November and December 2004 offset January 2005's 5.2% Iraq-turmoil-fueled drop.

You can see the months graphically on page 150. January by itself is impressive, up 2.6% on average. April, May, and June also shine, creating our NASDAQ Best Eight Months strategy. What appears as a Death Valley abyss occurs during NASDAQ's leanest months, August and September. NASDAQ's Best Eight Months seasonal strategy using MACD timing is displayed on page 62.

MONTHLY % CHANGES (JANUARY 1971–APRIL 2026)

NASDAQ Composite*					Dow Jones Industrials				
Month	Total % Change	Avg. % Change	# Up	# Down	Month	Total % Change	Avg. % Change	# Up	# Down
Jan	145.6%	2.6%	38	18	Jan	65.6%	1.2%	35	21
Feb	24.6	0.4	29	27	Feb	10.1	0.2	33	23
Mar	31.6	0.6	35	21	Mar	41.7	0.7	36	20
Apr	88.3	1.6	37	19	Apr	111.0	2.0	37	19
May	68.8	1.3	34	21	May	15.5	0.3	32	23
Jun	60.5	1.1	32	23	Jun	9.2	0.2	29	26
Jul	51.0	0.9	32	23	Jul	61.6	1.1	35	20
Aug	18.8	0.3	31	24	Aug	–6.8	–0.1	31	24
Sep	–42.1	–0.8	29	26	Sep	–56.0	–1.0	21	34
Oct	42.8	0.8	30	25	Oct	45.7	0.8	33	22
Nov	113.4	2.1	39	16	Nov	100.1	1.8	39	16
Dec	82.4	1.5	33	22	Dec	74.3	1.4	38	17
% Rank					**% Rank**				
Jan	145.6%	2.6%	38	18	Apr	111.0%	2.0%	37	19
Nov	113.4	2.1	39	16	Nov	100.1	1.8	39	16
Apr	88.3	1.6	37	19	Dec	74.3	1.4	38	17
Dec	82.4	1.5	33	22	Jan	65.6	1.2	35	21
May	68.8	1.3	34	21	Jul	61.6	1.1	35	20
Jun	60.5	1.1	32	23	Oct	45.7	0.8	33	22
Jul	51.0	0.9	32	23	Mar	41.7	0.7	36	20
Oct	42.8	0.8	30	25	May	15.5	0.3	32	23
Mar	31.6	0.6	35	21	Feb	10.1	0.2	33	23
Feb	24.6	0.4	29	27	Jun	9.2	0.2	29	26
Aug	18.8	0.3	31	24	Aug	–6.8	–0.1	31	24
Sep	–42.1	–0.8	29	26	Sep	–56.0	–1.0	21	34
Totals	**685.7%**	**12.4%**			**Totals**	**472.0%**	**8.6%**		
Average		**1.03%**			**Average**		**0.72%**		

**Based on NASDAQ composite, prior to Feb. 5, 1971, based on National Quotation Bureau indices.*

For comparison, Dow figures are shown. During this period NASDAQ averaged a 1.03% gain per month, 44.2% more than the Dow's 0.72% per month. Between January 1971 and January 1982 NASDAQ's composite index doubled in 12 years, while the Dow stayed flat. But while NASDAQ plummeted 77.9% from its 2000 highs to the 2002 bottom, the Dow only lost 37.8%. The Great Recession and bear market of 2007–2009 spread its carnage equally across Dow and NASDAQ. Recent market moves are increasingly more correlated, but NASDAQ still retains a sizable advantage.

2008 Second Worst June Ever, Dow -10.2%, S&P -8.6%,
Only 1930 Was Worse, NASDAQ June 2008 -9.1%, June 2002 -9.4%

MONDAY
D 61.9
S 38.1
N 42.9
7

It's not the strongest of the species [think "traders"] that survive, nor the most intelligent, but the one most responsive to change.
— Charles Darwin (English naturalist and biologist, *On the Origin of Species*, 1808-1882)

FOMC Meeting (2 Days)

TUESDAY
D 66.7
S 71.4
N 61.9
8

Bill [Gates] isn't afraid of taking long-term chances. He also understands that you have to try everything because the real secret to innovation is failing fast.
— Gary Starkweather (Inventor of laser printer in 1969 at Xerox, *Fortune*, July 8, 2002)

WEDNESDAY
D 42.9
S 42.9
N 42.9
9

I cannot give you a formula for success but I can give you a formula for failure: Try to please everybody.
— Herbert Swope (American journalist, 1882-1958)

THURSDAY
D 28.6
S 33.3
N 38.1
10

The whole problem with the world is that fools and fanatics are always so certain of themselves, but wiser people so full of doubts.
— Bertrand Russell (British mathematician and philosopher, 1872-1970)

FRIDAY
D 61.9
S 66.7
N 61.9
11

The reasonable man adapts himself to the world; the unreasonable one persists in trying to adapt the world to himself. Therefore, all progress depends on the unreasonable man.
— George Bernard Shaw (Irish dramatist, 1856-1950)

SATURDAY
12

SUNDAY
13

GET MORE OUT OF NASDAQ'S BEST EIGHT MONTHS WITH MACD TIMING

NASDAQ's amazing eight-month run from November through June is hard to miss on pages 60 and 150. A $10,000 investment in these eight months since 1971 gained $1,893,992 versus $2,810 during the void that is the four-month period July–October (as of May 11, 2026).

Using the same MACD timing indicators on the NASDAQ as is done for the Dow (page 54) has enabled us to capture much of October's improved performance, pumping up NASDAQ's results considerably. Over the 55 years since NASDAQ began, the gain on the same $10,000 more than doubles to $4,407,056 and the gain during the four-month void becomes a loss of $4,587. Only five double-digit losses occurred during the favorable period and the bulk of many NASDAQ's bear markets were avoided.

Updated signals are emailed to *Almanac Investor* subscribers as soon as they are triggered. Visit *www.stocktradersalmanac.com*, or see a special offer for new subscribers between pages 66 and 67.

BEST EIGHT MONTHS STRATEGY + TIMING

MACD Signal Date	Worst 4 Months July 1–Oct 31* NASDAQ	% Change	Investing $10,000	MACD Signal Date	Best 8 Months Nov 1–June 30* NASDAQ	% Change	Investing $10,000
22-Jul-71	109.54	–3.6	$9,640	4-Nov-71	105.56	24.1	$12,410
7-Jun-72	131.00	–1.8	9,466	23-Oct-72	128.66	–22.7	9,593
25-Jun-73	99.43	–7.2	8,784	7-Dec-73	92.32	–20.2	7,655
3-Jul-74	73.66	–23.2	6,746	7-Oct-74	56.57	47.8	11,314
11-Jun-75	83.60	–9.2	6,125	7-Oct-75	75.88	20.8	13,667
22-Jul-76	91.66	–2.4	5,978	19-Oct-76	89.45	13.2	15,471
27-Jul-77	101.25	–4.0	5,739	4-Nov-77	97.21	26.6	19,586
7-Jun-78	123.10	–6.5	5,366	6-Nov-78	115.08	19.1	23,327
3-Jul-79	137.03	–1.1	5,307	30-Oct-79	135.48	15.5	26,943
20-Jun-80	156.51	26.2	6,697	9-Oct-80	197.53	11.2	29,961
4-Jun-81	219.68	–17.6	5,518	1-Oct-81	181.09	–4.0	28,763
7-Jun-82	173.84	12.5	6,208	7-Oct-82	195.59	57.4	45,273
1-Jun-83	307.95	–10.7	5,544	3-Nov-83	274.86	–14.2	38,844
1-Jun-84	235.90	5.0	5,821	15-Oct-84	247.67	17.3	45,564
3-Jun-85	290.59	–3.0	5,646	1-Oct-85	281.77	39.4	63,516
10-Jun-86	392.83	–10.3	5,064	1-Oct-86	352.34	20.5	76,537
30-Jun-87	424.67	–22.7	3,914	2-Nov-87	328.33	20.1	91,921
8-Jul-88	394.33	–6.6	3,656	29-Nov-88	368.15	22.4	112,511
13-Jun-89	450.73	0.7	3,682	9-Nov-89	454.07	1.9	114,649
11-Jun-90	462.79	–23.0	2,835	2-Oct-90	356.39	39.3	159,706
11-Jun-91	496.62	6.4	3,016	1-Oct-91	528.51	7.4	171,524
11-Jun-92	567.68	1.5	3,061	14-Oct-92	576.22	20.5	206,686
7-Jun-93	694.61	9.9	3,364	1-Oct-93	763.23	–4.4	197,592
17-Jun-94	729.35	5.0	3,532	11-Oct-94	765.57	13.5	224,267
1-Jun-95	868.82	17.2	4,140	13-Oct-95	1018.38	21.6	272,709
3-Jun-96	1238.73	1.0	4,181	7-Oct-96	1250.87	10.3	300,798
4-Jun-97	1379.67	24.4	5,201	3-Oct-97	1715.87	1.8	306,212
1-Jun-98	1746.82	–7.8	4,795	15-Oct-98	1611.01	49.7	458,399
1-Jun-99	2412.03	18.5	5,682	6-Oct-99	2857.21	35.7	622,047
29-Jun-00	3877.23	–18.2	4,648	18-Oct-00	3171.56	–32.2	421,748
1-Jun-01	2149.44	–31.1	3,202	1-Oct-01	1480.46	5.5	444,944
3-Jun-02	1562.56	–24.0	2,434	2-Oct-02	1187.30	38.5	616,247
20-Jun-03	1644.72	15.1	2,802	6-Oct-03	1893.46	4.3	642,746
21-Jun-04	1974.38	–1.6	2,757	1-Oct-04	1942.20	6.1	681,954
8-Jun-05	2060.18	1.5	2,798	19-Oct-05	2091.76	2.9	701,731
7-Jun-06	2151.80	7.2	2,999	5-Oct-06	2306.34	10.2	773,308
7-Jun-07	2541.38	7.9	3,236	1-Oct-07	2740.99	–9.1	702,937
2-Jun-08	2491.53	–31.3	2,223	17-Oct-08	1711.29	6.1	745,816
15-Jun-09	1816.38	17.8	2,619	9-Oct-09	2139.28	1.6	757,749
7-Jun-10	2173.90	18.6	3,106	4-Nov-10	2577.34	7.4	813,822
1-Jun-11	2769.19	–10.5	2,780	7-Oct-11	2479.35	10.8	901,715
1-Jun-12	2747.48	9.6	3,047	6-Nov-12	3011.93	14.4	1,031,562
4-Jun-13	3445.26	10.1	3,355	15-Oct-13	3794.01	15.4	1,190,423
26-Jun-14	4379.05	0.9	3,385	21-Oct-14	4419.48	14.5	1,363,034
4-Jun-15	5059.12	–5.5	3,199	5-Oct-15	4781.26	1.4	1,382,116
13-Jun-16	4848.44	9.5	3,503	24-Oct-16	5309.83	16.9	1,615,694
9-Jun-17	6207.92	11.3	3,899	28-Nov-17	6912.36	11.6	1,803,115
21-Jun-18	7712.95	–5.3	3,692	31-Oct-18	7305.90	11.5	2,010,473
19-Jul-19	8146.49	–1.1	3,651	11-Oct-19	8057.04	17.8	2,368,337
11-Jun-20	9492.73	25.3	4,575	5-Nov-20	11890.93	23.2	2,917,791
14-Jul-21	14644.95	–0.4	4,557	8-Oct-21	14579.54	–25.9	2,162,083
13-Jun-22	10809.23	3.4	4,712	4-Oct-22	11176.41	20.7	2,609,634
23-Jun-23	13492.52	–0.1	4,707	9-Oct-23	13484.24	31.4	3,429,059
25-Jun-24	17717.65	3.5	4,872	11-Oct-24	18342.94	12.5	3,857,691
14-Jul-25	20640.33	11.1	5,413	6-Oct-25	22941.67	14.5**	4,417,056**
11-May-26**	26274.12						
	Average	–0.2%				13.2%	
	55-Year (Loss)		($4,587)		55-Year Gain		$4,407,056

*** As of 5/11/2026 – NASDAQ Seasonal Sell NOT triggered yet*

** MACD-generated entry and exit points (earlier or later) can lengthen or shorten eight-month periods.*

JUNE 2027

Monday of Triple-Witching Week Mixed, Dow Down 15 of Last 29

MONDAY
D 47.6
S 57.1
N 66.7
14

The game [or market] can be reduced to a social science; that it is simply a matter of figuring out the odds, and exploiting the laws of probability; that baseball players [or investors] follow strikingly predictable patterns.
— Michael Lewis (American author & journalist, what Oakland A's GM Billy Beane claims to believe, *Moneyball: The Art of Winning an Unfair Game*, b. 1960)

Triple-Witching Week Often Up in Bull Markets and Down in Bears (Page 108)

TUESDAY
D 61.9
S 66.7
N 66.7
15

It's a lot of fun finding a country nobody knows about. The only thing better is finding a country everybody's bullish on and shorting it.
— Jim Rogers (Financier, *Investment Biker*, b. 1942)

WEDNESDAY
D 52.4
S 52.4
N 52.4
16

There's no such thing as a loss, it's just an unmonetized lesson.
— Ted Weschler (Investment Manager at Berkshire Hathaway, b. 1962)

June Triple-Witching Day Mixed, But Dow Down 8 of Last 11

THURSDAY
D 47.6
S 47.6
N 61.9
17

I am young, powerful and successful, and I produce at least $10,000 a month.
— (Mantra of Suze Orman, *The 9 Steps to Financial Freedom*, as a young Merrill Lynch broker)

(Market Closed - Juneteenth National Independence Day Observed)

FRIDAY
18

When you get into a tight place and everything goes against you, till it seems as though you could not hang on a minute longer, never give up then, for that is just the place and time that the tide will turn.
— Harriet Beecher Stowe (American writer and abolitionist)

Juneteenth National Independence Day

SATURDAY
19

Father's Day

SUNDAY
20

TRIPLE RETURNS, FEWER TRADES: BEST 6 + 4-YEAR CYCLE

We first introduced this strategy to *Almanac Investor* subscribers in October 2006. Recurring seasonal stock market patterns and the Four-Year Presidential Election/Stock Market Cycle (page 132) have been integral to our research since the first *Almanac* 60 years ago. Yale Hirsch discovered the Best Six Months in 1986 (page 54), and it has been a cornerstone of our seasonal investment analysis and strategies ever since.

Most of the market's gains have occurred during the Best Six Months and the market generally hits a low point every four years in the first (post-election) or second (midterm) year and exhibits the greatest gains in the third (pre-election) year. This strategy combines the best of these two market phenomena, the Best Six Months and the 4-Year Cycle, timing entries and exits with MACD (pages 56 and 62).

We've gone back to 1949 to include the full four-year cycle that began with post-election year 1949. Only four trades every four years are needed to more than triple the results of the Best Six Months. Buy and sell during the post-election and midterm years and then hold from the midterm MACD seasonal buy signal sometime on/after October 1 until the post-election MACD seasonal sell signal sometime on/after April 1, approximately 2.5 years. Solid returns, less effort, lower transaction fees and fewer taxable events.

FOUR TRADES EVERY FOUR YEARS

Year	Worst Six Months May–Oct	Best Six Months Nov–April
Post-election	Sell	Buy
Midterm	Sell	Buy
Pre-election	Hold	Hold
Election	Hold	Hold

BEST SIX MONTHS+TIMING+4-YEAR CYCLE STRATEGY

	DJIA % Change May 1–Oct 31*	Investing $10,000	DJIA % Change Nov 1–Apr 30*	Investing $10,000
1949	3.0%	$10,300	17.5%	$11,750
1950	7.3	11,052	19.7	14,065
1951		11,052		14,065
1952		11,052		14,065
1953	0.2	11,074	17.1	16,470
1954	13.5	12,569	35.7	22,350
1955		12,569		22,350
1956		12,569		22,350
1957	−12.3	11,023	4.9	23,445
1958	17.3	12,930	27.8	29,963
1959		12,930		29,963
1960		12,930		29,963
1961	2.9	13,305	−1.5	29,514
1962	−15.3	11,269	58.5	46,780
1963		11,269		46,780
1964		11,269		46,780
1965	2.6	11,562	−2.5	45,611
1966	−16.4	9,666	22.2	55,737
1967		9,666		55,737
1968		9,666		55,737
1969	−11.9	8,516	−6.7	52,003
1970	−1.4	8,397	21.5	63,184
1971		8,397		63,184
1972		8,397		63,184
1973	−11.0	7,473	0.1	63,247
1974	−22.4	5,799	42.5	90,127
1975		5,799		90,127
1976		5,799		90,127
1977	−11.4	5,138	0.5	90,578
1978	−4.5	4,907	26.8	114,853
1979		4,907		114,853
1980		4,907		114,853
1981	−14.6	4,191	0.4	115,312
1982	15.5	4,841	25.9	145,178
1983		4,841		145,178
1984		4,841		145,178
1985	7.0	5,180	38.1	200,491
1986	−2.8	5,035	33.2	267,054
1987		5,035		267,054
1988		5,035		267,054
1989	9.8	5,528	3.3	275,867
1990	−6.7	5,158	35.1	372,696
1991		5,158		372,696
1992		5,158		372,696
1993	5.5	5,442	5.6	393,455
1994	3.7	5,643	88.2	740,482
1995		5,643		740,482
1996		5,643		740,482
1997	3.6	5,846	18.5	877,471
1998	−12.4	5,121	36.3	1,195,993
1999		5,121		1,195,993
2000		5,121		1,195,993
2001	−17.3	4,235	15.8	1,384,960
2002	−25.2	3,168	34.2	1,858,616
2003		3,168		1,858,616
2004		3,168		1,858,616
2005	−0.5	3,152	7.7	2,001,729
2006	4.7	3,300	−31.7	1,367,181
2007		3,300		1,367,181
2008		3,300		1,367,181
2009	23.8	4,085	10.8	1,514,738
2010	4.6	4,273	27.4	1,929,777
2011		4,273		1,929,777
2012		4,273		1,929,777
2013	4.1	4,448	7.1	2,066,791
2014	2.3	4,550	24.0	2,562,820
2015		4,550		2,562,820
2016		4,550		2,562,820
2017	15.7	5,265	0.4	2,573,072
2018	5.0	5,528	34.6	3,463,354
2019		5,528		3,463,354
2020		5,528		3,463,354
2021	2.8	5,683	−0.5	3,446,038
2022	−12.3	4,984	33.7	4,607,352
2023		4,984		4,607,352
2024		4,984		4,607,352
2025	15.2	5,741	6.4	4,902,223
2026	−0.6**	5,707**		
Average	**−0.4%**		**9.7%**	
# Up	**22**		**34**	
# Down	**17**		**5**	
77-Year Gain (Loss)		**($4,259)**		**$4,892,223**

* *MACD and 2.5-year hold lengthen and shorten six-month periods.*
** *As of May 19, 2026 Close – Switching – Not in totals.*

Week After June Triple-Witching, Dow Down 29 of Last 36
Average Loss Since 1990, 0.7%

MONDAY
D 57.1
S 52.4
N 47.6
21

Those who cannot remember the past are condemned to repeat it.
— George Santayana (Spanish-American philosopher, poet, 1863-1952)

TUESDAY
D 38.1
S 38.1
N 42.9
22

To find one man in a thousand who is your true friend from unselfish motives is to find one of the great wonders of the world.
— Leopold Mozart (Quoted by Maynard Solomon, *Mozart*)

WEDNESDAY
D 47.6
S 52.4
N 47.6
23

The most probable hypothesis is usually the one with the least evidence against it, not the one with the most evidence for it.
— Richards J. Heuer, Jr (CIA analyst, *Psychology of Intelligence Analysis*, 1927-2018)

THURSDAY
D 33.3
S 28.6
N 23.8
24

Of a stock's move, 31% can be attributed to the general stock market, 12% to the industry influence, 37% to the influence of other groupings, and the remaining 20% is peculiar to the one stock.
— Benjamin F. King ("Market and Industry Factors in Stock Price Behavior," *Journal of Business*, January 1966)

FRIDAY
D 47.6
S 57.1
N 57.1
25

The first human who hurled an insult instead of a stone was the founder of civilization.
— Sigmund Freud (Austrian neurologist, psychiatrist, father of psychoanalysis, 1856-1939)

SATURDAY
26

July Almanac Investor Sector Seasonalities: See Pages 94, 96, and 98

SUNDAY
27

JULY ALMANAC

JULY

S	M	T	W	T	F	S
				1	2	3
4	5	6	7	8	9	10
11	12	13	14	15	16	17
18	19	20	21	22	23	24
25	26	27	28	29	30	31

AUGUST

S	M	T	W	T	F	S
1	2	3	4	5	6	7
8	9	10	11	12	13	14
15	16	17	18	19	20	21
22	23	24	25	26	27	28
29	30	31				

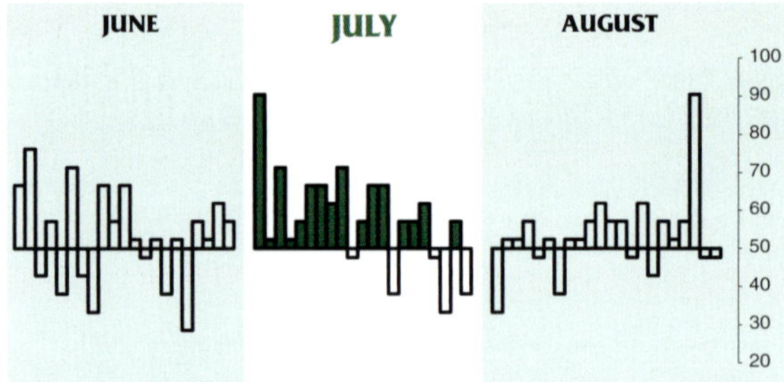

Market Probability Chart above is a graphic representation of the S&P 500 Recent Market Probability Calendar on page 126.

◆ July is the best month of the third quarter (page 68) ◆ Start of 2nd half brings an inflow of retirement funds ◆ First trading day S&P up 32 of last 37 ◆ Graph above shows strength in the first half of July ◆ Huge gain in July usually provides better buying opportunity over next four months ◆ Start of NASDAQ's worst four months of the year (page 60 & 150) ◆ Pre-election Julys are ranked #6 Dow (up 12, down 7), #6 S&P (up 12, down 7), and #9 NASDAQ (up 8, down 6)

July Vital Statistics

	DJIA	S&P 500	NASDAQ	Russell 1K	Russell 2K
Rank	4	4	7	4	9
Up	51	46	32	27	26
Down	25	30	23	20	21
Average % Change	1.4	1.3	0.9	1.2	0.4
Pre-Election Yr Avg % Chg	1.2	1.0	1.2	0.8	0.8
Best & Worst July					
	% Change	% Change	% Change	% Change	% Change
Best	1989 9.0	2022 9.1	2022 12.3	2022 9.2	1980 11.0
Worst	1969 –6.6	2002 –7.9	2002 –9.2	2002 –7.5	2002 –15.2
Best & Worst July Weeks					
Best	7/17/09 7.3	7/17/09 7.0	7/17/09 7.4	7/17/09 7.0	7/17/09 8.0
Worst	7/19/02 –7.7	7/19/02 –8.0	7/28/00 –10.5	7/19/02 –7.4	7/2/10 –7.2
Best & Worst July Days					
Best	7/24/02 6.4	7/24/02 5.7	7/29/02 5.8	7/24/02 5.6	7/29/02 4.9
Worst	7/19/02 –4.6	7/19/02 –3.8	7/28/00 –4.7	7/19/02 –3.6	7/23/02 –4.1
First Trading Day of Monthly Options Expiration Week: 1980–2026					
Record (#Up–#Down)	30-16	29-17	31-15	29-17	26-20
Current streak	U3	U3	U3	U3	U3
Avg % Change	0.13	0.02	0.001	–0.001	–0.03
Monthly Options Expiration Day: 1980–2026					
Record (#Up–#Down)	19-25	22-24	19-27	23-23	17-29
Current streak	D2	D2	U1	U1	D3
Avg % Change	–0.21	–0.22	–0.34	–0.23	–0.39
Monthly Options Expiration Week: 1980–2026					
Record (#Up–#Down)	28-18	26-20	22-24	26-20	26-20
Current streak	D1	U1	U1	U1	U3
Avg % Change	0.48	0.11	–0.05	0.06	–0.04
Week After Monthly Options Expiration: 1980–2026					
Record (#Up–#Down)	27-19	24-22	22-24	25-21	20-26
Current streak	U5	U1	U1	U1	U5
Avg % Change	0.12	0.04	–0.18	0.03	–0.07
First Trading Day Performance					
% of Time Up	68.4	73.7	65.5	76.6	68.1
Avg % Change	0.28	0.28	0.18	0.33	0.16
Last Trading Day Performance					
% of Time Up	51.3	60.5	50.9	57.4	61.7
Avg % Change	0.02	0.09	0.05	0.03	–0.02

Dow & S&P 1950–May 1, 2026; NASDAQ 1971–May 1, 2026; Russell 1K & 2K 1979–May 1, 2026.

When Dow and S&P in July are inferior,
NASDAQ days tend to be even drearier.

MONDAY
D 52.4
S 52.4
N 66.7
28

Under capitalism, the seller chases after the buyer, and that makes both of them work better; under socialism, the buyer chases the seller, and neither has time to work.
— Andrei Sakharov's Uncle Ivan

TUESDAY
D 61.9
S 61.9
N 61.9
29

If you spend more than 14 minutes a year worrying about the market, you've wasted 12 minutes.
— Peter Lynch (Fidelity Investments, *One Up On Wall Street*, b. 1944)

Last Day of Q2 Bearish for Dow, Down 19 of Last 35, but Up 11 of Last 15, Bullish for NASDAQ, Up 23 of 34

WEDNESDAY
D 57.1
S 57.1
N 52.4
30

If you don't keep [your employees] happy, they're not going to keep the [customers] happy.
— David Longest (Red Lobster VP, *NY Times* 4/23/89)

First Trading Day in July, S&P Up 32 of Last 37, Average Gain 0.5%

THURSDAY
D 85.7
S 90.5
N 85.7
1

There is a perfect inverse correlation between inflation rates and price/earnings ratios... When inflation has been very high...P/E has been [low].
— Liz Ann Sonders (Chief Investment Strategist Charles Schwab, June 2006)

July Is the Best Performing Dow and S&P Month of Third Quarter (Page 68)

FRIDAY
D 38.1
S 52.4
N 52.4
2

When new money is created on a grand scale, it must go somewhere and have some major consequences. One of these will be greatly increased volatility and instability in the economy and financial system.
— J. Anthony Boeckh, Ph.D (Chairman Bank Credit Analyst 1968-2002, *The Great Reflation*, *Boeckh Investment Letter*)

SATURDAY
3

Independence Day

SUNDAY
4

FIRST MONTH OF QUARTERS IS THE MOST BULLISH

We have observed over the years that the investment calendar reflects the annual, semi-annual, and quarterly operations of institutions during January, April, and July. The opening month of the first three quarters produces the greatest gains in the Dow Jones Industrials, S&P 500, and NASDAQ. Recent January weakness has given March the advantage in Q1 for Dow Jones Industrials and S&P 500 from 1991 through April 2026.

The fourth quarter had behaved quite differently since it is affected by year-end portfolio adjustments and Presidential and Congressional elections in even-numbered years. Since 1991 major turnarounds have helped October join the ranks of bullish first months of quarters. October transformed into a bear-killing-turnaround month, posting Dow gains in 19 of the last 28 years, 2008 was a significant exception. (See pages 156–173.)

After experiencing the most powerful bull market of all time during the 1990s, followed by two ferocious bear markets early in the millennium, we divided the monthly average percent changes into two groups: before 1991 and after. Comparing the month-by-month quarterly behavior of the three major U.S. averages in the table, you'll see that first months of the first three quarters perform best overall. Nasty selloffs in April 2000, 2002, 2004, 2005, and 2022 and July 2000–2002, and 2004 hit the NASDAQ hardest. The bear market of October 2007–March 2009, which more than cut the markets in half, took a toll on every first month except April. October 2008 was the worst month in a decade. January was also a difficult month in 13 of the last 27 years pulling its performance lower. (See pages 156–173.)

Between 1950 and 1990, the S&P 500 gained 1.3% (Dow, 1.4%) on average in first months of the first three quarters. Second months barely eked out any gain, while third months, thanks to March, moved up 0.23% (Dow, 0.07%) on average. NASDAQ's first month of the first three quarters averages 1.67% from 1971–1990 with July being a negative drag.

DOW JONES INDUSTRIALS, S&P 500 AND NASDAQ
AVERAGE MONTHLY % CHANGES BY QUARTER

	DJIA 1950–1990			S&P 500 1950–1990			NASDAQ 1971–1990		
	1st Mo	2nd Mo	3rd Mo	1st Mo	2nd Mo	3rd Mo	1st Mo	2nd Mo	3rd Mo
1Q	1.5%	−0.01%	1.0%	1.5%	−0.1%	1.1%	3.8%	1.2%	0.9%
2Q	1.6	−0.4	0.1	1.3	−0.1	0.3	1.7	0.8	1.1
3Q	1.1	0.3	−0.9	1.1	0.3	−0.7	−0.5	0.1	−1.6
Tot	**4.2%**	**−0.1%**	**0.2%**	**3.9%**	**0.1%**	**0.7%**	**5.0%**	**2.1%**	**0.4%**
Avg	**1.40%**	**−0.04%**	**0.07%**	**1.30%**	**0.03%**	**0.23%**	**1.67%**	**0.70%**	**0.13%**
4Q	*−0.1%*	*1.4%*	*1.7%*	*0.4%*	*1.7%*	*1.6%*	*−1.4%*	*1.6%*	*1.4%*
	DJIA 1991-April 2026			**S&P 500 1991-April 2026**			**NASDAQ 1991-April 2026**		
1Q	0.4%	0.1%	0.6%	0.6%	0.02%	0.8%	1.9%	−0.003%	0.4%
2Q	2.1	0.5	−0.3	1.9	0.9	0.16	1.5	1.5	1.1
3Q	1.7	−0.5	−0.7	1.5	−0.2	−0.6	1.8	0.5	−0.3
Tot	**4.2%**	**0.1%**	**−0.4%**	**4.0%**	**0.7%**	**0.4%**	**5.2%**	**2.0%**	**1.2%**
Avg	**1.40%**	**0.05%**	**−0.13%**	**1.33%**	**0.24%**	**0.12%**	**1.73%**	**0.67%**	**0.40%**
4Q	*1.8%*	*2.4%*	*1.2%*	*1.5%*	*2.1%*	*1.2%*	*2.0%*	*2.3%*	*1.5%*
	DJIA 1950-April 2026			**S&P 500 1950-April 2026**			**NASDAQ 1971-April 2026**		
1Q	1.0%	0.1%	0.8%	1.1%	−0.04%	1.0%	2.6%	0.4%	0.6%
2Q	1.8	0.03	−0.1	1.6	0.4	0.2	1.6	1.3	1.1
3Q	1.4	−0.1	−0.8	1.3	0.04	−0.6	0.9	0.3	−0.8
Tot	**4.2%**	**0.08%**	**−0.1%**	**4.0%**	**0.4%**	**0.6%**	**5.1%**	**2.0%**	**0.9%**
Avg	**1.40%**	**0.03%**	**−0.03%**	**1.33%**	**0.14%**	**0.21%**	**1.71%**	**0.68%**	**0.30%**
4Q	*0.8%*	*1.9%*	*1.5%*	*0.9%*	*1.8%*	*1.4%*	*0.8%*	*2.1%*	*1.5%*

(Market Closed - Independence Day Observed)

MONDAY
5

Fortune favors the brave.
— Virgil (Roman Poet, *Aeneid*, 70-19 B.C.)

Market Subject to Elevated Volatility After July 4th

TUESDAY
D 61.9
S 71.4
N 71.4
6

Companies already dominant in a field rarely produce the breakthroughs that transform it.
— George Gilder

WEDNESDAY
D 52.4
S 52.4
N 57.1
7

There has never been a commercial technology like this [Internet] in the history of the world, whereby the minute you adopt it, it forces you to think and act globally.
— Robert D. Hormats (Under Secretary of State Economic, Energy and the Environment 2009-2013, Goldman Sachs 1982-2009, b.1943)

Beware the "Summer Rally" Hype
Historically the Weakest Rally of All Seasons (Page 76)

THURSDAY
D 52.4
S 57.1
N 66.7
8

Institutions tend to dump stock in a single transaction and buy, if possible, in smaller lots, gradually accumulating a position. Therefore, many more big blocks are traded on downticks than on upticks.
— Justin Mamis (Technical analyst and author, *The Mamis Letter, When To Sell*, 1929-2019)

FRIDAY
D 61.9
S 66.7
N 76.2
9

The game is lost only when we stop trying.
— Mario Cuomo (Former NY Governor, *C-SPAN*)

SATURDAY
10

SUNDAY
11

2025 DAILY DOW POINT CHANGES (DOW JONES INDUSTRIAL AVERAGE)

Week #		Monday**	Tuesday	Wednsday	Thursday	Friday**	Weekly Dow Close	Net Point Change
						2024 Close	42544.22	
1				Holiday	– 151.95	339.86	42732.13	187.91
2	J	– 25.57	– 178.20	106.84	Holiday	– 696.75	41938.45	– 793.68
3	A	358.67	221.16	703.27	– 68.42	334.70	43487.83	1549.38
4	N	Holiday	537.98	130.92	408.34	– 140.82	44424.25	936.42
5		289.33	136.77	– 136.83	168.61	**– 337.47**	44544.66	120.41
6		**– 122.75**	134.13	317.24	– 125.65	– 444.23	44303.40	– 241.26
7	F	167.01	123.24	– 225.09	342.87	– 165.35	44546.08	242.68
8	E	Holiday	10.26	71.25	– 450.94	– 748.63	43428.02	– 1118.06
9	B	33.19	159.95	– 188.04	– 193.62	601.41	43840.91	412.89
10		– 649.67	– 670.25	485.60	– 427.51	222.64	42801.72	– 1039.19
11	M	– 890.01	– 478.23	– 82.55	– 537.36	674.62	41488.19	– 1313.53
12	A	353.44	– 260.32	383.32	– 11.31	32.03	41985.35	497.16
13	R	597.97	4.18	– 132.71	– 155.09	– 715.80	41583.90	– 401.45
14		417.86	– 11.80	235.36	– 1679.39	**– 2231.07**	38314.86	– 3269.04
15	A	**– 349.26**	– 320.01	2962.86	– 1014.79	619.05	40212.71	1897.85
16	P	312.08	– 155.83	– 699.57	**– 527.16**	Holiday	39142.23	– 1070.48
17	R	**– 971.82**	1016.57	419.59	486.83	20.10	40113.50	971.27
18		114.09	300.03	141.74	83.60	564.47	41317.43	1203.93
19		– 98.60	– 389.83	284.97	254.48	– 119.07	41249.38	– 68.05
20	M	1160.72	– 269.67	– 89.37	271.69	331.99	42654.74	1405.36
21	A	137.33	– 114.83	– 816.80	– 1.35	– 256.02	41603.07	– 1051.67
22	Y	Holiday	740.58	– 244.95	117.03	54.34	42270.07	667.00
23		35.41	214.16	– 91.90	– 108.00	443.13	42762.87	492.80
24	J	– 1.11	105.11	– 1.10	101.85	– 769.83	42197.79	– 565.08
25	U	317.30	– 299.29	– 44.14	Holiday	35.16	42206.82	9.03
26	N	374.96	507.24	– 106.59	404.41	432.43	43819.27	1612.45
27		275.50	400.17	– 10.52	344.11*	Holiday	44828.53	1009.26
28	J	– 422.17	– 165.60	217.54	192.34	– 279.13	44371.51	– 457.02
29	U	88.14	– 436.36	231.49	229.71	**– 142.30**	44342.19	– 29.32
30	L	**– 19.12**	179.37	507.85	– 316.38	208.01	44901.92	559.73
31		– 64.36	– 204.57	– 171.71	– 330.30	– 542.40	43588.58	– 1313.34
32		585.06	– 61.90	81.38	– 224.48	206.97	44175.61	587.03
33	A	– 200.52	483.52	463.66	– 11.01	34.86	44946.12	770.51
34	U	– 34.30	10.45	16.04	– 152.81	846.24	45631.74	685.62
35	G	– 349.27	135.60	147.16	71.67	**– 92.02**	45544.88	– 86.86
36		Holiday	**– 249.07**	– 24.58	350.06	– 220.43	45400.86	– 144.02
37	S	114.09	196.39	– 220.42	617.08	– 273.78	45834.22	433.36
38	E	49.23	– 125.55	260.42	124.10	172.85	46315.27	481.05
39	P	66.27	– 88.76	– 171.50	– 173.96	299.97	46247.29	– 67.98
40		68.78	81.82	43.21	78.62	238.56	46758.28	510.99
41		– 63.31	– 91.99	– 1.20	– 243.36	– 878.82	45479.60	– 1278.68
42	O	587.98	202.88	– 17.15	– 301.07	238.37	46190.61	711.01
43	C	515.97	218.16	– 334.33	144.20	472.51	47207.12	1016.51
44	T	337.47	161.78	– 74.37	– 109.88	40.75	47562.87	355.75
45	N	– 226.19	– 251.44	225.76	– 398.70	74.80	46987.10	– 575.77
46	O	381.53	559.33	326.86	– 797.60	**– 309.74**	47147.48	160.38
47	V	**– 557.24**	– 498.50	47.03	– 386.51	493.15	46245.41	– 902.07
48		202.86	664.18	314.67	Holiday	289.30*	47716.42	1471.01
49		– 427.09	185.13	408.44	– 31.96	104.05	47954.99	238.57
50	D	– 215.67	– 179.03	497.46	646.26	**– 245.96**	48458.05	503.06
51	E	**– 41.49**	– 302.30	– 228.29	65.88	183.04	48134.89	– 323.16
52	C	227.79	79.73	288.75*	Holiday	**– 20.19**	48710.97	576.08
53		**– 249.04**	– 94.87	– 303.77		**Year Close:**	**48063.29**	– 647.68
TOTALS		**3231.22**	**831.92**	**5903.20**	**– 3243.77**	**– 1203.50**		

Outline Bold Color: Down Friday, Down Monday

**Shortened trading day: Jul 3, Nov 28, & Dec 24*

*** Monday denotes first trading day of week, Friday denotes last trading day of week*

Monday Before July Monthly Expiration, Dow Up 18 of Last 23

MONDAY
D 57.1
S 66.7
N 71.4
12

All there is to investing is picking good stocks at good times and staying with them as long as they remain good companies.
— Warren Buffett (CEO Berkshire Hathaway, investor & philanthropist, b. 1930)

TUESDAY
D 71.4
S 61.9
N 52.4
13

Don't be scared to take big steps—you can't cross a chasm in two small jumps.
— David Lloyd George (British Prime Minister, 1916-1922)

WEDNESDAY
D 81.0
S 71.4
N 76.2
14

Selling a soybean contract short is worth two years at the Harvard Business School.
— Robert Stovall (60-year veteran Wall Street analyst and strategist, Father of Sam, 1926-2020)

THURSDAY
D 71.4
S 47.6
N 61.9
15

A president is elected and tries to get rid of the dirty stuff in the economy as quickly as possible, so that by the time the next election comes around, he looks like a hero. The stock market is reacting to what the politicians are doing.
— Yale Hirsch (Creator of *Stock Trader's Almanac, NY Times* 10/10/2010, 1923-2021)

July Monthly Expiration Day, Dow Down 17 of Last 26, -4.6% 2002, -2.5% 2010

FRIDAY
D 57.1
S 57.1
N 61.9
16

There is nothing more powerful than a market that has changed its mind.
— Arthur D. Cashin, Jr. (Legendary NYSE floor trader, director of floor operations UBS Financial Services, 1941-2024)

SATURDAY
17

SUNDAY
18

MARKET GAINS MORE ON SUPER-8 DAYS EACH MONTH THAN ON ALL 13 REMAINING DAYS COMBINED

For many years the last day plus the first four days were the best days of the month. The market currently exhibits greater bullish bias from the last three trading days of the previous month through the first two days of the current month, and shows significant bullishness during the middle three trading days, nine to eleven, due to 401(k) cash inflows (see pages 147 and 148). This pattern was not as pronounced during the boom years of the 1990s, with market strength all month long. Since the 2009 market bottom, the Super-8 advantage has been sporadic. So far in 2026, the Super 8 have not performed well. The Super 8 lagged badly in 2024 after soaring in 2023. When compared to the last 27 and third-year record (at the bottom of the page), the Super-8 edge has faltered since 2018 .

SUPER-8 DAYS* S&P 500 % CHANGES VS. REST OF MONTH

	2018 Super 8 Days	2018 Rest of Month	2019 Super 8 Days	2019 Rest of Month	2020 Super 8 Days	2020 Rest of Month
Jan	2.49%	4.57%	–0.04%	7.19%	0.71%	0.40%
Feb	–1.13	–3.28	4.22	1.47	0.38	–4.88
Mar	–3.30	0.07	0.99	–0.19	–16.43	0.61
Apr	–0.33	–0.39	2.34	1.45	–2.60	12.37
May	–0.57	3.69	–1.35	–2.92	–1.46	5.48
Jun	0.68	–0.61	0.37	3.72	–1.01	4.13
Jul	0.04	4.16	2.05	1.64	3.44	0.90
Aug	–0.88	3.03	–4.31	–0.90	2.79	5.16
Sep	–0.30	0.93	2.26	1.73	4.31	–9.10
Oct	–0.99	–7.90	–1.36	3.24	0.05	2.74
Nov	2.57	–1.65	2.22	0.87	0.87	6.29
Dec	–3.30	–4.86	0.27	3.11	1.65	1.08
Totals	**–5.02%**	**–2.24%**	**7.65%**	**20.39%**	**–7.30%**	**25.17%**
Average	**–0.42%**	**–0.19%**	**0.64%**	**1.70%**	**–0.61%**	**2.10%**

	2021 Super 8 Days	2021 Rest of Month	2022 Super 8 Days	2022 Rest of Month	2023 Super 8 Days	2023 Rest of Month
Jan	–0.51%	3.59%	–3.01%	–6.30%	–0.75%	6.84%
Feb	–0.03	0.85	4.73	–7.25	4.38	–5.33
Mar	1.51	0.88	3.88	4.24	0.01	–1.03
Apr	3.69	1.59	0.02	–8.77	3.47	–0.91
May	1.93	–1.86	1.86	–6.44	1.14	0.80
Jun	0.65	1.55	2.00	–3.89	5.22	0.23
Jul	0.70	2.11	–1.01	1.56	2.57	1.68
Aug	1.22	0.34	6.49	–2.83	–1.85	–1.09
Sep	1.61	–2.18	–4.75	–5.63	1.12	–4.67
Oct	–0.52	3.51	6.87	–1.73	–1.11	–2.11
Nov	2.01	0.75	–0.97	6.14	6.44	3.34
Dec	–2.69	4.62	–1.27	–3.67	2.06	2.81
Totals	**9.55%**	**15.75%**	**14.84%**	**–34.57%**	**22.70%**	**0.58%**
Average	**0.80%**	**1.31%**	**1.24%**	**–2.88%**	**1.89%**	**0.05%**

	2024 Super 8 Days	2024 Rest of Month	2025 Super 8 Days	2025 Rest of Month	2026 Super 8 Days	2026 Rest of Month
Jan	–2.31%	4.86%	1.01%	–0.51%	–0.74%	1.45%
Feb	1.54	2.08	0.78	–2.62	–2.27	1.03
Mar	0.07	2.86	–1.66	–2.46	–2.18	–3.90
Apr	–2.15	–1.13	1.70	–4.89	3.92	6.58
May	1.95	3.09	4.20	2.85		
Jun	0.68	2.38	1.01	1.86		
Jul	2.22	–2.35	2.28	2.54		
Aug	1.58	1.45	–0.87	2.08		
Sep	–1.20	2.95	0.02	2.13		
Oct	0.39	1.38	3.51	0.79		
Nov	–3.76	6.83	–4.29	1.67		
Dec	0.88	–0.04	0.82	2.52		
Totals	**–0.10%**	**24.35%**	**8.52%**	**5.95%**	**–1.28%**	**5.17%**
Average	**–0.01%**	**2.03%**	**0.71%**	**0.50%**	**–0.32%**	**1.29%**

	Super Eight Days		**Rest of Month (13 days)**	
328	Net % Changes	182.99%	Net % Changes	25.80%
Month	Average Period	0.56%	Average Period	0.08%
Totals	Average Day	0.07%	Average Day	0.01%

** Super 8 Days = Last 3 + First 2 + Middle 3*

MONDAY
D 71.4
S 66.7
N 66.7
19

It is wise to remember that too much success [in the stock market] is in itself an excellent warning.
— Gerald M. Loeb (E.F. Hutton, *The Battle for Investment Survival*, predicted 1929 Crash, 1900-1974)

TUESDAY
D 71.4
S 66.7
N 71.4
20

My best shorts come from research reports where there are recommendations to buy stocks on weakness; also, where a brokerage firm changes its recommendation from a buy to a hold.
— Marc Howard (Hedge fund manager, *New York Magazine* 1976, b. 1941)

Week After July Monthly Expiration Prone to Swings, Dow Up 18 of Last 24
2002 +3.1%, 2006 +3.2%, 2007 -4.2%, 2009 +4.0%, 2010 +3.2, 2015 -2.9%

WEDNESDAY
D 28.6
S 38.1
N 23.8
21

Every new high ever seen in the indexes has been retraced, at least twice, save for those since August 2020 until now.
— Ralph Vince (Trader, programmer, author, 12/7/2021, b. 1958)

THURSDAY
D 52.4
S 57.1
N 52.4
22

Successful investing is anticipating the anticipations of others.
— John Maynard Keynes (British economist, 1883-1946)

FRIDAY
D 38.1
S 57.1
N 52.4
23

Get to the Point! Blurt it out! Tell me plainly what's in it for me!
— Roy H. Williams (*The Wizard of Ads*, A reader's mental response to a poorly constructed advertisement. Quoted in *Your Company*, 12/98)

SATURDAY
24

SUNDAY
25

AUGUST ALMANAC

AUGUST						
S	M	T	W	T	F	S
1	2	3	4	5	6	7
8	9	10	11	12	13	14
15	16	17	18	19	20	21
22	23	24	25	26	27	28
29	30	31				

SEPTEMBER						
S	M	T	W	T	F	S
			1	2	3	4
5	6	7	8	9	10	11
12	13	14	15	16	17	18
19	20	21	22	23	24	25
26	27	28	29	30		

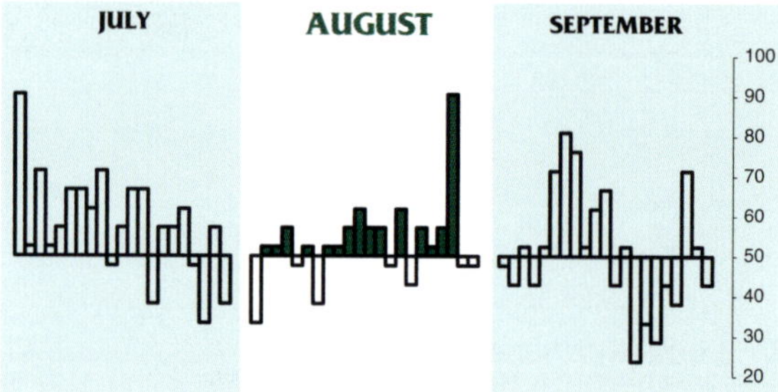

Market Probability Chart above is a graphic representation of the S&P 500 Recent Market Probability Calendar on page 126.

◆ Harvesting made August the best stock market month 1901–1951 ◆ Now about 2% farm, August is the second worst Dow, S&P, and NASDAQ (2000 up 11.7%, 2001 down 10.9%) month since 1988 ◆ Second-shortest bear in history (45 days) caused by turmoil in Russia, currency crisis, and hedge-fund debacle ended here in 1998, 1344.22-point drop in the Dow, 16th worst monthly point loss, off 15.1% second worst percent loss since 1941 ◆ Saddam Hussein triggered a 10.0% slide in 1990 ◆ Best Dow gains: 1982 (11.5%) and 1984 (9.8%) as bear markets ended ◆ Next to last day S&P down 19 times last 30 years ◆ Pre-election year Augusts' rankings #9 S&P, #9 Dow, and #10 NASDAQ

August Vital Statistics

	DJIA	S&P 500	NASDAQ	Russell 1K	Russell 2K
Rank	10	10	11	10	10
Up	43	42	31	29	26
Down	33	34	24	18	21
Average % Change	–0.1	0.04	0.3	0.4	0.3
Pre-Election Yr Avg % Chg	0.6	0.3	0.3	–0.1	–0.9
Best & Worst August					
	% Change	% Change	% Change	% Change	% Change
Best	1982 11.5	1982 11.6	2000 11.7	1982 11.3	1984 11.5
Worst	1998 –15.1	1998 –14.6	1998 –19.9	1998 –15.1	1998 –19.5
Best & Worst August Weeks					
Best	8/20/82 10.3	8/20/82 8.8	8/3/84 7.4	8/20/82 8.5	8/3/84 7.0
Worst	8/23/74 –6.1	8/5/11 –7.2	8/28/98 –8.8	8/5/11 –7.7	8/5/11 –10.3
Best & Worst August Days					
Best	8/17/82 4.9	8/17/82 4.8	8/9/11 5.3	8/9/11 5.0	8/9/11 6.9
Worst	8/31/98 –6.4	8/31/98 –6.8	8/31/98 –8.6	8/8/11 –6.9	8/8/11 –8.9
First Trading Day of Monthly Options Expiration Week: 1980–2026					
Record (#Up–#Down)	28-18	33-13	33-13	32-14	27-19
Current streak	D2	D1	D1	D2	D3
Avg % Change	0.19	0.24	0.32	0.22	0.20
Monthly Options Expiration Day: 1980–2026					
Record (#Up–#Down)	25-21	24-22	25-21	26-20	26-20
Current streak	U3	D1	D1	D1	D1
Avg % Change	–0.07	–0.04	–0.11	–0.04	0.09
Monthly Options Expiration Week: 1980–2026					
Record (#Up–#Down)	21-25	25-21	24-22	25-21	26-20
Current streak	U2	U2	U2	U2	U2
Avg % Change	0.02	0.18	0.32	0.19	0.23
Week After Monthly Options Expiration: 1980–2026					
Record (#Up–#Down)	28-18	31-15	29-17	31-15	30-16
Current streak	U2	U3	D1	U3	U2
Avg % Change	0.27	0.33	0.54	0.35	0.33
First Trading Day Performance					
% of Time Up	44.7	46.1	50.9	40.4	42.6
Avg % Change	–0.02	–0.01	–0.11	0.001	–0.13
Last Trading Day Performance					
% of Time Up	56.6	60.5	63.6	55.3	63.8
Avg % Change	0.08	0.10	0.05	–0.04	0.03

Dow & S&P 1950–May 1, 2026; NASDAQ 1971–May 1, 2026; Russell 1K & 2K 1979–May 1, 2026.

August's a good month to go on vacation;
Trading stocks will likely lead to frustration.

MONDAY
D 71.4
S 61.9
N 57.1
26

Between two evils, I always pick the one I never tried before.
— Mae West (American actress and playwright, 1893-1980)

FOMC Meeting (2 Days)

TUESDAY
D 47.6
S 47.6
N 47.6
27

You win some, you lose some. And then there's that little-known third category.
— Albert Gore (U.S. Vice President 1993-2000, former 2000 presidential candidate, quoted at the 2004 DNC)

WEDNESDAY
D 38.1
S 33.3
N 42.9
28

The principles of successful stock speculation are based on the supposition that people will continue in the future to make the mistakes that they have made in the past.
— Thomas F. Woodlock (*Wall Street Journal* editor & columnist, quoted in *Reminiscences of a Stock Operator*, 1866-1945)

THURSDAY
D 47.6
S 57.1
N 71.4
29

When you're one step ahead of the crowd, you're a genius. When you're two steps ahead, you're a crackpot.
— Shlomo Riskin (Rabbi, author, b. 1940)

Last Trading Day in July, NASDAQ and S&P Down 13 of Last 21, Dow Down 14 of Last 21

FRIDAY
D 33.3
S 38.1
N 38.1
30

Brevity is the soul of wit.
— William Shakespeare (English playwright, 1564-1616)

SATURDAY
31

August Almanac Investor Sector Seasonalities: See Pages 94, 96, and 98

SUNDAY
1

A RALLY FOR ALL SEASONS

Most years, especially when the market sells off during the first half, prospects for the perennial summer rally become the buzz on the street. Parameters for this "rally" were defined by the late Ralph Rotnem as the lowest close in the Dow Jones Industrials in May or June to the highest close in July, August, or September. Such a big deal is made of the "summer rally" that one might get the impression the market puts on its best performance in the summertime. Nothing could be further from the truth! Not only does the market "rally" in every season of the year, but it does so with more gusto in the winter, spring, and fall than in the summer.

Winters in 63 years averaged a 12.9% gain as measured from the low in November or December to the first quarter closing high. Spring rose 11.6% followed by fall with 11.3%. Last and least was the average 9.5% "summer rally." Even 2020's impressive 25.2% "summer rally" was outmatched by spring. Nevertheless, no matter how thick the gloom or grim the outlook, don't despair! There's always a rally for all seasons, statistically.

SEASONAL GAINS IN DOW JONES INDUSTRIALS

	WINTER RALLY Nov/Dec Low to Q1 High	SPRING RALLY Feb/Mar Low to Q2 High	SUMMER RALLY May/Jun Low to Q3 High	FALL RALLY Aug/Sep Low to Q4 High
1964	15.3%	6.2%	9.4%	8.3%
1965	5.7	6.6	11.6	10.3
1966	5.9	4.8	3.5	7.0
1967	11.6	8.7	11.2	4.4
1968	7.0	11.5	5.2	13.3
1969	0.9	7.7	1.9	6.7
1970	5.4	6.2	22.5	19.0
1971	21.6	9.4	5.5	7.4
1972	19.1	7.7	5.2	11.4
1973	8.6	4.8	9.7	15.9
1974	13.1	8.2	1.4	11.0
1975	36.2	24.2	8.2	8.7
1976	23.3	6.4	5.9	4.6
1977	8.2	3.1	2.8	2.1
1978	2.1	16.8	11.8	5.2
1979	11.0	8.9	8.9	6.1
1980	13.5	16.8	21.0	8.5
1981	11.8	9.9	0.4	8.3
1982	4.6	9.3	18.5	37.8
1983	15.7	17.8	6.3	10.7
1984	5.9	4.6	14.1	9.7
1985	11.7	7.1	9.5	19.7
1986	31.1	18.8	9.2	11.4
1987	30.6	13.6	22.9	5.9
1988	18.1	13.5	11.2	9.8
1989	15.1	12.9	16.1	5.7
1990	8.8	14.5	12.4	8.6
1991	21.8	11.2	6.6	9.3
1992	14.9	6.4	3.7	3.3
1993	8.9	7.7	6.3	7.3
1994	9.7	5.2	9.1	5.0
1995	13.6	19.3	11.3	13.9
1996	19.2	7.5	8.7	17.3
1997	17.7	18.4	18.4	7.3
1998	20.3	13.6	8.2	24.3
1999	15.1	21.6	8.2	12.6
2000	10.8	15.2	9.8	3.5
2001	6.4	20.8	1.7	23.1
2002	14.8	7.9	2.8	17.6
2003	6.5	23.9	14.3	15.7
2004	11.6	5.2	4.4	10.6
2005	9.0	2.1	5.6	5.3
2006	8.8	8.3	9.5	13.0
2007	6.7	13.5	6.6	10.3
2008	2.5	11.2	3.8	4.5
2009	19.6	34.4	19.7	15.5
2010	11.6	13.1	11.1	16.0
2011	12.6	10.3	7.0	14.7
2012	18.0	4.5	12.4	5.7
2013	16.2	11.8	6.9	12.2
2014	6.0	10.2	5.5	10.3
2015	7.1	5.5	3.0	14.4
2016	3.4	15.6	8.7	10.8
2017	18.0	8.3	8.8	14.6
2018	14.4	7.6	11.8	6.6
2019	19.7	6.8	10.3	12.4
2020	8.1	48.3	25.2	14.8
2021	23.2	15.1	7.0	7.8
2022	8.2	7.7	14.3	20.4
2023	7.2	8.1	8.7	12.5
2024	19.6	4.5	11.7	16.3
2025	7.4	8.0	13.9	11.8
2026	9.7	9.6*		
Totals	**810.2%**	**728.4%**	**591.3%**	**698.2%**
Average	**12.9%**	**11.6%**	**9.5%**	**11.3%**

** As of 4/24/2026*

AUGUST 2027

First Trading Day in August, Dow Down 20 of Last 29
First Nine Trading Days of August Are Historically Weak (Pages 74 and 138)

MONDAY
D 33.3
S 33.3
N 47.6
2

It was never my thinking that made the big money for me. It was always my sitting. Got that? My sitting tight!
— Jesse Livermore (Early 20th century stock trader & speculator, *How to Trade in Stocks*, 1877-1940)

TUESDAY
D 47.6
S 52.4
N 47.6
3

Your chances for success in any undertaking can be measured by your belief in yourself.
— Robert Collier (Direct marketing copywriter & author, 1885-1950)

WEDNESDAY
D 52.4
S 52.4
N 57.1
4

Even being right 3 or 4 times out of 10 should yield a person a fortune, if he has the sense to cut his losses quickly on the ventures where he has been wrong.
— Bernard Baruch (Financier, speculator, statesman, presidential adviser, 1870-1965)

THURSDAY
D 52.4
S 57.1
N 61.9
5

Seek not the paths of the ancients, seek that which the ancients sought.
— Matsuo Bashō (Japanese poet and philosopher, 1644-1694)

FRIDAY
D 52.4
S 47.6
N 42.9
6

Keep me away from the wisdom which does not cry, the philosophy which does not laugh and the greatness which does not bow before children.
— Kahlil Gibran (Lebanese-born American mystic, poet and artist, 1883-1931)

SATURDAY
7

SUNDAY
8

TAKE ADVANTAGE OF DOWN FRIDAY/ DOWN MONDAY WARNING

Fridays* and Mondays* are the most important days of the week. Friday* is the day for squaring positions—trimming longs or covering shorts before taking off for the weekend. Traders want to limit their exposure (particularly to stocks that are not acting well) since there could be unfavorable developments before trading resumes two or more days later.

Monday* is important because the market then has the chance to reflect any weekend news, plus what traders think after digesting the previous week's action and the many Monday* morning research and strategy comments.

For over 30 years, a down Friday* followed by down Monday* has frequently corresponded with important market inflection points that typically exhibit a negative bias, often coinciding with market tops and on a few climactic occasions, such as in October 2002, March 2009, March 2020, and August–October 2022, near major market bottoms.

One simple way to get a quick reading on which way the market may be heading is to keep track of the performance of the Dow Jones Industrial Average on Fridays* and the following Mondays*. Since 1995 there have been 309 occurrences of Down Friday/Down Monday* (DF/DM) with 92 falling in the bear market years of 2001, 2002, 2008, 2011, 2015, 2020, and 2022, producing an average decline of 12.5% (shaded).

To illustrate how DF/DM* can telegraph market infection points we created the chart below of the Dow Jones Industrials from November 2023 to April 24, 2026, with arrows pointing to occurrences of DF/DM*. Use DF/DM* as a warning to examine market conditions carefully.

DOWN FRIDAY/DOWN MONDAY

Year	Total Number Down Friday/ Down Monday	Subsequent Average % Dow Loss*	Average Number of Days it took
1995	8	−1.2%	18
1996	9	−3.0%	28
1997	6	−5.1%	45
1998	9	−6.4%	47
1999	9	−6.4%	39
2000	11	−6.6%	32
2001	13	−13.5%	53
2002	18	−11.9%	54
2003	9	−3.0%	17
2004	9	−3.7%	51
2005	10	−3.0%	37
2006	11	−2.0%	14
2007	8	−6.0%	33
2008	15	−17.0%	53
2009	10	−8.7%	15
2010	7	−3.1%	10
2011	11	−9.0%	53
2012	11	−4.0%	38
2013	7	−2.4%	15
2014	7	−2.5%	8
2015	12	−9.2%	44
2016	10	−2.7%	25
2017	11	−1.2%	18
2018	14	−5.8%	45
2019	7	−4.3%	32
2020	8	−19.0%	27
2021	7	−4.4%	38
2022	15	−7.8%	46
2023	8	−3.1%	21
2024	9	−3.8%	47
2025	8	−4.8%	36
2026**	2	−3.7%	43
Average	**10**	**−5.9%**	**34**

** Over next 3 months, ** Ending April 24, 2026*

DOW JONES INDUSTRIALS (November 2024 - April 24, 2026)

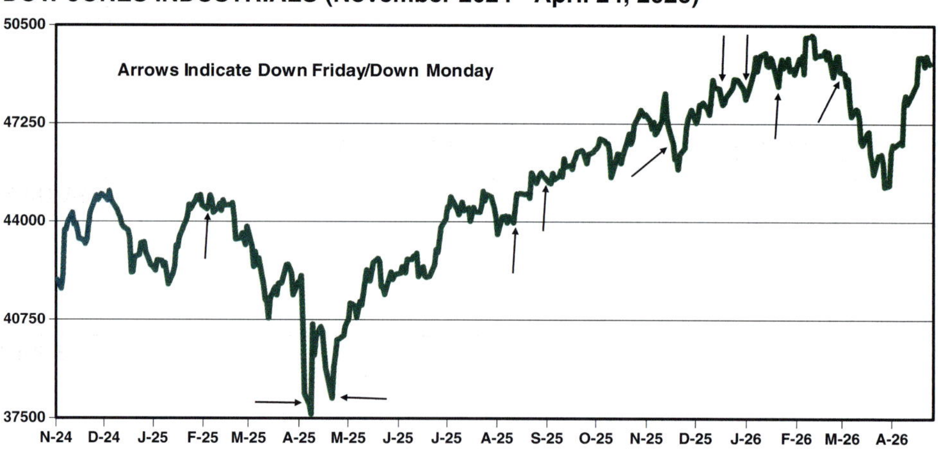

** Monday denotes first trading day of week, Friday denotes last trading day of week.*

AUGUST 2027

August Second-Worst Dow, S&P, NASDAQ & Russell 2000 Month 1988-2025
Harvesting Made August Best Dow Month 1901-1951

MONDAY **9**
D 57.1
S 52.4
N 52.4

Oil has fostered massive corruption in almost every country that has been "blessed" with it, and the expectation that oil wealth will transform economies has lead to disastrous policy choices.
— Ted Tyson (Chief Investment Officer, Mastholm Asset Management)

TUESDAY **10**
D 33.3
S 38.1
N 38.1

A cynic is a man who knows the price of everything and the value of nothing.
— Oscar Wilde (Irish-born writer and wit, 1845-1900)

WEDNESDAY **11**
D 38.1
S 52.4
N 47.6

Never lend money to someone who must borrow money to pay interest [on other money owed].
— (A Swiss Banker's First Rule quoted by Lester Thurow)

Mid-August Stronger Than Beginning and End

THURSDAY **12**
D 66.7
S 52.4
N 61.9

There are three principal means of acquiring knowledge…observation of nature, reflection, and experimentation. Observation collects facts; reflection combines them; experimentation verifies the result of that combination.
— Denis Diderot (French philosopher, edited first modern Encyclopedia in 1745, 1713-1784)

FRIDAY **13**
D 61.9
S 57.1
N 57.1

The difference between life and the movies is that a script has to make sense, and life doesn't.
— Joseph L. Mankiewicz (Film director, writer, producer, 1909-1993)

SATURDAY **14**

SUNDAY **15**

MARKET BEHAVIOR THREE DAYS BEFORE AND THREE DAYS AFTER HOLIDAYS

The *Stock Trader's Almanac* has tracked holiday seasonality annually since the first edition in 1968. Stocks used to rise on the day before holidays and sell off the day after, but nowadays each holiday moves to its own rhythm. Eight holidays are separated into five groups. Average percent changes for the Dow, S&P 500, NASDAQ, and Russell 2000 are shown.

The Dow and S&P consist of blue chips and the largest cap stocks, whereas NASDAQ represents tech stocks and the Russell 2000 would be more representative of smaller cap stocks. This is evident on the last day of the year with NASDAQ and the Russell 2000 having a field day, while their larger brethren in the Dow and S&P are showing losses on average.

Thanks to the Santa Claus Rally the three days before and after New Year's Day and Christmas are best. NASDAQ and the Russell 2000 average gains of 1.0% and 0.9% over the six-day spans respectively. However, trading around the first day of the year has been mixed recently. Traders have been selling more the first trading day of the year, pushing gains and losses into the New Year.

Bullishness before Labor Day and after Memorial Day is often affected by strength the first day of September and June. The second worst day after a holiday is the day after Easter. Surprisingly, the following day is the best second day after a holiday, eclipsing the second day after New Year's Day.

Presidents' Day is the least bullish of all the holidays, bearish the day before and three days after. NASDAQ has dropped 24 of the last 37 days before Presidents' Day (Dow, 20 of 37; S&P 22 of 37; Russell 2000, 18 of 37).

HOLIDAYS: 3 DAYS BEFORE, 3 DAYS AFTER (Average % change 1980–April 2026)

	−3	−2	−1		+1	+2	+3
S&P 500	−0.01	0.15	−0.12	**Mixed Before &**	0.16	0.23	0.04
DJIA	−0.02	0.10	−0.15	**Positive After**	0.27	0.22	0.17
NASDAQ	0.00	0.20	0.06	**New Year's Day**	0.16	0.42	0.12
Russell 2K	−0.06	0.33	0.26	*1/1/27*	0.03	0.21	0.12
S&P 500	0.34	−0.04	−0.10	**Negative Before & After**	−0.20	−0.05	−0.05
DJIA	0.29	−0.05	−0.04	**Presidents'**	−0.16	−0.07	−0.12
NASDAQ	0.53	0.16	−0.25	**Day**	−0.45	−0.05	0.02
Russell 2K	0.42	0.13	−0.02	*2/15/27*	−0.38	−0.16	−0.02
S&P 500	0.13	0.02	0.36	**Positive Before &**	−0.21	0.43	0.14
DJIA	0.10	0.02	0.25	**Negative After**	−0.18	0.39	0.15
NASDAQ	0.30	0.21	0.43	**Good Friday**	−0.28	0.50	0.23
Russell 2K	0.21	0.17	0.56	*3/26/27*	−0.38	0.39	0.11
S&P 500	0.05	0.06	0.09	**Positive Before**	0.26	0.08	0.25
DJIA	0.01	−0.02	0.01	**& After**	0.28	0.09	0.13
NASDAQ	0.14	0.24	0.18	**Memorial Day**	0.26	−0.04	0.43
Russell 2K	0.01	0.23	0.22	*5/31/27*	0.29	0.03	0.38
S&P 500	0.20	0.18	0.15	**Positive Before**	−0.08	0.01	0.10
DJIA	0.20	0.12	0.13	**& Negative After**	−0.07	0.0004	0.07
NASDAQ	0.30	0.20	0.14	**Independence Day**	−0.02	−0.10	0.28
Russell 2K	0.30	0.07	0.07	*7/4/27*	−0.26	−0.13	0.14
S&P 500	0.21	−0.19	0.09	**Labor Day**	−0.09	0.14	−0.07
DJIA	0.18	−0.22	0.09	*9/6/27*	−0.07	0.17	−0.12
NASDAQ	0.39	−0.06	0.08		−0.19	0.04	0.05
Russell 2K	0.48	0.02	0.10		−0.17	0.16	0.03
S&P 500	0.16	0.09	0.25	**Positive Before**	0.12	−0.36	0.25
DJIA	0.17	0.10	0.22	**& After**	0.09	−0.35	0.25
NASDAQ	0.09	−0.10	0.41	**Thanksgiving**	0.34	−0.32	0.12
Russell 2K	0.26	0.01	0.39	*11/25/27*	0.21	−0.56	0.18
S&P 500	0.20	0.17	0.18	**Christmas**	0.28	−0.04	0.21
DJIA	0.24	0.19	0.20	*12/25/27*	0.31	−0.01	0.17
NASDAQ	0.03	0.30	0.34		0.26	−0.05	0.25
Russell 2K	0.30	0.27	0.32		0.30	−0.10	0.39

Monday Before August Monthly Expiration, Dow Up 19 of Last 31, Average Gain 0.2%

MONDAY
D 57.1
S 61.9
N 52.4
16

Every age has a blind eye and sees nothing wrong in practices and institutions, which its successors view with just horror.
— Sir Richard Livingstone (*On Education*, 1880-1960)

TUESDAY
D 47.6
S 57.1
N 52.4
17

In Wall Street, the man who does not change his mind will soon have no change to mind.
— William D. Gann (Trader, technical analyst, author, publisher, 1878-1955)

WEDNESDAY
D 61.9
S 57.1
N 52.4
18

Ideas are easy; it's execution that's hard.
— Jeff Bezos (Amazon.com)

THURSDAY
D 57.1
S 47.6
N 47.6
19

Savor the joy of others. It is abundant and free and it will lift your spirits and boost your wellbeing even as you add positive energy to the world.
— Phil Pearlman (Founder, Pearl Institute, b. 1967)

August Monthly Expiration Day Improving Lately, Dow Up 15 of Last 23 Down 7 of 8, 2010–2017

FRIDAY
D 57.1
S 61.9
N 76.2
20

Almost any insider purchase is worth investigating for a possible lead to a superior speculation. But very few insider sales justify concern.
— William Chidester (*Scientific Investing*)

SATURDAY
21

SUNDAY
22

FOURTH-QUARTER MARKET MAGIC

Examining market performance on a quarterly basis reveals several intriguing and helpful patterns. Fourth-quarter market gains have been magical, providing the greatest and most consistent gains over the years. First-quarter performance runs a respectable second. This should not be surprising as cash inflows, trading volume, and buying bias are generally elevated during these two quarters.

Positive market psychology hits a fever pitch as the holiday season approaches and does not begin to wane until spring. Professionals drive the market higher as they make portfolio adjustments to maximize year-end numbers. Bonuses are paid and invested around the turn of the year.

The market's sweet spot of the Four-Year Cycle begins in the fourth quarter of the midterm year. The best two-quarter span runs from the fourth quarter of the midterm year through the first quarter of the pre-election year, averaging 13.8% for the Dow, 14.4% for the S&P 500 and an amazing 19.5% for NASDAQ. Pre-election Q2 is smoking too, the third best quarter of the cycle, creating a three-quarter sweet spot from midterm Q4 to pre-election Q2 (see page 34).

Quarterly strength fades in the latter half of the pre-election year, but stays impressively positive through the election year. Weakness is most consistent in the second and third quarters of midterm years. Post-election year Q1 has weakened recently.

QUARTERLY % CHANGES

	Q1	Q2	Q3	Q4	Year	Q2–Q3	Q4–Q1	Q4–Q2
Dow Jones Industrials (1949–March 2026)								
Average	**1.9%**	**1.6%**	**0.7%**	**4.2%**	**8.7%**	**2.4%**	**6.3%**	**8.2%**
Post Election	0.2%	2.0%	0.6%	4.3%	7.7%	2.7%	5.1%	3.4%
Midterm	0.6%	– 1.9%	– 0.2%	6.6%	5.2%	– 2.0%	13.8%	19.3%
Pre-Election	6.9%	4.7%	0.8%	3.3%	16.1%	5.5%	3.2%	4.6%
Election	– 0.2%	1.7%	1.5%	2.7%	5.8%	3.3%	3.1%	5.6%
S&P 500 (1949–March 2026)								
Average	**2.0%**	**2.0%**	**0.9%**	**4.2%**	**9.6%**	**3.0%**	**6.5%**	**8.9%**
Post Election	–0.2%	2.9%	1.2%	3.9%	8.4%	4.2%	4.4%	2.0%
Midterm	0.4%	– 2.8%	0.2%	6.6%	4.6%	– 1.5%	14.4%	20.2%
Pre-Election	7.4%	5.0%	0.4%	3.9%	17.2%	5.4%	4.7%	7.4%
Election	0.7%	2.8%	1.7%	2.5%	8.1%	4.7%	2.6%	5.8%
NASDAQ Composite (1971–March 2026)								
Average	**3.9%**	**3.8%**	**0.7%**	**4.6%**	**13.7%**	**4.8%**	**8.6%**	**12.5%**
Post Election	– 1.6%	7.4%	2.9%	5.0%	13.8%	10.4%	5.5%	2.8%
Midterm	0.5%	– 3.5%	– 3.6%	5.8%	– 0.5%	– 6.6%	19.5%	29.4%
Pre-Election	13.4%	7.6%	0.5%	6.5%	30.3%	8.1%	9.4%	11.9%
Election	2.5%	3.3%	2.5%	1.0%	10.3%	6.4%	– 0.1%	6.2%

Week After August Monthly Expiration Mixed, Dow Up 11 of Last 21, Down 4.2% in 2022

MONDAY
D 47.6
S 42.9
N 38.1
23

Everything possible today was at one time impossible. Everything impossible today may at some time in the future be possible.
— Edward Lindaman (Apollo space project, president Whitworth College, 1920-1982)

TUESDAY
D 61.9
S 57.1
N 61.9
24

Never attribute to malevolence what is merely due to incompetence.
— Arthur C. Clarke (British sci-fi writer, *3001: The Final Odyssey*, 1917-2008)

WEDNESDAY
D 52.4
S 52.4
N 57.1
25

Writing a book is an adventure. To begin with it is a toy, an amusement; then it is a mistress, and then a master, and then a tyrant.
— Winston Churchill (British statesman, 1874-1965)

THURSDAY
D 52.4
S 57.1
N 61.9
26

Politics ought to be the part-time profession of every citizen who would protect the rights and privileges of free people and who would preserve what is good and fruitful in our national heritage.
— Dwight D. Eisenhower (34th U.S. President, 1890-1969)

August's Third-to-Last Trading Day, S&P Up 19 Years In A Row 2003-2021, Down 0.7% in 2022, Up 1.5% in 2023, Down 0.6% in 2024, Up 0.2% in 2025

FRIDAY
D 90.5
S 90.5
N 81.0
27

There are two kinds of people who lose money: those who know nothing and those who know everything.
— Henry Kaufman (German-American economist, b. 1927, to Robert Lenzner in *Forbes* 10/19/98 who added, "With two Nobel Prize winners in the house, Long-Term Capital clearly fits the second case.")

SATURDAY
28

September Almanac Investor Sector Seasonalities: See Pages 94, 96, and 98

SUNDAY
29

SEPTEMBER ALMANAC

SEPTEMBER						
S	M	T	W	T	F	S
		1	2	3	4	
5	6	7	8	9	10	11
12	13	14	15	16	17	18
19	20	21	22	23	24	25
26	27	28	29	30		

OCTOBER						
S	M	T	W	T	F	S
					1	2
3	4	5	6	7	8	9
10	11	12	13	14	15	16
17	18	19	20	21	22	23
24	25	26	27	28	29	30
31						

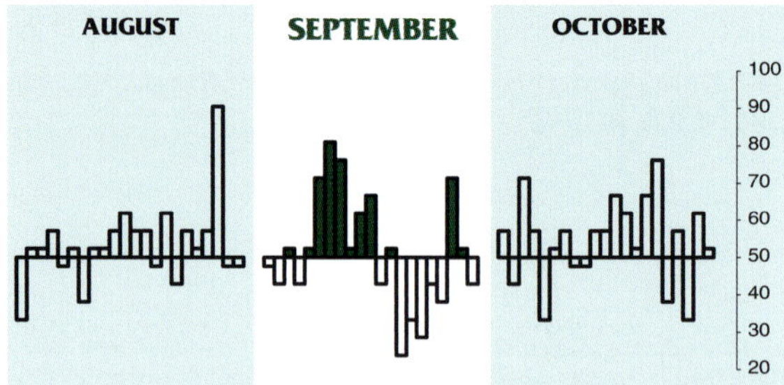

Market Probability Chart above is a graphic representation of the S&P 500 Recent Market Probability Calendar on page 126.

◆ Portfolio managers back after Labor Day tend to clean house in September ◆ Biggest % loser on the S&P, Dow and NASDAQ since 1950 (pages 52 & 60) ◆ Streak of four great Dow Septembers averaging 4.2% gains ended in 1999 with six losers in a row averaging –5.9% (page 156), up four straight 2005–2007, down 6% in 2008 and 2011, up 7.7% in 2010, down big in four of last six years ◆ Day after Labor Day Dow down 14 of last 18 ◆ S&P opened strong 18 of last 31 years but tends to close weak due to end-of-quarter mutual fund portfolio restructuring, last trading day: S&P down 18 of past 29 ◆ September Triple-Witching Week can be dangerous; week after is pitiful (page 108)

September Vital Statistics

	DJIA		S&P 500		NASDAQ		Russell 1K		Russell 2K	
Rank		12		12		12		12		12
Up		31		34		29		23		25
Down		45		41		26		24		22
Average % Change		–0.8		–0.6		–0.8		–0.8		–0.7
Pre-Election Yr Avg % Chg		–0.9		–1.0		–1.2		–1.1		–1.7
Best & Worst September										
	% Change		% Change		% Change		% Change		% Change	
Best	2010	7.7	2010	8.8	1998	13.0	2010	9.0	2010	12.3
Worst	2002	–12.4	1974	–11.9	2001	–17.0	2002	–10.9	2001	–13.6
Best & Worst September Weeks										
Best	9/28/01	7.4	9/28/01	7.8	9/16/11	6.3	9/28/01	7.6	9/28/01	6.9
Worst	9/21/01	–14.3	9/21/01	–11.6	9/21/01	–16.1	9/21/01	–11.7	9/21/01	–14.0
Best & Worst September Days										
Best	9/8/98	5.0	9/30/08	5.4	9/8/98	6.0	9/30/08	5.3	9/18/08	7.0
Worst	9/17/01	–7.1	9/29/08	–8.8	9/29/08	–9.1	9/29/08	–8.7	9/29/08	–6.7
First Trading Day of Monthly Options Expiration Week: 1980–2026										
Record (#Up–#Down)		31-15		27-19		19-27		27-19		23-23
Current streak		U6		U6		U1		U6		U7
Avg % Change		0.05		0.02		–0.14		0.002		–0.04
Monthly Options Expiration Day: 1980–2026										
Record (#Up–#Down)		22-24		21-25		25-21		22-24		25-21
Current streak		U2		U1		U1		U1		D4
Avg % Change		–0.09		–0.02		–0.03		–0.04		–0.01
Monthly Options Expiration Week: 1980–2026										
Record (#Up–#Down)		25-21		26-20		25-21		26-20		25-21
Current streak		U2		U2		U2		U2		U2
Avg % Change		–0.12		–0.001		0.03		0.00		0.17
Week After Monthly Options Expiration: 1980–2026										
Record (#Up–#Down)		16-30		14-32		20-26		14-31		15-31
Current streak		D1		D1		D1		D1		D4
Avg % Change		–0.73		–0.80		–0.90		–0.82		–1.42
First Trading Day Performance										
% of Time Up		57.9		59.2		52.7		53.2		48.9
Avg % Change		–0.02		–0.05		–0.11		–0.11		–0.08
Last Trading Day Performance										
% of Time Up		42.1		43.4		52.7		51.1		61.7
Avg % Change		–0.12		–0.05		0.03		0.03		0.20

Dow & S&P 1950–May 1, 2026; NASDAQ 1971–May 1, 2026; Russell 1K & 2K 1979–May 1, 2026.

September is when leaves and stocks tend to fall;
On Wall Street it's the worst month of all.

AUGUST/SEPTEMBER 2027

August's Next-to-Last Trading Day, S&P Down 19 of Last 30 Years

MONDAY
D 47.6
S 47.6
N 61.9
30

To succeed in the markets, it is essential to make your own decisions. Numerous traders cited listening to others as their worst blunder.
— Jack D. Schwager (Investment manager, author, *Stock Market Wizards: Interviews with America's Top Stock Traders*, b. 1948)

Last Trading Day in August, S&P Up 14 of Last 26 Years,
But Down 7 of Last 11

TUESDAY
D 42.9
S 47.6
N 47.6
31

During the first period of a man's life the greatest danger is not to take the risk.
— Søren Kierkegaard (Danish philosopher, 1813-1855)

First Trading Day in September, S&P Up 18 of Last 31, But Down 11 of Last 18

WEDNESDAY
D 42.9
S 47.6
N 47.6
1

So much hangs on the decisions of a small number of poorly educated people. That's democracy.
A terrible way to run a country, but every other system is worse.
— Kenneth Martin Follett (Welsh author, *Fall of Giants*, b. 1949)

THURSDAY
D 61.9
S 42.9
N 42.9
2

I have a simple philosophy. Fill what's empty. Empty what's full. And scratch where it itches.
— Alice Roosevelt Longworth (American writer, socialite, daughter of Teddy, 1884-1980)

FRIDAY
D 57.1
S 52.4
N 57.1
3

Cooperation is essential to address 21st-century challenges; you can't fire cruise missiles at the global financial crisis.
— Nicholas D. Kristof (*NY Times* columnist, 10/23/2008)

SATURDAY
4

SUNDAY
5

BEST INVESTMENT BOOKS OF THE YEAR

Shout out to strong works from the usual suspects this year. Andrew Ross Sorkin's *1929*, Stephen Witt's *The Thinking Machine* on Nvidia and Jensen Huang, Jeremy Grantham's *The Making of a Permabear*, Jim Cramer's *How to Make Money in Any Market*, Jack Schwager's *Market Wizards: The Next Generation*, and two from our friends at Ritholtz Wealth — Nick Maggiulli's *The Wealth Ladder* and Ben Carlson's *Risk and Reward*. For the 60th we focused on six titles that help frame the future of the AI Super Boom and a few savvy practical market navigation manuals.

A Century of Plenty: A Story of Progress for Generations to Come, Sven Smit, Chris Bradley, Nick Leung, Marc Canal, et al., McKinsey Global Institute, $24.99. A major research effort from McKinsey's independent research arm and a powerful long-arc counterpoint to the doom narrative dominating financial media. The book examines the "progress machine" that drove a six-fold rise in global income per capita from 1925 to 2025, then stress-tests whether the global economy can grow eight-fold by 2100. Smit and Bradley are McKinsey senior partners and co-authors of the international bestseller *Strategy Beyond the Hockey Stick*. Math holds. Endorsed by 2025 Nobel laureate Joel Mokyr. Intellectual foundation of the AI Super Boom thesis.

The AI Ideal: AIdealism and the Governance of AI, Niklas Lidströmer, PhD, MD, Morgan Kaufmann, $180.00. Philosophical counterweight to the productivity case. Lidströmer is a physician, scientist, and thought leader at the intersection of medicine, AI, and societal transformation. While most experts focus on AI doom, Lidströmer presents an actionable framework for how civilization governs the most consequential enabling technology since electricity. Rooted in European Enlightenment ideals, Scandinavian liberalism, and Swiss direct democracy, *AIdealism* rejects extreme ideologies and offers concrete prompts for guiding AI toward human betterment.

AI in Asset Management: Tools, Applications, and Frontiers, Joseph Simonian, PhD, editor, CFA Institute Research Foundation, complimentary for CFA members, $29.99. Institutional bridge between AI as theory and practice. Practitioner case studies on deploying machine learning in real investment processes — ML pipelines, alpha decay, model interpretability, and the new sources of risk that come with letting algorithms drive allocation decisions. For the serious investor who wants to understand what institutions are actually doing with AI right now, not what they say at conferences.

The QQQ and TQQQ ETF Profit Machine: A Roadmap for Trading and Investing in Cutting-Edge AI-Focused Tech Titans, Leslie N. Masonson, Notion Press, $39.95. Former VP at Citibank, Bank of America, and Irving Trust, applies seasonal swing trades and six technical analysis tools to NASDAQ ETF trading. Honored that our longtime friend covers our Best Months Switching Strategies and other Almanac seasonality work in depth in Chapter 5. He distills complex strategies into clear, disciplined, data-driven steps — a roadmap for returns and a framework for protecting capital. Game-changer for ETF traders.

Value Options: How Warren Buffett Uses Options to Buy Wonderful Businesses at Better-Than-Fair Prices, Tobias Carlisle and Tim Travis, Acquirers Funds, $16.99. Value investor's response to an era of speculation. Carlisle, CIO of Acquirers Funds and author of *Deep Value and Quantitative Value*, teams with Tim Travis to reveal what most retail investors don't know — Warren Buffett has quietly used options for decades to express his deepest convictions about value, price, and patience. Drawing on Berkshire's actual Coca-Cola and Burlington Northern trades, the authors reframe options not as speculative instruments but as a disciplined extension of value investing. The big money isn't in the buying or the selling — it's in the waiting.

The Art and Business of Professional Trading, Ryan Wright, Wiley, $41.00. Trading desk view of an algorithmic, AI-dominated market. Wright is founder and CEO of Raen Trading, a global proprietary trading firm and hedge fund whose traders include veterans of Jane Street, Point72, and DRW. He argues the amateur's obsession with predicting price direction is a trap — in a market dominated by algorithms and institutional flow, prediction is fragile, structure is robust. Organized into Foundations, Mental Models, The Professional's Edge, and The Business of Trading, the book draws on decision science, behavioral economics, and lessons from aviation and military strategy. Built for traders looking to level up.

SEPTEMBER 2027

Labor Day *(Market Closed)*

MONDAY
6

A good manager is a man who isn't worried about his own career but rather the careers of those who work for him… Don't worry about yourself! Take care of those who work for you and you'll float to greatness on their achievements.
— H.S.M. Burns (Scottish CEO Shell Oil 1947-1960, 1900-1971)

Day After Labor Day, Dow Down 14 of Last 18, and Last 9 in a Row

TUESDAY
7

D 42.9
S 42.9
N 47.6

I'm not nearly so concerned about the return on my capital as I am the return of my capital.
— Will Rogers (American humorist and showman, 1879-1935)

WEDNESDAY
8

D 61.9
S 52.4
N 57.1

Wise men are instructed by reason, men of less understanding by experience, the most ignorant by necessity, the beasts by nature.
— Marcus Tullius Cicero (Great Roman orator, politician, 106-43 B.C.)

THURSDAY
9

D 66.7
S 71.4
N 66.7

Capitalism without bankruptcy is like Christianity without hell.
— Frank Borman (*Apollo 8* astronaut, CEO Eastern Airlines, April 1986)

2001 4-Day Closing, Longest Since 9-Day Banking Moratorium in March 1933

FRIDAY
10

D 76.2
S 81.0
N 71.4

The generally accepted view is that markets are always right—that is, market prices tend to discount future developments accurately even when it is unclear what those developments are. I start with the opposite point of view. I believe that market prices are always wrong in the sense that they present a biased view of the future.
— George Soros (Financier, philanthropist, political activist, author and philosopher, 1987, b. 1930)

SATURDAY
11

SUNDAY
12

A CORRECTION FOR ALL SEASONS

While there's a rally for every season (page 76), almost always there's a decline or correction, too. Fortunately, corrections tend to be smaller than rallies, and that's what gives the stock market its long-term upward bias. In each season, the average bounce outdoes the average setback. On average, the net gain between the rally and the correction is smallest in summer and fall.

The summer setback tends to be slightly outdone by the average correction in the fall. Tax selling and portfolio cleaning are the usual explanations—individuals sell to register a tax loss and institutions like to get rid of their losers before preparing year-end statements. The October jinx also plays a major part. Since 1964, there have been 20 fall declines of over 10%, and in 11 of them (1966, 1974, 1978, 1979, 1987, 1990, 1997, 2000, 2002, 2008, and 2018) much damage was done in October, where so many bear markets end. Recent October lows were also seen in 1998, 1999, 2004, 2005, 2011, and 2023. Most often, it has paid to buy after fourth-quarter or late third-quarter "waterfall declines" for a rally that may continue into January or even beyond. The Covid-19 pandemic economic shutdown in late Q1/early Q2 of 2020 caused the worst winter and spring slumps since 1932. Easy monetary policy and strong corporate earnings spared Q1 2011 and 2012 from a seasonal slump. Tax cut expectations lifted the market in Q4 2017.

SEASONAL CORRECTIONS IN DOW JONES INDUSTRIALS

	WINTER SLUMP Nov/Dec High to Q1 Low	SPRING SLUMP Feb/Mar High to Q2 Low	SUMMER SLUMP May/Jun High to Q3 Low	FALL SLUMP Aug/Sep High to Q4 Low
1964	−0.1%	−2.4%	−1.0%	−2.1%
1965	−2.5	−7.3	−8.3	−0.9
1966	−6.0	−13.2	−17.7	−12.7
1967	−4.2	−3.9	−5.5	−9.9
1968	−8.8	−0.3	−5.5	+0.4
1969	−8.7	−8.7	−17.2	−8.1
1970	−13.8	−20.2	−8.8	−2.5
1971	−1.4	−4.8	−10.7	−13.4
1972	−0.5	−2.6	−6.3	−5.3
1973	−11.0	−12.8	−10.9	−17.3
1974	−15.3	−10.8	−29.8	−27.6
1975	−6.3	−5.5	−9.9	−6.7
1976	−0.2	−5.1	−4.7	−8.9
1977	−8.5	−7.2	−11.5	−10.2
1978	−12.3	−4.0	−7.0	−13.5
1979	−2.5	−5.8	−3.7	−10.9
1980	−10.0	−16.0	−1.7	−6.8
1981	−6.9	−5.1	−18.6	−12.9
1982	−10.9	−7.5	−10.6	−3.3
1983	−4.1	−2.8	−6.8	−3.6
1984	−11.9	−10.5	−8.4	−6.2
1985	−4.8	−4.4	−2.8	−2.3
1986	−3.3	−4.7	−7.3	−7.6
1987	−1.4	−6.6	−1.7	−36.1
1988	−6.7	−7.0	−7.6	−4.5
1989	−1.7	−2.4	−3.1	−6.6
1990	−7.9	−4.0	−17.3	−18.4
1991	−6.3	−3.6	−4.5	−6.3
1992	+0.1	−3.3	−5.4	−7.6
1993	−2.7	−3.1	−3.0	−2.0
1994	−4.4	−9.6	−4.4	−7.1
1995	−0.8	−0.1	−0.2	−2.0
1996	−3.5	−4.6	−7.5	+0.2
1997	−1.8	−9.8	−2.2	−13.3
1998	−7.0	−3.1	−18.2	−13.1
1999	−2.7	−1.7	−8.0	−11.5
2000	−14.8	−7.4	−4.1	−11.8
2001	−14.5	−13.6	−27.4	−16.2
2002	−5.1	−14.2	−26.7	−19.5
2003	−15.8	−5.3	−3.1	−2.1
2004	−3.9	−7.7	−6.3	−5.7
2005	−4.5	−8.5	−3.3	−4.5
2006	−2.4	−5.4	−7.8	−0.4
2007	−3.7	−3.2	−6.1	−8.4
2008	−14.5	−11.0	−20.6	−35.9
2009	−32.0	−6.3	−7.4	−3.5
2010	−6.1	−10.4	−13.1	−1.0
2011	+0.2	−4.0	−16.3	−12.2
2012	+0.5	−8.7	−5.3	−7.8
2013	−0.2	−0.3	−4.1	−5.7
2014	−7.3	−2.6	−3.4	−6.7
2015	−4.9	−3.8	−14.4	−7.6
2016	−12.6	−3.3	−0.9	−4.0
2017	−1.2	−3.4	−1.0	+0.6
2018	−5.3	−9.7	−4.5	−18.5
2019	−13.4	−4.9	−4.8	−4.2
2020	−35.1	−29.1	−6.8	−8.9
2021	−2.0	−0.1	−2.7	−4.6
2022	−10.6	−16.4	−15.7	−14.5
2023	−8.0	−4.3	−2.6	−9.0
2024	−1.2	−5.2	−3.3	−1.3
2025	−9.3	−16.1	−1.1	−2.0
2026*	−7.3	−7.3*		
Totals	**−435.8%**	**−436.7%**	**−510.6%**	**−535.9%**
Average	**−6.9%**	**−6.9%**	**−8.2%**	**−8.6%**

** As of 4/24/2026*

Monday Before September Triple Witching, NASDAQ Down 15 of Last 27

MONDAY **13**
D 66.7
S 76.2
N 66.7

It's a buy when the 10-week moving average crosses the 30-week moving average and the slope of both averages is up.
— Victor Sperandeo *(Trader Vic—Methods of a Wall Street Master)*

FOMC Meeting (2 Days)

TUESDAY **14**
D 57.1
S 52.4
N 66.7

Around the world, red tape is being cut. Whether it's telecom in Europe, water in South America, or power in Illinois, governments are stepping back, and competition is thriving where regulated monopolies once dominated.
— (*Fortune*, 12/20/99)

Monthly Expiration Week 2001, Dow Lost 1370 Points (14.3%)
16th Worst Weekly Point Loss Ever, 6th Worst Week Overall

WEDNESDAY **15**
D 66.7
S 61.9
N 47.6

In Washington people tell the truth off the record and lie on the record. In the Middle East they lie off the record and tell the truth on the record.
— Thomas L. Friedman (*NY Times* foreign affairs columnist, "Meet the Press" 12/17/06)

THURSDAY **16**
D 71.4
S 66.7
N 76.2

The world hates change, but it is the only thing that has brought progress.
— Charles Kettering (Inventor of electric ignition, founded Delco in 1909, 1876-1958)

September Triple Witching, Dow Up 13 of Last 22, But Down 9 of Last 14

FRIDAY **17**
D 47.6
S 42.9
N 38.1

Today's generation of young people holds more power than any generation before it to make a positive impact on the world.
— William J. Clinton (42nd U.S. President, Clinton Global Initiative, b. 1946)

SATURDAY **18**

SUNDAY **19**

FIRST-TRADING-DAY-OF-THE-MONTH PHENOMENON

Dow Jones Industrial Average has gained 41608.29 points between September 2, 1997 (7622.42), and April 24, 2026 (49230.71), it is incredible that 9021.65 points were gained on the first trading days of these 344 months. The remaining 6817 trading days combined gained 32586.64 points during the period. This averages out to gains of 26.23 points on first days, in contrast to just 4.78 points on all others.

Note: September 1997 through October 2000 racked up a total gain of 2632.39 Dow points on the first trading days of these 38 months (winners except for seven occasions). But between November 2000 and September 2002, when the 2000–2002 bear markets did the bulk of their damage, frightened investors switched from pouring money into the market on that day to pulling it out, 14 months out of 23, netting a 404.80 Dow point loss. The 2007–2009 bear market lopped off 964.14 Dow points on first days in 17 months November 2007–March 2009. First days had their worst year in 2025, declining eight times for a total loss of 1818.53 Dow points.

First days of August have performed worst, declining 19 times in the last 28 years. July's first trading day is second best by points but best based upon frequency of gains with only six declines in the last 37 years (since 1989). In rising market trends first days tend to perform much better as institutions are likely anticipating strong performance at each month's outset. S&P 500 and NASDAQ first days differ just slightly from Dow's pattern. August's first trading day is worst for S&P 500 and NASDAQ. September is also a net point decliner for S&P 500 and NASDAQ while December is positive for NASDAQ and negative for S&P 500.

DOW POINTS GAINED FIRST DAY OF MONTH SEPTEMBER 1997–APRIL 24, 2026

	Jan	Feb	Mar	Apr	May	Jun	Jul	Aug	Sep	Oct	Nov	Dec	Totals
1997									257.36	70.24	232.31	189.98	**749.89**
1998	56.79	201.28	4.73	68.51	83.70	22.42	96.65	−96.55	288.36	−210.09	114.05	16.99	**646.84**
1999	2.84	−13.13	18.20	46.35	225.65	36.52	95.62	−9.19	108.60	−63.95	−81.35	120.58	**486.74**
2000	−139.61	100.52	9.62	300.01	77.87	129.87	112.78	84.97	23.68	49.21	−71.67	−40.95	**636.30**
2001	−140.70	96.27	−45.14	−100.85	163.37	78.47	91.32	−12.80	47.74	−10.73	188.76	−87.60	**268.11**
2002	51.90	−12.74	262.73	−41.24	113.41	−215.46	−133.47	−229.97	−355.45	346.86	120.61	−33.52	**−126.34**
2003	265.89	56.01	−53.22	77.73	−25.84	47.55	55.51	−79.83	107.45	194.14	57.34	116.59	**819.32**
2004	−44.07	11.11	94.22	15.63	88.43	14.20	−101.32	39.45	−5.46	112.38	26.92	162.20	**413.69**
2005	−53.58	62.00	63.77	−99.46	59.19	82.39	28.47	−17.76	−21.97	−33.22	−33.30	106.70	**143.23**
2006	129.91	89.09	60.12	35.62	−23.85	91.97	77.80	−59.95	83.00	−8.72	−49.71	−27.80	**397.48**
2007	11.37	51.99	−34.29	27.95	73.23	40.47	126.81	150.38	91.12	191.92	−362.14	−57.15	**311.66**
2008	−220.86	92.83	−7.49	391.47	189.87	−134.50	32.25	−51.70	−26.63	−19.59	−5.18	−679.95	**−439.48**
2009	258.30	−64.03	−299.64	152.68	44.29	221.11	57.06	114.95	−185.68	−203.00	76.71	126.74	**299.49**
2010	155.91	118.20	78.53	70.44	143.22	−112.61	−41.49	208.44	254.75	41.63	6.13	249.76	**1172.91**
2011	93.24	148.23	−168.32	56.99	−3.18	−279.65	168.43	−10.75	−119.96	−258.08	−297.05	−25.65	**−695.75**
2012	179.82	83.55	28.23	52.45	65.69	−274.88	−8.70	−37.62	−54.90	77.98	136.16	−59.98	**187.80**
2013	308.41	149.21	35.17	−5.69	−138.85	138.46	65.36	128.48	23.65	62.03	69.80	−77.64	**758.39**
2014	−135.31	−326.05	−153.68	74.95	−21.97	26.46	129.47	−69.93	−30.89	−238.19	−24.28	−51.44	**−820.86**
2015	9.92	196.09	155.93	−77.94	185.54	29.69	138.40	−91.66	−469.68	−11.99	165.22	168.43	**395.95**
2016	−276.09	−17.12	348.58	107.66	117.52	2.47	19.38	−27.73	18.42	−54.30	−105.32	68.35	**201.82**
2017	119.16	26.85	303.31	−13.01	−27.05	135.53	129.64	72.80	39.46	152.51	57.77	−40.76	**956.21**
2018	104.79	37.32	−420.22	−458.92	−64.10	219.37	35.77	−81.37	−12.34	192.90	264.98	287.97	**106.15**
2019	18.78	64.22	110.32	329.74	−162.77	4.74	117.47	−280.85	−285.26	−343.79	301.13	−268.37	**−394.64**
2020	330.36	143.78	1293.96	−973.65	−622.03	91.91	−77.91	236.08	215.61	35.20	423.45	185.28	**1282.04**
2021	−382.59	229.29	603.14	171.66	238.38	45.86	131.02	−97.31	−48.20	482.54	94.28	−461.68	**1006.39**
2022	246.76	273.38	−597.65	139.92	84.29	−176.89	321.83	−46.73	145.99	765.38	−79.75	−194.76	**881.77**
2023	−10.88	6.92	5.14	327.00	−46.46	153.30	10.87	71.15	115.80	−74.15	221.71	294.61	**1075.01**
2024	25.50	369.54	91.49	−240.52	87.37	−115.29	50.66	−494.82	−626.15	−173.18	288.73	−128.65	**−865.32**
2025	−151.95	−122.75	−649.67	−11.80	83.60	35.41	400.17	−542.40	−249.07	43.21	−226.19	−427.09	**−1818.53**
2026	319.10	515.19	−73.14	224.23									**985.38**
Totals	**1133.11**	**2567.05**	**1064.73**	**647.91**	**986.52**	**338.89**	**2129.85**	**−1232.22**	**−670.65**	**1115.15**	**1510.12**	**−568.81**	**9021.65**

SUMMARY FIRST DAYS VS. OTHER DAYS OF MONTH

	# of Days	Total Points Gained	Average Daily Point Gain
First days	344	9021.65	26.23
Other days	6817	32586.64	4.78

SEPTEMBER 2027

MONDAY

D 57.1
S 52.4
N 52.4

20

A small debt produces a debtor; a large one, an enemy.
— Publilius Syrus (Syrian-born Roman mime and former slave, 83-43 B.C.)

Week After September Triple Witching Dow Down 27 of Last 36, Average Loss Since 1990, 1.0%

TUESDAY

D 42.9
S 23.8
N 38.1

21

Patriotism is when love of your own people comes first. Nationalism is when hate for people other than your own comes first.
— Charles De Gaulle (French president and WWII general, 1890-1970, May 1969)

WEDNESDAY

D 42.9
S 33.3
N 33.3

22

When a falling stock becomes a screaming buy because it cannot conceivably drop further, try to buy it 30 percent lower.
— Al Rizzo (Investment Advisor, *Dynamic Growth Letter,* 1986)

End of September Prone to Weakness From End-of-Q3 Institutional Portfolio Restructuring

THURSDAY

D 28.6
S 28.6
N 33.3

23

Six words that spell business success: create concept, communicate concept, sustain momentum.
— Yale Hirsch (Creator of *Stock Trader's Almanac*, 1923-2021)

FRIDAY

D 42.9
S 42.9
N 52.4

24

The words "I am…" are potent words; be careful what you hitch them to.
The thing you're claiming has a way of reaching back and claiming you.
— A. L. Kitselman (Author, math teacher)

SATURDAY

25

October Almanac Investor Sector Seasonalities: See Pages 94, 96, and 98

SUNDAY

26

OCTOBER ALMANAC

OCTOBER						
S	M	T	W	T	F	S
					1	2
3	4	5	6	7	8	9
10	11	12	13	14	15	16
17	18	19	20	21	22	23
24	25	26	27	28	29	30
31						

NOVEMBER						
S	M	T	W	T	F	S
	1	2	3	4	5	6
7	8	9	10	11	12	13
14	15	16	17	18	19	20
21	22	23	24	25	26	27
28	29	30				

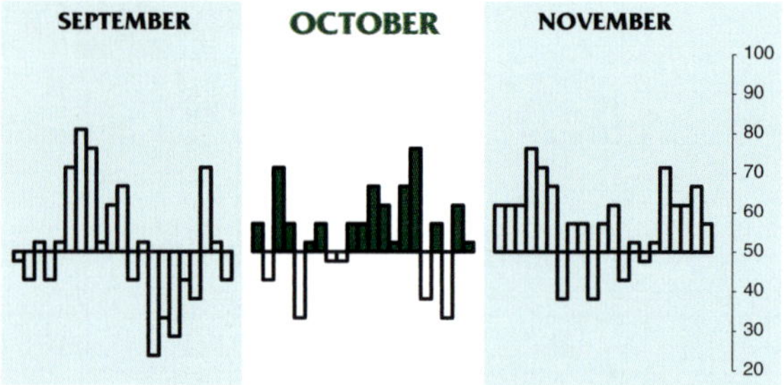

Market Probability Chart above is a graphic representation of the S&P 500 Recent Market Probability Calendar on page 126.

◆ Beware "Octoberphobia" from crashes in 1929, 1987, 554-point drop October 27, 1997, back-to-back massacres 1978 and 1979, Friday the 13th, 1989, and the 2008 meltdown ◆ Yet October is a "Bear Killer" and turned the tide in 13 post-WWII bear markets: 1946, 1957, 1960, 1962, 1966, 1974, 1987, 1990, 1998, 2001, 2002, 2011, and 2022 ◆ First October Dow top in 2007 ◆ Worst six months of the year ends with October (page 54) ◆ No longer worst month (pages 52 & 60) ◆ Best Dow, S&P and NASDAQ month from 1993 to 2007 ◆ Pre-election year Octobers since 1950, #10 Dow (+0.5), #10 S&P (+0.1%) and #11 NASDAQ (+0.1%) ◆ October is a great time to buy ◆ Big October Dow gains five years 1999–2003 after atrocious Septembers ◆ Enter Best Six Months earlier using MACD (page 56) ◆ October 2022, best Dow month by points, up over 4000 (+14.0%)

October Vital Statistics

	DJIA		S&P 500		NASDAQ		Russell 1K		Russell 2K	
Rank		7		7		8		7		11
Up		45		45		30		29		27
Down		31		31		25		18		20
Average % Change		0.8		0.9		0.8		1.0		–0.2
Pre-Election Yr Avg % Chg		–0.5		0.1		0.1		0.2		–1.9
Best & Worst October										
	% Change		% Change		% Change		% Change		% Change	
Best	2022	14.0	1974	16.3	1974	17.2	1982	11.3	2011	15.0
Worst	1987	–23.2	1987	–21.8	1987	–27.2	1987	–21.9	1987	–30.8
Best & Worst October Weeks										
Best	10/11/74	12.6	10/11/74	14.1	10/31/08	10.9	10/31/08	10.8	10/31/08	14.1
Worst	10/10/08	–18.2	10/10/08	–18.2	10/23/87	–19.2	10/10/08	–18.2	10/23/87	–20.4
Best & Worst October Days										
Best	10/13/08	11.1	10/13/08	11.6	10/13/08	11.8	10/13/08	11.7	10/13/08	9.3
Worst	10/19/87	–22.6	10/19/87	–20.5	10/19/87	–11.4	10/19/87	–19.0	10/19/87	–12.5
First Trading Day of Monthly Options Expiration Week: 1980–2026										
Record (#Up-#Down)		35-11		33-13		31-15		34-12		33-13
Current streak		U4		U4		U4		U4		U4
Avg % Change		0.67		0.68		0.62		0.66		0.49
Monthly Options Expiration Day: 1980–2026										
Record (#Up-#Down)		24-22		25-21		26-20		24-22		17-29
Current streak		U2		U2		U2		U2		D3
Avg % Change		–0.04		–0.11		–0.05		–0.10		–0.18
Monthly Options Expiration Week: 1980–2026										
Record (#Up-#Down)		33-13		34-12		28-18		33-13		28-18
Current streak		U2		U2		U2		U2		U2
Avg % Change		0.69		0.71		0.75		0.70		0.51
Week After Monthly Options Expiration: 1980–2026										
Record (#Up-#Down)		23-23		21-25		25-21		21-25		22-24
Current streak		U1		U1		U2		U1		U1
Avg % Change		–0.21		–0.24		–0.23		–0.26		–0.44
First Trading Day Performance										
% of Time Up		50.0		52.6		50.9		55.3		48.9
Avg % Change		0.10		0.08		–0.07		0.23		–0.19
Last Trading Day Performance										
% of Time Up		52.6		53.9		61.8		61.7		66.0
Avg % Change		0.05		0.10		0.36		0.23		0.45

Dow & S&P 1950–May 1, 2026; NASDAQ 1971–May 2, 2026; Russell 1K & 2K 1979–May 2, 2026.

October has killed many a bear;
Buy techs and small caps and soon wear a grin ear to ear.

SEPTEMBER/OCTOBER 2027

Start Looking for MACD BUY Signals on October 1 (Pages 56, 62, and 64)
***Almanac Investor* Subscribers Emailed When It Triggers (Learn More Page 67)**

MONDAY
D 47.6
S 38.1
N 52.4
27

The average man is always waiting for something to happen to him instead of setting to work to make things happen. For one person who dreams of making 50,000 pounds, a hundred people dream of being left 50,000 pounds.
— A. A. Milne (British author, *Winnie-the-Pooh*, 1882-1956)

TUESDAY
D 66.7
S 71.4
N 61.9
28

Under capitalism man exploits man: under socialism the reverse is true.
— Polish proverb

WEDNESDAY
D 57.1
S 52.4
N 38.1
29

As for it being different this time, it is different every time. The question is in what way, and to what extent.
— Tom McClellan (Market analyst and technician, *The McClellan Market Report*)

Last Day of Q3, S&P Down 18 of Last 29, But Up 7 of Last 11, Massive 5.4% Rally in 2008

THURSDAY
D 47.6
S 42.9
N 52.4
30

The market can stay irrational longer than you can stay solvent.
— John Maynard Keynes (British economist, 1883-1946)

First Trading Day in October Mixed, Dow Down 11 of Last 22, Up 2.7% in 2022

FRIDAY
D 47.6
S 57.1
N 52.4
1

I never buy at the bottom and I always sell too soon.
— Baron Nathan Rothchild's success formula (London financier, 1777-1836)

Rosh Hashanah

SATURDAY
2

SUNDAY
3

SECTOR SEASONALITY: SELECTED PERCENTAGE PLAYS

Sector seasonality was featured in the first 1968 *Almanac*. A Merrill Lynch study showed that buying seven sectors around September or October and selling in the first few months of 1954–1964 tripled the gains of holding them for 10 years. Over the years we have honed this strategy significantly and now devote a significant portion of our time and resources to investing and trading during positive and negative seasonal periods for the different sector indexes below with highly correlated exchange-traded funds (ETFs).

Updated seasonalities appear in the table below. We specify whether the seasonality starts or finishes in the beginning third (B), middle third (M), or last third (E) of the month. These Selected Percentage Plays are geared to take advantage of the bulk of seasonal sector strength or weakness.

By design, entry points are in advance of the major seasonal moves, providing traders ample opportunity to accumulate positions at favorable prices. Conversely, exit points have been selected to capture the majority of the move.

From the major seasonalities in the table below, we created the Sector Index Seasonality Strategy Calendar on pages 96 and 98. Note the concentration of bullish sector seasonalities during the Best Six Months, November–April, and bearish sector seasonalities during the Worst Six Months, May–October.

Almanac Investor subscribers receive specific entry and exit points for highly correlated ETFs and detailed analysis in our *ETF Trades* email Issue. Visit *www.stocktradersalmanac.com* or see a special offer for new subscribers between pages 66 and 67.

SECTOR INDEX SEASONALITY TABLE

			Seasonality				Average % Return†		
Ticker	Sector Index	Type	Start		Finish		25-Year	10-Year	5-Year
XCI	Computer Tech	Short	January	B	March	B	–4.55	–1.88	–4.20
XNG	Natural Gas	Long	February	E	June	B	13.72	18.04	16.83
S5INFT	InfoTech	Long	March	M	July	M	11.83	19.29	20.08
UTY	Utilities	Long	March	M	October	B	7.59	9.90	8.22
XCI	Computer Tech	Long	April	M	July	M	10.21	16.22	19.94
BKX	Banking	Short	May	B	July	B	–5.63	–2.87	–1.91
XAU	Gold & Silver	Short	May	M	June	E	–6.28	–4.90	–9.78
S5MATR	Materials	Short	May	M	October	M	–3.96	–0.43	–5.30
XOI	Oil	Short	June	B	August	E	–5.46	–6.41	–4.40
XNG	Natural Gas	Short	June	M	July	E	–6.63	–6.16	–3.82
XAU	Gold & Silver	Long	July	E	December	E	11.07	10.29	20.23
S5INDU	Industrials	Short	July	M	October	B	–3.73	–1.00	–2.87
DJT	Transports	Short	July	M	October	M	–4.24	–2.24	–6.27
BTK	Biotech	Long	August	B	March	B	12.51	9.27	8.16
S5INFT	InfoTech	Long	August	M	January	M	11.17	11.53	10.25
SOX	Semiconductor	Short	August	M	October	E	–5.39	–2.21	–5.11
BKX	Banking	Long	October	B	May	B	12.20	12.06	20.94
XBD	Broker/Dealer	Long	October	B	January	B	15.84	15.86	12.67
XCI	Computer Tech	Long	October	B	January	B	12.07	9.58	10.97
S5COND	Consumer Discretionary	Long	October	B	June	B	13.21	10.99	9.16
S5CONS	Consumer Staples	Long	October	B	June	B	8.85	8.45	10.97
S5HLTH	Healthcare	Long	October	B	May	B	7.93	6.40	7.78
S5INDU	Industrials	Long	October	E	May	M	10.96	10.12	16.59
S5MATR	Materials	Long	October	B	May	B	13.74	9.76	14.60
DRG	Pharmaceutical	Long	October	M	January	B	6.47	6.56	8.26
RMZ	Real Estate	Long	October	E	May	B	9.76	4.62	10.09
SOX	Semiconductor	Long	October	E	February	M	17.19	23.30	22.34
XTC	Telecom	Long	October	M	December	E	5.67	2.01	3.73
DJT	Transports	Long	October	B	May	B	14.24	6.68	12.11
XOI	Oil	Long	December	M	July	B	11.50	10.86	22.07

† *Average % return based on full seasonality completion through May 1, 2026*

OCTOBER 2027

October Ends Dow and S&P "Worst Six Months" (Pages 52, 54, 56, 64, and 149)
And NASDAQ "Worst Four Months" (Pages 60, 62, and 150)

MONDAY
D 38.1
S 42.9
N 47.6
4

The public may boo me, but when I go home and think of my money, I clap.
— Horace (Roman poet-critic, *Epistles*, c. 20 BC)

TUESDAY
D 71.4
S 71.4
N 66.7
5

If there is something you really want to do, make your plan and do it. Otherwise, you'll just regret it forever.
— Richard Rocco (PostNet franchisee, *Entrepreneur Magazine* 12/2006, b. 1946)

October 2011, Second Dow Month to Gain 1000 Points

WEDNESDAY
D 57.1
S 57.1
N 52.4
6

Low volatility is where trends are born, high volatility is where they go to die.
— John Bollinger, CMT, CFA (American author, technical/financial analyst, developer of Bollinger Bands, Bollinger Capital Management, *Capital Growth Letter, Bollinger on Bollinger Bands*, b. 1950)

THURSDAY
D 33.3
S 33.3
N 42.9
7

Whoso neglects learning in his youth, loses the past and is dead for the future.
— Euripides (Greek tragedian, *Medea*, 485-406 BC)

Dow Lost 18.2% (1874 points) on the Week Ending 10/10/2008
Worst Dow Week in the History of Wall Street

FRIDAY
D 52.4
S 52.4
N 57.1
8

Financial genius is a rising stock market.
— John Kenneth Galbraith (Canadian/American economist and diplomat, 1908-2006)

SATURDAY
9

SUNDAY
10

SECTOR INDEX SEASONALITY STRATEGY CALENDAR*

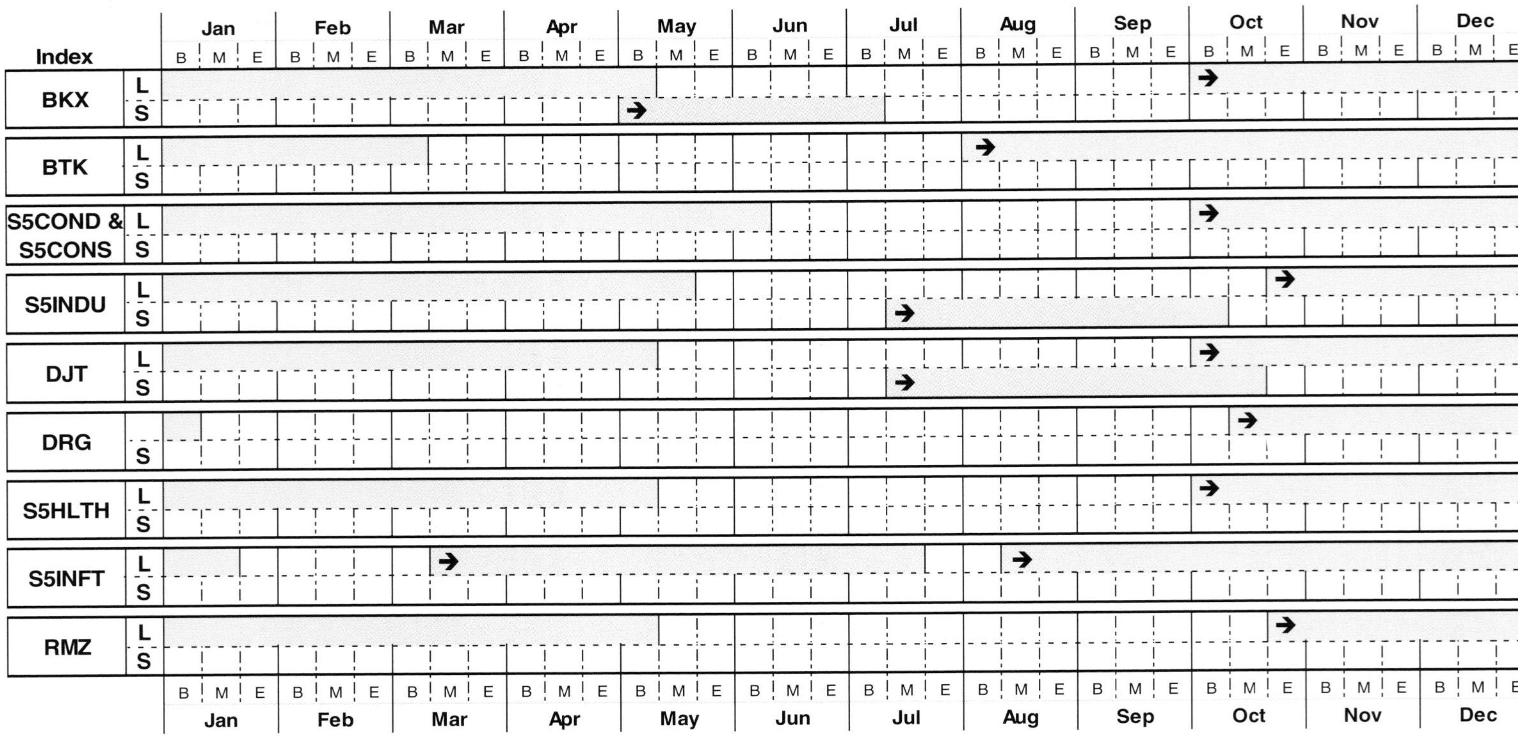

* Graphic representation of the Sector Index Seasonality Percentage Plays on page 94.
L = Long Trade, S = Short Trade, → = Start of Trade

(continued on page 98)

Columbus Day *(Bond Market Closed)*, **Yom Kippur**
Monday Before October Monthly Expiration, Dow Up 34 of 44

MONDAY
D 61.9
S 57.1
N 57.1
11

The future now belongs to societies that organize themselves for learning.
What we know and can do holds the key to economic progress.
— Ray Marshall (b. 1928) and Marc Tucker (b. 1939) (*Thinking for a Living: Education and the Wealth of Nations*, 1992)

TUESDAY
D 47.6
S 47.6
N 47.6
12

It's not what you say. It's what they hear.
— (A sign in an advertising office)

WEDNESDAY
D 38.1
S 47.6
N 57.1
13

At the end of the day, the most important thing is how good are you at risk control.
Ninety-percent of any great trader is going to be the risk control.
— Paul Tudor Jones II (Founder Tudor Investment Corporation, b. 1954)

THURSDAY
D 66.7
S 57.1
N 57.1
14

When investment decisions need to consider the speed of light, something is seriously wrong.
— Frank M. Bifulco (Senior Portfolio Manager Alcott Capital Management, *Barron's*, "Letters to the Editor," 5/24/2010)

October Monthly Expiration Day, Dow Down 6 Straight 2005–2010,
But Up 11 of Last 15

FRIDAY
D 47.6
S 57.1
N 57.1
15

He who knows nothing is confident of everything.
— Anonymous

SATURDAY
16

SUNDAY
17

(continued from page 96)

SECTOR INDEX SEASONALITY STRATEGY CALENDAR*

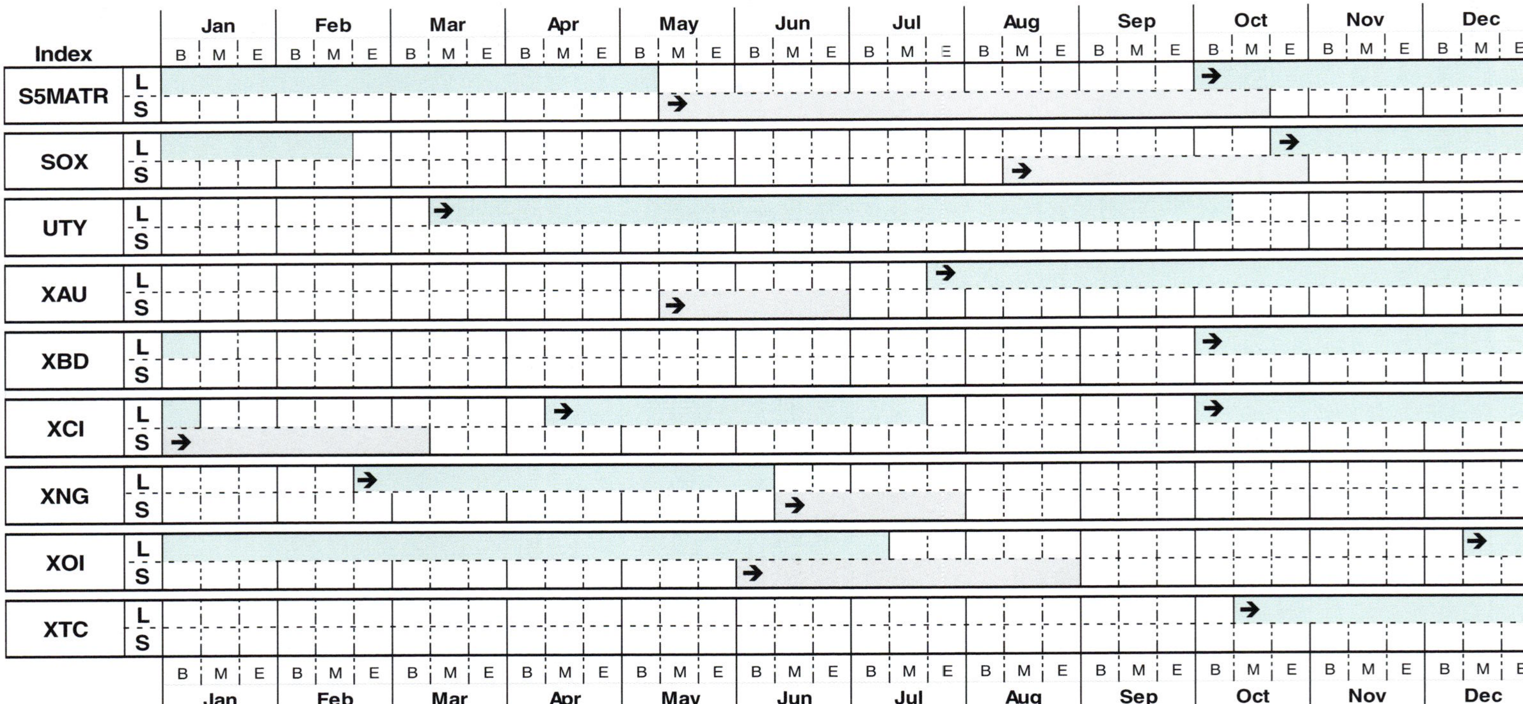

* Graphic representation of the Sector Index Seasonality Percentage Plays on page 94.
L = Long Trade, S = Short Trade, ⟶ = Start of Trade

MONDAY
18
D 61.9
S 66.7
N 57.1

Whenever you find the key to the market, they change the locks.
— Lucien Hooper (Securities analyst, *Forbes* columnist,"Dean of Wall Street," *Hooper Letter,* 1896-1988)

Crash of October 19, 1987, Dow Down 22.6% in One Day

TUESDAY
19
D 57.1
S 61.9
N 61.9

What investors really get paid for is holding dogs. Small stocks tend to have higher average returns than big stocks, and value stocks tend to have higher average returns than growth stocks.
— Kenneth R. French (Economist, Dartmouth, NBER, b. 1954)

WEDNESDAY
20
D 52.4
S 52.4
N 42.9

Never mind telling me what stocks to buy; tell me when to buy them.
— Humphrey B. Neill (Investor, analyst, author, *Neill Letters of Contrary Opinion*, 1895-1977)

Late October is Time to Buy Depressed Stocks
Especially Techs and Small Caps

THURSDAY
21
D 57.1
S 66.7
N 71.4

I'm very big on having clarified principles. I don't believe in being reactive. You can't do that in the markets effectively. I can't. I need perspective. I need a game plan.
— Ray Dalio (Money manager, founder Bridgewater Associates, *Fortune* 3/16/2009, b. 1949)

FRIDAY
22
D 61.9
S 76.2
N 71.4

It is impossible to please all the world and one's father.
— Jean de La Fontaine (French poet, 1621-1695)

SATURDAY
23

SUNDAY
24

NASDAQ 74000: WELCOME TO THE AI SUPER BOOM

The AI Super Boom began with the November 2022 ChatGPT launch — the Windows 3.1 moment of this cycle. Today, May 2026, AI is approaching mass-adoption akin to the PC/Windows 95 inflection point. The current secular bull launched at the October 4, 2011, NASDAQ intraday low of ~2,300, the structural equivalent of the August 1982 low that kicked off the prior secular bull.

Yale's 1976 Dow call was a 500% move. Our 2010 Dow call was a 500% move. NASDAQ is forecasted for a 32x move this cycle — NASDAQ gained +3,100% off the 1982 launching pad while the Dow rose +1,400%. Same cycle, same secular bull, bigger multiple because NASDAQ captures the enabling technology. Repeating the 1982–2000 move off the 2011 launching pad takes the NASDAQ to 74,000 by 2036.

Three things distinguish this leg of the cycle:

New inflation regime. Higher structural inflation than the pre-2020 normal. Sticky elevated inflation boosts nominal returns. NASDAQ, which captures AI productivity gains, benefits most.

New tokenization demand layer. DTCC and the major exchanges are building rails for blockchain-settled, 24/7-traded, globally-accessible U.S. equity tokens. Same supply, more buyers. Mutual funds expanded the buyer base in the 1950s and '60s. 401(k)s in the 1980s and '90s. ETFs in the 2000s and 2010s. Tokenization is next.

More powerful tech stack. AI is arguably the most enabling technology since electricity. AI plus quantum plus tokenization is exponentially more enabling than any prior cycle's engine. Secular bulls have been getting longer and higher; bears shorter and faster.

How It Ends

Every secular bull ends. The 1982–2000 cycle had its scares — 1987 crash, 1990 Gulf War, 1997 Asian crisis, 1998 LTCM — before the dot-com bubble finally unwound on its own internal excess. This cycle will too. Likely interim shocks: a geopolitical correction around 2030 (China–Taiwan most likely), or a tokenization-driven crash on digital-asset excess. The real top, most likely 2034–2036, comes from excess — overvaluation, overinvestment, regulatory constraint. After that: prolonged consolidation, not collapse. Until then, the risk isn't being too early for the end. It's being too early against the trend. Welcome to the AI Super Boom.

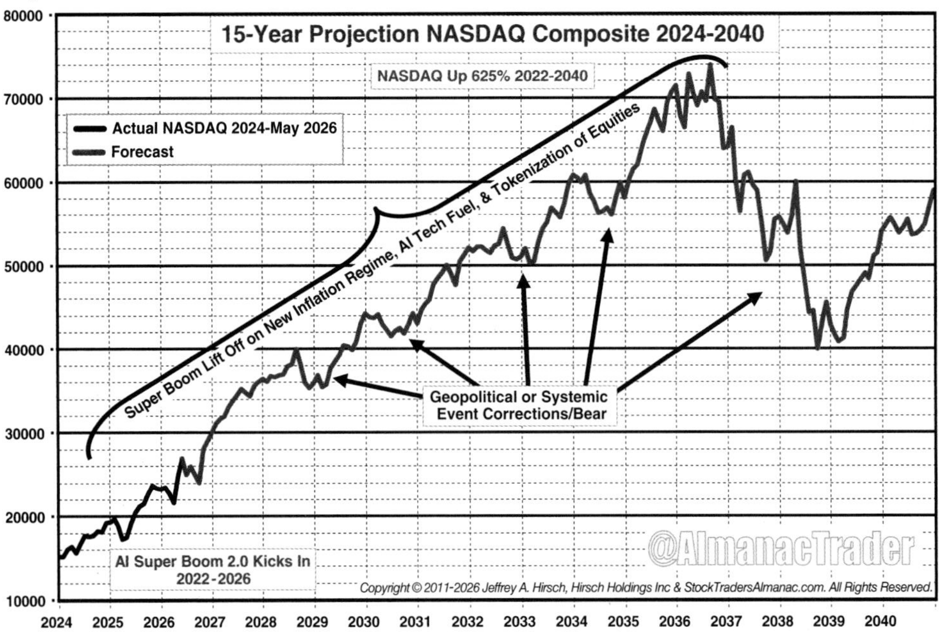

MONDAY
D 42.9
S 38.1
N 52.4
25

If a man can see both sides of a problem, you know that none of his money is tied up in it.
— Verda Ross

FOMC Meeting (2 Days)

TUESDAY
D 66.7
S 57.1
N 52.4
26

My grandfather always said, in low interest rate environments, borrow as little as you need. In high interest rate environments, borrow as much as you can afford.
— Anthony E. Malkin (Chairman & CEO Empire State Realty Trust, b. 1962)

WEDNESDAY
D 33.3
S 33.3
N 57.1
27

If there's anything duller than being on a board in Corporate America, I haven't found it.
— H. Ross Perot (American businessman, *NY Times,* 10/28/92, 2-time 3rd-party presidential candidate 1992 & 1996, 1930-2019)

98th Anniversary of 1929 Crash, Dow Down 23.0% in Two Days, October 28 & 29

THURSDAY
D 57.1
S 61.9
N 61.9
28

I'd be a bum on the street with a tin cup, if the markets were always efficient.
— Warren Buffett (CEO Berkshire Hathaway, investor & philanthropist, b. 1930)

FRIDAY
D 47.6
S 52.4
N 52.4
29

Learn from the mistakes of others; you can't live long enough to make them all yourself.
— Eleanor Roosevelt (First Lady, 1884-1962)

SATURDAY
30

Halloween

November Almanac Investor Sector Seasonalities: See Pages 94, 96, and 98

SUNDAY
31

NOVEMBER ALMANAC

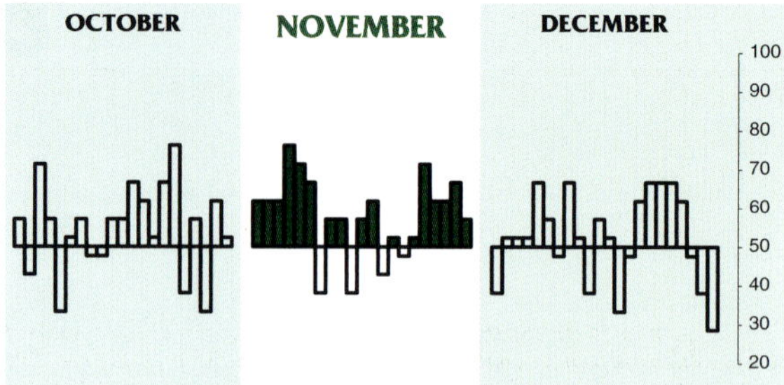

NOVEMBER

S	M	T	W	T	F	S
		1	2	3	4	5	6
7	8	9	10	11	12	13
14	15	16	17	18	19	20
21	22	23	24	25	26	27
28	29	30				

DECEMBER

S	M	T	W	T	F	S
			1	2	3	4
5	6	7	8	9	10	11
12	13	14	15	16	17	18
19	20	21	22	23	24	25
26	27	28	29	30	31	

Market Probability Chart above is a graphic representation of the S&P 500 Recent Market Probability Calendar on page 126.

◆ #1 S&P and Dow month since 1950, #2 on NASDAQ since 1971 (pages 52 & 60) ◆ Start of the "Best Six Months" of the year (page 54), NASDAQ's Best Eight Months and Best Three (pages 149 & 150) ◆ Simple MACD timing indicator nearly triples "Best Six Months" strategy (page 56), about triples NASDAQ's Best Eight (page 62) ◆ Day before and after Thanksgiving Day combined, only 19 losses in 74 years (page 106) ◆ Week before Thanksgiving Dow up 21 of last 33, but down 7 of the last 9 ◆ Pre-election year Novembers rank #8 Dow (+0.9%), #8 S&P (+0.9%), NASDAQ #7 (+1.9%) ◆ NASDAQ down 22.9% in November 2000 (undecided election, tech bubble burst) (page 167)

November Vital Statistics

	DJIA		S&P 500		NASDAQ		Russell 1K		Russell 2K	
Rank		1		1		2		1		1
Up		53		53		39		36		33
Down		23		23		16		11		14
Average % Change		1.9		1.8		2.1		2.2		2.6
Pre-Election Yr Avg % Chg		0.9		0.9		1.9		0.9		2.1
Best & Worst November										
	% Change		% Change		% Change		% Change		% Change	
Best	2020	11.8	2020	10.8	2001	14.2	2020	11.6	2020	18.3
Worst	1973	–14.0	1973	–11.4	2000	–22.9	2000	–9.3	2008	–12.0
Best & Worst November Weeks										
Best	11/28/08	9.7	11/28/08	12.0	11/28/08	10.9	11/28/08	12.5	11/28/08	16.4
Worst	11/21/08	–5.3	11/21/08	–8.4	11/10/00	–12.2	11/21/08	–8.8	11/21/08	–11.0
Best & Worst November Days										
Best	11/13/08	6.7	11/13/08	6.9	11/10/22	7.4	11/13/08	7.0	11/13/08	8.5
Worst	11/20/08	–5.6	11/20/08	–6.7	11/19/08	–6.5	11/20/08	–6.9	11/19/08	–7.9
First Trading Day of Monthly Options Expiration Week: 1980–2026										
Record (#Up–#Down)		25-21		20-26		17-29		22-24		20-26
Current streak		D1		D1		D1		D1		D1
Avg % Change		–0.04		–0.09		–0.20		–0.09		–0.09
Monthly Options Expiration Day: 1980–2026										
Record (#Up–#Down)		29-17		27-19		25-21		27-19		27-18
Current streak		U1		U1		U1		U1		U1
Avg % Change		0.20		0.14		0.01		0.14		0.20
Monthly Options Expiration Week: 1980–2026										
Record (#Up–#Down)		27-19		26-20		25-21		25-21		22-24
Current streak		D2		D2		D2		D2		D2
Avg % Change		0.18		0.03		–0.02		0.02		–0.17
Week After Monthly Options Expiration: 1980–2026										
Record (#Up–#Down)		28-18		30-16		30-15		30-16		29-17
Current streak		U4		U4		U4		U4		U4
Avg % Change		0.66		0.65		0.74		0.67		0.90
First Trading Day Performance										
% of Time Up		64.5		65.8		67.3		74.5		63.8
Avg % Change		0.30		0.32		0.34		0.41		0.34
Last Trading Day Performance										
% of Time Up		56.6		53.9		61.8		48.9		66.0
Avg % Change		0.14		0.15		0.01		0.07		0.11

Dow & S&P 1950–May 1, 2026; NASDAQ 1971–May 1, 2026; Russell 1K & 2K 1979–May 1, 2026.

Astute investors always smile and remember,
When stocks seasonally start soaring, and salute November.

NOVEMBER 2027

First Trading Day in November, Dow Up 12 of Last 17

MONDAY
1
D 57.1
S 61.9
N 61.9

There is no one who can replace America. Without American leadership, there is no leadership. That puts a tremendous burden on the American people to do something positive. You can't be tempted by the usual nationalism.
— Lee Hong-koo (South Korean prime minister 1994-1995 and ambassador to U.S. 1998-2000, *NY Times* 2/25/2009)

Election Day

TUESDAY
2
D 61.9
S 61.9
N 57.1

I know nothing grander, better exercise…more positive proof of the past, the triumphant result of faith in humankind, than a well-contested national election.
— Walt Whitman (American poet, 1819-1892)

November Begins Dow and S&P "Best Six Months" (Pages 52, 54, 56, 64, and 149)
And NASDAQ "Best Eight Months" (Pages 60, 62, and 150)

WEDNESDAY
3
D 66.7
S 61.9
N 57.1

On Wall Street, to know what everyone else knows is to know nothing.
— Newton Zinder (Investment advisor and analyst, E.F. Hutton, b. 1927)

THURSDAY
4
D 66.7
S 76.2
N 66.7

The difference between the almost right word [or trade] and the right word [trade] is really a large matter— 'tis the difference between the lightning-bug and the lightning.
— Mark Twain (American novelist and satirist, pen name of Samuel Longhorne Clemens, 1835-1910)

FRIDAY
5
D 76.2
S 71.4
N 71.4

That's the American way. If little kids don't aspire to make money like I did, what the hell good is this country?
— Lee Iacocca (American industrialist, Former Chrysler CEO, 1924-2019)

SATURDAY
6

Daylight Saving Time Ends

SUNDAY
7

TRADERS FEAST ON SMALL STOCKS THANKSGIVING THROUGH SANTA CLAUS RALLY

Thanksgiving kicks off a run of solid bullish seasonal patterns. November–January is the year's best consecutive 3-month span (page 149). Then there's the January Effect (pages 112 & 114) of small caps outperforming large caps in January, which nowadays begins in mid-December.

And of course, the "Santa Claus Rally," (page 118) invented and named by our late founder Yale Hirsch in 1972 in the *Almanac* and often misunderstood, is the short, sweet rally that runs from the last five trading days of the year to the first two trading days of the New Year. Pop also coined the phrase: *"If Santa Claus should fail to call, bears may come to Broad and Wall."*

We have combined these seasonal occurrences into one trade: Buy the Tuesday before Thanksgiving and hold until the second trading day of the New Year. Our good friend and renowned technician and options guru Larry McMillan of the *Options Strategist* opened our eyes to this trade and runs it with options on iShares Russell 2000 (IWM) starting on the day before Thanksgiving.

We feature the Russell 2000 here as this trade produces a higher magnitude of returns for the small cap index with practically the same plurality of gains as the S&P. Since 1979 the Russell 2000 is up 76.6% of the time, 36 of 47 years, with an average gain of 3.1% from the Tuesday before Thanksgiving to the second trading day of the year. For comparison S&P 500 is up 78.9% of the time, 60 of 76 years, average gain 2.5% and NASDAQ is up 76.4% of the time, 42 of 55 years, average gain 2.8%.

RUSSELL 2000 THANKSGIVING–SANTA CLAUS RALLY TRADE

Year	Tuesday B4 Thanksgiving	2nd Trading Day New Year	% Change
1979	50.00	54.11	8.22%
1980	76.92	76.28	−0.83
1981	73.94	72.78	−1.57
1982	85.36	89.08	4.36
1983	113.40	113.66	0.23
1984	101.01	101.27	0.26
1985	123.42	130.88	6.04
1986	138.49	140.76	1.64
1987	115.58	126.13	9.13
1988	139.87	148.39	6.09
1989	166.62	170.79	2.50
1990	124.13	130.35	5.01
1991	175.50	192.09	9.45
1992	210.79	220.08	4.41
1993	248.12	256.97	3.57
1994	242.26	247.65	2.22
1995	301.12	315.21	4.68
1996	351.37	361.85	2.98
1997	426.91	437.06	2.38
1998	396.60	422.09	6.43
1999	454.45	478.38	5.27
2000	466.79	484.39	3.77
2001	453.90	495.51	9.17
2002	398.32	390.31	−2.01
2003	543.18	568.92	4.74
2004	624.53	628.54	0.64
2005	682.55	689.25	0.98
2006	792.17	789.95	−0.28
2007	749.33	745.01	−0.58
2008	443.18	505.03	13.96
2009	592.58	638.49	7.75
2010	719.92	785.83	9.16
2011	696.26	747.28	7.33
2012	793.81	872.60	9.93
2013	1134.53	1156.09	1.90
2014	1186.33	1181.35	−0.42
2015	1188.81	1110.44	−6.59
2016	1334.34	1387.95	4.02
2017	1518.89	1552.58	2.22
2018	1469.01	1330.83	−9.41
2019	1624.23	1660.87	2.26
2020	1853.53	1979.11	6.78
2021	2327.86	2268.87	−2.53
2022	1860.44	1772.54	−4.72
2023	1783.26	1959.20	9.87
2024	2424.31	2268.47	−6.43
2025	2465.98	2547.92	3.32
		Average	**3.13%**
		Median	**3.32%**
		Up	**36**
		Down	**11**
		Win %	**76.60%**
		Avg Win	**5.07%**
		Avg Loss	**−3.22%**

NOVEMBER 2027

MONDAY
D 66.7
S 66.7
N 66.7
8

A realist believes that what is done or left undone in the short run determines the long run.
— Sydney J. Harris (American journalist and author, 1917-1986)

Week Before November Options Monthly Expiration, S&P 500 Up 12 of Last 17

TUESDAY
D 52.4
S 38.1
N 28.6
9

The longer you can look back, the farther you can look forward.
— Winston Churchill (British statesman, 1874-1965)

WEDNESDAY
D 42.9
S 57.1
N 57.1
10

Bitcoin is digital photography. Before you know it, it will digitize and dematerialize the entire financial system, and the same thing that happened to Kodak will happen to many traditional financial institutions.
— Peter Diamandis (American engineer, physician, entrepreneur, futurist, b. 1961)

Veterans' Day

THURSDAY
D 61.9
S 57.1
N 57.1
11

Never tell people how to do things. Tell them what to do and they will surprise you with their ingenuity.
— General George S. Patton, Jr. (U.S. Army field commander WWII, 1885-1945)

FRIDAY
D 38.1
S 38.1
N 38.1
12

When Amercia sneezes, the rest of the world catches cold.
— Anonymous (circa 1929)

SATURDAY
13

SUNDAY
14

TRADING THE THANKSGIVING MARKET

For 35 years the "holiday spirit" gave Wednesday before Thanksgiving and Friday after a great track record, except for two occasions. Publishing it in the 1987 *Almanac* was the "kiss of death." Since 1988 Wednesday–Friday gained 22 of 38 times with a total Dow point gain of 685.82. The best strategy appears to be coming into the week long and exiting into strength before the holiday. Omicron Covid-19 variant cancelled Thanksgiving in 2021.

DOW JONES INDUSTRIALS BEFORE AND AFTER THANKSGIVING

	Tuesday Before	Wednesday Before		Friday After	Total Gain Dow Points	Dow Close	Next Monday
1952	–0.18	1.54		1.22	2.76	283.66	0.04
1953	1.71	0.65		2.45	3.10	280.23	1.14
1954	3.27	1.89		3.16	5.05	387.79	0.72
1955	4.61	0.71		0.26	0.97	482.88	–1.92
1956	–4.49	–2.16		4.65	2.49	472.56	–2.27
1957	–9.04	10.69		3.84	14.53	449.87	–2.96
1958	–4.37	8.63		8.31	16.94	557.46	2.61
1959	2.94	1.41		1.42	2.83	652.52	6.66
1960	–3.44	1.37		4.00	5.37	606.47	–1.04
1961	–0.77	1.10		2.18	3.28	732.60	–0.61
1962	6.73	4.31		7.62	11.93	644.87	–2.81
1963	32.03	–2.52		9.52	7.00	750.52	1.39
1964	–1.68	–5.21		–0.28	–5.49	882.12	–6.69
1965	2.56	N/C		–0.78	–0.78	948.16	–1.23
1966	–3.18	1.84		6.52	8.36	803.34	–2.18
1967	13.17	3.07		3.58	6.65	877.60	4.51
1968	8.14	–3.17	T	8.76	5.59	985.08	–1.74
1969	–5.61	3.23		1.78	5.01	812.30	–7.26
1970	5.21	1.98		6.64	8.62	781.35	12.74
1971	–5.18	0.66	H	17.96	18.62	816.59	13.14
1972	8.21	7.29		4.67	11.96	1025.21	–7.45
1973	–17.76	10.08		–0.98	9.10	854.00	–29.05
1974	5.32	2.03	A	–0.63	1.40	618.66	–15.64
1975	9.76	3.15		2.12	5.27	860.67	–4.33
1976	–6.57	1.66		5.66	7.32	956.62	–6.57
1977	6.41	0.78	N	1.12	1.90	844.42	–4.85
1978	–1.56	2.95		3.12	6.07	810.12	3.72
1979	–6.05	–1.80	K	4.35	2.55	811.77	16.98
1980	3.93	7.00		3.66	10.66	993.34	–23.89
1981	18.45	7.90		7.80	15.70	885.94	3.04
1982	–9.01	9.01	S	7.36	16.37	1007.36	–4.51
1983	7.01	–0.20		1.83	1.63	1277.44	–7.62
1984	9.83	6.40		18.78	25.18	1220.30	–7.95
1985	0.12	18.92	G	–3.56	15.36	1472.13	–14.22
1986	6.05	4.64		–2.53	2.11	1914.23	–1.55
1987	40.45	–16.58	I	–36.47	–53.05	1910.48	–76.93
1988	11.73	14.58		–17.60	–3.02	2074.68	6.76
1989	7.25	17.49		18.77	36.26	2675.55	19.42
1990	–35.15	9.16	V	–12.13	–2.97	2527.23	5.94
1991	14.08	–16.10		–5.36	–21.46	2894.68	40.70
1992	25.66	17.56		15.94	33.50	3282.20	22.96
1993	3.92	13.41	I	–3.63	9.78	3683.95	–6.15
1994	–91.52	–3.36		33.64	30.28	3708.27	31.29
1995	40.46	18.06		7.23*	25.29	5048.84	22.04
1996	–19.38	–29.07	N	22.36*	–6.71	6521.70	N/C
1997	41.03	–14.17		28.35*	14.18	7823.13	189.98
1998	–73.12	13.13	G	18.80*	31.93	9333.08	–216.53
1999	–93.89	12.54		–19.26*	–6.72	10988.91	–40.99
2000	31.85	–95.18		70.91*	–24.27	10470.23	75.84
2001	–75.08	–66.70		125.03*	58.33	9959.71	23.04
2002	–172.98	255.26		–35.59*	219.67	8896.09	–33.52
2003	16.15	15.63		2.89*	18.52	9782.46	116.59
2004	3.18	27.71	D	1.92*	29.63	10522.23	–46.33
2005	51.15	44.66		15.53*	60.19	10931.62	–40.90
2006	5.05	5.36		–46.78*	–41.42	12280.17	–158.46
2007	51.70	–211.10	A	181.84*	–29.26	12980.88	–237.44
2008	36.08	247.14		102.43*	349.57	8829.04	–679.95
2009	–17.24	30.69	Y	–154.48*	–123.79	10309.92	34.92
2010	–142.21	150.91		–95.28*	55.63	11092.00	–39.51
2011	–53.59	–236.17		–25.77*	–261.94	11231.78	291.23
2012	–7.45	48.38		172.79*	221.17	13009.68	–42.31
2013	0.26	24.53		–10.92*	13.61	16086.41	–77.64
2014	–2.96	–2.69		15.99*	13.30	17828.24	–51.44
2015	19.51	1.20		–14.90*	–13.70	17798.49	–78.57
2016	67.18	59.31		68.96*	128.27	19152.14	–54.24
2017	160.50	–64.65		31.81*	–32.84	23557.99	22.79
2018	–551.80	–0.95		–178.74*	–179.69	24285.95	354.29
2019	55.21	42.32		–112.59*	–70.27	28051.41	–268.37
2020	454.97	–173.77		37.90*	–135.87	29910.37	–271.73
2021	194.55	–9.42		–905.04*	–914.46	34899.34	236.60
2022	397.82	95.96		152.97*	248.93	34347.03	–497.57
2023	–62.75	184.74		117.12*	301.86	35390.15	–56.68
2024	123.74	–138.28		188.62*	50.34	44910.65	–128.65
2025	664.18	314.67		289.30*	603.97	47716.42	–427.09

**Shortened trading day*

Monday Before November Monthly Expiration, Dow Up 14 of Last 22, 2008 –2.6%, 2018 –2.3%

MONDAY
D 61.9
S 57.1
N 52.4
15

The "canonical" market bottom typically features below-average valuations, falling interest rates, new lows in some major indices on diminished trading volume…and finally, a quick high-volume reversal in breadth….
— John P. Hussman, Ph.D. (Hussman Funds, 5/22/06)

Week Before Thanksgiving, Dow Up 21 of Last 33, Down 7 of Last 9

TUESDAY
D 57.1
S 61.9
N 66.7
16

Best technical buy signal: Is when you have to add another sheet of chart paper to the top of old chart.
— Larry Williams (Legendary trader, author, politician, b. 1942)

Trading Thanksgiving Market: Long into Weakness Prior, Exit into Strength (Page 106)

WEDNESDAY
D 33.3
S 42.9
N 42.9
17

Setting a goal is not the main thing. It is deciding how you will go about achieving it and staying with that plan.
— Tom Landry (Head Coach Dallas Cowboys 1960-1988)

THURSDAY
D 47.6
S 52.4
N 52.4
18

We like what's familiar, and we dislike change. So, we push the familiar until it starts working against us big-time—a crisis. Then, MAYBE we can accept change.
— Kevin Cameron (Journalist, *Cycle World*, April 2013)

November Monthly Expiration Day, Dow Up 17 of Last 24
Dow Surged in 2008, Up 494 Points (6.5%)

FRIDAY
D 42.9
S 47.6
N 47.6
19

I have learned as a composer chiefly through my mistakes and pursuits of false assumptions, not by my exposure to founts of wisdom and knowledge.
— Igor Stravinsky (Russian composer)

SATURDAY
20

SUNDAY
21

AURA OF THE TRIPLE WITCH—4TH QUARTER MOST BULLISH: DOWN WEEKS TRIGGER MORE WEAKNESS WEEK AFTER

Options expire the third Friday of every month but in March, June, September, and December a powerful coven gathers. Since the S&P index futures began trading on April 21, 1982, stock options, index options, and index futures, all expire at the same time four times each year—known as Triple Witching. Traders have long sought to understand and master the magic of this quarterly phenomenon.

We have analyzed what the market does prior, during, and following Triple-Witching expirations in search of consistent trading patterns. Here are some of our findings of how the Dow Jones Industrials perform around Triple-Witching Week (TWW).

- Since 1991, TWW is most bullish in Q1 and Q4.
- Following weeks became more bearish. Since Q1 2000 only 45 of 104 were up, and 21 occurred in December, 12 in March, 7 in September, 5 in June.
- TWWs have tended to be down in flat periods and dramatically so during bear markets.
- Down weeks tend to follow down TWWs, creating an interesting pattern. Since 1991, of 52 down TWWs, 30 following weeks were also down. This is surprising inasmuch as the previous decade had an exactly opposite pattern: There were 13 down TWWs then, but 12 up weeks followed them.
- TWWs in Q2 and Q3 (Worst Six Months May–October) are much weaker and the weeks following, horrendous. But in Q1 and Q4 (Best Six Months November–April) only the week after Q1 expiration is negative.

Throughout the *Almanac* you will see notations on the performance of Mondays and Fridays of TWW as we place considerable significance on the beginnings and ends of weeks (pages 78 and 143–146).

TRIPLE-WITCHING WEEK AND WEEK AFTER DOW POINT CHANGES

	Expiration Week Q1	Week After	Expiration Week Q2	Week After	Expiration Week Q3	Week After	Expiration Week Q4	Week After
1991	−6.93	−89.36	−34.98	−58.81	33.54	−13.19	20.12	167.04
1992	40.48	−44.95	−69.01	−2.94	21.35	−76.73	9.19	12.97
1993	43.76	−31.60	−10.24	−3.88	−8.38	−70.14	10.90	6.15
1994	32.95	−120.92	3.33	−139.84	58.54	−101.60	116.08	26.24
1995	38.04	65.02	86.80	75.05	96.85	−33.42	19.87	−78.76
1996	114.52	51.67	55.78	−50.60	49.94	−15.54	179.53	76.51
1997	−130.67	−64.20	14.47	−108.79	174.30	4.91	−82.01	−76.98
1998	303.91	−110.35	−122.07	231.67	100.16	133.11	81.87	314.36
1999	27.20	−81.31	365.05	−303.00	−224.80	−524.30	32.73	148.33
2000	666.41	517.49	−164.76	−44.55	−293.65	−79.63	−277.95	200.60
2001	−821.21	−318.63	−353.36	−19.05	−1369.70	611.75	224.19	101.65
2002	34.74	−179.56	−220.42	−10.53	−326.67	−284.57	77.61	−207.54
2003	662.26	−376.20	83.63	−211.70	173.27	−331.74	236.06	46.45
2004	−53.48	26.37	6.31	−44.57	−28.61	−237.22	106.70	177.20
2005	−144.69	−186.80	110.44	−325.23	−36.62	−222.35	97.01	7.68
2006	203.31	0.32	122.63	−25.46	168.66	−52.67	138.03	−102.30
2007	−165.91	370.60	215.09	−279.22	377.67	75.44	110.80	−84.78
2008	410.23	−144.92	−464.66	−496.18	−33.55	−245.31	−50.57	−63.56
2009	54.40	497.80	−259.53	−101.34	214.79	−155.01	−142.61	191.21
2010	117.29	108.38	239.57	−306.83	145.08	252.41	81.59	81.58
2011	−185.88	362.07	52.45	−69.78	516.96	−737.61	−317.87	427.61
2012	310.60	−151.89	212.97	−126.39	−13.90	−142.34	55.83	−252.73
2013	117.04	−2.08	−270.78	110.20	75.03	−192.85	465.78	257.27
2014	237.10	20.29	171.34	−95.24	292.23	−166.59	523.97	248.91
2015	378.34	−414.99	117.11	−69.27	−48.51	−69.91	−136.66	423.62
2016	388.99	−86.57	−190.18	−274.41	38.35	137.65	86.56	90.40
2017	11.64	−317.90	112.31	10.48	470.55	81.25	322.58	102.32
2018	−389.23	−1413.31	−226.05	−509.59	588.83	−285.19	−1655.14	617.03
2019	398.63	−346.55	629.52	−119.17	−284.45	−114.82	319.71	190.17
2020	−4011.64	2462.80	265.92	−855.91	−8.22	−483.46	132.68	20.82
2021	−150.67	444.91	−1189.52	1143.76	−22.84	213.12	−605.55	585.12
2022	1810.74	106.31	−1504.01	1611.90	−1329.29	−1232.01	−556.00	283.47
2023	−47.66	375.55	422.34	−571.69	41.65	−654.40	1057.29	80.81
2024	−7.92	761.13	561.17	−31.47	669.58	249.64	−987.80	151.95
2025	497.16	−401.45	9.03	1612.45	481.05	−67.97	−323.16	576.01
2026	−981.00	−410.83						
Up	**23**	**15**	**21**	**7**	**21**	**9**	**24**	**28**
Down	**13**	**21**	**14**	**28**	**14**	**26**	**11**	**7**

NOVEMBER 2027

MONDAY
D 57.1
S 52.4
N 61.9
22

Absorb what is useful, discard what is useless, and add what is specifically your own.
— Bruce Lee (Hong Kong-American martial artist, actor, philosopher and filmmaker, founder of Jeet Kune Do, 1940-1973)

TUESDAY
D 71.4
S 71.4
N 61.9
23

If we did all the things we are capable of doing, we would literally astound ourselves.
— Thomas Alva Edison (American inventor, 1093 patents, 1847-1931)

WEDNESDAY
D 71.4
S 61.9
N 66.7
24

Executives owe it to the organization and to their fellow workers not to tolerate nonperforming individuals in important jobs.
— Peter Drucker (Austria-born pioneer management theorist, 1909-2005)

Thanksgiving *(Market Closed)*

THURSDAY
25

To affect the quality of the day, that is the highest of the arts.
— Henry David Thoreau (American writer, naturalist and philosopher, 1817-1862)

(Shortened Trading Day)

FRIDAY
D 66.7
S 61.9
N 71.4
26

Life is like riding a bicycle. You don't fall off unless you stop peddling.
— Claude D. Pepper (U.S. Senator Florida 1936-1951, 1900-1989)

SATURDAY
27

December Almanac Investor Sector Seasonalities: See Pages 94, 96, and 98

SUNDAY
28

DECEMBER ALMANAC

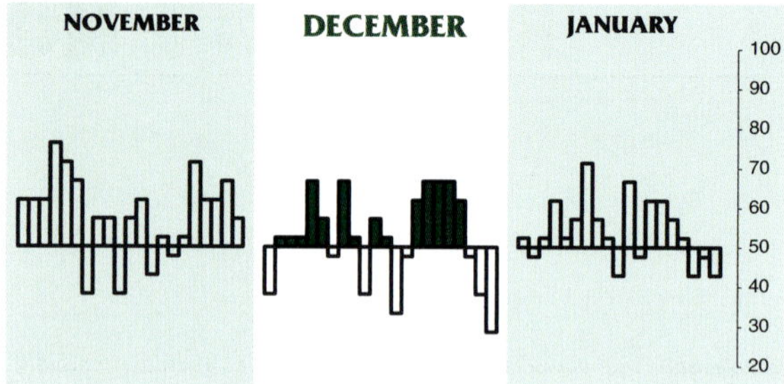

DECEMBER

S	M	T	W	T	F	S
			1	2	3	4
5	6	7	8	9	10	11
12	13	14	15	16	17	18
19	20	21	22	23	24	25
26	27	28	29	30	31	

JANUARY

S	M	T	W	T	F	S
						1
2	3	4	5	6	7	8
9	10	11	12	13	14	15
16	17	18	19	20	21	22
23	24	25	26	27	28	29
30	31					

Market Probability Chart above is a graphic representation of the S&P 500 Recent Market Probability Calendar on page 126.

◆ #3 S&P (+1.4%) and Dow (+1.5%) month since 1950 (page 52), #4 NASDAQ (+1.5%) since 1971 ◆ 2018 worst December since 1931, Dow –8.7%, S&P –9.2%, NASDAQ –9.5% (pages 156, 162, & 166) ◆ "Free lunch" served on Wall Street before Christmas (page 116) ◆ Small caps start to outperform larger caps near middle of month (pages 112 and 114) ◆ "Santa Claus Rally" visible in graph above and on page 118 ◆ In 1998 was part of best fourth quarter since 1928 (page 180) ◆ Fourth quarter expiration week most bullish Triple-Witching Week, Dow up 24 of last 35 (page 108) ◆ Pre-election year December rankings: #3 Dow (+2.8%), #3 S&P (+3.0%) and #2 NASDAQ (+4.3%)

December Vital Statistics

	DJIA		S&P 500		NASDAQ		Russell 1K		Russell 2K	
Rank		3		3		4		3		2
Up		53		55		33		34		34
Down		23		21		22		13		13
Average % Change		1.5		1.4		1.5		1.2		2.0
Pre-Election Yr Avg % Chg		2.8		3.0		4.3		3.1		3.8
Best & Worst December										
	% Change		% Change		% Change		% Change		% Change	
Best	1991	9.5	1991	11.2	1999	22.0	1991	11.2	1999	11.2
Worst	2018	–8.7	2018	–9.2	2002	–9.7	2018	–9.3	2018	–12.0
Best & Worst December Weeks										
Best	12/2/11	7.0	12/2/11	7.4	12/8/00	10.3	12/2/11	7.4	12/2/11	10.3
Worst	12/4/87	–7.5	12/6/74	–7.1	12/15/00	–9.1	12/21/18	–7.1	12/21/18	–8.4
Best & Worst December Days										
Best	12/26/18	5.0	12/16/08	5.1	12/5/00	10.5	12/16/08	5.2	12/16/08	6.7
Worst	12/1/08	–7.7	12/1/08	–8.9	12/1/08	–9.0	12/1/08	–9.1	12/1/08	–11.9
First Trading Day of Monthly Options Expiration Week: 1980–2026										
Record (#Up–#Down)		26-20		27-19		22-24		27-19		21-25
Current streak		D2		D1		D1		D1		D1
Avg % Change		0.12		0.10		–0.04		0.07		–0.20
Monthly Options Expiration Day: 1980–2026										
Record (#Up–#Down)		28-18		30-16		30-16		30-16		28-18
Current streak		U3		U2		U3		U2		U2
Avg % Change		0.16		0.23		0.24		0.23		0.32
Monthly Options Expiration Week: 1980–2026										
Record (#Up–#Down)		32-14		31-15		26-20		30-16		23-23
Current streak		D2		U1		U1		U1		D2
Avg % Change		0.43		0.46		0.09		0.42		0.36
Week After Monthly Options Expiration: 1980–2026										
Record (#Up–#Down)		35-10		30-16		32-14		30-16		33-13
Current streak		U13		U3		U3		U3		U3
Avg % Change		0.82		0.61		0.78		0.64		0.95
First Trading Day Performance										
% of Time Up		46.1		48.7		58.2		48.9		46.8
Avg % Change		–0.06		–0.03		0.10		–0.04		–0.13
Last Trading Day Performance										
% of Time Up		50.0		56.6		63.6		46.8		59.6
Avg % Change		0.05		0.07		0.20		–0.09		0.26

Dow & S&P 1950–May 1, 2026; NASDAQ 1971–May 1, 2026; Russell 1K & 2K 1979–May 1, 2026.

If Santa Claus should fail to call,
Bears may come to Broad and Wall.

MONDAY
29
D 66.7
S 66.7
N 57.1

It is impossible to produce superior performance unless you do something different from the majority.
— Sir John Templeton (Founder Templeton Funds, philanthropist, 1912-2008)

Last Trading Day of November, S&P Down 16 of Last 28

TUESDAY
30
D 61.9
S 57.1
N 52.4

Bill Gates' One-Minus Staffing: For every project, figure out the bare minimum of people needed to staff it. Cut to the absolute muscle and bones, then take out one more. When you understaff, people jump on the loose ball. You find out who the real performers are. Not so when you're overstaffed. People sit around waiting for somebody else to do it.
— Quoted by Rich Karlgaard (Publisher, *Forbes* Dec. 25, 2000)

First Trading Day in December, NASDAQ Up 22 of 36, But Down 8 of Last 15

WEDNESDAY
1
D 38.1
S 38.1
N 47.6

In order to be great writer (or "investor") a person must have a built-in, shockproof crap detector.
— Ernest Hemingway (American writer, 1954 Nobel Prize, 1899-1961)

THURSDAY
2
D 42.9
S 52.4
N 52.4

A person's greatest virtue is his ability to correct his mistakes and continually make a new person of himself.
— Yang-Ming Wang (Chinese philosopher, 1472-1529)

FRIDAY
3
D 57.1
S 52.4
N 66.7

What's money? A man is a success if he gets up in the morning and goes to bed at night and in between does what he wants to do.
— Bob Dylan (American singer-songwriter, musician and artist, b. 1941)

SATURDAY
4

SUNDAY
5

MOST OF THE SO-CALLED JANUARY EFFECT TAKES PLACE IN THE LAST HALF OF DECEMBER

Over the years we reported annually on the fascinating January Effect, showing that small-cap stocks handily outperformed large-cap stocks during January 40 out of 43 years between 1953 and 1995. Readers saw that "Cats and Dogs" on average quadrupled the returns of blue chips in this period. Then, the January Effect disappeared over the next four years.

Looking at the graph on page 114, comparing the Russell 1000 index of large capitalization stocks to the Russell 2000 smaller capitalization stocks, shows small cap stocks beginning to outperform the blue chips in mid-December. Narrowing the comparison down to half-month segments was an inspiration and proved to be quite revealing, as you can see in the table below.

39-YEAR AVERAGE RATES OF RETURN (DEC 1987–FEB 2026)

	Russell 1000		Russell 2000	
Mid-Dec*	**Change**	**Annualized**	**Change**	**Annualized**
12/15–12/31	1.3%	34.4%	2.4%	72.2%
12/15–01/15	1.8	22.7	3.1	41.9
12/15–01/31	2.0	17.5	3.1	28.2
12/15–02/15	3.3	21.5	5.1	34.8
12/15–02/28	2.3	12.1	4.2	23.0
End-Dec*				
12/31–01/15	0.5	11.0	0.7	15.8
12/31–01/31	0.7	8.7	0.7	8.7
12/31–02/15	1.9	16.0	2.6	22.4
12/31–02/28	0.9	5.8	1.8	11.9

47-YEAR AVERAGE RATES OF RETURN (DEC 1979–FEB 2026)

	Russell 1000		Russell 2000	
Mid-Dec*	**Change**	**Annualized**	**Change**	**Annualized**
12/15–12/31	1.3%	34.4%	2.3%	68.4%
12/15–01/15	2.0	25.5	3.5	48.3
12/15–01/31	2.3	20.3	3.7	34.4
12/15–02/15	3.4	22.2	5.5	37.9
12/15–02/28	2.6	13.8	4.8	26.7
End-Dec*				
12/31–01/15	0.7	15.8	1.2	28.5
12/31–01/31	1.1	14.0	1.4	18.2
12/31–02/15	2.1	17.8	3.2	28.2
12/31–02/28	1.3	8.5	2.5	16.8

** Mid-month dates are the 11th trading day of the month, month end dates are monthly closes.*

Small-cap strength in the last half of December became even more magnified after the 1987 market crash. Note the dramatic shift in gains in the last half of December during the 39-year period starting in 1987, versus the 47 years from 1979 to 2026. With all the beaten-down small stocks being dumped for tax loss purposes, it generally pays to get a head start on the January Effect in mid-December. You don't have to wait until December either; the small-cap sector often begins to turn around near the end of October (page 114).

DECEMBER 2027

MONDAY
6
D 47.6
S 52.4
N 57.1

Let me tell you the secret that has led me to my goal. My strength lies solely in my tenacity.
— Louis Pasteur (French chemist, founder of microbiology, 1822-1895)

FOMC Meeting (2 Days)

TUESDAY
7
D 71.4
S 66.7
N 61.9

We're not believers that the government is bigger than the business cycle.
— David Rosenberg (Economist, Merrill Lynch, *Barron's* 4/21/2008)

Small Cap Strength Starts in Mid-December (Pages 112 and 114)

WEDNESDAY
8
D 57.1
S 57.1
N 61.9

Leadership is the ability to hide your panic from others
— Lao Tzu (Chinese philosopher, Shaolin monk, founder of Taoism, 6th century BCE)

THURSDAY
9
D 42.9
S 47.6
N 57.1

Drawing on my fine command of language, I said nothing.
— Robert Benchley (American writer, actor and humorist, 1889-1945)

FRIDAY
10
D 61.9
S 66.7
N 61.9

Never doubt that a small group of thoughtful, committed citizens can change the world: indeed it's the only thing that ever has.
— Margaret Mead (American anthropologist)

SATURDAY
11

SUNDAY
12

JANUARY EFFECT NOW STARTS IN MID-DECEMBER

Small-cap stocks tend to outperform big caps in January. Known as the "January Effect," the tendency is clearly revealed by the graph below. Daily data for the Russell 2000 index of smaller companies are divided by the Russell 1000 index of largest companies since July 1, 1979, and then compressed into a single year to show an idealized yearly pattern. When the graph is descending, big blue chips are outperforming smaller companies; when the graph is rising, smaller companies are moving up faster than their larger brethren.

In a typical year the smaller fry stay on the sidelines while the big boys are on the field. Then, around early November, small stocks begin to wake up and in mid-December, they take off. Anticipated year-end dividends, payouts, and bonuses could be a factor. Other major moves are quite evident around Labor Day—possibly because individual investors are back from vacations and from mid-April through early June. Small caps tend to hold the lead through early June, though the bulk of the move is usually complete by early March.

RUSSELL 2000/RUSSELL 1000 ONE-YEAR SEASONAL PATTERN

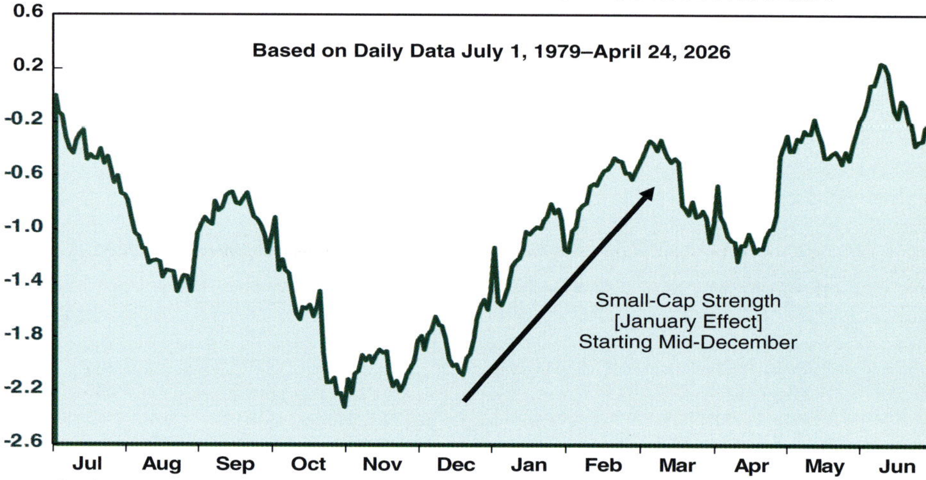

The bottom graph shows the actual ratio of the Russell 2000 divided by the Russell 1000 from 1979. Smaller companies had the upper hand for five years into 1983 as the last major bear trend wound to a close and the nascent bull market logged its first year. After falling behind for about eight years, they came back after the Persian Gulf War bottom in 1990, moving up until 1994 when big caps ruled the latter stages of the millennial bull. For six years the picture was bleak for small fry as the blue chips and tech stocks moved to stratospheric PE ratios. Small caps spiked in late 2020 and early 2021 and have been in retreat since. Note how the small cap advantage has waned during major bull moves and intensified during periods of uncertainty as traders may begin bargain hunting early.

RUSSELL 2000/RUSSELL 1000 (1979–MARCH 2026)

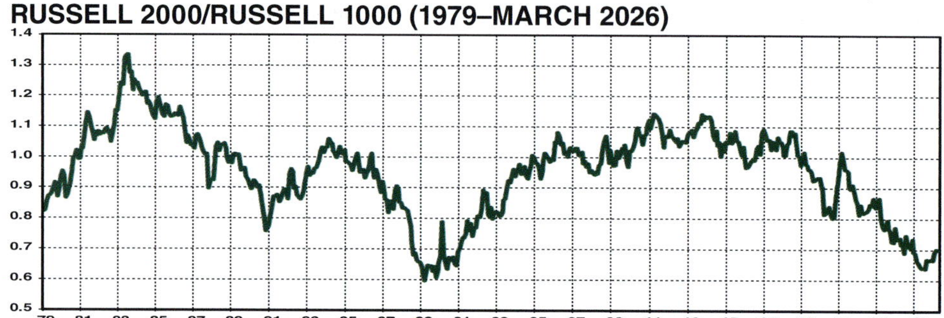

Monday Before December Triple Witching S&P Up 16 of Last 26, 2018 Down 2.1%

MONDAY **13**
D 61.9
S 52.4
N 38.1

Buy when others are despondently selling and sell when others are greedily buying.
— Mark Mobius (Fund manager Templeton Investments, on investing in foreign countries)

TUESDAY **14**
D 42.9
S 38.1
N 47.6

Capitalism is the legitimate racket of the ruling class.
— Al Capone (American gangster, 1899-1947)

December Triple-Witching Week, S&P Up 30 of Last 42, 2018 Down 7.1%

WEDNESDAY **15**
D 57.1
S 57.1
N 61.9

At the age of 24, I began setting clear, written goals for each area of my life. I accomplished more in the following year than I had in the previous 24.
— Brian Tracy (Motivational speaker)

THURSDAY **16**
D 38.1
S 52.4
N 57.1

We are humans, and as humans, we have a tendency of agreeing with each other and of trying to find further supporting evidence for something that is thought to be correct.
— Thomas C. Südhof (German-American biochemist, 2013 Nobel Prize in Physiology or Medicine, b. 1955)

December Triple-Witching Day, S&P Up 28 of Last 44, But Down 7 of Last 11, 2018 –2.1%

FRIDAY **17**
D 28.6
S 33.3
N 38.1

Liberal institutions straightaway cease from being liberal the moment they are firmly established.
— Friedrich Nietzsche (German philosopher, 1844-1900)

The Only FREE LUNCH on Wall Street is Served (Page 116)
***Almanac Investors* Emailed Before the Open, Monday (Learn More Page 67)**

SATURDAY **18**

SUNDAY **19**

WALL STREET'S ONLY "FREE LUNCH" SERVED BEFORE CHRISTMAS

Investors tend to get rid of their losers near year-end for tax purposes, often hammering these stocks down to bargain levels. Over the years, the *Almanac* has shown that NYSE stocks selling at their lows on December 15 will usually outperform the market by February 15 in the following year. Preferred stocks, closed-end funds, splits, and new issues are eliminated.

BARGAIN STOCKS VS. THE MARKET*

Short Span* Late Dec–Jan/Feb	New Lows Late Dec	% Change Jan/Feb	% Change NYSE Composite	Bargain Stocks Advantage
1974–75	112	48.9%	22.1%	26.8%
1975–76	21	34.9	14.9	20.0
1976–77	2	1.3	−3.3	4.6
1977–78	15	2.8	−4.5	7.3
1978–79	43	11.8	3.9	7.9
1979–80	5	9.3	6.1	3.2
1980–81	14	7.1	−2.0	9.1
1981–82	21	−2.6	−7.4	4.8
1982–83	4	33.0	9.7	23.3
1983–84	13	−3.2	−3.8	0.6
1984–85	32	19.0	12.1	6.9
1985–86	4	−22.5	3.9	−26.4
1986–87	22	9.3	12.5	−3.2
1987–88	23	13.2	6.8	6.4
1988–89	14	30.0	6.4	23.6
1989–90	25	−3.1	−4.8	1.7
1990–91	18	18.8	12.6	6.2
1991–92	23	51.1	7.7	43.4
1992–93	9	8.7	0.6	8.1
1993–94	10	−1.4	2.0	−3.4
1994–95	25	14.6	5.7	8.9
1995–96	5	−11.3	4.5	−15.8
1996–97	16	13.9	11.2	2.7
1997–98	29	9.9	5.7	4.2
1998–99	40	−2.8	4.3	−7.1
1999–00	26	8.9	−5.4	14.3
2000–01	51	44.4	0.1	44.3
2001–02	12	31.4	−2.3	33.7
2002–03	33	28.7	3.9	24.8
2003–04	15	16.7	2.3	14.4
2004–05	36	6.8	−2.8	9.6
2005–06	71	12.0	2.6	9.4
2006–07	43	5.1	−0.5	5.6
2007–08	71	−3.2	−9.4	6.2
2008–09	88	11.4	−2.4	13.8
2009–10	25	1.8	−3.0	4.8
2010–11	20	8.3	3.4	4.9
2011–12	65	18.1	6.1	12.0
2012–13	17	20.9	3.4	17.5
2013–14	18	25.7	1.7	24.0
2014–15	17	0.2	−0.4	0.6
2015–16	38	−9.2	5.6	−14.8
2016–17	19	2.8	0.6	2.2
2017–18	18	3.3	1.2	2.1
2018–19	23	24.9	15.1	9.8
2019–20	13	−1.1	−0.3	−0.7
2020–21	3	−4.9	3.6	−8.5
2021–22	26	−1.5	−0.02	−1.5
2022–23	38	−0.3	3.7	−4.0
2023–24	13	−0.4	4.0	−4.4
2024–25	26	−2.1	5.3	−7.4
2025–26	21	0.4	6.4	−6.0
	52-Year Totals	**539.9%**	**169.3%**	**370.5%**
	Average	**10.4%**	**3.3%**	**7.1%**

** Dec 15–Feb 15 (1974–1999), Dec 1999–2026 based on actual newsletter portfolio*

In response to changing market conditions, we tweaked the strategy the last 27 years adding selections from NASDAQ and AMEX, and selling sooner in some years. We email the list of stocks to our *Almanac Investor* subscribers. Visit *www.stocktradersalmanac.com* or see a special offer for new subscribers between pages 66 and 67.

We have concluded that the most prudent course of action is to compile our list from the stocks making new lows on Triple-Witching Friday before Christmas, capitalizing on the Santa Claus Rally (page 118). This also gives us the weekend to evaluate the stocks in greater depth and weed out any glaringly problematic ones. *Almanac Investor* subscribers will receive the list of stocks selected from the new lows made on December 18, 2026, and December 17, 2027, via email.

This "Free Lunch" strategy is an extremely short-term strategy reserved for the nimblest traders. It has performed better after market corrections and when there are more new lows to choose from. The object is to buy bargain stocks near their 52-week lows and sell any quick, generous gains, as these issues can be real dogs.

DECEMBER 2027

Week After December Triple Witching Dow Up 28 of Last 35, Average Gain 0.8% Since 1991

MONDAY
D 52.4
S 47.6
N 47.6
20

A loss never bothers me after I take it. I forget it overnight. But being wrong—not taking the loss—that is what does damage to the pocketbook and to the soul.
— Jesse Livermore (Early 20th century stock trader and speculator, *How to Trade in Stocks*, 1877-1940)

TUESDAY
D 71.4
S 61.9
N 61.9
21

With enough inside information and a million dollars, you can go broke in a year.
— Warren Buffett (CEO Berkshire Hathaway, investor and philanthropist, b. 1930)

WEDNESDAY
D 66.7
S 66.7
N 66.7
22

In a bear market everyone loses. And the winner is the one who loses the least.
— Richard Russell (*Dow Theory Letters*, 1924-2015)

Last Trading Day Before Christmas, NASDAQ Up 15 of Last 19, 2018 Down 2.2%

THURSDAY
D 71.4
S 66.7
N 57.1
23

A man isn't a man until he has to meet a payroll.
— Ivan Shaffer (*The Stock Promotion Game*)

(Market Closed - Christmas Observed)

FRIDAY
24

Friendship renders prosperity more brilliant, while it lightens adversity by sharing it and making its burden common.
— Marcus Tullius Cicero (Great Roman Orator, Politician, 106-43 B.C.)

Christmas Day
Chanukah

SATURDAY
25

SUNDAY
26

IF SANTA CLAUS SHOULD FAIL TO CALL, BEARS MAY COME TO BROAD AND WALL

Santa Claus tends to come to Wall Street nearly every year, bringing a short, sweet, respectable rally within the last five days of the year and the first two in January. This has been good for an average 1.2% gain since 1969 (1.2% since 1950). Santa's failure to show tends to precede bear markets, or times stocks could be purchased later in the year at much lower prices. We discovered this phenomenon in 1972. See page 20 for more.

DAILY % CHANGE IN S&P 500 AT YEAR-END

	Trading Days Before Year-End						First Days in January			Rally % Change
	6	5	4	3	2	1	1	2	3	
1969	−0.4	1.1	0.8	−0.7	0.4	0.5	1.0	0.5	−0.7	3.6
1970	0.1	0.6	0.5	1.1	0.2	−0.1	−1.1	0.7	0.6	1.9
1971	−0.4	0.2	1.0	0.3	−0.4	0.3	−0.4	0.4	1.0	1.3
1972	−0.3	−0.7	0.6	0.4	0.5	1.0	0.9	0.4	−0.1	3.1
1973	−1.1	−0.7	3.1	2.1	−0.2	0.01	0.1	2.2	−0.9	6.7
1974	−1.4	1.4	0.8	−0.4	0.03	2.1	2.4	0.7	0.5	7.2
1975	0.7	0.8	0.9	−0.1	−0.4	0.5	0.8	1.8	1.0	4.3
1976	0.1	1.2	0.7	−0.4	0.5	0.5	−0.4	−1.2	−0.9	0.8
1977	0.8	0.9	N/C	0.1	0.2	0.2	−1.3	−0.3	−0.8	−0.3
1978	0.03	1.7	1.3	−0.9	−0.4	−0.2	0.6	1.1	0.8	3.3
1979	−0.6	0.1	0.1	0.2	−0.1	0.1	−2.0	−0.5	1.2	−2.2
1980	−0.4	0.4	0.5	−1.1	0.2	0.3	0.4	1.2	0.1	2.0
1981	−0.5	0.2	−0.2	−0.5	0.5	0.2	0.2	−2.2	−0.7	−1.8
1982	0.6	1.8	−1.0	0.3	−0.7	0.2	−1.6	2.2	0.4	1.2
1983	−0.2	−0.03	0.9	0.3	−0.2	0.05	−0.5	1.7	1.2	2.1
1984	−0.5	0.8	−0.2	−0.4	0.3	0.6	−1.1	−0.5	−0.5	−0.6
1985	−1.1	−0.7	0.2	0.9	0.5	0.3	−0.8	0.6	0.1	1.1
1986	−1.0	0.2	0.1	−0.9	−0.5	−0.5	1.8	2.3	0.2	2.4
1987	1.3	−0.5	−2.6	−0.4	1.3	−0.3	3.6	1.1	0.1	2.2
1988	−0.2	0.3	−0.4	0.1	0.8	−0.6	−0.9	1.5	0.2	0.9
1989	0.6	0.8	−0.2	0.6	0.5	0.8	1.8	−0.3	−0.9	4.1
1990	0.5	−0.6	0.3	−0.8	0.1	0.5	−1.1	−1.4	−0.3	−3.0
1991	2.5	0.6	1.4	0.4	2.1	0.5	0.04	0.5	−0.3	5.7
1992	−0.3	0.2	−0.1	−0.3	0.2	−0.7	−0.1	−0.2	0.04	−1.1
1993	0.01	0.7	0.1	−0.1	−0.4	−0.5	−0.2	0.3	0.1	−0.1
1994	0.01	0.2	0.4	−0.3	0.1	−0.4	−0.03	0.3	−0.1	0.2
1995	0.8	0.2	0.4	0.04	−0.1	0.3	0.8	0.1	−0.6	1.8
1996	−0.3	0.5	0.6	0.1	−0.4	−1.7	−0.5	1.5	−0.1	0.1
1997	−1.5	−0.7	0.4	1.8	1.8	−0.04	0.5	0.2	−1.1	4.0
1998	2.1	−0.2	−0.1	1.3	−0.8	−0.2	−0.1	1.4	2.2	1.3
1999	1.6	−0.1	0.04	0.4	0.1	0.3	−1.0	−3.8	0.2	−4.0
2000	0.8	2.4	0.7	1.0	0.4	−1.0	−2.8	5.0	−1.1	5.7
2001	0.4	−0.02	0.4	0.7	0.3	−1.1	0.6	0.9	0.6	1.8
2002	0.2	−0.5	−0.3	−1.6	0.5	0.05	3.3	−0.05	2.2	1.2
2003	0.3	−0.2	0.2	1.2	0.01	0.2	−0.3	1.2	0.1	2.4
2004	0.1	−0.4	0.7	−0.01	0.01	−0.1	−0.8	−1.2	−0.4	−1.8
2005	0.4	0.04	−1.0	0.1	−0.3	−0.5	1.6	0.4	0.002	0.4
2006	−0.4	−0.5	0.4	0.7	−0.1	−0.5	−0.1	0.1	−0.6	0.003
2007	1.7	0.8	0.1	−1.4	0.1	−0.7	−1.4	N/C	−2.5	−2.5
2008	−1.0	0.6	0.5	−0.4	2.4	1.4	3.2	−0.5	0.8	7.4
2009	0.2	0.5	0.1	−0.1	0.02	−1.0	1.6	0.3	0.05	1.4
2010	−0.2	0.1	0.1	0.1	−0.2	−0.02	1.1	−0.1	0.5	1.1
2011	0.8	0.9	0.01	−1.3	1.1	−0.4	1.6	0.02	0.3	1.9
2012	−0.9	−0.2	−0.5	−0.1	−1.1	1.7	2.5	−0.2	0.5	2.0
2013	0.5	0.3	0.5	−0.03	−0.02	0.4	−0.9	−0.03	−0.3	0.2
2014	0.2	−0.01	0.3	0.1	−0.5	−1.0	−0.03	−1.8	−0.9	−3.0
2015	1.2	−0.2	−0.2	1.1	−0.7	−0.9	−1.5	0.2	−1.3	−2.3
2016	−0.2	0.1	0.2	−0.8	−0.03	−0.5	0.9	0.6	−0.1	0.4
2017	0.2	−0.05	−0.1	0.1	0.2	−0.5	0.8	0.6	0.4	1.1
2018	−2.1	−2.7	5.0	0.9	−0.1	0.9	0.1	−2.5	3.4	1.3
2019	0.1	−0.02	0.5	0.003	−0.6	0.3	0.8	−0.7	0.4	0.3
2020	0.1	0.4	0.9	−0.2	0.1	0.6	−1.5	0.7	0.6	1.0
2021	0.6	1.4	−0.1	0.1	−0.3	−0.3	0.6	−0.1	−1.9	1.4
2022	−1.4	0.6	−0.4	−1.2	1.7	−0.3	−0.4	0.8	−1.2	0.8
2023	1.0	0.2	0.4	0.1	0.04	−0.3	−0.6	−0.8	−0.3	−0.9
2024	0.7	1.1	−0.04	−1.1	−1.1	−0.4	−0.2	1.3	0.6	−0.5
2025	0.5	0.3	−0.03	−0.4	−0.1	−0.7	0.2	0.6	0.6	−0.1
Avg	**0.09**	**0.27**	**0.33**	**0.01**	**0.13**	**0.012**	**0.18**	**0.30**	**0.04**	**1.2**

The couplet above was certainly on the mark in 1999, as the period suffered a horrendous 4.0% loss. On January 14, 2000, the Dow started its 33-month 37.8% slide to the October 2002 midterm election-year bottom. NASDAQ cracked eight weeks later falling 37.3% in 10 weeks, eventually dropping 77.9% by October 2002. Energy prices and Middle East terror woes may have grounded Santa in 2004. In 2007 the fourth-worst reading since 1950 was recorded as a full-blown financial crisis led to the second-worst bear market in history. In 2016, the period was hit again as global growth concerns escalated and the market digested the first interest rate hike in nearly a decade. Inflation, interest rate, and new administration concerns weighed down Santa in 2024 and 2025. Market valuation issues hindered 2026.

DECEMBER 2027/JANUARY 2028

Santa Claus Rally Begins (Page 118)

MONDAY
D 57.1
S 66.7
N 81.0
27

I never met anyone, or heard of anyone, or read of anyone who was successful who was a pessimist. You have to be positive, or you'll never get anywhere.
— William J. O'Neil (Founder *Investors Business Daily*, investment adivisor, CANSLIM, *How to Make Money in Stocks*, 1933-2023)

TUESDAY
D 71.4
S 61.9
N 57.1
28

Pullbacks near the 30-week moving average are often good times to take action.
— Michael L. Burke (*Investors Intelligence*, 1935-2014)

WEDNESDAY
D 42.9
S 47.6
N 38.1
29

Have not great merchants, great manufacturers, great inventors done more for the world than preachers and philanthropists. Can there be any doubt that cheapening the cost of necessities and conveniences of life is the most powerful agent of civilization and progress?
— Charles Elliott Perkins (Railroad magnate, 1888, 1840-1907)

THURSDAY
D 42.9
S 38.1
N 33.3
30

Explosive growth of shadow banking was about the invisible hand having a party, a non-regulated drinking party, with rating agencies handing out fake IDs.
— Paul McCulley (Economist, bond investor, PIMCO, coined "shadow banking" in 2007, *NY Times* 4/26/2010, b. 1957)

Last Trading Day of the Year, NASDAQ Down 20 of last 26
NASDAQ Was Up 29 Years in a Row 1971–1999

FRIDAY
D 33.3
S 28.6
N 28.6
31

The knowledge of past times… is both an ornament and nutriment to the human mind.
— Leonardo da Vinci (Italian Renaissance polymath, 1452-1519)

New Year's Day

SATURDAY
1

January Almanac Investor Sector Seasonalities: See Pages 94, 96, and 98

SUNDAY
2

2028 STRATEGY CALENDAR

(Option expiration dates circled)

	MONDAY	TUESDAY	WEDNESDAY	THURSDAY	FRIDAY	SATURDAY	SUNDAY
	27	28	29	30	31	1 JANUARY New Year's Day	2
	3	4	5	6	7	8	9
JANUARY	10	11	12	13	14	15	16
	17 Martin Luther King Jr. Day	18	19	20	21	22	23
	24	25	26	27	28	29	30
	31	1 FEBRUARY	2	3	4	5	6
	7	8	9	10	11	12	13
FEBRUARY	14 ♥	15	16	17	18	19	20
	21 Presidents' Day	22	23	24	25	26	27
	28	29	1 MARCH Ash Wednesday	2	3	4	5
	6	7	8	9	10	11	12 Daylight Saving Time Begins
MARCH	13	14	15	16	17 ♣ St. Patrick's Day	18	19
	20	21	22	23	24	25	26
	27	28	29	30	31	1 APRIL	2
	3	4	5	6	7	8	9
APRIL	10	11 Passover	12	13	14 Good Friday	15	16 Easter
	17	18 Tax Deadline	19	20	21	22	23
	24	25	26	27	28	29	30
	1 MAY	2	3	4	5	6	7
	8	9	10	11	12	13	14 Mother's Day
MAY	15	16	17	18	19	20	21
	22	23	24	25	26	27	28
	29 Memorial Day	30	31	1 JUNE	2	3	4
	5	6	7	8	9	10	11
JUNE	12	13	14	15	16	17	18 Father's Day
	19 Juneteenth	20	21	22	23	24	25
	26	27	28	29	30	1 JULY	2

Market closed on shaded weekdays; closes early when half-shaded.

2028 STRATEGY CALENDAR

(Option expiration dates circled)

MONDAY	TUESDAY	WEDNESDAY	THURSDAY	FRIDAY	SATURDAY	SUNDAY	
3	4 Independence Day	5	6	7	8	9	
10	11	12	13	14	15	16	JULY
17	18	19	20	(21)	22	23	
24	25	26	27	28	29	30	
31	1 AUGUST	2	3	4	5	6	
7	8	9	10	11	12	13	AUGUST
14	15	16	17	(18)	19	20	
21	22	23	24	25	26	27	
28	29	30	31	1 SEPTEMBER	2	3	
4 Labor Day	5	6	7	8	9	10	SEPTEMBER
11	12	13	14	(15)	16	17	
18	19	20	21 Rosh Hashanah	22	23	24	
25	26	27	28	29	30 Yom Kippur	1 OCTOBER	
2	3	4	5	6	7	8	
9 Columbus Day	10	11	12	13	14	15	OCTOBER
16	17	18	19	(20)	21	22	
23	24	25	26	27	28	29	
30	31	1 NOVEMBER	2	3	4	5 Daylight Saving Time Ends	
6	7 Election Day	8	9	10	11 Veterans' Day	12	NOVEMBER
13	14	15	16	(17)	18	19	
20	21	22	23 Thanksgiving Day	24	25	26	
27	28	29	30	1 DECEMBER	2	3	
4	5	6	7	8	9	10	
11	12	13 Chanukah	14	(15)	16	17	DECEMBER
18	19	20	21	22	23	24	
25 Christmas	26	27	28	29	30	31	

DIRECTORY OF TRADING PATTERNS AND DATABANK

CONTENTS

DOW JONES INDUSTRIALS MARKET PROBABILITY CALENDAR 2027

THE % CHANCE OF THE MARKET RISING ON ANY TRADING DAY OF THE YEAR*

(Based on the number of times the DJIA rose on a particular trading day during **January 1953–December 2025**)

Date	Jan	Feb	Mar	Apr	May	Jun	Jul	Aug	Sep	Oct	Nov	Dec
1	H	63.0	65.8	58.9	S	60.3	68.5	S	56.2	49.3	63.0	43.8
2	S	56.2	58.9	60.3	S	57.5	56.2	42.5	60.3	S	53.4	52.1
3	S	42.5	57.5	S	56.2	49.3	S	45.2	57.5	S	68.5	61.6
4	58.9	54.8	49.3	S	64.4	60.3	S	47.9	S	56.2	58.9	S
5	71.2	47.9	46.6	49.3	52.1	S	H	53.4	S	56.2	52.1	S
6	47.9	S	S	58.9	45.2	S	60.3	54.8	H	58.9	S	54.8
7	56.2	S	S	52.1	50.7	56.2	56.2	S	43.8	43.8	S	52.1
8	46.6	43.8	50.7	60.3	S	47.9	58.9	S	50.7	52.1	63.0	46.6
9	S	46.6	61.6	58.9	S	37.0	57.5	47.9	47.9	S	53.4	50.7
10	S	60.3	50.7	S	54.8	50.7	S	43.8	58.9	S	54.8	58.9
11	47.9	47.9	53.4	S	46.6	58.9	S	47.9	S	46.6	49.3	S
12	50.7	49.3	54.8	57.5	50.7	S	53.4	52.1	S	41.1	46.6	S
13	50.7	S	S	56.2	42.5	S	46.6	64.4	60.3	50.7	S	47.9
14	56.2	S	S	69.9	54.8	53.4	68.5	S	49.3	60.3	S	47.9
15	52.1	H	61.6	58.9	S	52.1	53.4	S	56.2	52.1	58.9	50.7
16	S	58.9	61.6	56.2	S	49.3	47.9	57.5	56.2	S	50.7	53.4
17	S	43.8	57.5	S	57.5	49.3	S	50.7	42.5	S	46.6	45.2
18	H	46.6	53.4	S	45.2	H	S	47.9	S	54.8	49.3	S
19	58.9	47.9	42.5	52.1	50.7	S	53.4	54.8	S	46.6	56.2	S
20	42.5	S	S	53.4	43.8	S	54.8	58.9	49.3	58.9	S	54.8
21	42.5	S	S	54.8	35.6	46.6	39.7	S	45.2	43.8	S	60.3
22	42.5	41.1	47.9	50.7	S	47.9	47.9	S	43.8	52.1	64.4	58.9
23	S	47.9	39.7	54.8	S	45.2	43.8	49.3	38.4	S	63.0	54.8
24	S	58.9	52.1	S	52.1	38.4	S	53.4	49.3	S	67.1	H
25	57.5	45.2	46.6	S	45.2	47.9	S	50.7	S	31.5	H	S
26	58.9	46.6	H	52.1	45.2	S	61.6	46.6	S	54.8	60.3	S
27	49.3	S	S	57.5	56.2	S	53.4	63.0	52.1	50.7	S	60.3
28	60.3	S	S	57.5	54.8	46.6	45.2	S	53.4	60.3	S	71.2
29	54.8		53.4	54.8	S	57.5	57.5	S	50.7	52.1	56.2	47.9
30	S		46.6	47.9	S	56.2	50.7	43.8	42.5	S	54.8	53.4
31	S		43.8		H		S	56.2		S		50.7

See developing trends on pages 72, 90, 143-148

H = Holiday, S = Saturday/Sunday

RECENT DOW JONES INDUSTRIALS MARKET PROBABILITY CALENDAR 2027

THE % CHANCE OF THE MARKET RISING ON ANY TRADING DAY OF THE YEAR*

(Based on the number of times the DJIA rose on a particular trading day during **January 2005–December 2025****)

Date	Jan	Feb	Mar	Apr	May	Jun	Jul	Aug	Sep	Oct	Nov	Dec
1	H	81.0	61.9	61.9	S	71.4	85.7	S	42.9	47.6	57.1	38.1
2	S	57.1	33.3	71.4	S	66.7	38.1	33.3	61.9	S	61.9	42.9
3	S	52.4	52.4	S	57.1	33.3	S	47.6	57.1	S	66.7	57.1
4	66.7	61.9	47.6	S	66.7	66.7	S	52.4	S	38.1	66.7	S
5	61.9	57.1	47.6	42.9	52.4	S	H	52.4	S	71.4	76.2	S
6	47.6	S	S	52.4	38.1	S	61.9	52.4	H	57.1	S	47.6
7	61.9	S	S	47.6	71.4	61.9	52.4	S	42.9	33.3	S	71.4
8	42.9	52.4	38.1	66.7	S	66.7	52.4	S	61.9	52.4	66.7	57.1
9	S	52.4	66.7	47.6	S	42.9	61.9	57.1	66.7	S	52.4	42.9
10	S	57.1	47.6	S	71.4	28.6	S	33.3	76.2	S	42.9	61.9
11	52.4	61.9	52.4	S	33.3	61.9	S	38.1	S	61.9	61.9	S
12	61.9	47.6	66.7	47.6	57.1	S	57.1	66.7	S	47.6	38.1	S
13	57.1	S	S	57.1	28.6	S	71.4	61.9	66.7	38.1	S	61.9
14	47.6	S	S	61.9	52.4	47.6	81.0	S	57.1	66.7	S	42.9
15	38.1	H	66.7	47.6	S	61.9	71.4	S	66.7	47.6	61.9	57.1
16	S	71.4	57.1	61.9	S	52.4	57.1	57.1	71.4	S	57.1	38.1
17	S	66.7	61.9	S	71.4	47.6	S	47.6	47.6	S	33.3	28.6
18	H	42.9	61.9	S	47.6	H	S	61.9	S	61.9	47.6	S
19	57.1	38.1	52.4	47.6	42.9	S	71.4	57.1	S	57.1	42.9	S
20	47.6	S	S	61.9	38.1	S	71.4	57.1	57.1	52.4	S	52.4
21	52.4	S	S	57.1	42.9	57.1	28.6	S	42.9	57.1	S	71.4
22	47.6	52.4	47.6	61.9	S	38.1	52.4	S	42.9	61.9	57.1	66.7
23	S	52.4	47.6	66.7	S	47.6	38.1	47.6	28.6	S	71.4	71.4
24	S	52.4	61.9	S	47.6	33.3	S	61.9	42.9	S	71.4	H
25	57.1	42.9	47.6	S	57.1	47.6	S	52.4	S	42.9	H	S
26	61.9	28.6	H	57.1	52.4	S	71.4	52.4	S	66.7	66.7	S
27	52.4	S	S	52.4	66.7	S	47.6	90.5	47.6	33.3	S	57.1
28	47.6	S	S	71.4	33.3	52.4	38.1	S	66.7	57.1	S	71.4
29	38.1		42.9	76.2	S	61.9	47.6	S	57.1	47.6	66.7	42.9
30	S		61.9	33.3	S	57.1	33.3	47.6	47.6	S	61.9	42.9
31	S		52.4		H		S	42.9		S		33.3

** See developing trends on pages 72, 90, 143–148 ** Based on most recent 21-year period*

H = Holiday, S = Saturday/Sunday

S&P 500 MARKET PROBABILITY CALENDAR 2027

THE % CHANCE OF THE MARKET RISING ON ANY TRADING DAY OF THE YEAR*

(Based on the number of times the S&P 500 rose on a particular trading day during **January 1953–December 2025**)

Date	Jan	Feb	Mar	Apr	May	Jun	Jul	Aug	Sep	Oct	Nov	Dec
1	H	63.0	61.6	63.0	S	57.5	74.0	S	58.9	52.1	64.4	46.6
2	S	61.6	56.2	61.6	S	65.8	57.5	43.8	53.4	S	56.2	52.1
3	S	47.9	60.3	S	57.5	52.1	S	45.2	56.2	S	68.5	58.9
4	47.9	53.4	47.9	S	65.8	56.2	S	47.9	S	63.0	58.9	S
5	67.1	49.3	47.9	50.7	54.8	S	H	54.8	S	57.5	52.1	S
6	52.1	S	S	56.2	42.5	S	57.5	54.8	H	60.3	S	56.2
7	52.1	S	S	53.4	49.3	47.9	58.9	S	43.8	45.2	S	47.9
8	46.6	47.9	52.1	60.3	S	49.3	60.3	S	50.7	50.7	61.6	50.7
9	S	45.2	60.3	60.3	S	41.1	57.5	46.6	56.2	S	56.2	52.1
10	S	60.3	52.1	S	52.1	53.4	S	49.3	60.3	S	57.5	52.1
11	50.7	56.2	60.3	S	47.9	63.0	S	49.3	S	43.8	47.9	S
12	56.2	47.9	45.2	52.1	53.4	S	54.8	47.9	S	45.2	47.9	S
13	54.8	S	S	53.4	42.5	S	50.7	64.4	65.8	52.1	S	47.9
14	58.9	S	S	61.6	53.4	56.2	71.2	S	50.7	53.4	S	41.1
15	58.9	H	60.3	58.9	S	57.5	52.1	S	54.8	53.4	52.1	50.7
16	S	57.5	63.0	57.5	S	47.9	46.6	61.6	56.2	S	52.1	56.2
17	S	39.7	56.2	S	56.2	53.4	S	54.8	46.6	S	52.1	42.5
18	H	47.9	50.7	S	49.3	H	S	52.1	S	58.9	53.4	S
19	57.5	41.1	46.6	52.1	52.1	S	49.3	50.7	S	45.2	56.2	S
20	50.7	S	S	52.1	41.1	S	53.4	58.9	52.1	64.4	S	46.6
21	52.1	S	S	49.3	42.5	42.5	41.1	S	43.8	45.2	S	52.1
22	49.3	41.1	42.5	54.8	S	50.7	49.3	S	46.6	50.7	61.6	56.2
23	S	42.5	52.1	49.3	S	46.6	46.6	46.6	35.6	S	63.0	52.1
24	S	58.9	45.2	S	52.1	35.6	S	52.1	47.9	S	67.1	H
25	53.4	49.3	47.9	S	52.1	43.8	S	49.3	S	34.2	H	S
26	52.1	52.1	H	52.1	47.9	S	57.5	47.9	S	57.5	60.3	S
27	43.8	S	S	56.2	57.5	S	53.4	63.0	47.9	53.4	S	61.6
28	61.6	S	S	52.1	56.2	50.7	46.6	S	60.3	60.3	S	68.5
29	60.3		53.4	53.4	S	60.3	61.6	S	50.7	53.4	58.9	52.1
30	S		41.1	53.4	S	53.4	60.3	46.6	43.8	S	52.1	58.9
31	S		43.8		H		S	60.3		S		57.5

See developing trends on pages 72, 90, 143–148

H = Holiday, S = Saturday/Sunday

RECENT S&P 500 MARKET PROBABILITY CALENDAR 2027

THE % CHANCE OF THE MARKET RISING ON ANY TRADING DAY OF THE YEAR*

(Based on the number of times the S&P 500 rose on a particular trading day during **January 2005–December 2025****)

Date	Jan	Feb	Mar	Apr	May	Jun	Jul	Aug	Sep	Oct	Nov	Dec
1	H	76.2	61.9	66.7	S	66.7	90.5	S	47.6	57.1	61.9	38.1
2	S	71.4	38.1	76.2	S	76.2	52.4	33.3	42.9	S	61.9	52.4
3	S	42.9	57.1	S	61.9	42.9	S	52.4	52.4	S	61.9	52.4
4	52.4	71.4	47.6	S	52.4	57.1	S	52.4	S	42.9	76.2	S
5	47.6	52.4	47.6	47.6	42.9	S	H	57.1	S	71.4	71.4	S
6	52.4	S	S	57.1	42.9	S	71.4	47.6	H	57.1	S	52.4
7	61.9	S	S	47.6	71.4	38.1	52.4	S	42.9	33.3	S	66.7
8	52.4	66.7	38.1	61.9	S	71.4	57.1	S	52.4	52.4	66.7	57.1
9	S	57.1	61.9	52.4	S	42.9	66.7	52.4	71.4	S	38.1	47.6
10	S	52.4	61.9	S	57.1	33.3	S	38.1	81.0	S	57.1	66.7
11	57.1	76.2	57.1	S	42.9	66.7	S	52.4	S	57.1	57.1	S
12	71.4	61.9	42.9	57.1	57.1	S	66.7	52.4	S	47.6	38.1	S
13	57.1	S	S	61.9	33.3	S	61.9	57.1	76.2	47.6	S	52.4
14	52.4	S	S	57.1	52.4	57.1	71.4	S	52.4	57.1	S	38.1
15	42.9	H	52.4	52.4	S	66.7	47.6	S	61.9	57.1	57.1	57.1
16	S	71.4	61.9	61.9	S	52.4	57.1	61.9	66.7	S	61.9	52.4
17	S	57.1	61.9	S	61.9	47.6	S	57.1	42.9	S	42.9	33.3
18	H	38.1	52.4	S	52.4	H	S	57.1	S	66.7	52.4	S
19	66.7	33.3	52.4	52.4	42.9	S	66.7	47.6	S	61.9	47.6	S
20	47.6	S	S	47.6	38.1	S	66.7	61.9	52.4	52.4	S	47.6
21	61.9	S	S	38.1	42.9	52.4	38.1	S	23.8	66.7	S	61.9
22	61.9	38.1	42.9	66.7	S	38.1	57.1	S	33.3	76.2	52.4	66.7
23	S	52.4	52.4	61.9	S	52.4	57.1	42.9	28.6	S	71.4	66.7
24	S	61.9	57.1	S	47.6	28.6	S	57.1	42.9	S	61.9	H
25	57.1	42.9	47.6	S	71.4	57.1	S	52.4	S	38.1	H	S
26	52.4	28.6	H	66.7	57.1	S	61.9	57.1	S	57.1	61.9	S
27	42.9	S	S	47.6	71.4	S	47.6	90.5	38.1	33.3	S	66.7
28	47.6	S	S	61.9	42.9	52.4	33.3	S	71.4	61.9	S	61.9
29	42.9		42.9	76.2	S	61.9	57.1	S	52.4	52.4	66.7	47.6
30	S		57.1	38.1	S	57.1	38.1	47.6	42.9	S	57.1	38.1
31	S		52.4		H		S	47.6		S		28.6

** See developing trends on pages 72, 90, 143–148 ** Based on most recent 21-year period*

H = Holiday, S = Saturday/Sunday

NASDAQ COMPOSITE MARKET PROBABILITY CALENDAR 2027

THE % CHANCE OF THE MARKET RISING ON ANY TRADING DAY OF THE YEAR*

(Based on the number of times the NASDAQ rose on a particular trading day during **January 1971–December 2025**)

Date	Jan	Feb	Mar	Apr	May	Jun	Jul	Aug	Sep	Oct	Nov	Dec
1	H	70.9	61.8	49.1	S	60.0	65.5	S	52.7	50.9	67.3	58.2
2	S	69.1	52.7	65.5	S	76.4	50.9	50.9	58.2	S	52.7	58.2
3	S	52.7	65.5	S	60.0	56.4	S	41.8	58.2	S	69.1	65.5
4	54.5	65.5	47.3	S	67.3	60.0	S	50.9	S	58.2	60.0	S
5	61.8	52.7	49.1	58.2	54.5	S	H	61.8	S	60.0	54.5	S
6	56.4	S	S	52.7	50.9	S	52.7	54.5	H	60.0	S	58.2
7	63.6	S	S	47.3	56.4	52.7	54.5	S	54.5	54.5	S	50.9
8	58.2	56.4	52.7	63.6	S	52.7	63.6	S	56.4	58.2	58.2	56.4
9	S	52.7	58.2	60.0	S	43.6	69.1	43.6	52.7	S	50.9	49.1
10	S	61.8	49.1	S	61.8	52.7	S	47.3	54.5	S	60.0	49.1
11	61.8	61.8	67.3	S	56.4	61.8	S	50.9	S	50.9	52.7	S
12	60.0	69.1	49.1	58.2	43.6	S	63.6	58.2	S	49.1	50.9	S
13	60.0	S	S	52.7	56.4	S	63.6	61.8	61.8	67.3	S	43.6
14	60.0	S	S	58.2	60.0	63.6	74.5	S	60.0	60.0	S	41.8
15	60.0	H	54.5	49.1	S	58.2	63.6	S	40.0	52.7	45.5	52.7
16	S	65.5	67.3	61.8	S	49.1	50.9	56.4	54.5	S	50.9	56.4
17	S	47.3	60.0	S	54.5	54.5	S	52.7	49.1	S	50.9	47.3
18	H	49.1	67.3	S	56.4	H	S	54.5	S	52.7	52.7	S
19	69.1	36.4	47.3	49.1	47.3	S	54.5	49.1	S	45.5	50.9	S
20	58.2	S	S	52.7	43.6	S	61.8	69.1	60.0	61.8	S	50.9
21	49.1	S	S	56.4	49.1	47.3	36.4	S	47.3	52.7	S	56.4
22	52.7	45.5	54.5	58.2	S	47.3	49.1	S	47.3	52.7	65.5	61.8
23	S	50.9	54.5	54.5	S	50.9	52.7	50.9	41.8	S	60.0	63.6
24	S	65.5	49.1	S	52.7	40.0	S	54.5	50.9	S	61.8	H
25	47.3	56.4	45.5	S	58.2	49.1	S	54.5	S	40.0	H	S
26	65.5	50.9	H	54.5	60.0	S	56.4	58.2	S	45.5	69.1	S
27	56.4	S	S	45.5	58.2	S	49.1	65.5	47.3	56.4	S	70.9
28	54.5	S	S	61.8	60.0	60.0	45.5	S	52.7	60.0	S	67.3
29	61.8		50.9	69.1	S	67.3	58.2	S	45.5	61.8	63.6	47.3
30	S		56.4	56.4	S	67.3	50.9	60.0	52.7	S	61.8	58.2
31	S		61.8		H		S	63.6		S		63.6

** See developing trends on pages 72, 90, 143–148*

Based on NASDAQ composite, prior to Feb. 5, 1971 based on National Quotation Bureau indices. H = Holiday, S = Saturday/Sunday

<u>RECENT</u> NASDAQ COMPOSITE MARKET PROBABILITY CALENDAR 2027

THE % CHANCE OF THE MARKET RISING ON ANY TRADING DAY OF THE YEAR*

(Based on the number of times the NASDAQ rose on a particular trading day during **January 2005–December 2025****)

Date	Jan	Feb	Mar	Apr	May	Jun	Jul	Aug	Sep	Oct	Nov	Dec
1	H	81.0	57.1	61.9	S	61.9	85.7	S	47.6	52.4	61.9	47.6
2	S	66.7	42.9	71.4	S	76.2	52.4	47.6	42.9	S	57.1	52.4
3	S	38.1	52.4	S	61.9	47.6	S	47.6	57.1	S	57.1	66.7
4	57.1	61.9	33.3	S	57.1	57.1	S	57.1	S	47.6	66.7	S
5	38.1	52.4	38.1	52.4	38.1	S	H	61.9	S	66.7	71.4	S
6	47.6	S	S	52.4	47.6	S	71.4	42.9	H	52.4	S	57.1
7	57.1	S	S	38.1	61.9	42.9	57.1	S	47.6	42.9	S	61.9
8	66.7	66.7	42.9	61.9	S	61.9	66.7	S	57.1	57.1	66.7	61.9
9	S	57.1	57.1	47.6	S	42.9	76.2	52.4	66.7	S	28.6	57.1
10	S	57.1	47.6	S	71.4	38.1	S	38.1	71.4	S	57.1	61.9
11	66.7	76.2	61.9	S	52.4	61.9	S	47.6	S	57.1	57.1	S
12	66.7	85.7	47.6	61.9	47.6	S	71.4	61.9	S	47.6	38.1	S
13	61.9	S	S	52.4	52.4	S	52.4	57.1	66.7	57.1	S	38.1
14	47.6	S	S	47.6	61.9	66.7	76.2	S	66.7	57.1	S	47.6
15	42.9	H	52.4	42.9	S	66.7	61.9	S	47.6	57.1	52.4	61.9
16	S	71.4	66.7	61.9	S	52.4	61.9	52.4	76.2	S	66.7	57.1
17	S	47.6	71.4	S	47.6	61.9	S	52.4	38.1	S	42.9	38.1
18	H	38.1	76.2	S	57.1	H	S	52.4	S	57.1	52.4	S
19	66.7	33.3	61.9	33.3	38.1	S	66.7	47.6	S	61.9	47.6	S
20	47.6	S	S	52.4	42.9	S	71.4	76.2	52.4	42.9	S	47.6
21	52.4	S	S	61.9	47.6	47.6	23.8	S	38.1	71.4	S	61.9
22	57.1	42.9	47.6	61.9	S	42.9	52.4	S	33.3	71.4	61.9	66.7
23	S	42.9	52.4	52.4	S	47.6	52.4	38.1	33.3	S	61.9	57.1
24	S	76.2	66.7	S	42.9	23.8	S	61.9	52.4	S	66.7	H
25	52.4	57.1	38.1	S	71.4	57.1	S	57.1	S	52.4	H	S
26	66.7	38.1	H	66.7	61.9	S	57.1	61.9	S	52.4	71.4	S
27	57.1	S	S	38.1	66.7	S	47.6	81.0	52.4	57.1	S	81.0
28	47.6	S	S	52.4	38.1	66.7	42.9	S	61.9	61.9	S	57.1
29	52.4		42.9	85.7	S	61.9	71.4	S	38.1	52.4	57.1	38.1
30	S		66.7	28.6	S	52.4	38.1	61.9	52.4	S	52.4	33.3
31	S		52.4		H		S	47.6		S		28.6

** See developing trends on pages 72, 90, 143–148 ** Based on most recent 21-year period*
H = Holiday, S = Saturday/Sunday

RUSSELL 1000 INDEX MARKET PROBABILITY CALENDAR 2027

THE % CHANCE OF THE MARKET RISING ON ANY TRADING DAY OF THE YEAR*

(Based on the number of times the Russell 1000 rose on a particular trading day during **January 1979–December 2025**)

Date	Jan	Feb	Mar	Apr	May	Jun	Jul	Aug	Sep	Oct	Nov	Dec
1	H	68.1	59.6	59.6	S	61.7	76.6	S	53.2	55.3	74.5	48.9
2	S	63.8	46.8	63.8	S	66.0	46.8	40.4	48.9	S	55.3	53.2
3	S	55.3	59.6	S	57.4	51.1	S	42.6	51.1	S	61.7	59.6
4	44.7	57.4	40.4	S	61.7	57.4	S	46.8	S	55.3	63.8	S
5	57.4	53.2	44.7	51.1	51.1	S	H	53.2	S	59.6	53.2	S
6	57.4	S	S	57.4	38.3	S	51.1	53.2	H	57.4	S	44.7
7	55.3	S	S	46.8	51.1	42.6	57.4	S	40.4	40.4	S	51.1
8	53.2	55.3	51.1	68.1	S	51.1	57.4	S	51.1	53.2	61.7	51.1
9	S	46.8	57.4	57.4	S	42.6	55.3	55.3	59.6	S	46.8	48.9
10	S	70.2	46.8	S	55.3	48.9	S	42.6	66.0	S	57.4	53.2
11	61.7	66.0	57.4	S	55.3	57.4	S	48.9	S	40.4	53.2	S
12	59.6	51.1	42.6	48.9	53.2	S	61.7	46.8	S	42.6	53.2	S
13	57.4	S	S	51.1	51.1	S	61.7	61.7	70.2	59.6	S	46.8
14	57.4	S	S	55.3	55.3	55.3	76.6	S	57.4	59.6	S	38.3
15	61.7	H	57.4	59.6	S	61.7	51.1	S	53.2	57.4	53.2	57.4
16	S	66.0	61.7	57.4	S	51.1	53.2	63.8	51.1	S	48.9	55.3
17	S	42.6	57.4	S	59.6	59.6	S	61.7	46.8	S	57.4	44.7
18	H	40.4	51.1	S	55.3	H	S	59.6	S	57.4	51.1	S
19	63.8	36.2	48.9	46.8	51.1	S	51.1	61.7	S	46.8	53.2	S
20	44.7	S	S	51.1	46.8	S	61.7	66.0	46.8	68.1	S	44.7
21	44.7	S	S	44.7	40.4	40.4	40.4	S	36.2	48.9	S	53.2
22	51.1	42.6	44.7	55.3	S	51.1	48.9	S	44.7	51.1	59.6	68.1
23	S	44.7	46.8	57.4	S	46.8	44.7	46.8	36.2	S	68.1	61.7
24	S	59.6	53.2	S	59.6	34.0	S	57.4	40.4	S	66.0	H
25	53.2	53.2	42.6	S	61.7	42.6	S	48.9	S	36.2	H	S
26	59.6	48.9	H	53.2	55.3	S	72.3	55.3	S	55.3	70.2	S
27	48.9	S	S	53.2	57.4	S	53.2	61.7	44.7	48.9	S	63.8
28	57.4	S	S	57.4	53.2	53.2	44.7	S	66.0	63.8	S	66.0
29	55.3		46.8	61.7	S	63.8	61.7	S	55.3	61.7	66.0	55.3
30	S		46.8	51.1	S	57.4	57.4	53.2	51.1	S	48.9	59.6
31	S		51.1		H		S	55.3		S		46.8

** See developing trends on pages 72, 90, 143–148*
H = Holiday, S = Saturday/Sunday

RUSSELL 2000 INDEX MARKET PROBABILITY CALENDAR 2027

THE % CHANCE OF THE MARKET RISING ON ANY TRADING DAY OF THE YEAR*

(Based on the number of times the Russell 2000 rose on a particular trading day during **January 1979–December 2025**)

Date	Jan	Feb	Mar	Apr	May	Jun	Jul	Aug	Sep	Oct	Nov	Dec
1	H	68.1	66.0	48.9	S	66.0	68.1	S	48.9	48.9	63.8	46.8
2	S	61.7	55.3	59.6	S	72.3	48.9	42.6	55.3	S	70.2	59.6
3	S	53.2	61.7	S	63.8	48.9	S	44.7	51.1	S	63.8	61.7
4	46.8	63.8	48.9	S	66.0	55.3	S	48.9	S	48.9	59.6	S
5	61.7	57.4	57.4	44.7	57.4	S	H	51.1	S	55.3	55.3	S
6	55.3	S	S	53.2	53.2	S	46.8	51.1	H	63.8	S	59.6
7	59.6	S	S	46.8	59.6	61.7	55.3	S	57.4	40.4	S	48.9
8	55.3	61.7	48.9	59.6	S	46.8	53.2	S	57.4	48.9	57.4	55.3
9	S	51.1	57.4	59.6	S	42.6	59.6	48.9	57.4	S	51.1	48.9
10	S	68.1	44.7	S	51.1	51.1	S	51.1	61.7	S	63.8	48.9
11	59.6	66.0	59.6	S	57.4	55.3	S	46.8	S	48.9	46.8	S
12	59.6	63.8	51.1	59.6	48.9	S	57.4	51.1	S	46.8	48.9	S
13	63.8	S	S	53.2	53.2	S	57.4	66.0	61.7	63.8	S	44.7
14	63.8	S	S	55.3	48.9	55.3	63.8	S	57.4	57.4	S	38.3
15	61.7	H	53.2	57.4	S	61.7	55.3	S	42.6	63.8	51.1	44.7
16	S	61.7	61.7	59.6	S	48.9	51.1	57.4	48.9	S	31.9	48.9
17	S	53.2	66.0	S	53.2	44.7	S	57.4	46.8	S	57.4	57.4
18	H	42.6	55.3	S	57.4	H	S	55.3	S	48.9	48.9	S
19	68.1	38.3	44.7	48.9	48.9	S	51.1	46.8	S	46.8	36.2	S
20	63.8	S	S	53.2	59.6	S	53.2	63.8	42.6	61.7	S	57.4
21	38.3	S	S	51.1	53.2	46.8	36.2	S	40.4	48.9	S	63.8
22	53.2	48.9	55.3	61.7	S	44.7	44.7	S	48.9	51.1	63.8	68.1
23	S	51.1	51.1	57.4	S	53.2	46.8	48.9	36.2	S	68.1	63.8
24	S	59.6	55.3	S	59.6	42.6	S	61.7	44.7	S	63.8	H
25	48.9	61.7	48.9	S	53.2	48.9	S	61.7	S	36.2	H	S
26	66.0	55.3	H	53.2	61.7	S	66.0	55.3	S	42.6	59.6	S
27	51.1	S	S	57.4	63.8	S	59.6	68.1	38.3	51.1	S	76.6
28	51.1	S	S	66.0	55.3	53.2	46.8	S	57.4	55.3	S	63.8
29	68.1		48.9	59.6	S	70.2	57.4	S	53.2	66.0	70.2	51.1
30	S		55.3	55.3	S	68.1	61.7	63.8	61.7	S	66.0	57.4
31	S		78.7		H		S	63.8		S		59.6

* See new trends developing on pages 72, 90, 143–148

H = Holiday, S = Saturday/Sunday

DECENNIAL CYCLE: A MARKET PHENOMENON

By arranging each year's market gain or loss so the first and succeeding years of each decade fall into the same column, certain interesting patterns emerge—strong fifth and eighth years; weak second, seventh, and zero years.

This fascinating phenomenon was first presented by Edgar Lawrence Smith in *Common Stocks and Business Cycles* (William-Frederick Press, 1959). Anthony Gaubis co-pioneered the decennial pattern with Smith.

When Smith first cut graphs of market prices into 10-year segments and placed them above one another, he observed that each decade tended to have three bull market cycles and that the longest and strongest bull markets seem to favor the middle years of a decade.

Don't place too much emphasis on the decennial cycle nowadays, other than the extraordinary fifth and zero years, as the stock market is more influenced by the quadrennial presidential election cycle, shown on page 132. Also, the last half-century, which has been the most prosperous in U.S. history, has distributed the returns among most years of the decade. Interestingly, NASDAQ suffered its worst bear market ever in a zero year.

Seventh years are the second worst in the decennial cycle with an average loss of –0.5%, only zero years are weaker. However, 2027 is a pre-election year, the best year of the four-year-presidential-election cycle since 1833. Of the seven years ending in seven that were also pre-election years (2007, 1987, 1967, 1947, 1927, 1907, and 1887), five were up and two were down with an average gain of +1.3%. Excluding the oldest and two down (1907 & 1887) results in the average gain jumping to +11.0%.

THE 10-YEAR STOCK MARKET CYCLE

Annual % Change in Dow Jones Industrial Average

Year of Decade

DECADES	1st	2nd	3rd	4th	5th	6th	7th	8th	9th	10th
1881–1890	3.0%	–2.9%	–8.5%	–18.8%	20.1%	12.4%	–8.4%	4.8%	5.5%	–14.1%
1891–1900	17.6	–6.6	–24.6	–0.6	2.3	–1.7	21.3	22.5	9.2	7.0
1901–1910	–8.7	–0.4	–23.6	41.7	38.2	–1.9	–37.7	46.6	15.0	–17.9
1911–1920	0.4	7.6	–10.3	–5.4	81.7	–4.2	–21.7	10.5	30.5	–32.9
1921–1930	12.7	21.7	–3.3	26.2	30.0	0.3	28.8	48.2	–17.2	–33.8
1931–1940	–52.7	–23.1	66.7	4.1	38.5	24.8	–32.8	28.1	–2.9	–12.7
1941–1950	–15.4	7.6	13.8	12.1	26.6	–8.1	2.2	–2.1	12.9	17.6
1951–1960	14.4	8.4	–3.8	44.0	20.8	2.3	–12.8	34.0	16.4	–9.3
1961–1970	18.7	–10.8	17.0	14.6	10.9	–18.9	15.2	4.3	–15.2	4.8
1971–1980	6.1	14.6	–16.6	–27.6	38.3	17.9	–17.3	–3.1	4.2	14.9
1981–1990	–9.2	19.6	20.3	–3.7	27.7	22.6	2.3	11.8	27.0	–4.3
1991–2000	20.3	4.2	13.7	2.1	33.5	26.0	22.6	16.1	25.2	–6.2
2001–2010	–7.1	–16.8	25.3	3.1	–0.6	16.3	6.4	–33.8	18.8	11.0
2011–2020	5.5	7.3	26.5	7.5	–2.2	13.4	25.1	–5.6	22.3	7.2
2021–2030	18.7	–8.8	13.7	12.9	13.0					
Total % Change	**24.3%**	**21.6%**	**106.3%**	**112.3%**	**378.8%**	**101.2%**	**–6.8%**	**182.3%**	**151.7%**	**–68.7%**
Avg % Change	**1.6%**	**1.4%**	**6.6%**	**7.5%**	**25.3%**	**7.2%**	**–0.5%**	**13.0%**	**10.8%**	**–4.9%**
Up Years	10	8	8	10	13	9	8	10	11	6
Down Years	5	7	7	5	2	5	6	4	3	8

Based on annual close; Cowles indices 1881–1885; 12 Mixed Stocks, 10 Rails, 2 Inds 1886–1889;

20 Mixed Stocks, 18 Rails, 2 Inds 1890–1896; Railroad average 1897 (First industrial average published May 26, 1896).

PRESIDENTIAL ELECTION/STOCK MARKET CYCLE: THE 193-YEAR SAGA CONTINUES

It is no mere coincidence that the last two years (pre-election year and election year) of the 48 presidential terms since 1833 produced a total net market gain of 798.6%, dwarfing the 349.5% gain of the first two years of these terms.

Presidential elections every four years have a profound impact on the economy and the stock market. Wars, recessions, and bear markets tend to start or occur in the first half of the term (2022 Russia–Ukraine War and bear market); prosperous times and bull markets, in the latter half. A millennial bull market, financial crisis, and a global pandemic had temporarily overridden the four-year cycle in recent decades, but the four-year cycle continues to reassert its overarching domination of market behavior as incumbents incessantly seek re-election or to keep the party in power.

STOCK MARKET ACTION SINCE 1833

Annual % Change in Dow Jones Industrial Average[1]

4-Year Cycle Beginning	President Elected	Post-Election Year	Midterm Year	Pre-Election Year	Election Year
1833	Jackson (D)	–0.9	13.0	3.1	–11.7
1837	Van Buren (D)	–11.5	1.6	–12.3	5.5
1841*	W.H. Harrison (W)**	–13.3	–18.1	45.0	15.5
1845*	Polk (D)	8.1	–14.5	1.2	–3.6
1849*	Taylor (W)	N/C	18.7	–3.2	19.6
1853*	Pierce (D)	–12.7	–30.2	1.5	4.4
1857	Buchanan (D)	–31.0	14.3	–10.7	14.0
1861*	Lincoln (R)	–1.8	55.4	38.0	6.4
1865	Lincoln (R)**	–8.5	3.6	1.6	10.8
1869	Grant (R)	1.7	5.6	7.3	6.8
1873	Grant (R)	–12.7	2.8	–4.1	–17.9
1877	Hayes (R)	–9.4	6.1	43.0	18.7
1881	Garfield (R)**	3.0	–2.9	–8.5	–18.8
1885*	Cleveland (D)	20.1	12.4	–8.4	4.8
1889*	B. Harrison (R)	5.5	–14.1	17.6	–6.6
1893*	Cleveland (D)	–24.6	–0.6	2.3	–1.7
1897*	McKinley (R)	21.3	22.5	9.2	7.0
1901	McKinley (R)**	–8.7	–0.4	–23.6	41.7
1905	T. Roosevelt (R)	38.2	–1.9	–37.7	46.6
1909	Taft (R)	15.0	–17.9	0.4	7.6
1913*	Wilson (D)	–10.3	–5.4	81.7	–4.2
1917	Wilson (D)	–21.7	10.5	30.5	–32.9
1921*	Harding (R)**	12.7	21.7	–3.3	26.2
1925	Coolidge (R)	30.0	0.3	28.8	48.2
1929	Hoover (R)	–17.2	–33.8	–52.7	–23.1
1933*	F. Roosevelt (D)	66.7	4.1	38.5	24.8
1937	F. Roosevelt (D)	–32.8	28.1	–2.9	–12.7
1941	F. Roosevelt (D)	–15.4	7.6	13.8	12.1
1945	F. Roosevelt (D)**	26.6	–8.1	2.2	–2.1
1949	Truman (D)	12.9	17.6	14.4	8.4
1953*	Eisenhower (R)	–3.8	44.0	20.8	2.3
1957	Eisenhower (R)	–12.8	34.0	16.4	–9.3
1961*	Kennedy (D)**	18.7	–10.8	17.0	14.6
1965	Johnson (D)	10.9	–18.9	15.2	4.3
1969*	Nixon (R)	–15.2	4.8	6.1	14.6
1973	Nixon (R)***	–16.6	–27.6	38.3	17.9
1977*	Carter (D)	–17.3	–3.1	4.2	14.9
1981*	Reagan (R)	–9.2	19.6	20.3	–3.7
1985	Reagan (R)	27.7	22.6	2.3	11.8
1989	G. H. W. Bush (R)	27.0	–4.3	20.3	4.2
1993*	Clinton (D)	13.7	2.1	33.5	26.0
1997	Clinton (D)	22.6	16.1	25.2	–6.2
2001*	G. W. Bush (R)	–7.1	–16.8	25.3	3.1
2005	G. W. Bush (R)	–0.6	16.3	6.4	–33.8
2009*	Obama (D)	18.8	11.0	5.5	7.3
2013	Obama (D)	26.5	7.5	–2.2	13.4
2017*	Trump (R)	25.1	–5.6	22.3	7.2
2021*	Biden (D)	18.7	–8.8	13.7	12.9
2025*	Trump (R)	13.0			
Total % Gain		**169.4%**	**180.1%**	**503.3%**	**295.3%**
Average % Gain		**3.5%**	**3.8%**	**10.5%**	**6.2%**
# Up		24	28	36	33
# Down		24	20	12	15

*****Party in power ousted   ******Died in office   *******Resigned   ***D***–Democrat, ***W***–Whig, ***R***–Republican

[1] *Based on annual close; prior to 1886 based on Cowles and other indices; 12 Mixed Stocks, 10 Rails, 2 Inds 1886–1889; 20 Mixed Stocks, 18 Rails, 2 Inds 1890–1896; Railroad average 1897 (First industrial average published May 26, 1896).*

DOW JONES INDUSTRIALS BULL AND BEAR MARKETS SINCE 1900

Bear markets begin at the end of one bull market and end at the start of the next bull market (1/4/2022 to 9/30/2022 as an example). The longest bull market on record ended on 7/17/98, and the shortest bear market on record ended on 3/23/2020, when the new bull market began. The greatest bull super cycle in history that began 8/12/82 ended in 2000 after the Dow gained 1409% and NASDAQ climbed 3072%. The Dow gained only 497% in the eight-year super bull from 1921 to the top in 1929. NASDAQ suffered its worst loss ever from the 2000 top to the 2002 bottom, down 77.9%, nearly as much as the 89.2% drop in the Dow from the 1929 top to the 1932 bottom. The third longest Dow bull since 1900 that began 10/9/02 ended on its fifth anniversary. The ensuing bear market was the second worst bear market since 1900, slashing the Dow 53.8%. At press time, Dow was in a bull market, trading around 48,500, rebounding after a pullback from all-time highs triggered by war with Iran. (See page 134 for S&P 500 and NASDAQ bulls and bears.)

DOW JONES INDUSTRIALS BULL AND BEAR MARKETS SINCE 1900

— Beginning —		— Ending —		Bull		Bear	
Date	DJIA	Date	DJIA	% Gain	Days	% Change	Days
9/24/00	38.80	6/17/01	57.33	47.8%	266	–46.1%	875
11/9/03	30.88	1/19/06	75.45	144.3	802	–48.5	665
11/15/07	38.83	11/19/09	73.64	89.6	735	–27.4	675
9/25/11	53.43	9/30/12	68.97	29.1	371	–24.1	668
7/30/14	52.32	11/21/16	110.15	110.5	845	–40.1	393
12/19/17	65.95	11/3/19	119.62	81.4	684	–46.6	660
8/24/21	63.90	3/20/23	105.38	64.9	573	–18.6	221
10/27/23	85.76	9/3/29	381.17	344.5	2138	–47.9	71
11/13/29	198.69	4/17/30	294.07	48.0	155	–86.0	813
7/8/32	41.22	9/7/32	79.93	93.9	61	–37.2	173
2/27/33	50.16	2/5/34	110.74	120.8	343	–22.8	171
7/26/34	85.51	3/10/37	194.40	127.3	958	–49.1	386
3/31/38	98.95	11/12/38	158.41	60.1	226	–23.3	147
4/8/39	121.44	9/12/39	155.92	28.4	157	–40.4	959
4/28/42	92.92	5/29/46	212.50	128.7	1492	–23.2	133
10/9/46	163.12	6/15/48	193.16	18.4	615	–16.3	363
6/13/49	161.60	1/5/53	293.79	81.8	1302	–13.0	252
9/14/53	255.49	4/6/56	521.05	103.9	935	–19.4	564
10/22/57	419.79	1/5/60	685.47	63.3	805	–17.4	294
10/25/60	566.05	12/13/61	734.91	29.8	414	–27.1	195
6/26/62	535.76	2/9/66	995.15	85.7	1324	–25.2	240
10/7/66	744.32	12/3/68	985.21	32.4	788	–35.9	539
5/26/70	631.16	4/28/71	950.82	50.6	337	–16.1	209
11/23/71	797.97	1/11/73	1051.70	31.8	415	–45.1	694
12/6/74	577.60	9/21/76	1014.79	75.7	655	–26.9	525
2/28/78	742.12	9/8/78	907.74	22.3	192	–16.4	591
4/21/80	759.13	4/27/81	1024.05	34.9	371	–24.1	472
8/12/82	776.92	11/29/83	1287.20	65.7	474	–15.6	238
7/24/84	1086.57	8/25/87	2722.42	150.6	1127	–36.1	55
10/19/87	1738.74	7/17/90	2999.75	72.5	1002	–21.2	86
10/11/90	2365.10	7/17/98	9337.97	294.8	2836	–19.3	45
8/31/98	7539.07	1/14/00	11722.98	55.5	501	–29.7	616
9/21/01	8235.81	3/19/02	10635.25	29.1	179	–31.5	204
10/9/02	7286.27	10/9/07	14164.53	94.4	1826	–53.8	517
3/9/09	6547.05	4/29/11	12810.54	95.7	781	–16.8	157
10/3/11	10655.30	5/19/15	18312.39	71.9	1324	–14.5	268
2/11/16	15660.18	2/12/20	29551.42	88.7	1462	–37.1	40
3/23/20	18591.93	1/4/22	36799.65	97.9	652	–21.9	269
9/30/22	28725.51	2/10/26	50188.14	74.7*	1229*		
			Average	**86.0%**	**793**	**–30.6%**	**380**

** As of April 14, 2026—not in averages*

Based on Dow Jones Industrial Average.
The NYSE was closed from 7/31/1914 to 12/11/1914 due to World War I.
DJIA figures were then adjusted back to reflect the composition change from 12 to 20 stocks in September 1916.

1900–2000 Data: Ned Davis Research

STANDARD & POOR'S 500 BULL AND BEAR MARKETS SINCE 1929 NASDAQ COMPOSITE SINCE 1971

A constant debate of the definition and timing of bull and bear markets permeates Wall Street like the bell that signals the open and close of every trading day. We have relied on the Ned Davis Research parameters for years to track bulls and bears on the Dow (see page 133). Standard & Poor's 500 index has been a stalwart indicator for decades and at times marched to a slightly different beat than the Dow. The moves of the S&P 500 and NASDAQ have been correlated to the bull & bear dates on page 133. Many dates line up for the three indices, but you will notice quite a lag or lead on several occasions, especially NASDAQ's independent cadence from 1975 to 1980. The 2022 bear market ended on different days for the three indices.

STANDARD & POOR'S 500 BULL AND BEAR MARKETS

— Beginning —		— Ending —		Bull		Bear	
Date	S&P 500	Date	S&P 500	% Gain	Days	% Change	Days
11/13/29	17.66	4/10/30	25.92	46.8%	148	–83.0%	783
6/1/32	4.40	9/7/32	9.31	111.6	98	–40.6	173
2/27/33	5.53	2/6/34	11.82	113.7	344	–31.8	401
3/14/35	8.06	3/6/37	18.68	131.8	723	–49.0	390
3/31/38	8.50	11/9/38	13.79	62.2	223	–26.2	150
4/8/39	10.18	10/25/39	13.21	29.8	200	–43.5	916
4/28/42	7.47	5/29/46	19.25	157.7	1492	–28.8	353
5/17/47	13.71	6/15/48	17.06	24.4	395	–20.6	363
6/13/49	13.55	1/5/53	26.66	96.8	1302	–14.8	252
9/14/53	22.71	8/2/56	49.74	119.0	1053	–21.6	446
10/22/57	38.98	8/3/59	60.71	55.7	650	–13.9	449
10/25/60	52.30	12/12/61	72.64	38.9	413	–28.0	196
6/26/62	52.32	2/9/66	94.06	79.8	1324	–22.2	240
10/7/66	73.20	11/29/68	108.37	48.0	784	–36.1	543
5/26/70	69.29	4/28/71	104.77	51.2	337	–13.9	209
11/23/71	90.16	1/11/73	120.24	33.4	415	–48.2	630
10/3/74	62.28	9/21/76	107.83	73.1	719	–19.4	531
3/6/78	86.90	9/12/78	106.99	23.1	190	–8.2	562
3/27/80	98.22	11/28/80	140.52	43.1	246	–27.1	622
8/12/82	102.42	10/10/83	172.65	68.6	424	–14.4	288
7/24/84	147.82	8/25/87	336.77	127.8	1127	–33.5	101
12/4/87	223.92	7/16/90	368.95	64.8	955	–19.9	87
10/11/90	295.46	7/17/98	1186.75	301.7	2836	–19.3	45
8/31/98	957.28	3/24/00	1527.46	59.6	571	–36.8	546
9/21/01	965.80	1/4/02	1172.51	21.4	105	–33.8	278
10/9/02	776.76	10/9/07	1565.15	101.5	1826	–56.8	517
3/9/09	676.53	4/29/11	1363.61	101.6	781	–19.4	157
10/3/11	1099.23	5/21/15	2130.82	93.8	1326	–14.2	266
2/11/16	1829.08	2/19/20	3386.15	85.1	1469	–33.9	33
3/23/20	2237.40	1/3/22	4796.56	114.4	651	–25.4	282
10/12/22	3577.03	4/15/26	7022.95	96.3*	1281*	*As of April 15 2026—not in averages	
			Average	**82.7%**	**771**	**–29.7%**	**360**

NASDAQ COMPOSITE BULL AND BEAR MARKETS

— Beginning —		— Ending —		Bull		Bear	
Date	NASDAQ	Date	NASDAQ	% Gain	Days	% Change	Days
11/23/71	100.31	1/11/73	136.84	36.4%	415	–59.9%	630
10/3/74	54.87	7/15/75	88.00	60.4	285	–16.2	63
9/16/75	73.78	9/13/78	139.25	88.7	1093	–20.4	62
11/14/78	110.88	2/8/80	165.25	49.0	451	–24.9	48
3/27/80	124.09	5/29/81	223.47	80.1	428	–28.8	441
8/13/82	159.14	6/24/83	328.91	106.7	315	–31.5	397
7/25/84	225.30	8/26/87	455.26	102.1	1127	–35.9	63
10/28/87	291.88	10/9/89	485.73	66.4	712	–33.0	372
10/16/90	325.44	7/20/98	2014.25	518.9	2834	–29.5	80
10/8/98	1419.12	3/10/00	5048.62	255.8	519	–71.8	560
9/21/01	1423.19	1/4/02	2059.38	44.7	105	–45.9	278
10/9/02	1114.11	10/31/07	2859.12	156.6	1848	–55.6	495
3/9/09	1268.64	4/29/11	2873.54	126.5	781	–18.7	157
10/3/11	2335.83	7/20/15	5218.86	123.4	1386	–18.2	206
2/11/16	4266.84	2/19/20	9817.18	130.1	1469	–30.1	33
3/23/20	6860.67	11/19/21	16057.44	134.1	606	–36.4	404
12/28/22	10213.29	4/15/26	24016.02	135.1*	1204*	*As of April 15, 2026—not in averages	
			Average	**130.0%**	**898**	**–34.8%**	**268**

JANUARY DAILY POINT CHANGES DOW JONES INDUSTRIALS

Previous Month Close	2017	2018	2019	2020	2021	2022	2023	2024	2025	2026
	19762.60	**24719.22**	**23327.46**	**28538.44**	**30606.48**	**36338.30**	**33147.25**	**37689.54**	**42544.22**	**48063.29**
1	S	H	H	H	H	S	S	H	H	H
2	H	104.79	18.78	330.36	S	S	H	25.50	−151.95	319.10
3	119.16	98.67	−660.02	−233.92	S	246.76	−10.88	−284.85	339.86	S
4	60.40	152.45	746.94	S	−382.59	214.59	133.40	10.15	S	S
5	−42.87	220.74	S	S	167.71	−392.54	−339.69	25.77	S	594.79
6	64.51	S	S	68.50	437.80	−170.64	700.53	S	−25.57	484.90
7	S	S	98.19	−119.70	211.73	−4.81	S	S	−178.20	−466.00
8	S	−12.87	256.10	161.41	56.84	S	S	216.90	106.84	270.03
9	−76.42	102.80	91.67	211.81	S	S	−112.96	−157.85	H*	237.96
10	−31.85	−16.67	122.80	−133.13	S	−162.79	186.45	170.57	−696.75	S
11	98.75	205.60	−5.97	S	−89.28	183.15	268.91	15.29	S	S
12	−63.28	228.46	S	S	60.00	38.30	216.96	−118.04	S	86.13
13	−5.27	S	S	83.28	−8.22	−176.70	112.64	S	358.67	−398.21
14	S	S	−86.11	32.62	−68.95	−201.81	S	S	221.16	−42.36
15	S	H	155.75	90.55	−177.26	S	S	H	703.27	292.81
16	H	−10.33	141.57	267.42	S	S	H	−231.86	−68.42	−83.11
17	−58.96	322.79	162.94	50.46	S	H	−391.76	−94.45	334.70	S
18	−22.05	−97.84	336.25	S	H	−543.34	−613.89	201.94	S	S
19	−72.32	53.91	S	S	116.26	−339.82	−252.40	395.19	S	H
20	94.85	S	S	H	257.86	−313.26	330.93	S	H	−870.74
21	S	S	H	−152.06	−12.37	−450.02	S	S	537.98	588.64
22	S	142.88	−301.87	−9.77	−179.03	S	S	138.01	130.92	306.78
23	−27.40	−3.79	171.14	−26.18	S	S	254.07	−96.36	408.34	−285.30
24	112.86	41.31	−22.38	−170.36	S	99.13	104.40	−99.06	−140.82	S
25	155.80	140.67	183.96	S	−36.98	−66.77	9.88	242.74	S	S
26	32.40	223.92	S	S	−22.96	−129.64	205.57	60.30	S	313.69
27	−7.13	S	S	−453.93	−633.87	−7.31	28.67	S	289.33	−408.99
28	S	S	−208.98	187.05	300.19	564.69	S	S	136.77	12.19
29	S	−177.23	51.74	11.60	−620.74	S	S	224.02	−136.83	55.96
30	−122.65	−362.59	434.90	124.99	S	S	−260.99	133.86	168.61	−179.09
31	−107.04	72.50	−15.19	−603.41	S	406.39	368.95	−317.01	−337.47	S
Close	**19864.09**	**26149.39**	**24999.67**	**28256.03**	**29982.62**	**35131.86**	**34086.04**	**38150.30**	**44544.66**	**48892.47**
Change	**101.49**	**1430.17**	**1672.21**	**−282.41**	**−623.86**	**−1206.44**	**938.79**	**460.76**	**2000.44**	**829.18**

FEBRUARY DAILY POINT CHANGES DOW JONES INDUSTRIALS

Previous Month Close	2017	2018	2019	2020	2021	2022	2023	2024	2025	2026
	19864.09	**26149.39**	**24999.67**	**28256.03**	**29982.62**	**35131.86**	**34086.04**	**38150.30**	**44544.66**	**48892.47**
1	26.85	37.32	64.22	S	229.29	273.38	6.92	369.54	S	S
2	−6.03	−665.75	S	S	475.57	224.09	−39.02	134.58	S	515.19
3	186.55	S	S	143.78	36.12	−518.17	−127.93	S	−122.75	−166.67
4	S	S	175.48	407.82	332.26	−21.42	S	S	134.13	260.31
5	S	−1175.21	172.15	483.22	92.38	S	S	−274.30	317.24	−592.58
6	−19.04	567.02	−21.22	88.92	S	S	−34.99	141.24	−125.65	1206.95
7	37.87	−19.42	−220.77	−277.26	S	1.39	265.67	156.00	−444.23	S
8	−35.95	−1032.89	−63.20	S	237.52	371.65	−207.68	48.97	S	S
9	118.06	330.44	S	S	−9.93	305.28	−249.13	−54.64	S	20.20
10	96.97	S	S	174.31	61.97	−526.47	169.39	S	167.01	52.27
11	S	S	−53.22	−0.48	−7.10	−503.53	S	S	123.24	−66.74
12	S	410.37	372.65	275.08	27.70	S	S	125.69	−225.09	−669.42
13	142.79	39.18	117.51	−128.11	S	S	376.66	−524.63	342.87	48.95
14	92.25	253.04	−103.88	−25.23	S	−171.89	−156.66	151.52	−165.35	S
15	107.45	306.88	443.86	S	H	422.67	38.78	348.85	S	S
16	7.91	19.01	S	S	64.35	−54.57	−431.20	−145.13	S	H
17	4.28	S	S	H	90.27	−622.24	129.84	S	H	32.26
18	S	S	H	−165.89	−119.68	−232.85	S	S	10.26	129.47
19	S	H	8.07	115.84	0.98	S	S	H	71.25	−267.50
20	H	−254.63	63.12	−128.05	S	S	H	−64.19	−450.94	230.81
21	118.95	−166.97	−103.81	−227.57	S	H	−697.10	48.44	−748.63	S
22	32.60	164.70	181.18	S	27.37	−482.57	−84.50	456.87	S	S
23	34.72	347.51	S	S	15.66	−464.85	108.82	62.42	S	−821.91
24	11.44	S	S	−1031.61	424.51	92.07	−336.99	S	33.19	370.44
25	S	S	60.14	−879.44	−559.85	834.92	S	S	159.95	307.65
26	S	399.28	−33.97	−123.77	−469.64	S	S	−62.30	−188.04	17.05
27	15.68	−299.24	−72.82	−1190.95	S	S	72.17	−96.82	−193.62	−521.28
28	−25.20	−380.83	−69.16	−357.28	S	−166.15	−232.39	−23.39	601.41	S
29	—	—	—	—	—	—	—	47.37	—	—
Close	**20812.24**	**25029.20**	**25916.00**	**25409.36**	**30932.37**	**33892.60**	**32656.70**	**38996.39**	**43840.91**	**48977.92**
Change	**948.15**	**−1120.19**	**916.33**	**−2846.67**	**949.75**	**−1239.26**	**−1429.34**	**846.09**	**−703.75**	**85.45**

** President Carter Funeral*

MARCH DAILY POINT CHANGES DOW JONES INDUSTRIALS

Previous Month	2017	2018	2019	2020	2021	2022	2023	2024	2025	2026
Close	**20812.24**	**25029.20**	**25916.00**	**25409.36**	**30932.37**	**33892.60**	**32656.70**	**38996.39**	**43840.91**	**48977.92**
1	303.31	– 420.22	110.32	S	603.14	– 597.65	5.14	90.99	S	S
2	– 112.58	– 70.92	S	1293.96	– 143.99	596.40	341.73	S	S	– 73.14
3	2.74	S	S	– 785.91	– 121.43	– 96.69	387.40	S	– 649.67	– 403.51
4	S	S	– 206.67	1173.45	– 345.95	– 179.86	S	– 97.55	– 670.25	238.14
5	S	336.70	– 13.02	– 969.58	572.16	S	S	– 404.64	485.60	– 784.67
6	– 51.37	9.36	– 133.17	– 256.50	S	S	40.47	75.86	– 427.51	– 453.19
7	– 29.58	– 82.76	– 200.23	S	S	– 797.42	– 574.98	130.30	222.64	S
8	– 69.03	93.85	– 22.99	S	306.14	– 184.74	– 58.06	– 68.66	S	S
9	2.46	440.53	S	– 2013.76	30.30	653.61	– 543.54	S	S	239.25
10	44.79	S	S	1167.14	464.28	– 112.18	– 345.22	S	– 890.01	– 34.29
11	S	S	200.64	– 1464.94	188.57	– 229.88	S	46.97	– 478.23	– 289.24
12	S	– 157.13	– 96.22	–2352.60	293.05	S	S	235.83	– 82.55	– 739.42
13	– 21.50	– 171.58	148.23	1985.00	S	S	– 90.50	37.83	– 537.36	– 119.38
14	– 44.11	– 248.91	7.05	S	S	1.05	336.26	– 137.66	674.62	S
15	112.73	115.54	138.93	S	174.82	599.10	– 280.83	– 190.89	S	S
16	– 15.55	72.85	S	– 2997.10	– 127.51	518.76	371.98	S	S	387.94
17	– 19.93	S	S	1048.86	189.42	417.66	– 384.57	S	353.44	46.85
18	S	S	65.23	– 1338.46	– 153.07	274.17	S	75.66	– 260.32	– 768.11
19	S	– 335.60	– 26.72	188.27	– 234.33	S	S	320.33	383.32	– 203.72
20	– 8.76	116.36	– 141.71	– 913.21	S	S	382.60	401.37	– 11.31	– 443.96
21	– 237.85	– 44.96	216.84	S	S	– 201.94	316.02	269.24	32.03	S
22	– 6.71	– 724.42	– 460.19	S	103.23	254.47	– 530.49	– 305.47	S	S
23	– 4.72	– 424.69	S	– 582.05	– 308.05	– 448.96	75.14	S	S	631.00
24	– 59.86	S	S	2112.98	– 3.09	349.44	132.28	S	597.97	– 84.41
25	S	S	14.51	495.64	199.42	153.30	S	– 162.26	4.18	125.43
26	S	669.40	140.90	1351.62	453.40	S	S	– 31.31	– 132.71	– 289.38
27	– 45.74	– 344.89	– 32.14	– 915.39	S	S	194.55	477.75	– 155.09	– 793.47
28	150.52	– 9.29	91.87	S	S	94.65	– 37.83	47.29	– 715.80	S
29	– 42.18	254.69	211.22	S	98.49	338.30	323.35	H	S	S
30	69.17	H	S	690.70	– 104.41	– 65.38	141.43	S	S	49.50
31	– 65.27	S	S	– 410.32	– 85.41	– 550.46	415.12	S	417.86	1125.37
Close	**20663.22**	**24103.11**	**25928.68**	**21917.16**	**32981.55**	**34678.35**	**33274.15**	**39807.37**	**42001.76**	**46341.51**
Change	**– 149.02**	**– 926.09**	**12.68**	**– 3492.20**	**2049.18**	**785.75**	**617.45**	**810.98**	**– 1839.15**	**– 2636.41**

APRIL DAILY POINT CHANGES DOW JONES INDUSTRIALS

Previous Month	2017	2018	2019	2020	2021	2022	2023	2024	2025	2026
Close	**20663.22**	**24103.11**	**25928.68**	**21917.16**	**32981.55**	**34678.35**	**33274.15**	**39807.37**	**42001.76**	**46341.51**
1	S	S	329.74	– 973.65	171.66	139.92	S	– 240.52	– 11.80	224.23
2	S	– 458.92	– 79.29	469.93	H	S	S	– 396.61	235.36	– 61.07
3	– 13.01	389.17	39.00	– 360.91	S	S	327.00	– 43.10	– 1679.39	H
4	39.03	230.94	166.50	S	S	103.61	– 198.77	– 530.16	– 2231.07	S
5	– 41.09	240.92	40.36	S	373.98	– 280.70	80.34	307.06	S	S
6	14.80	– 572.46	S	1627.46	– 96.95	– 144.67	2.57	S	S	165.21
7	– 6.85	S	S	– 26.13	16.02	87.06	H	S	– 349.26	– 85.42
8	S	S	– 83.97	779.71	57.31	137.55	S	– 11.24	– 320.01	1325.46
9	S	46.34	– 190.44	285.80	297.03	S	S	– 9.13	2962.86	275.88
10	1.92	428.90	6.58	H	S	S	101.23	– 422.16	– 1014.79	– 269.23
11	– 6.72	– 218.55	– 14.11	S	S	– 413.04	98.27	– 2.43	619.05	S
12	– 59.44	293.60	269.25	S	– 55.20	– 87.72	– 38.29	– 475.84	S	S
13	– 138.61	– 122.91	S	– 328.60	– 68.13	344.23	383.19	S	S	301.68
14	H	S	S	558.99	53.62	– 113.36	– 143.22	S	312.08	135.74
15	S	S	– 27.53	– 445.41	305.10	H	S	– 248.13	– 155.83	109.73
16	S	212.90	67.89	33.33	164.68	S	S	63.86	– 699.57	115.00
17	183.67	213.59	– 3.12	704.81	S	S	100.71	– 45.66	– 527.16	868.71
18	– 113.64	– 38.56	110.00	S	S	– 39.54	– 10.55	22.07	H	S
19	– 118.79	– 83.18	H	S	– 123.04	499.51	– 79.62	211.02	S	S
20	174.22	– 201.95	S	– 592.05	– 256.33	249.59	– 110.39	S	S	– 4.87
21	– 30.95	S	S	– 631.56	316.01	– 368.03	22.34	S	– 971.82	– 293.18
22	S	S	– 48.49	456.94	– 321.41	– 981.36	S	253.58	1016.57	340.65
23	S	– 14.25	145.34	39.44	227.59	S	S	263.71	419.59	– 179.71
24	216.13	– 424.56	– 59.34	260.01	S	S	66.44	– 42.77	486.83	– 79.61
25	232.23	59.70	– 134.97	S	S	238.06	– 344.57	– 375.12	20.10	S
26	– 21.03	238.51	81.25	S	– 61.92	– 809.28	– 228.96	153.86	S	S
27	6.24	– 11.15	S	358.51	3.36	61.75	524.29	S	S	– 62.92
28	– 40.82	S	S	– 32.23	– 164.55	614.46	272.00	S	114.09	– 25.86
29	S	S	11.06	532.31	239.98	– 939.18	S	146.43	300.03	– 280.12
30	S	– 148.04	38.52	– 288.14	– 185.51	S	S	– 570.17	141.74	790.33
Close	**20940.51**	**24163.15**	**26592.91**	**24345.72**	**33874.85**	**32977.21**	**34098.16**	**37815.92**	**40669.36**	**49652.14**
Change	**277.29**	**60.04**	**664.23**	**2428.56**	**893.30**	**– 1701.14**	**824.01**	**– 1991.45**	**– 1332.40**	**3310.63**

MAY DAILY POINT CHANGES DOW JONES INDUSTRIALS

Previous Month	2016	2017	2018	2019	2020	2021	2022	2023	2024	2025
Close	**17773.64**	**20940.51**	**24163.15**	**26592.91**	**24345.72**	**33874.85**	**32977.21**	**34098.16**	**37815.92**	**40669.36**
1	S	–27.05	–64.10	–162.77	–622.03	S	S	–46.46	87.37	83.60
2	117.52	36.43	–174.07	–122.35	S	S	84.29	–367.17	322.37	564.47
3	–140.25	8.01	5.17	197.16	S	238.38	67.29	–270.29	450.02	S
4	–99.65	–6.43	332.36	S	26.07	19.80	932.27	–286.50	S	S
5	9.45	55.47	S	S	133.33	97.31	–1063.09	546.64	S	–98.60
6	79.92	S	S	–66.47	–218.45	318.19	–98.60	S	176.59	–389.83
7	S	S	94.81	–473.39	211.25	229.23	S	S	31.99	284.97
8	S	5.34	2.89	2.24	455.43	S	S	–55.69	172.13	254.48
9	–34.72	–36.50	182.33	–138.97	S	S	–653.67	–56.88	331.37	–119.07
10	222.44	–32.67	196.99	114.01	S	–34.94	–84.96	–30.48	125.08	S
11	–217.23	–23.69	91.64	S	–109.33	–473.66	–326.63	–221.82	S	S
12	9.38	–22.81	S	S	–457.21	–681.50	–103.81	–8.89	S	1160.72
13	–185.18	S	S	–617.38	–516.81	433.79	466.36	S	–81.33	–269.67
14	S	S	68.24	207.06	377.37	360.68	S	S	126.60	–89.37
15	S	85.33	–193.00	115.97	60.08	S	S	47.98	349.89	271.69
16	175.39	–2.19	62.52	214.66	S	S	26.76	–336.46	–38.62	331.99
17	–180.73	–372.82	–54.95	–98.68	S	–54.34	431.17	408.63	134.21	S
18	–3.36	56.09	1.11	S	911.95	–267.13	–1164.52	115.14	S	S
19	–91.22	141.82	S	S	–390.51	–164.62	–236.94	–109.28	S	137.33
20	65.54	S	S	–84.10	369.04	188.11	8.77	S	–196.82	–114.83
21	S	S	298.20	197.43	–101.78	123.69	S	S	66.22	–816.80
22	S	89.99	–178.88	–100.72	–8.96	S	S	–140.05	–201.95	–1.35
23	–8.01	43.08	52.40	–286.14	S	S	618.34	–231.07	–605.78	–256.02
24	213.12	74.51	–75.05	95.22	S	186.14	58.38	–255.59	4.33	S
25	145.46	70.53	–58.67	S	H	–81.52	181.66	–35.27	S	S
26	–23.22	–2.67	S	S	529.95	10.59	516.91	328.69	S	H
27	44.93	S	S	H	553.16	141.59	575.77	S	H	740.58
28	S	S	H	–237.92	–147.63	64.81	S	S	–216.73	–244.95
29	S	H	–391.64	–221.36	–17.53	S	S	H	–411.32	117.03
30	H	–50.81	306.33	43.47	S	S	H	–50.56	–330.06	54.34
31	–86.02	–20.82	–251.94	–354.84	S	H	–222.84	–134.51	574.84	S
Close	**17787.20**	**21008.65**	**24415.84**	**24815.04**	**25383.11**	**34529.45**	**32990.12**	**32908.27**	**38686.32**	**42270.07**
Change	**13.56**	**68.14**	**252.69**	**–1777.87**	**1037.39**	**654.60**	**12.91**	**–1189.89**	**870.40**	**1600.71**

JUNE DAILY POINT CHANGES DOW JONES INDUSTRIALS

Previous Month	2016	2017	2018	2019	2020	2021	2022	2023	2024	2025
Close	**17787.20**	**21008.65**	**24415.84**	**24815.04**	**25383.11**	**34529.45**	**32990.12**	**32908.27**	**38686.32**	**42270.07**
1	2.47	135.53	219.37	S	91.91	45.86	–176.89	153.30	S	S
2	48.89	62.11	S	S	267.63	25.07	435.05	701.19	S	35.41
3	–31.50	S	S	4.74	527.24	–23.34	–348.58	S	–115.29	214.16
4	S	S	178.48	512.40	11.93	179.35	S	S	140.26	–91.90
5	S	–22.25	–13.71	207.39	829.16	S	S	–199.90	96.04	–108.00
6	113.27	–47.81	346.41	181.09	S	S	16.08	10.42	78.84	443.13
7	17.95	37.46	95.02	263.28	S	–126.15	264.36	91.74	–87.18	S
8	66.77	8.84	75.12	S	461.46	–30.42	–269.24	168.59	S	S
9	–19.86	89.44	S	S	–300.14	–152.68	–638.11	43.17	S	–1.11
10	–119.85	S	S	78.74	–282.31	19.10	–880.00	S	69.05	105.11
11	S	S	5.78	–14.17	–1861.82	13.36	S	S	–120.62	–1.10
12	S	–36.30	–1.58	–43.68	477.37	S	S	189.55	–35.21	101.85
13	–132.86	92.80	–119.53	101.94	S	S	–876.05	145.79	–65.11	–769.83
14	–57.66	46.09	–25.89	–17.16	S	–85.85	–151.91	–232.79	–57.94	S
15	–34.65	–14.66	–84.83	S	157.62	–94.42	303.70	428.73	S	S
16	92.93	24.38	S	S	526.82	–265.66	–741.46	–108.94	S	317.30
17	–57.94	S	S	22.92	–170.37	–210.22	–38.29	S	188.94	–299.29
18	S	S	–103.01	353.01	–39.51	–533.37	S	S	56.76	–44.14
19	S	144.71	–287.26	38.46	–208.64	S	S	H	H	H
20	129.71	–61.85	–42.41	249.17	S	S	H	–245.25	299.90	35.16
21	24.86	–57.11	–196.10	–34.04	S	586.89	641.47	–102.35	15.57	S
22	–48.90	–12.74	119.19	S	153.50	68.61	–47.12	–4.81	S	S
23	230.24	–2.53	S	S	131.14	–71.34	194.23	–219.28	S	374.96
24	–610.32	S	S	8.41	–710.16	322.58	823.32	S	260.88	507.24
25	S	S	–328.09	–179.32	299.66	237.02	S	S	–299.05	–106.59
26	S	14.79	30.31	–11.40	–730.05	S	S	–12.72	15.64	404.41
27	–260.51	–98.89	–165.52	–10.24	S	S	–62.42	212.03	36.26	432.43
28	269.48	143.95	98.46	73.38	S	–150.57	–491.27	–74.08	–45.20	S
29	284.96	–167.58	55.36	S	580.25	9.02	82.32	269.76	S	S
30	235.31	62.60	S	S	217.08	210.22	–253.88	285.18	S	275.50
Close	**17929.99**	**21349.63**	**24271.41**	**26599.96**	**25812.88**	**34502.51**	**30775.43**	**34407.60**	**39118.86**	**44094.77**
Change	**142.79**	**340.98**	**–144.43**	**1784.92**	**429.77**	**–26.94**	**–2214.69**	**1499.33**	**432.54**	**1824.70**

JULY DAILY POINT CHANGES DOW JONES INDUSTRIALS

Previous Month	2016	2017	2018	2019	2020	2021	2022	2023	2024	2025
Close	**17929.99**	**21349.63**	**24271.41**	**26599.96**	**25812.88**	**34502.51**	**30775.43**	**34407.60**	**39118.86**	**44094.77**
1	19.38	S	S	117.47	–77.91	131.02	321.83	S	50.66	400.17
2	S	S	35.77	69.25	92.39	152.82	S	S	162.33	–10.52
3	S	129.64*	–132.36*	179.32*	H	S	S	10.87*	–23.85*	344.11*
4	H	H	H	H	S	S	H	H	H	H
5	–108.75	–1.10	181.92	–43.88	S	H	–129.44	–129.83	67.87	S
6	78.00	–158.13	99.74	S	459.67	–208.98	69.86	–366.38	S	S
7	–22.74	94.30	S	S	–396.85	104.42	346.87	–187.38	S	–422.17
8	250.86	S	S	–115.98	177.10	–259.86	–46.40	S	–31.08	–165.60
9	S	S	320.11	–22.65	–361.19	448.23	S	S	–52.82	217.54
10	S	–5.82	143.07	76.71	369.21	S	S	209.52	429.39	192.34
11	80.19	0.55	–219.21	227.88	S	S	–164.31	317.02	32.39	–279.13
12	120.74	123.07	224.44	243.95	S	126.02	–192.51	86.01	247.15	S
13	24.45	20.95	94.52	S	10.50	–107.39	–208.54	47.71	S	S
14	134.29	84.65	S	S	556.79	44.44	–142.62	113.89	S	88.14
15	10.14	S	S	27.13	227.51	53.79	658.09	S	210.82	–436.36
16	S	S	44.95	–23.53	–135.39	–299.17	S	S	742.76	231.49
17	S	–8.02	55.53	–115.78	–62.76	S	S	76.32	243.60	229.71
18	16.50	–54.99	79.40	3.12	S	S	–215.65	366.58	–533.06	–142.30
19	25.96	66.02	–134.79	–68.77	S	–725.81	754.44	109.28	–377.49	S
20	36.02	–28.97	–6.38	S	8.92	549.95	47.79	163.97	S	S
21	–77.80	–31.71	S	S	159.53	286.01	162.06	2.51	S	–19.12
22	53.62	S	S	17.70	165.44	25.35	–137.61	S	127.91	179.37
23	S	S	–13.83	177.29	–353.51	238.20	S	S	–57.35	507.85
24	S	–66.90	197.65	–79.22	–182.44	S	S	183.55	–504.22	–316.38
25	–77.79	100.26	172.16	–128.99	S	S	90.75	26.83	81.20	208.01
26	–19.31	97.58	112.97	51.47	S	82.76	–228.50	82.05	654.27	S
27	–1.58	85.54	–76.01	S	114.88	–85.79	436.05	–237.40	S	S
28	–15.82	33.76	S	S	–205.49	–127.59	332.04	176.57	S	–64.36
29	–24.11	S	S	28.90	160.29	153.60	315.50	S	–49.41	–204.57
30	S	S	–144.23	–23.33	–225.92	–149.06	S	S	203.40	–171.71
31	S	60.81	108.36	–333.75	114.67	S	S	100.24	99.46	–330.30
Close	**18432.24**	**21891.12**	**25415.19**	**26864.27**	**26428.32**	**34935.47**	**32845.13**	**35559.53**	**40842.79**	**44130.98**
Change	**502.25**	**541.49**	**1143.78**	**264.31**	**615.44**	**432.96**	**2069.70**	**1151.93**	**1723.93**	**36.21**

*Shortened trading day

AUGUST DAILY POINT CHANGES DOW JONES INDUSTRIALS

Previous Month	2016	2017	2018	2019	2020	2021	2022	2023	2024	2025
Close	**18432.24**	**21891.12**	**25415.19**	**26864.27**	**26428.32**	**34935.47**	**32845.13**	**35559.53**	**40842.79**	**44130.98**
1	–27.73	72.80	–81.37	–280.85	S	S	–46.73	71.15	–494.82	–542.40
2	–90.74	52.32	–7.66	–98.41	S	–97.31	–402.23	–348.16	–610.71	S
3	41.23	9.86	136.42	S	236.08	278.24	416.33	–66.63	S	S
4	–2.95	66.71	S	S	164.07	–323.73	–85.68	–150.27	S	585.06
5	191.48	S	S	–767.27	373.05	271.58	76.65	S	–1033.99	–61.90
6	S	S	39.60	311.78	185.46	144.26	S	S	294.39	81.38
7	S	25.61	126.73	–22.45	46.50	S	S	407.51	–234.21	–224.48
8	–14.24	–33.08	–45.16	371.12	S	S	29.07	–158.64	683.04	206.97
9	3.76	–36.64	–74.52	–90.75	S	–106.66	–58.13	–191.13	51.05	S
10	–37.39	–204.69	–196.09	S	357.96	162.82	535.10	52.79	S	S
11	117.86	14.31	S	S	–104.53	220.30	27.16	105.25	S	–200.52
12	–37.05	S	S	–380.07	289.93	14.88	424.38	S	–140.53	483.52
13	S	S	–125.44	372.54	–80.12	15.53	S	S	408.63	463.66
14	S	135.39	112.22	–800.49	34.30	S	S	26.23	242.75	–11.01
15	59.58	5.28	–137.51	99.97	S	S	151.39	–361.24	554.67	34.86
16	–84.03	25.88	396.32	306.62	S	110.02	239.57	–180.65	96.70	S
17	21.92	–274.14	110.59	S	–86.11	–282.12	–171.69	–290.91	S	S
18	23.76	–76.22	S	S	–66.84	–382.59	18.72	25.83	S	–34.30
19	–45.13	S	S	249.78	–85.19	–66.57	–292.30	S	236.77	10.45
20	S	S	89.37	–173.35	46.85	225.96	S	S	–61.56	16.04
21	S	29.24	63.60	240.29	190.60	S	S	–36.97	55.52	–152.81
22	–23.15	196.14	–88.69	49.51	S	S	–643.13	–174.86	–177.71	846.24
23	17.88	–87.80	–76.62	–623.34	S	215.63	–154.02	184.15	462.30	S
24	–65.82	–28.69	133.37	S	378.13	30.55	59.64	–373.56	S	S
25	–33.07	30.27	S	S	–60.02	39.24	322.55	247.48	S	–349.27
26	–53.01	S	S	269.93	83.48	–192.38	–1008.38	S	65.44	135.60
27	S	S	259.29	–120.93	160.35	242.68	S	S	9.98	147.16
28	S	–5.27	14.38	258.20	161.60	S	S	213.08	–159.08	71.67
29	107.59	56.97	60.55	326.15	S	S	–184.41	292.69	243.63	–92.02
30	–48.69	27.06	–137.65	41.03	S	–55.96	–308.12	37.57	228.03	S
31	–53.42	55.67	–22.10	S	–223.82	–39.11	–280.44	–168.33	S	S
Close	**18400.88**	**21948.10**	**25964.82**	**26403.28**	**28430.05**	**35360.73**	**31510.43**	**34721.91**	**41563.08**	**45544.88**
Change	**–31.36**	**56.98**	**549.63**	**–460.99**	**2001.73**	**425.26**	**–1334.70**	**–837.62**	**720.29**	**1413.90**

SEPTEMBER DAILY POINT CHANGES DOW JONES INDUSTRIALS

Previous Month	2016	2017	2018	2019	2020	2021	2022	2023	2024	2025
Close	**18400.88**	**21948.10**	**25964.82**	**26403.28**	**28430.05**	**35360.73**	**31510.43**	**34721.91**	**41563.08**	**45544.88**
1	18.42	39.46	S	S	215.61	– 48.20	145.99	115.80	S	H
2	72.66	S	S	H	454.84	131.29	– 337.98	S	H	– 249.07
3	S	S	H	– 285.26	– 807.77	– 74.73	S	S	– 626.15	– 24.58
4	S	H	– 12.34	237.45	– 159.42	S	S	H	38.04	350.06
5	H	– 234.25	22.51	372.68	S	S	H	– 195.74	– 219.22	– 220.43
6	46.16	54.33	20.88	69.31	S	H	– 173.14	– 198.78	– 410.34	S
7	– 11.98	– 22.86	– 79.33	S	H	– 269.09	435.98	57.54	S	S
8	– 46.23	13.01	S	S	– 632.42	– 68.93	193.24	75.86	S	114.09
9	– 394.46	S	S	38.05	439.58	– 151.69	377.19	S	484.18	196.39
10	S	S	– 59.47	73.92	– 405.89	– 271.66	S	S	– 92.63	– 220.42
11	S	259.58	113.99	227.61	131.06	S	S	87.13	124.75	617.08
12	239.62	61.49	27.86	45.41	S	S	229.63	– 17.73	235.06	– 273.78
13	– 258.32	39.32	147.07	37.07	S	261.91	–1276.37	– 70.46	297.01	S
14	– 31.98	45.30	8.68	S	327.69	– 312.06	30.12	331.58	S	S
15	177.71	64.86	S	S	2.27	256.82	– 173.27	– 288.87	S	49.23
16	– 88.68	S	S	– 142.70	36.78	– 63.07	– 139.40	S	228.30	– 125.55
17	S	S	– 92.55	33.98	– 130.40	– 166.44	S	S	– 15.90	260.42
18	S	63.01	184.84	36.28	– 244.56	S	S	6.06	– 103.08	124.10
19	– 3.63	39.45	158.80	– 52.29	S	S	197.26	– 106.57	522.09	172.85
20	9.79	41.79	251.22	– 159.72	S	– 614.41	– 313.45	– 76.85	38.17	S
21	163.74	– 53.36	86.52	S	– 509.72	– 50.63	– 522.45	– 370.46	S	S
22	98.76	– 9.64	S	S	140.48	338.48	– 107.10	– 106.58	S	66.27
23	– 131.01	S	S	14.92	– 525.05	506.50	– 486.27	S	61.29	– 88.76
24	S	S	– 181.45	– 142.22	52.31	33.18	S	S	83.57	– 171.50
25	S	– 53.50	– 69.84	162.94	358.52	S	S	43.04	– 293.47	– 173.96
26	– 166.62	– 11.77	– 106.93	– 79.59	S	S	– 329.60	– 388.00	260.36	299.97
27	133.47	56.39	54.65	– 70.87	S	71.37	– 125.82	– 68.61	137.89	S
28	110.94	40.49	18.38	S	410.10	– 569.38	548.75	116.07	S	S
29	– 195.79	23.89	S	S	– 131.40	90.73	– 458.13	– 158.84	S	68.78
30	164.70	S	S	96.58	329.04	– 546.80	– 500.10	S	17.15	81.82
Close	**18308.15**	**22405.09**	**26458.31**	**26916.83**	**27781.70**	**33843.92**	**28725.51**	**33507.50**	**42330.15**	**46397.89**
Change	**– 92.73**	**456.99**	**493.49**	**513.55**	**– 648.35**	**– 1516.81**	**– 2784.92**	**– 1214.41**	**767.07**	**853.01**

OCTOBER DAILY POINT CHANGES DOW JONES INDUSTRIALS

Previous Month	2016	2017	2018	2019	2020	2021	2022	2023	2024	2025
Close	**18308.15**	**22405.09**	**26458.31**	**26916.83**	**27781.70**	**33843.92**	**28725.51**	**33507.50**	**42330.15**	**46397.89**
1	S	S	192.90	– 343.79	35.20	482.54	S	S	– 173.18	43.21
2	S	152.51	122.73	– 494.42	– 134.09	S	S	– 74.15	39.55	78.62
3	– 54.30	84.07	54.45	122.42	S	S	765.38	– 430.97	– 184.93	238.56
4	– 85.40	19.97	– 200.91	372.68	S	– 323.54	825.43	127.17	341.16	S
5	112.58	113.75	– 180.43	S	465.83	311.75	– 42.45	– 9.98	S	S
6	– 12.53	– 1.72	S	S	– 375.88	102.32	– 346.93	288.01	S	– 63.31
7	– 28.01	S	S	– 95.70	530.70	337.95	– 630.15	S	– 398.51	– 91.99
8	S	S	39.73	– 313.98	122.05	– 8.69	S	S	126.13	– 1.20
9	S	– 12.60	– 56.21	181.97	161.39	S	S	197.07	431.63	– 243.36
10	88.55	69.61	– 831.83	150.66	S	S	– 93.91	134.65	– 57.88	– 878.82
11	– 200.38	42.21	– 545.91	319.92	S	– 250.19	36.31	65.57	409.74	S
12	15.54	– 31.88	287.16	S	250.62	– 117.72	– 28.34	– 173.73	S	S
13	– 45.26	30.71	S	S	– 157.71	– 0.53	827.87	39.15	S	587.98
14	39.44	S	S	– 29.23	– 165.81	534.75	– 403.89	S	201.36	202.88
15	S	S	– 89.44	237.44	– 19.80	382.20	S	S	– 324.80	– 17.15
16	S	85.24	547.87	– 22.82	112.11	S	S	314.25	337.28	– 301.07
17	– 51.98	40.48	– 91.74	23.90	S	S	550.99	13.11	161.35	238.37
18	75.54	160.16	– 327.23	– 255.68	S	– 36.15	337.98	– 332.57	36.86	S
19	40.68	5.44	64.89	S	– 410.89	198.70	– 99.99	– 250.91	S	S
20	– 40.27	165.59	S	S	113.37	152.03	– 90.22	– 286.89	S	515.97
21	– 16.64	S	S	57.44	– 97.97	– 6.26	748.97	S	– 344.31	218.16
22	S	S	– 126.93	– 39.54	152.84	73.94	S	S	– 6.71	– 334.33
23	S	– 54.67	– 125.98	45.85	– 28.09	S	S	– 190.87	– 409.94	144.20
24	77.32	167.80	– 608.01	– 28.42	S	S	417.06	204.97	– 140.59	472.51
25	– 53.76	– 112.30	401.13	152.53	S	64.13	337.12	– 105.45	– 259.96	S
26	30.06	71.40	– 296.24	S	– 650.19	15.73	2.37	– 251.63	S	S
27	– 29.65	33.33	S	S	– 222.19	– 266.19	194.17	– 366.71	S	337.47
28	– 8.49	S	S	132.66	– 943.24	239.79	828.52	S	273.17	161.78
29	S	S	– 245.39	– 19.26	139.16	89.08	S	S	– 154.52	– 74.37
30	S	– 85.45	431.72	115.23	– 157.51	S	S	511.37	– 91.51	– 109.88
31	– 18.77	28.50	241.12	– 140.46	S	S	– 128.85	123.91	– 378.08	40.75
Close	**18142.42**	**23377.24**	**25115.76**	**27046.23**	**26501.60**	**35819.56**	**32732.95**	**33052.87**	**41763.46**	**47562.87**
Change	**– 165.73**	**972.15**	**– 1342.55**	**129.40**	**– 1280.10**	**1975.64**	**4007.44**	**– 454.63**	**– 566.69**	**1164.98**

NOVEMBER DAILY POINT CHANGES DOW JONES INDUSTRIALS

Previous Month	2016	2017	2018	2019	2020	2021	2022	2023	2024	2025
Close	**18142.42**	**23377.24**	**25115.76**	**27046.23**	**26501.60**	**35819.56**	**32732.95**	**33052.87**	**41763.46**	**47562.87**
1	-105.32	57.77	264.98	301.13	S	94.28	-79.75	221.71	288.73	S
2	-77.46	81.25	-109.91	S	423.45	138.79	-505.44	564.50	S	S
3	-28.97	22.93	S	S	554.98	104.95	-146.51	222.24	S	-226.19
4	-42.39	S	S	114.75	367.63	-33.35	401.97	S	-257.59	-251.44
5	S	S	190.87	30.52	542.52	203.72	S	S	427.28	225.76
6	S	9.23	173.31	-0.07	-66.78	S	S	34.54	1508.05	-398.70
7	371.32	8.81	545.29	182.24	S	S	423.78	56.74	-0.59	74.80
8	73.14	6.13	10.92	6.44	S	104.27	333.83	-40.33	259.65	S
9	256.95	-101.42	-201.92	S	834.57	-112.24	-646.89	-220.33	S	S
10	218.19	-39.73	S	S	262.95	-240.04	1201.43	391.16	S	381.53
11	39.78	S	S	10.25	-23.29	-158.71	32.49	S	304.14	559.33
12	S	S	-602.12	0.00	-317.46	179.08	S	S	-382.15	326.86
13	S	17.49	-100.69	92.10	399.64	S	S	54.77	47.21	-797.60
14	21.03	-30.23	-205.99	-1.63	S	S	-211.16	489.83	-207.33	-309.74
15	54.37	-138.19	208.77	222.93	S	-12.86	56.22	163.51	-305.87	S
16	-54.92	187.08	123.95	S	470.63	54.77	-39.09	-45.74	S	S
17	35.68	-100.12	S	S	-167.09	-211.17	-7.51	1.81	S	-557.24
18	-35.89	S	S	31.33	-344.93	-60.10	199.37	S	-55.39	-498.50
19	S	S	-395.78	-102.20	44.81	-268.97	S	S	-120.66	47.03
20	S	72.09	-551.80	-112.93	-219.75	S	S	203.76	139.53	-386.51
21	88.76	160.50	-0.95	-54.80	S	S	-45.41	-62.75	461.88	493.15
22	67.18	-64.65	H	109.33	S	17.27	397.82	184.74	426.16	S
23	59.31	H	-178.74*	S	327.79	194.55	95.96	H	S	S
24	H	31.81*	S	S	454.97	-9.42	H	117.12*	S	202.86
25	68.96*	S	S	190.85	-173.77	H	152.97*	S	440.06	664.18
26	S	S	354.29	55.21	H	-905.04*	S	S	123.74	314.67
27	S	22.79	108.49	42.32	37.90*	S	S	-56.68	-138.28	H
28	-54.24	255.93	617.70	H	S	S	-497.57	83.51	H	289.30*
29	23.70	103.97	-27.59	-112.59*	S	236.60	3.07	13.44	188.62*	S
30	1.98	331.67	199.62	S	-271.73	-652.22	737.24	520.47	S	S
Close	**19123.58**	**24272.35**	**25538.46**	**28051.41**	**29638.64**	**34483.72**	**34589.77**	**35950.89**	**44910.65**	**47716.42**
Change	**981.16**	**895.11**	**422.70**	**1005.18**	**3137.04**	**-1335.84**	**1856.82**	**2898.02**	**3147.19**	**153.55**

**Shortened trading day*

DECEMBER DAILY POINT CHANGES DOW JONES INDUSTRIALS

Previous Month	2016	2017	2018	2019	2020	2021	2022	2023	2024	2025
Close	**19123.58**	**24272.35**	**25538.46**	**28051.41**	**29638.64**	**34483.72**	**34589.77**	**35950.89**	**44910.65**	**47716.42**
1	68.35	-40.76	S	S	185.28	-461.68	-194.76	294.61	S	-427.09
2	-21.51	S	S	-268.37	59.87	617.75	34.87	S	-128.65	185.13
3	S	S	287.97	-280.23	85.73	-59.71	S	S	-76.47	408.44
4	S	58.46	-799.36	146.97	248.74	S	S	-41.06	308.51	-31.96
5	45.82	-109.41	H**	28.01	S	S	-482.78	-79.88	-248.33	104.05
6	35.54	-39.73	-79.40	337.27	S	646.95	-350.76	-70.13	-123.19	S
7	297.84	70.57	-558.72	S	-148.47	492.40	1.58	62.95	S	S
8	65.19	117.68	S	S	104.09	35.32	183.56	130.49	S	-215.67
9	142.04	S	S	-105.46	-105.07	-0.06	-305.02	S	-240.59	-179.03
10	S	S	34.31	-27.88	-69.55	216.30	S	S	-154.10	497.46
11	S	56.87	-53.02	29.58	47.11	S	S	157.06	-99.27	646.26
12	39.58	118.77	157.03	220.75	S	S	528.58	173.01	-234.44	-245.96
13	114.78	80.63	70.11	3.33	S	-320.04	103.60	512.30	-86.06	S
14	-118.68	-76.77	-496.87	S	-184.82	-106.77	-142.29	158.11	S	S
15	59.71	143.08	S	S	337.76	383.25	-764.13	56.81	S	-41.49
16	-8.83	S	S	100.51	-44.77	-29.79	-281.76	S	-110.58	-302.30
17	S	S	-507.53	31.27	148.83	-532.20	S	S	-267.58	-228.29
18	S	140.46	82.66	-27.88	-124.32	S	S	0.86	-1123.03	65.88
19	39.65	-37.45	-351.98	137.68	S	S	-162.92	251.90	15.37	183.04
20	91.56	-28.10	-464.06	78.13	S	-433.28	92.20	-475.92	498.02	S
21	-32.66	55.64	-414.23	S	37.40	560.54	526.74	322.35	S	S
22	-23.08	-28.23	S	S	-200.94	261.19	-348.99	-18.38	S	227.79
23	14.93	S	S	96.44	114.32	196.67	176.44	S	66.69	79.73
24	S	S	-653.17*	-36.08*	70.04*	H	S	S	390.08*	288.75*
25	S	H	H	H	H	S	S	H	H	H
26	H	-7.85	1086.25	105.94	S	S	H	159.36	28.77	-20.19
27	11.23	28.09	260.37	23.87	S	351.82	37.63	111.19	-333.59	S
28	-111.36	63.21	-76.42	S	204.10	95.83	-365.85	53.58	S	S
29	-13.90	-118.29	S	S	-68.30	90.42	345.09	-20.56	S	-249.04
30	-57.18	S	S	-183.12	73.89	-90.55	-73.55	S	-418.48	-94.87
31	S	S	265.06	76.30	196.92	-59.78	S	S	-29.51	-303.77
Close	**19762.60**	**24719.22**	**23327.46**	**28538.44**	**30606.48**	**36338.30**	**33147.25**	**37689.54**	**42544.22**	**48063.29**
Change	**639.02**	**446.87**	**-2211.00**	**487.03**	**967.84**	**1854.58**	**-1442.52**	**1738.65**	**-2366.43**	**346.87**

** Shortened trading day, ** President H.W. Bush Funeral*

A TYPICAL DAY IN THE MARKET

Half-hourly data became available for the Dow Jones Industrial Average starting in January 1987. The NYSE switched 10:00 a.m. openings to 9:30 a.m. in October 1985. Below is the comparison between half-hourly performance 1987–April 10, 2026, and hourly November 1963 to June 1985. Stronger closings in a more bullish climate are evident. Morning and afternoon weaknesses appear an hour earlier.

MARKET % PERFORMANCE EACH HALF-HOUR OF THE DAY (January 1987–April 10, 2026)

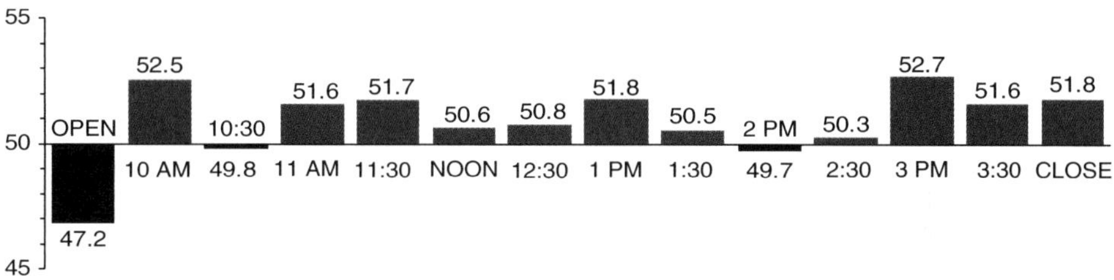

Based on the number of times the Dow Jones Industrial Average increased over the previous half-hour

MARKET % PERFORMANCE EACH HOUR OF THE DAY (November 1963–June 1985)

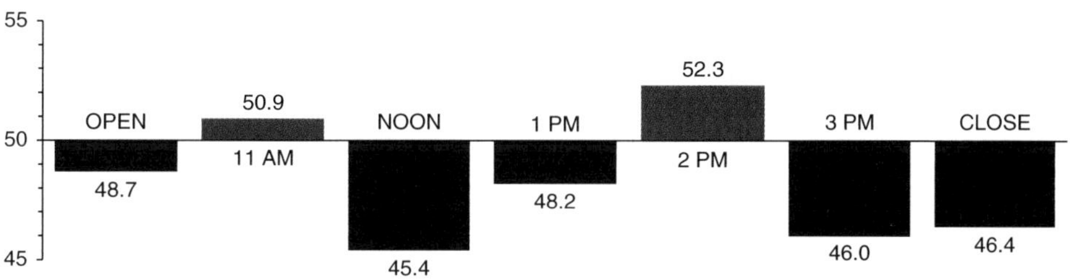

Based on the number of times the Dow Jones Industrial Average increased over the previous hour

On the next page, half-hourly movements since January 1987 are separated by day of the week. From 1953 to 1989 Monday was the worst day of the week, especially during long bear markets, but times changed. Monday was the best day of the week and on the plus side eleven years in a row from 1990 to 2000. Since the 2000 top Monday has been the worst day.

During the last 16 years (2010–April 10, 2026), Monday is the second weakest day of the week and Tuesday is the best. On all days stocks do tend to firm up near the close with weakness early morning and from around 1:30 to 2:30 frequently.

THROUGH THE WEEK ON A HALF-HOURLY BASIS

From the chart showing the percentage of times the Dow Jones Industrial Average rose over the preceding half-hour (January 1987 to April 10, 2026*), the typical week unfolds.

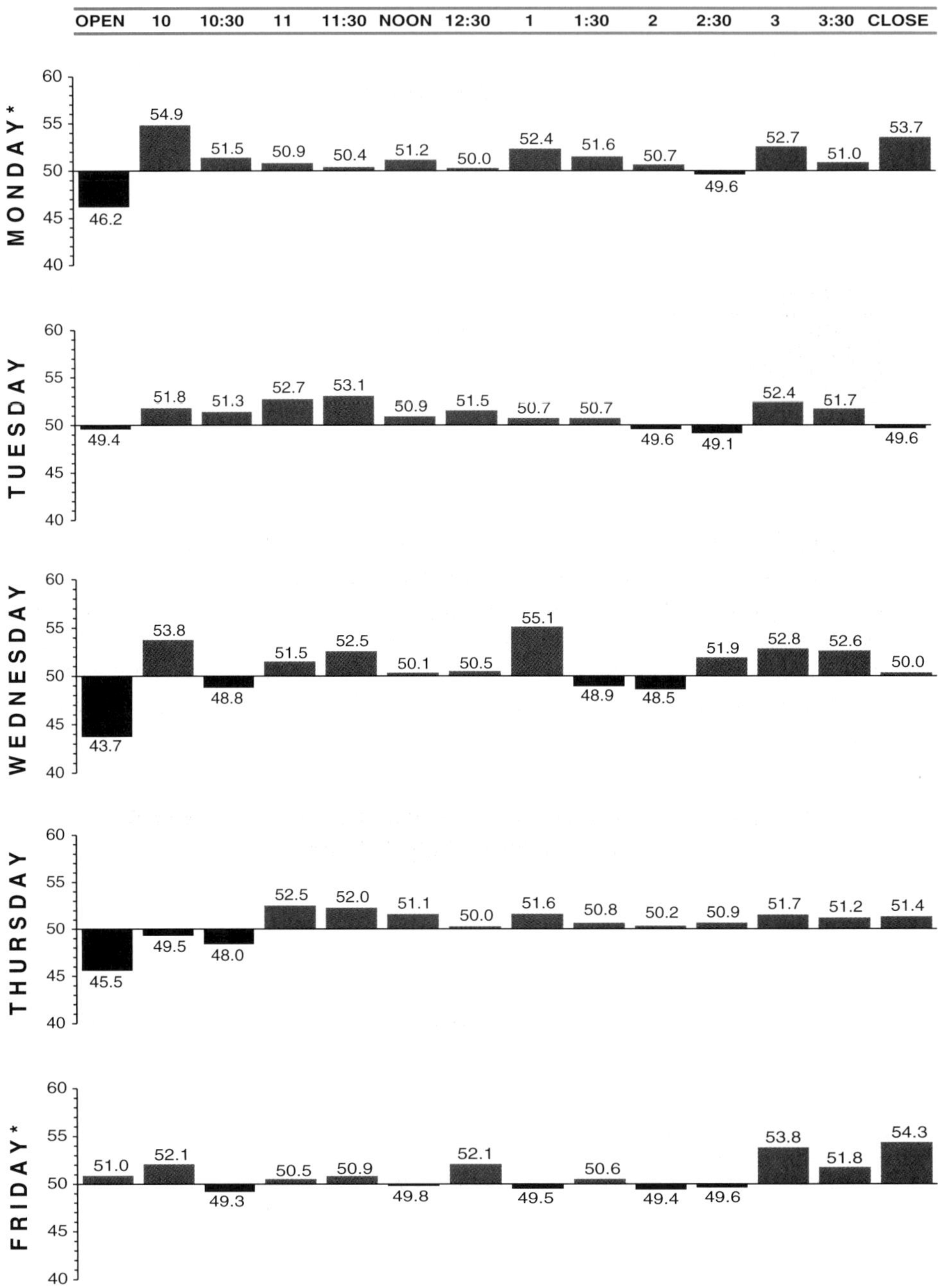

** Monday denotes first trading day of week, Friday denotes last trading day of week*

TUESDAY & WEDNESDAY, BEST DAYS OF WEEK

Between 1952 and 1989, Monday was the worst trading day of the week. The first trading day of the week (including Tuesday when Monday is a holiday) rose only 44.3% of the time, while the other trading days closed higher 54.8% of the time. (NYSE Saturday trading was discontinued in June 1952.)

MARKET % PERFORMANCE EACH DAY OF THE WEEK
(June 1952–December 1989)

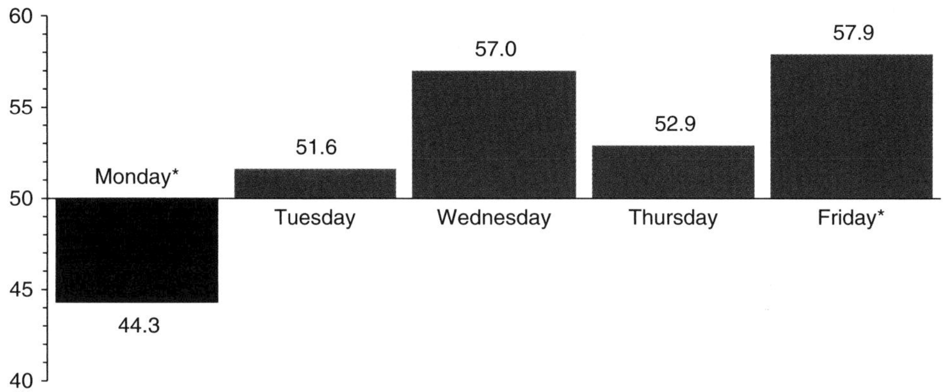

A dramatic reversal occurred in 1990—Monday became one of the most powerful days of the week. However, during the last 25 and a half years Tuesday has produced the greatest average gain ("Turn around Tuesdays") and Wednesday has the greatest frequency of advances. Weakness on Friday and/or Monday is common during uncertain market times. Monday was the worst day during the 2007–2009 bear and only Tuesday and Friday were net gainers. See pages 78 and 145.

MARKET % PERFORMANCE EACH DAY OF THE WEEK
(January 1990–May 1, 2026)

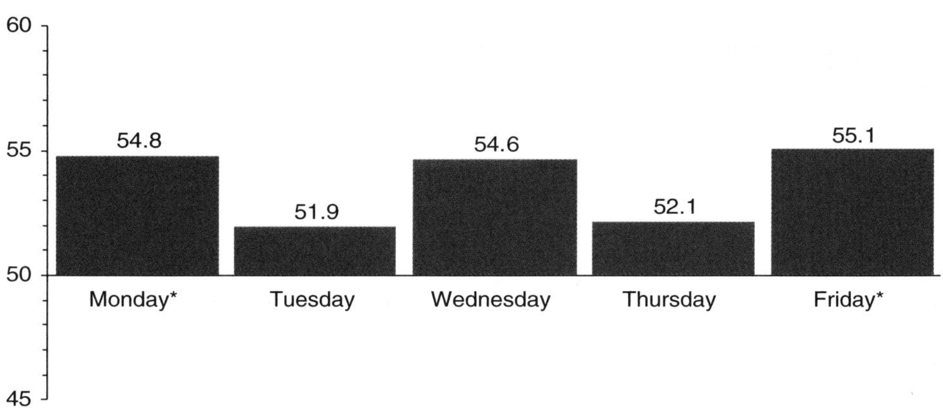

Charts based on the number of times S&P 500 closed higher than previous day
** Monday denotes first trading day of week, Friday denotes last trading day of week*

NASDAQ STRONGEST LAST THREE DAYS OF WEEK

Despite 20 years less data, daily trading patterns on NASDAQ through 1989 appear to be fairly similar to the S&P on page 143 except for more bullishness on Thursdays. During the mostly flat markets of the 1970s and early 1980s, it would appear that apprehensive investors decided to throw in the towel over weekends and sell on Mondays and Tuesdays.

NASDAQ % PERFORMANCE EACH DAY OF THE WEEK (1971–1989)

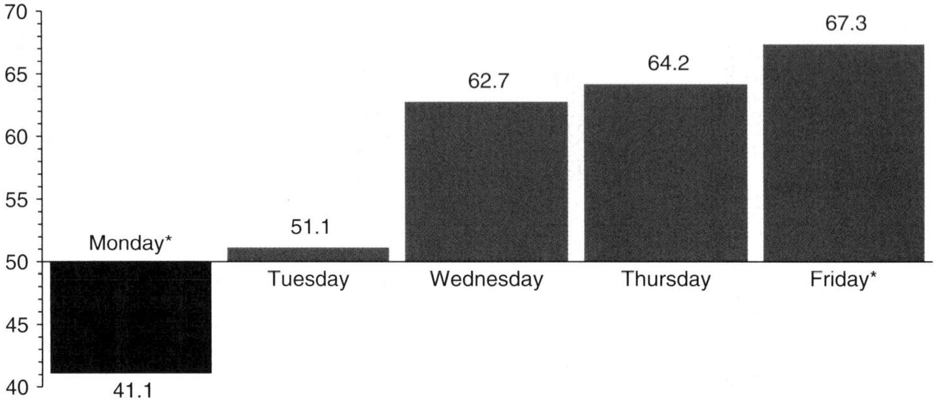

Notice the modest difference in the daily trading pattern between NASDAQ and S&P from January 1, 1990, to recent times. Technology has an ever-increasing role in the economy which is reflected in strength across NASDAQ's weekly pattern. Notice the similarities to the S&P since 2001 on pages 145 and 146, Monday and/or Friday weakness, mid-week strength during bear markets.

NASDAQ % PERFORMANCE EACH DAY OF THE WEEK (1990–May 1, 2026)

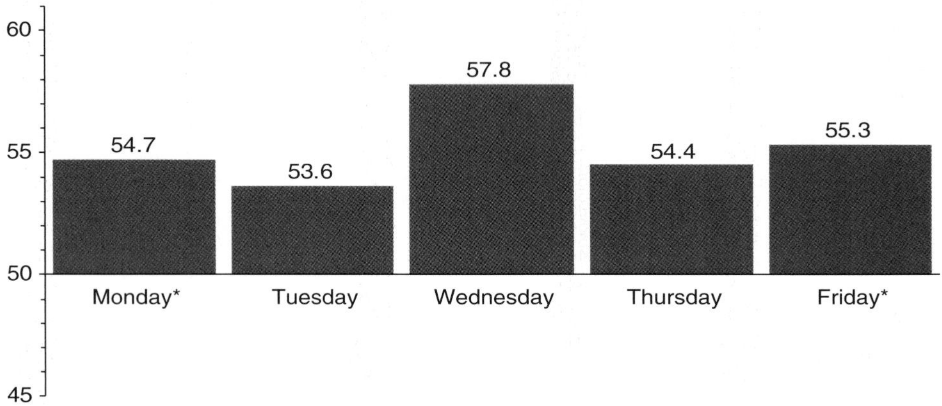

Based on NASDAQ composite, prior to Feb. 5, 1971 based on National Quotation Bureau indices
** Monday denotes first trading day of week, Friday denotes last trading day of week*

S&P DAILY PERFORMANCE EACH YEAR SINCE 1952

To determine if market trend alters performance of different days of the week, we separated 24 bear years—1953, '56, '57, '60, '62, '66, '69, '70, '73, '74, '77, '78, '81, '84, '87, '90, '94, 2000, '01, '02, '08, '11, '15, '22, and '24 from 50 bull market years. While Tuesdays and Thursdays did not vary much between bull and bear years, Mondays and Fridays were sharply affected. There was a swing of 11.1 percentage points in Monday's and 9.8 in Friday's performance.

PERCENTAGE OF TIMES MARKET CLOSED HIGHER THAN PREVIOUS DAY
(JUNE 1952–MAY 1, 2026)

	Monday*	Tuesday	Wednesday	Thursday	Friday**
1952	48.4%	55.6%	58.1%	51.9%	66.7%
1953	32.7	50.0	54.9	57.5	56.6
1954	50.0	57.5	63.5	59.2	73.1
1955	50.0	45.7	63.5	60.0	78.9
1956	36.5	39.6	46.9	50.0	59.6
1957	25.0	54.0	66.7	48.9	44.2
1958	59.6	52.0	59.6	68.1	72.6
1959	42.3	53.1	55.8	48.9	69.8
1960	34.6	50.0	44.2	54.0	59.6
1961	52.9	54.4	64.7	56.0	67.3
1962	28.3	52.1	54.0	51.0	50.0
1963	46.2	63.3	51.0	57.5	69.2
1964	40.4	48.0	61.5	58.7	77.4
1965	44.2	57.5	55.8	51.0	71.2
1966	36.5	47.8	53.9	42.0	57.7
1967	38.5	50.0	60.8	64.0	69.2
1968†	49.1	57.5	64.3	42.6	54.9
1969	30.8	45.8	50.0	67.4	50.0
1970	38.5	46.0	63.5	48.9	52.8
1971	44.2	64.6	57.7	55.1	51.9
1972	38.5	60.9	57.7	51.0	67.3
1973	32.1	51.1	52.9	44.9	44.2
1974	32.7	57.1	51.0	36.7	30.8
1975	53.9	38.8	61.5	56.3	55.8
1976	55.8	55.3	55.8	40.8	58.5
1977	40.4	40.4	46.2	53.1	53.9
1978	51.9	43.5	59.6	54.0	48.1
1979	54.7	53.2	58.8	66.0	44.2
1980	55.8	54.2	71.7	35.4	59.6
1981	44.2	38.8	55.8	53.2	47.2
1982	46.2	39.6	44.2	44.9	50.0
1983	55.8	46.8	61.5	52.0	55.8
1984	39.6	63.8	31.4	46.0	44.2
1985	44.2	61.2	54.9	56.3	53.9
1986	51.9	44.9	67.3	58.3	55.8
1987	51.9	57.1	63.5	61.7	49.1
1988	51.9	61.7	51.9	48.0	59.6
1989	51.9	47.8	69.2	58.0	69.2
1990	67.9	53.2	52.9	40.0	51.9
1991	44.2	46.9	52.9	49.0	51.9
1992	51.9	49.0	53.9	56.3	45.3
1993	65.4	41.7	55.8	44.9	48.1
1994	55.8	46.8	52.9	48.0	59.6
1995	63.5	56.5	63.5	62.0	63.5
1996	54.7	44.9	51.0	57.1	63.5
1997	67.3	67.4	42.3	41.7	57.7
1998	57.7	62.5	57.7	38.3	60.4
1999	46.2	29.8	67.3	53.1	57.7
2000	51.9	43.5	40.4	56.0	46.2
2001	45.3	51.1	44.0	59.2	43.1
2002	40.4	37.5	56.9	38.8	48.1
2003	59.6	62.5	42.3	58.3	50.0
2004	51.9	61.7	59.6	52.1	52.8
2005	59.6	47.8	59.6	56.0	55.8
2006	55.8	55.6	67.3	52.0	48.1
2007	47.2	50.0	64.0	50.0	61.5
2008	42.3	50.0	41.5	60.4	55.8
2009	53.9	50.0	57.7	63.8	52.8
2010	61.5	57.5	55.8	53.1	57.7
2011	48.1	56.5	55.8	56.0	57.7
2012	52.8	48.9	50.0	58.0	53.9
2013	51.9	60.4	54.9	59.2	65.4
2014	53.9	56.3	57.7	56.3	61.5
2015	51.9	43.8	44.2	53.2	43.4
2016	50.0	58.7	55.8	50.0	46.2
2017	55.8	55.6	61.5	50.0	61.5
2018	52.8	60.9	50.0	46.0	53.9
2019	50.0	54.2	60.8	65.3	67.3
2020	63.5	54.2	61.5	52.1	54.7
2021	51.9	44.7	61.5	65.3	59.6
2022	38.5	48.9	46.2	38.0	44.2
2023	61.5	54.6	44.2	52.0	65.4
2024	58.5	62.5	56.0	44.9	61.5
2025	65.4	47.9	67.3	52.2	53.9
2026‡	76.5	46.7	52.9	37.5	55.6
Average	**49.1%**	**51.8%**	**55.8%**	**52.7%**	**56.5%**
50 Bull Years	**52.7%**	**53.3%**	**58.1%**	**53.6%**	**59.7%**
24 Bear Years	**41.6%**	**48.7%**	**51.2%**	**50.8%**	**49.9%**

Based on S&P 500

† Most Wednesdays closed last 7 months of 1968 ‡ Through 5/1/2026 only, not included in averages
**Monday denotes first trading day of week, Friday denotes last trading day of week.*

NASDAQ DAILY PERFORMANCE EACH YEAR SINCE 1971

After dropping a hefty 77.9% from its 2000 high (versus –37.8% on the Dow and –49.1% on the S&P 500), NASDAQ tech stocks still lead. From January 1, 1971, through May 1, 2026, NASDAQ moved up an impressive 27986%. The Dow (up 5800%) and the S&P (up 7746%) gained less than a quarter and third as much, respectively.

Monday's performance on NASDAQ was lackluster during the three-year bear market of 2000–2002. As NASDAQ rebounded (up 50% in 2003), strength returned to Monday during 2003–2006. During the bear market from late 2007 to early 2009, weakness was most consistent on Monday and Friday. At press time, Monday and Wednesday have been best.

PERCENTAGE OF TIMES NASDAQ CLOSED HIGHER THAN PREVIOUS DAY (1971–MAY 1, 2026)

	Monday*	Tuesday	Wednesday	Thursday	Friday**
1971	51.9%	52.1%	59.6%	65.3%	71.2%
1972	30.8	60.9	63.5	57.1	78.9
1973	34.0	48.9	52.9	53.1	48.1
1974	30.8	44.9	52.9	51.0	42.3
1975	44.2	42.9	63.5	64.6	63.5
1976	50.0	63.8	67.3	59.2	58.5
1977	51.9	40.4	53.9	63.3	73.1
1978	48.1	47.8	73.1	72.0	84.6
1979	45.3	53.2	64.7	86.0	82.7
1980	46.2	64.6	84.9	52.1	73.1
1981	42.3	32.7	67.3	76.6	69.8
1982	34.6	47.9	59.6	51.0	63.5
1983	42.3	44.7	67.3	68.0	73.1
1984	22.6	53.2	35.3	52.0	51.9
1985	36.5	59.2	62.8	68.8	66.0
1986	38.5	55.1	65.4	72.9	75.0
1987	42.3	49.0	65.4	68.1	66.0
1988	50.0	55.3	61.5	66.0	63.5
1989	38.5	54.4	71.2	72.0	75.0
1990	54.7	42.6	60.8	46.0	55.8
1991	51.9	59.2	66.7	65.3	51.9
1992	44.2	53.1	59.6	60.4	45.3
1993	55.8	56.3	69.2	57.1	67.3
1994	51.9	46.8	54.9	52.0	55.8
1995	50.0	52.2	63.5	64.0	63.5
1996	50.9	57.1	64.7	61.2	63.5
1997	65.4	59.2	53.9	52.1	55.8
1998	59.6	58.3	65.4	44.7	58.5
1999	61.5	40.4	63.5	57.1	65.4
2000	40.4	41.3	42.3	60.0	57.7
2001	41.5	57.8	52.0	55.1	47.1
2002	44.2	37.5	56.9	46.9	46.2
2003	57.7	60.4	40.4	60.4	46.2
2004	57.7	59.6	53.9	50.0	50.9
2005	61.5	47.8	51.9	48.0	59.6
2006	55.8	51.1	65.4	50.0	44.2
2007	47.2	63.0	66.0	56.0	57.7
2008	34.6	52.1	49.1	54.2	42.3
2009	51.9	54.2	63.5	63.8	50.9
2010	61.5	53.2	61.5	55.1	61.5
2011	50.0	56.5	50.0	64.0	53.9
2012	49.1	53.3	50.0	54.0	51.9
2013	57.7	60.4	52.9	59.2	67.3
2014	57.7	58.3	57.7	52.1	59.6
2015	55.8	39.6	53.9	59.6	49.1
2016	51.9	52.2	55.8	50.0	57.7
2017	59.6	62.2	67.3	50.0	67.3
2018	54.7	69.6	50.0	46.0	50.0
2019	50.0	58.3	62.8	59.2	59.6
2020	69.2	58.3	67.3	60.4	54.7
2021	55.8	44.7	48.1	67.4	63.5
2022	40.4	51.1	44.2	44.0	42.3
2023	67.3	52.3	53.9	54.0	53.9
2024	64.2	64.6	52.0	51.0	59.6
2025	63.5	45.8	71.2	50.0	57.7
2026†	76.5	53.3	76.5	31.3	50.0
Average	**49.6%**	**52.7%**	**59.2%**	**58.2%**	**59.5%**
41 Bull Years	**52.2%**	**54.8%**	**61.4%**	**58.9%**	**62.1%**
14 Bear Years	**41.8%**	**46.7%**	**52.7%**	**55.9%**	**52.0%**

Based on NASDAQ composite; prior to Feb. 5, 1971 based on National Quotation Bureau indices
† Through 5/1/2026 only, not included in averages
**Monday denotes first trading day of week, Friday denotes last trading day of week*

MONTHLY CASH INFLOWS INTO S&P STOCKS

For many years, the last trading day of the month, plus the first four of the following month, were the best market days of the month. This pattern is quite clear in the first chart, showing these five consecutive trading days towering above the other 16 trading days of the average month in the 1953–1981 period. The rationale was that individuals and institutions tended to operate similarly, causing a massive flow of cash into stocks near beginnings of months.

MARKET % PERFORMANCE EACH DAY OF THE MONTH
(January 1953–December 1981)

Based on the number of times the S&P 500 closed higher than previous day.

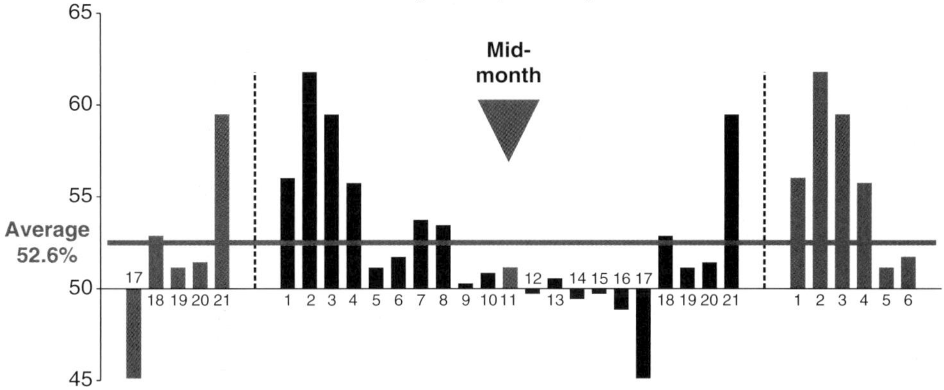

Clearly "front-running" traders took advantage of this phenomenon, drastically altering the previous pattern. The second chart from 1982 onward shows the trading shift caused by these "anticipators" to the end of the month plus the first two. Another development shows the 9th, 10th, 11th, and 12th trading days rising as well. Growth of 401(k) retirement plans, IRAs, and similar plans (participants' salaries are usually paid twice monthly) are likely responsible for this mid-month bulge. First trading days of the month have produced the greatest gains in recent years (see page 90). Last trading day of the month strength has faded substantially over the last 26 years.

MARKET % PERFORMANCE EACH DAY OF THE MONTH
(January 1982–December 2025)

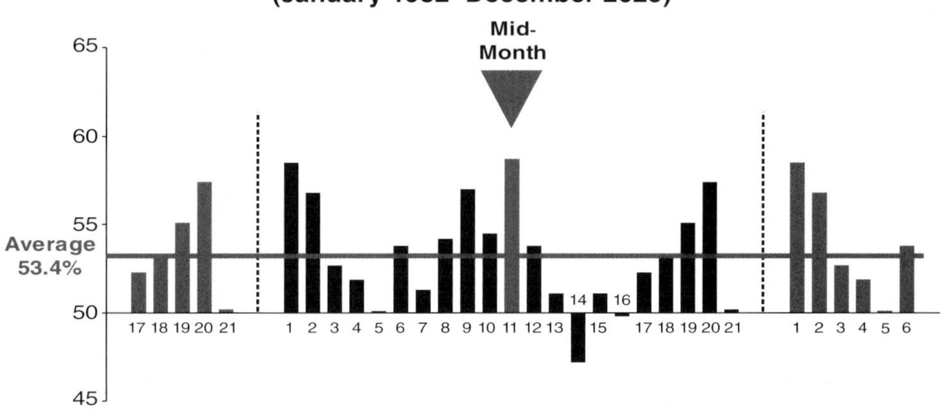

Trading days (excluding Saturdays, Sundays, and holidays).

MONTHLY CASH INFLOWS INTO NASDAQ STOCKS

NASDAQ stocks moved up 58.1% of the time through 1981 compared to 52.6% for the S&P on page 147. Ends and beginnings of the month are fairly similar, specifically the last plus the first four trading days. But notice how investors piled into NASDAQ stocks until midmonth. NASDAQ rose 118.6% from January 1, 1971, to December 31, 1981, compared to 33.0% for the S&P.

NASDAQ % PERFORMANCE EACH DAY OF THE MONTH
(January 1971–December 1981)
Based on the number of times the NASDAQ composite closed higher than previous day.

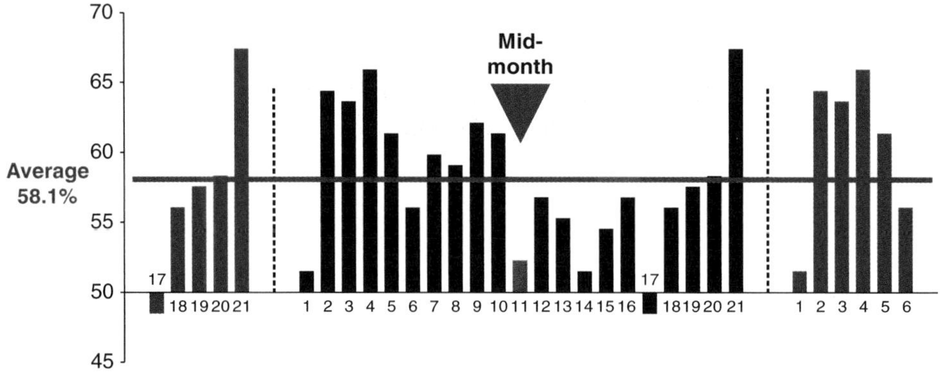

After the air was let out of the tech market in 2000–2002, S&P's 5486% gain over the last 44 years is less unevenly matched with NASDAQ's 11768% gain. Last three, first three, sixth, and middle ninth, and eleventh days rose the most. Where the S&P now has two days of the month that go down more often than up, NASDAQ has one. NASDAQ exhibits the most strength on the first trading day of the month. Over the past 26 years, last days have weakened considerably, down more frequently than not.

NASDAQ % PERFORMANCE EACH DAY OF THE MONTH
(January 1982–December 2025)

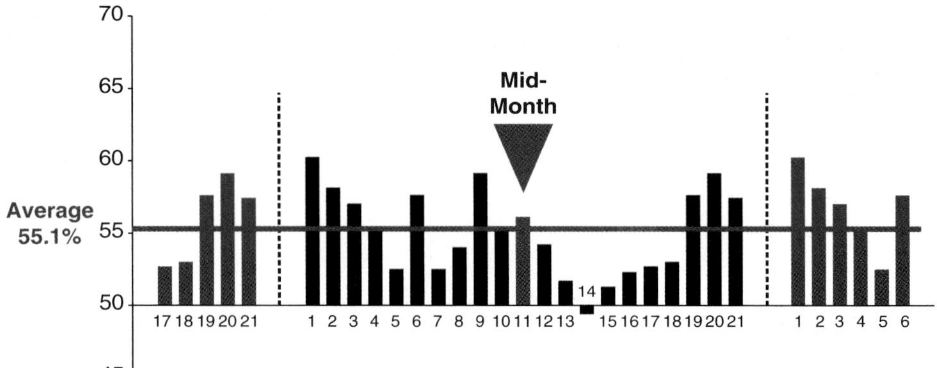

Trading days (excluding Saturdays, Sundays, and holidays).
Based on NASDAQ composite, prior to February 5, 1971, based on National Quotation Bureau indices.

NOVEMBER, DECEMBER, AND JANUARY: YEAR'S BEST THREE-MONTH SPAN

The most important observation to be made from a chart showing the average monthly percent change in market prices since 1950 is that institutions (mutual funds, pension funds, banks, etc.) determine the trading patterns in today's market.

The "investment calendar" reflects the annual, semiannual, and quarterly operations of institutions during January, April, and July. October, besides being the last campaign month before elections, is also the time when most bear markets seem to end, as in 1946, 1957, 1960, 1966, 1974, 1987, 1990, 1998, 2002, and 2022. (August and September tend to combine to make the worst consecutive two-month period.)

S&P 500 MONTHLY % PERFORMANCE (January 1950–April 2026)

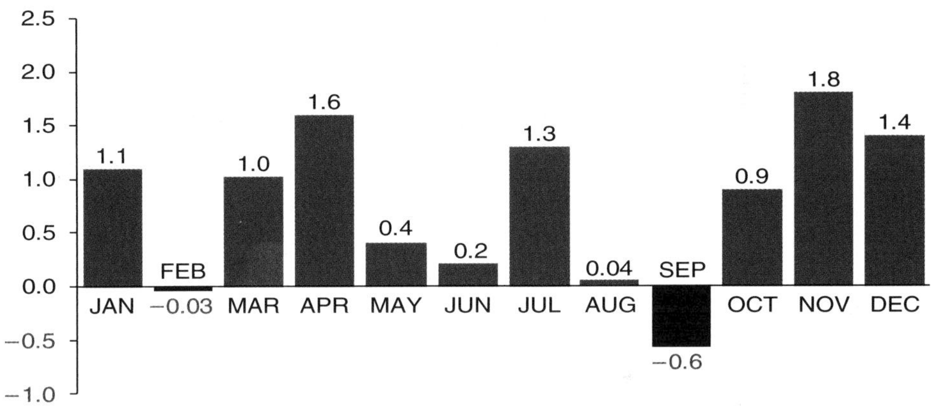

Average month-to-month % change in S&P 500. (Based on monthly closing prices.)

Unusual year-end strength comes from corporate and private pension funds, producing a 4.3% gain on average between November 1 and January 31. In 2007–2008, these three months were all down for the fourth time since 1930; previously in 1931–1932, 1940–1941 and 1969–1970, also bear markets. September's dismal performance makes it the worst month of the year. However, in the last 22 years, it has been up 13 times after being down five in a row 1999–2003, but down seven of the last twelve.

In pre-election years since 1950, January is the best month +4.2% (up 17, down 2). April is second best with an average 3.4% gain. February, March, June, July, August, October, November, and December are also positive on average. September is the worst month of pre-election years, average loss –1.0% (down 13, up 6). May is also a net loser (–0.1%).

See page 52 for monthly performance tables for the S&P 500 and the Dow Jones industrials. See pages 54, 56, 62, and 64 for unique switching strategies.

On page 68, you can see how the first month of the first three quarters far outperforms the second and third months since 1950, and note the improvement in May's and October's performance since 1991.

NOVEMBER THROUGH JUNE: NASDAQ'S EIGHT-MONTH RUN

The two-and-a-half-year plunge of 77.9% in NASDAQ stocks, between March 10, 2000, and October 9, 2002, brought several horrendous monthly losses (the two greatest were November 2000, –22.9% and February 2001, –22.4%), which trimmed average monthly performance over the $55^1/_3$-year period. Ample Octobers in 18 of the last 28 years, including three huge turnarounds in 2001 (+12.8%), 2002 (+13.5%) and 2011 (+11.1%) have put bear-killing October in the number two spot since 1998. January's 2.6% average gain is still awesome, and more than twice S&P's 1.1% January average since 1971.

NASDAQ MONTHLY PERFORMANCE
(January 1971–April 2026)

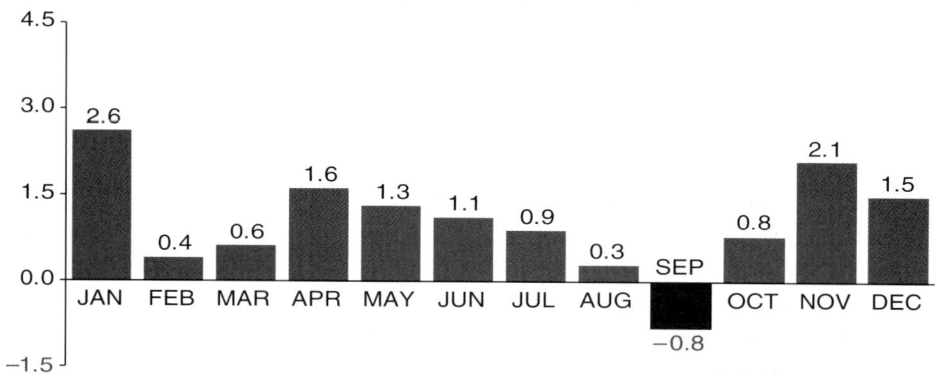

Average month-to-month % change in NASDAQ composite, prior to February 5, 1971, based on National Quotation Bureau indices. (Based on monthly closing prices.)

Bear in mind, when comparing NASDAQ to the S&P on page 149, that there are 23 fewer years of data here. During this $55^1/_3$-year (1971–April 2026) period, NASDAQ gained 27678%, while the S&P and the Dow rose only 7723% and 5819%, respectively. On page 60, you can see a statistical monthly comparison between NASDAQ and the Dow.

Year-end strength is even more pronounced in NASDAQ, producing a 6.2% gain on average between November 1 and January 31—nearly 1.5 times greater than that of the S&P 500 on page 149. September is the worst month of the year for the over-the-counter index as well, posting an average loss of –0.8%. These extremes underscore NASDAQ's higher volatility—and moves of greater magnitude.

In pre-election years since 1971, January is the best month with an average gain of 7.1% (up 12, down 2). December is second best, +4.3% (up 8, down 6). February through August plus October and November are also positive. September is the only negative month in pre-election years, down –1.2% on average (up 7, down 7).

DOW JONES INDUSTRIALS ANNUAL HIGHS, LOWS, & CLOSES SINCE 1901

	HIGH		LOW		YEAR		HIGH		LOW		YEAR
YEAR	DATE	CLOSE	DATE	CLOSE	CLOSE	YEAR	DATE	CLOSE	DATE	CLOSE	CLOSE
1901	6/17	57.33	12/24	45.07	47.29	1933	7/18	108.67	2/27	50.16	99.90
1902	4/24	50.14	12/15	43.64	47.10	1934	2/5	110.74	7/26	85.51	104.04
1903	2/16	49.59	11/9	30.88	35.98	1935	11/19	148.44	3/14	96.71	144.13
1904	12/5	53.65	3/12	34.00	50.99	1936	11/17	184.90	1/6	143.11	179.90
1905	12/29	70.74	1/25	50.37	70.47	1937	3/10	194.40	11/24	113.64	120.85
1906	1/19	75.45	7/13	62.40	69.12	1938	11/12	158.41	3/31	98.95	154.76
1907	1/7	70.60	11/15	38.83	43.04	1939	9/12	155.92	4/8	121.44	150.24
1908	11/13	64.74	2/13	42.94	63.11	1940	1/3	152.80	6/10	111.84	131.13
1909	11/19	73.64	2/23	58.54	72.56	1941	1/10	133.59	12/23	106.34	110.96
1910	1/3	72.04	7/26	53.93	59.60	1942	12/26	119.71	4/28	92.92	119.40
1911	6/19	63.78	9/25	53.43	59.84	1943	7/14	145.82	1/8	119.26	135.89
1912	9/30	68.97	2/10	58.72	64.37	1944	12/16	152.53	2/7	134.22	152.32
1913	1/9	64.88	6/11	52.83	57.71	1945	12/11	195.82	1/24	151.35	192.91
1914	3/20	61.12	7/30	52.32	54.58	1946	5/29	212.50	10/9	163.12	177.20
1915	12/27	99.21	2/24	54.22	99.15	1947	7/24	186.85	5/17	163.21	181.16
1916	11/21	110.15	4/22	84.96	95.00	1948	6/15	193.16	3/16	165.39	177.30
1917	1/3	99.18	12/19	65.95	74.38	1949	12/30	200.52	6/13	161.60	200.13
1918	10/18	89.07	1/15	73.38	82.20	1950	11/24	235.47	1/13	196.81	235.41
1919	11/3	119.62	2/8	79.15	107.23	1951	9/13	276.37	1/3	238.99	269.23
1920	1/3	109.88	12/21	66.75	71.95	1952	12/30	292.00	5/1	256.35	291.90
1921	12/15	81.50	8/24	63.90	81.10	1953	1/5	293.79	9/14	255.49	280.90
1922	10/14	103.43	1/10	78.59	98.73	1954	12/31	404.39	1/11	279.87	404.39
1923	3/20	105.38	10/27	85.76	95.52	1955	12/30	488.40	1/17	388.20	488.40
1924	12/31	120.51	5/20	88.33	120.51	1956	4/6	521.05	1/23	462.35	499.47
1925	11/6	159.39	3/30	115.00	156.66	1957	7/12	520.77	10/22	419.79	435.69
1926	8/14	166.64	3/30	135.20	157.20	1958	12/31	583.65	2/25	436.89	583.65
1927	12/31	202.40	1/25	152.73	202.40	1959	12/31	679.36	2/9	574.46	679.36
1928	12/31	300.00	2/20	191.33	300.00	1960	1/5	685.47	10/25	566.05	615.89
1929	9/3	381.17	11/13	198.69	248.48	1961	12/13	734.91	1/3	610.25	731.14
1930	4/17	294.07	12/16	157.51	164.58	1962	1/3	726.01	6/26	535.76	652.10
1931	2/24	194.36	12/17	73.79	77.90	1963	12/18	767.21	1/2	646.79	762.95
1932	3/8	88.78	7/8	41.22	59.93	1964	11/18	891.71	1/2	766.08	874.13

continued

DOW JONES INDUSTRIALS ANNUAL HIGHS, LOWS, & CLOSES SINCE 1901 (continued)

	HIGH		LOW		YEAR		HIGH		LOW		YEAR
YEAR	DATE	CLOSE	DATE	CLOSE	CLOSE	YEAR	DATE	CLOSE	DATE	CLOSE	CLOSE
1965	12/31	969.26	6/28	840.59	969.26	1996	12/27	6560.91	1/10	5032.94	6448.27
1966	2/9	995.15	10/7	744.32	785.69	1997	8/6	8259.31	4/11	6391.69	7908.25
1967	9/25	943.08	1/3	786.41	905.11	1998	11/23	9374.27	8/31	7539.07	9181.43
1968	12/3	985.21	3/21	825.13	943.75	1999	12/31	11497.12	1/22	9120.67	11497.12
1969	5/14	968.85	12/17	769.93	800.36	2000	1/14	11722.98	3/7	9796.03	10786.85
1970	12/29	842.00	5/26	631.16	838.92	2001	5/21	11337.92	9/21	8235.81	10021.50
1971	4/28	950.82	11/23	797.97	890.20	2002	3/19	10635.25	10/9	7286.27	8341.63
1972	12/11	1036.27	1/26	889.15	1020.02	2003	12/31	10453.92	3/11	7524.06	10453.92
1973	1/11	1051.70	12/5	788.31	850.86	2004	12/28	10854.54	10/25	9749.99	10783.01
1974	3/13	891.66	12/6	577.60	616.24	2005	3/4	10940.55	4/20	10012.36	10717.50
1975	7/15	881.81	1/2	632.04	852.41	2006	12/27	12510.57	1/20	10667.39	12463.15
1976	9/21	1014.79	1/2	858.71	1004.65	2007	10/9	14164.53	3/5	12050.41	13264.82
1977	1/3	999.75	11/2	800.85	831.17	2008	5/2	13058.20	11/20	7552.29	8776.39
1978	9/8	907.74	2/28	742.12	805.01	2009	12/30	10548.51	3/9	6547.05	10428.05
1979	10/5	897.61	11/7	796.67	838.74	2010	12/29	11585.38	7/2	9686.48	11577.51
1980	11/20	1000.17	4/21	759.13	963.99	2011	4/29	12810.54	10/3	10655.30	12217.56
1981	4/27	1024.05	9/25	824.01	875.00	2012	10/5	13610.15	6/4	12101.46	13104.14
1982	12/27	1070.55	8/12	776.92	1046.54	2013	12/31	16576.66	1/8	13328.85	16576.66
1983	11/29	1287.20	1/3	1027.04	1258.64	2014	12/26	18053.71	2/3	15372.80	17823.07
1984	1/6	1286.64	7/24	1086.57	1211.57	2015	5/19	18312.39	8/25	15666.44	17425.03
1985	12/16	1553.10	1/4	1184.96	1546.67	2016	12/20	19974.62	2/11	15660.18	19762.60
1986	12/2	1955.57	1/22	1502.29	1895.95	2017	12/28	24837.51	1/19	19732.40	24719.22
1987	8/25	2722.42	10/19	1738.74	1938.83	2018	10/3	26828.39	12/24	21792.20	23327.46
1988	10/21	2183.50	1/20	1879.14	2168.57	2019	12/27	28645.26	1/3	22686.22	28538.44
1989	10/9	2791.41	1/3	2144.64	2753.20	2020	12/31	30606.48	3/23	18591.93	30606.48
1990	7/17	2999.75	10/11	2365.10	2633.66	2021	12/29	36488.63	1/29	29982.62	36338.30
1991	12/31	3168.83	1/9	2470.30	3168.83	2022	1/4	36799.65	9/30	28725.51	33147.25
1992	6/1	3413.21	10/9	3136.58	3301.11	2023	12/28	37710.10	3/13	31819.14	37689.54
1993	12/29	3794.33	1/20	3241.95	3754.09	2024	12/4	45014.04	1/17	37266.67	42544.22
1994	1/31	3978.36	4/4	3593.35	3834.44	2025	12/24	48731.16	4/8	37645.59	48063.29
1995	12/13	5216.47	1/30	3832.08	5117.12	2026*	2/10	50188.14	3/27	45166.64	*At press time*

*Through May 1, 2026

S&P 500 ANNUAL HIGHS, LOWS, & CLOSES SINCE 1930

	HIGH		LOW		YEAR
YEAR	DATE	CLOSE	DATE	CLOSE	CLOSE
1930	4/10	25.92	12/16	14.44	15.34
1931	2/24	18.17	12/17	7.72	8.12
1932	9/7	9.31	6/1	4.40	6.89
1933	7/18	12.20	2/27	5.53	10.10
1934	2/6	11.82	7/26	8.36	9.50
1935	11/19	13.46	3/14	8.06	13.43
1936	11/9	17.69	1/2	13.40	17.18
1937	3/6	18.68	11/24	10.17	10.55
1938	11/9	13.79	3/31	8.50	13.21
1939	1/4	13.23	4/8	10.18	12.49
1940	1/3	12.77	6/10	8.99	10.58
1941	1/10	10.86	12/29	8.37	8.69
1942	12/31	9.77	4/28	7.47	9.77
1943	7/14	12.64	1/2	9.84	11.67
1944	12/16	13.29	2/7	11.56	13.28
1945	12/10	17.68	1/23	13.21	17.36
1946	5/29	19.25	10/9	14.12	15.30
1947	2/8	16.20	5/17	13.71	15.30
1948	6/15	17.06	2/14	13.84	15.20
1949	12/30	16.79	6/13	13.55	16.76
1950	12/29	20.43	1/14	16.65	20.41
1951	10/15	23.85	1/3	20.69	23.77
1952	12/30	26.59	2/20	23.09	26.57
1953	1/5	26.66	9/14	22.71	24.81
1954	12/31	35.98	1/11	24.80	35.98
1955	11/14	46.41	1/17	34.58	45.48
1956	8/2	49.74	1/23	43.11	46.67
1957	7/15	49.13	10/22	38.98	39.99
1958	12/31	55.21	1/2	40.33	55.21
1959	8/3	60.71	2/9	53.58	59.89
1960	1/5	60.39	10/25	52.30	58.11
1961	12/12	72.64	1/3	57.57	71.55
1962	1/3	71.13	6/26	52.32	63.10
1963	12/31	75.02	1/2	62.69	75.02
1964	11/20	86.28	1/2	75.43	84.75
1965	11/15	92.63	6/28	81.60	92.43
1966	2/9	94.06	10/7	73.20	80.33
1967	9/25	97.59	1/3	80.38	96.47
1968	11/29	108.37	3/5	87.72	103.86
1969	5/14	106.16	12/17	89.20	92.06
1970	1/5	93.46	5/26	69.29	92.15
1971	4/28	104.77	11/23	90.16	102.09
1972	12/11	119.12	1/3	101.67	118.05
1973	1/11	120.24	12/5	92.16	97.55
1974	1/3	99.80	10/3	62.28	68.56
1975	7/15	95.61	1/8	70.04	90.19
1976	9/21	107.83	1/2	90.90	107.46
1977	1/3	107.00	11/2	90.71	95.10
1978	9/12	106.99	3/6	86.90	96.11

	HIGH		LOW		YEAR
YEAR	DATE	CLOSE	DATE	CLOSE	CLOSE
1979	10/5	111.27	2/27	96.13	107.94
1980	11/28	140.52	3/27	98.22	135.76
1981	1/6	138.12	9/25	112.77	122.55
1982	11/9	143.02	8/12	102.42	140.64
1983	10/10	172.65	1/3	138.34	164.93
1984	11/6	170.41	7/24	147.82	167.24
1985	12/16	212.02	1/4	163.68	211.28
1986	12/2	254.00	1/22	203.49	242.17
1987	8/25	336.77	12/4	223.92	247.08
1988	10/21	283.66	1/20	242.63	277.72
1989	10/9	359.80	1/3	275.31	353.40
1990	7/16	368.95	10/11	295.46	330.22
1991	12/31	417.09	1/9	311.49	417.09
1992	12/18	441.28	4/8	394.50	435.71
1993	12/28	470.94	1/8	429.05	466.45
1994	2/2	482.00	4/4	438.92	459.27
1995	12/13	621.69	1/3	459.11	615.93
1996	11/25	757.03	1/10	598.48	740.74
1997	12/5	983.79	1/2	737.01	970.43
1998	12/29	1241.81	1/9	927.69	1229.23
1999	12/31	1469.25	1/14	1212.19	1469.25
2000	3/24	1527.46	12/20	1264.74	1320.28
2001	2/1	1373.47	9/21	965.80	1148.08
2002	1/4	1172.51	10/9	776.76	879.82
2003	12/31	1111.92	3/11	800.73	1111.92
2004	12/30	1213.55	8/12	1063.23	1211.92
2005	12/14	1272.74	4/20	1137.50	1248.29
2006	12/15	1427.09	6/13	1223.69	1418.30
2007	10/9	1565.15	3/5	1374.12	1468.36
2008	1/2	1447.16	11/20	752.44	903.25
2009	12/28	1127.78	3/9	676.53	1115.10
2010	12/29	1259.78	7/2	1022.58	1257.64
2011	4/29	1363.61	10/3	1099.23	1257.60
2012	9/14	1465.77	1/3	1277.06	1426.19
2013	12/31	1848.36	1/8	1457.15	1848.36
2014	12/29	2090.57	2/3	1741.89	2058.90
2015	5/21	2130.82	8/25	1867.61	2043.94
2016	12/13	2271.72	2/11	1829.08	2238.83
2017	12/18	2690.16	1/3	2257.83	2673.61
2018	9/20	2930.75	12/24	2351.10	2506.85
2019	12/27	3240.02	1/3	2447.89	3230.78
2020	12/31	3756.07	3/23	2237.40	3756.07
2021	12/29	4793.06	1/4	3700.65	4766.18
2022	1/3	4796.56	10/12	3577.03	3839.50
2023	12/28	4783.35	1/5	3808.10	4769.83
2024	12/6	6090.27	1/4	4688.68	5881.63
2025	12/24	6932.05	4/8	4982.77	6845.50
2026*	5/1	7230.12	3/30	6343.72	*At press time*

*Through May 1, 2026

NASDAQ ANNUAL HIGHS, LOWS, & CLOSES SINCE 1971

YEAR	HIGH DATE	HIGH CLOSE	LOW DATE	LOW CLOSE	YEAR CLOSE
1971	12/31	114.12	1/5	89.06	114.12
1972	12/8	135.15	1/3	113.65	133.73
1973	1/11	136.84	12/24	88.67	92.19
1974	3/15	96.53	10/3	54.87	59.82
1975	7/15	88.00	1/2	60.70	77.62
1976	12/31	97.88	1/2	78.06	97.88
1977	12/30	105.05	4/5	93.66	105.05
1978	9/13	139.25	1/11	99.09	117.98
1979	10/5	152.29	1/2	117.84	151.14
1980	11/28	208.15	3/27	124.09	202.34
1981	5/29	223.47	9/28	175.03	195.84
1982	12/8	240.70	8/13	159.14	232.41
1983	6/24	328.91	1/3	230.59	278.60
1984	1/6	287.90	7/25	225.30	247.35
1985	12/16	325.16	1/2	245.91	324.93
1986	7/3	411.16	1/9	323.01	349.33
1987	8/26	455.26	10/28	291.88	330.47
1988	7/5	396.11	1/12	331.97	381.38
1989	10/9	485.73	1/3	378.56	454.82
1990	7/16	469.60	10/16	325.44	373.84
1991	12/31	586.34	1/14	355.75	586.34
1992	12/31	676.95	6/26	547.84	676.95
1993	10/15	787.42	4/26	645.87	776.80
1994	3/18	803.93	6/24	693.79	751.96
1995	12/4	1069.79	1/3	743.58	1052.13
1996	12/9	1316.27	1/15	988.57	1291.03
1997	10/9	1745.85	4/2	1201.00	1570.35
1998	12/31	2192.69	10/8	1419.12	2192.69
1999	12/31	4069.31	1/4	2208.05	4069.31
2000	3/10	5048.62	12/20	2332.78	2470.52
2001	1/24	2859.15	9/21	1423.19	1950.40
2002	1/4	2059.38	10/9	1114.11	1335.51
2003	12/30	2009.88	3/11	1271.47	2003.37
2004	12/30	2178.34	8/12	1752.49	2175.44
2005	12/2	2273.37	4/28	1904.18	2205.32
2006	11/22	2465.98	7/21	2020.39	2415.29
2007	10/31	2859.12	3/5	2340.68	2652.28
2008	1/2	2609.63	11/20	1316.12	1577.03
2009	12/30	2291.28	3/9	1268.64	2269.15
2010	12/22	2671.48	7/2	2091.79	2652.87
2011	4/29	2873.54	10/3	2335.83	2605.15
2012	9/14	3183.95	1/4	2648.36	3019.51
2013	12/31	4176.59	1/8	3091.81	4176.59
2014	12/29	4806.91	2/3	3996.96	4736.05
2015	7/20	5218.86	8/25	4506.49	5007.41
2016	12/27	5487.44	2/11	4266.84	5383.12
2017	12/18	6994.76	1/3	5429.08	6903.39
2018	8/29	8109.69	12/24	6192.92	6635.28
2019	12/26	9022.39	1/3	6463.50	8972.60
2020	12/28	12899.42	3/23	6860.67	12888.28
2021	11/29	16057.44	3/8	12609.16	15644.97
2022	1/3	15832.80	12/28	10213.29	10466.48
2023	12/27	15099.18	1/5	10305.24	15011.35
2024	12/16	20173.89	1/4	14510.30	19310.79
2025	10/29	23958.47	4/8	15267.91	23241.99
2026*	5/1	25114.44	3/30	20794.64	*At press time*

**Through May 1, 2026*

RUSSELL 1000 ANNUAL HIGHS, LOWS, & CLOSES SINCE 1979

	HIGH		LOW		YEAR		HIGH		LOW		YEAR
YEAR	DATE	CLOSE	DATE	CLOSE	CLOSE	YEAR	DATE	CLOSE	DATE	CLOSE	CLOSE
1979	10/5	61.18	2/27	51.83	59.87	2003	12/31	594.56	3/11	425.31	594.56
1980	11/28	78.26	3/27	53.68	75.20	2004	12/30	651.76	8/13	566.06	650.99
1981	1/6	76.34	9/25	62.03	67.93	2005	12/14	692.09	4/20	613.37	679.42
1982	11/9	78.47	8/12	55.98	77.24	2006	12/15	775.08	6/13	665.81	770.08
1983	10/10	95.07	1/3	76.04	90.38	2007	10/9	852.32	3/5	749.85	799.82
1984	1/6	92.80	7/24	79.49	90.31	2008	1/2	788.62	11/20	402.91	487.77
1985	12/16	114.97	1/4	88.61	114.39	2009	12/28	619.22	3/9	367.55	612.01
1986	7/2	137.87	1/22	111.14	130.00	2010	12/29	698.11	7/2	562.58	696.90
1987	8/25	176.22	12/4	117.65	130.02	2011	4/29	758.45	10/3	604.42	693.36
1988	10/21	149.94	1/20	128.35	146.99	2012	9/14	809.01	1/4	703.72	789.90
1989	10/9	189.93	1/3	145.78	185.11	2013	12/31	1030.36	1/8	807.95	1030.36
1990	7/16	191.56	10/11	152.36	171.22	2014	12/29	1161.45	2/3	972.95	1144.37
1991	12/31	220.61	1/9	161.94	220.61	2015	5/21	1189.55	8/25	1042.77	1131.88
1992	12/18	235.06	4/8	208.87	233.59	2016	12/13	1260.06	2/11	1005.89	1241.66
1993	10/15	252.77	1/8	229.91	250.71	2017	12/18	1490.06	1/3	1252.11	1481.81
1994	2/1	258.31	4/4	235.38	244.65	2018	9/20	1624.28	12/24	1298.02	1384.26
1995	12/13	331.18	1/3	244.41	328.89	2019	12/26	1789.56	1/3	1351.87	1784.21
1996	12/2	401.21	1/10	318.24	393.75	2020	12/31	2120.87	3/23	1224.45	2120.87
1997	12/5	519.72	4/11	389.03	513.79	2021	12/27	2660.44	1/4	2089.72	2645.91
1998	12/29	645.36	1/9	490.26	642.87	2022	1/3	2660.78	10/12	1969.25	2105.90
1999	12/31	767.97	2/9	632.53	767.97	2023	12/28	2631.33	1/5	2089.03	2622.14
2000	9/1	813.71	12/20	668.75	700.09	2024	12/6	3350.31	1/4	2573.83	3221.05
2001	1/30	727.35	9/21	507.98	604.94	2025	12/24	3781.96	4/8	2719.99	3732.87
2002	3/19	618.74	10/9	410.52	466.18	2026*	5/1	3933.95	3/30	3464.50	*At press time*

RUSSELL 2000 ANNUAL HIGHS, LOWS, & CLOSES SINCE 1979

	HIGH		LOW		YEAR		HIGH		LOW		YEAR
YEAR	DATE	CLOSE	DATE	CLOSE	CLOSE	YEAR	DATE	CLOSE	DATE	CLOSE	CLOSE
1979	12/31	55.91	1/2	40.81	55.91	2003	12/30	565.47	3/12	345.94	556.91
1980	11/28	77.70	3/27	45.36	74.80	2004	12/28	654.57	8/12	517.10	651.57
1981	6/15	85.16	9/25	65.37	73.67	2005	12/2	690.57	4/28	575.02	673.22
1982	12/8	91.01	8/12	60.33	88.90	2006	12/27	797.73	7/21	671.94	787.66
1983	6/24	126.99	1/3	88.29	112.27	2007	7/13	855.77	11/26	735.07	766.03
1984	1/12	116.69	7/25	93.95	101.49	2008	6/5	763.27	11/20	385.31	499.45
1985	12/31	129.87	1/2	101.21	129.87	2009	12/24	634.07	3/9	343.26	625.39
1986	7/3	155.30	1/9	128.23	135.00	2010	12/27	792.35	2/8	586.49	783.65
1987	8/25	174.44	10/28	106.08	120.42	2011	4/29	865.29	10/3	609.49	740.92
1988	7/15	151.42	1/12	121.23	147.37	2012	9/14	864.70	6/4	737.24	849.35
1989	10/9	180.78	1/3	146.79	168.30	2013	12/31	1163.64	1/3	872.60	1163.64
1990	6/15	170.90	10/30	118.82	132.16	2014	12/29	1219.11	10/13	1049.30	1204.70
1991	12/31	189.94	1/15	125.25	189.94	2015	6/23	1295.80	9/29	1083.91	1135.89
1992	12/31	221.01	7/8	185.81	221.01	2016	12/9	1388.07	2/11	953.72	1357.13
1993	11/2	260.17	2/23	217.55	258.59	2017	12/28	1548.93	4/13	1345.24	1535.51
1994	3/18	271.08	12/9	235.16	250.36	2018	8/31	1740.75	12/24	1266.92	1348.56
1995	9/14	316.12	1/30	246.56	315.97	2019	12/24	1678.01	1/3	1330.83	1668.47
1996	5/22	364.61	1/16	301.75	362.61	2020	12/23	2007.10	3/18	991.16	1974.86
1997	10/13	465.21	4/25	335.85	437.02	2021	11/8	2442.74	1/4	1945.91	2245.31
1998	4/21	491.41	10/8	310.28	421.96	2022	1/3	2272.56	6/16	1649.84	1761.25
1999	12/31	504.75	3/23	383.37	504.75	2023	12/27	2066.21	10/27	1636.94	2027.07
2000	3/9	606.05	12/20	443.80	483.53	2024	11/25	2442.03	1/17	1913.17	2230.16
2001	5/22	517.23	9/21	378.89	488.50	2025	12/11	2590.61	4/8	1760.71	2481.91
2002	4/16	522.95	10/9	327.04	383.09	2026*	5/1	2812.82	3/30	2414.01	*At press time*

**Through May 1, 2026*

DOW JONES INDUSTRIALS MONTHLY PERCENT CHANGES SINCE 1950

	Jan	Feb	Mar	Apr	May	Jun	Jul	Aug	Sep	Oct	Nov	Dec	Year
1950	0.8	0.8	1.3	4.0	4.2	−6.4	0.1	3.6	4.4	−0.6	1.2	3.4	17.6
1951	5.7	1.3	−1.6	4.5	−3.7	−2.8	6.3	4.8	0.3	−3.2	−0.4	3.0	14.4
1952	0.5	−3.9	3.6	−4.4	2.1	4.3	1.9	−1.6	−1.6	−0.5	5.4	2.9	8.4
1953	−0.7	−1.9	−1.5	−1.8	−0.9	−1.5	2.7	−5.1	1.1	4.5	2.0	−0.2	−3.8
1954	4.1	0.7	3.0	5.2	2.6	1.8	4.3	−3.5	7.3	−2.3	9.8	4.6	44.0
1955	1.1	0.7	−0.5	3.9	−0.2	6.2	3.2	0.5	−0.3	−2.5	6.2	1.1	20.8
1956	−3.6	2.7	5.8	0.8	−7.4	3.1	5.1	−3.0	−5.3	1.0	−1.5	5.6	2.3
1957	−4.1	−3.0	2.2	4.1	2.1	−0.3	1.0	−4.8	−5.8	−3.3	2.0	−3.2	−12.8
1958	3.3	−2.2	1.6	2.0	1.5	3.3	5.2	1.1	4.6	2.1	2.6	4.7	34.0
1959	1.8	1.6	−0.3	3.7	3.2	−0.03	4.9	−1.6	−4.9	2.4	1.9	3.1	16.4
1960	−8.4	1.2	−2.1	−2.4	4.0	2.4	−3.7	1.5	−7.3	0.04	2.9	3.1	−9.3
1961	5.2	2.1	2.2	0.3	2.7	−1.8	3.1	2.1	−2.6	0.4	2.5	1.3	18.7
1962	−4.3	1.1	−0.2	−5.9	−7.8	−8.5	6.5	1.9	−5.0	1.9	10.1	0.4	−10.8
1963	4.7	−2.9	3.0	5.2	1.3	−2.8	−1.6	4.9	0.5	3.1	−0.6	1.7	17.0
1964	2.9	1.9	1.6	−0.3	1.2	1.3	1.2	−0.3	4.4	−0.3	0.3	−0.1	14.6
1965	3.3	0.1	−1.6	3.7	−0.5	−5.4	1.6	1.3	4.2	3.2	−1.5	2.4	10.9
1966	1.5	−3.2	−2.8	1.0	−5.3	−1.6	−2.6	−7.0	−1.8	4.2	−1.9	−0.7	−18.9
1967	8.2	−1.2	3.2	3.6	−5.0	0.9	5.1	−0.3	2.8	−5.1	−0.4	3.3	15.2
1968	−5.5	−1.7	0.02	8.5	−1.4	−0.1	−1.6	1.5	4.4	1.8	3.4	−4.2	4.3
1969	0.2	−4.3	3.3	1.6	−1.3	−6.9	−6.6	2.6	−2.8	5.3	−5.1	−1.5	−15.2
1970	−7.0	4.5	1.0	−6.3	−4.8	−2.4	7.4	4.1	−0.5	−0.7	5.1	5.6	4.8
1971	3.5	1.2	2.9	4.1	−3.6	−1.8	−3.7	4.6	−1.2	−5.4	−0.9	7.1	6.1
1972	1.3	2.9	1.4	1.4	0.7	−3.3	−0.5	4.2	−1.1	0.2	6.6	0.2	14.6
1973	−2.1	−4.4	−0.4	−3.1	−2.2	−1.1	3.9	−4.2	6.7	1.0	−14.0	3.5	−16.6
1974	0.6	0.6	−1.6	−1.2	−4.1	0.03	−5.6	−10.4	−10.4	9.5	−7.0	−0.4	−27.6
1975	14.2	5.0	3.9	6.9	1.3	5.6	−5.4	0.5	−5.0	5.3	2.9	−1.0	38.3
1976	14.4	−0.3	2.8	−0.3	−2.2	2.8	−1.8	−1.1	1.7	−2.6	−1.8	6.1	17.9
1977	−5.0	−1.9	−1.8	0.8	−3.0	2.0	−2.9	−3.2	−1.7	−3.4	1.4	0.2	−17.3
1978	−7.4	−3.6	2.1	10.6	0.4	−2.6	5.3	1.7	−1.3	−8.5	0.8	0.7	−3.1
1979	4.2	−3.6	6.6	−0.8	−3.8	2.4	0.5	4.9	−1.0	−7.2	0.8	2.0	4.2
1980	4.4	−1.5	−9.0	4.0	4.1	2.0	7.8	−0.3	−0.02	−0.9	7.4	−3.0	14.9
1981	−1.7	2.9	3.0	−0.6	−0.6	−1.5	−2.5	−7.4	−3.6	0.3	4.3	−1.6	−9.2
1982	−0.4	−5.4	−0.2	3.1	−3.4	−0.9	−0.4	11.5	−0.6	10.7	4.8	0.7	19.6
1983	2.8	3.4	1.6	8.5	−2.1	1.8	−1.9	1.4	1.4	−0.6	4.1	−1.4	20.3
1984	−3.0	−5.4	0.9	0.5	−5.6	2.5	−1.5	9.8	−1.4	0.1	−1.5	1.9	−3.7
1985	6.2	−0.2	−1.3	−0.7	4.6	1.5	0.9	−1.0	−0.4	3.4	7.1	5.1	27.7
1986	1.6	8.8	6.4	−1.9	5.2	0.9	−6.2	6.9	−6.9	6.2	1.9	−1.0	22.6
1987	13.8	3.1	3.6	−0.8	0.2	5.5	6.3	3.5	−2.5	−23.2	−8.0	5.7	2.3
1988	1.0	5.8	−4.0	2.2	−0.1	5.4	−0.6	−4.6	4.0	1.7	−1.6	2.6	11.8
1989	8.0	−3.6	1.6	5.5	2.5	−1.6	9.0	2.9	−1.6	−1.8	2.3	1.7	27.0

continued

DOW JONES INDUSTRIALS MONTHLY PERCENT CHANGES SINCE 1950 (continued)

	Jan	Feb	Mar	Apr	May	Jun	Jul	Aug	Sep	Oct	Nov	Dec	Year
1990	–5.9	1.4	3.0	–1.9	8.3	0.1	0.9	–10.0	–6.2	–0.4	4.8	2.9	–4.3
1991	3.9	5.3	1.1	–0.9	4.8	–4.0	4.1	0.6	–0.9	1.7	–5.7	9.5	20.3
1992	1.7	1.4	–1.0	3.8	1.1	–2.3	2.3	–4.0	0.4	–1.4	2.4	–0.1	4.2
1993	0.3	1.8	1.9	–0.2	2.9	–0.3	0.7	3.2	–2.6	3.5	0.1	1.9	13.7
1994	6.0	–3.7	–5.1	1.3	2.1	–3.5	3.8	4.0	–1.8	1.7	–4.3	2.5	2.1
1995	0.2	4.3	3.7	3.9	3.3	2.0	3.3	–2.1	3.9	–0.7	6.7	0.8	33.5
1996	5.4	1.7	1.9	–0.3	1.3	0.2	–2.2	1.6	4.7	2.5	8.2	–1.1	26.0
1997	5.7	0.9	–4.3	6.5	4.6	4.7	7.2	–7.3	4.2	–6.3	5.1	1.1	22.6
1998	–0.02	8.1	3.0	3.0	–1.8	0.6	–0.8	–15.1	4.0	9.6	6.1	0.7	16.1
1999	1.9	–0.6	5.2	10.2	–2.1	3.9	–2.9	1.6	–4.5	3.8	1.4	5.7	25.2
2000	–4.8	–7.4	7.8	–1.7	–2.0	–0.7	0.7	6.6	–5.0	3.0	–5.1	3.6	–6.2
2001	0.9	–3.6	–5.9	8.7	1.6	–3.8	0.2	–5.4	–11.1	2.6	8.6	1.7	–7.1
2002	–1.0	1.9	2.9	–4.4	–0.2	–6.9	–5.5	–0.8	–12.4	10.6	5.9	–6.2	–16.8
2003	–3.5	–2.0	1.3	6.1	4.4	1.5	2.8	2.0	–1.5	5.7	–0.2	6.9	25.3
2004	0.3	0.9	–2.1	–1.3	–0.4	2.4	–2.8	0.3	–0.9	–0.5	4.0	3.4	3.1
2005	–2.7	2.6	–2.4	–3.0	2.7	–1.8	3.6	–1.5	0.8	–1.2	3.5	–0.8	–0.6
2006	1.4	1.2	1.1	2.3	–1.7	–0.2	0.3	1.7	2.6	3.4	1.2	2.0	16.3
2007	1.3	–2.8	0.7	5.7	4.3	–1.6	–1.5	1.1	4.0	0.2	–4.0	–0.8	6.4
2008	–4.6	–3.0	–0.03	4.5	–1.4	–10.2	0.2	1.5	–6.0	–14.1	–5.3	–0.6	–33.8
2009	–8.8	–11.7	7.7	7.3	4.1	–0.6	8.6	3.5	2.3	0.005	6.5	0.8	18.8
2010	–3.5	2.6	5.1	1.4	–7.9	–3.6	7.1	–4.3	7.7	3.1	–1.0	5.2	11.0
2011	2.7	2.8	0.8	4.0	–1.9	–1.2	–2.2	–4.4	–6.0	9.5	0.8	1.4	5.5
2012	3.4	2.5	2.0	0.01	–6.2	3.9	1.0	0.6	2.6	–2.5	–0.5	0.6	7.3
2013	5.8	1.4	3.7	1.8	1.9	–1.4	4.0	–4.4	2.2	2.8	3.5	3.0	26.5
2014	–5.3	4.0	0.8	0.7	0.8	0.7	–1.6	3.2	–0.3	2.0	2.5	–0.03	7.5
2015	–3.7	5.6	–2.0	0.4	1.0	–2.2	0.4	–6.6	–1.5	8.5	0.3	–1.7	–2.2
2016	–5.5	0.3	7.1	0.5	0.1	0.8	2.8	–0.2	–0.5	–0.9	5.4	3.3	13.4
2017	0.5	4.8	–0.7	1.3	0.3	1.6	2.5	0.3	2.1	4.3	3.8	1.8	25.1
2018	5.8	–4.3	–3.7	0.2	1.0	–0.6	4.7	2.2	1.9	–5.1	1.7	–8.7	–5.6
2019	7.2	3.7	0.1	2.6	–6.7	7.2	1.0	–1.7	1.9	0.5	3.7	1.7	22.3
2020	–1.0	–10.1	–13.7	11.1	4.3	1.7	2.4	7.6	–2.3	–4.6	11.8	3.3	7.2
2021	–2.0	3.2	6.6	2.7	1.9	–0.1	1.3	1.2	–4.3	5.8	–3.7	5.4	18.7
2022	–3.3	–3.5	2.3	–4.9	0.04	–6.7	6.7	–4.1	–8.8	14.0	5.7	–4.2	–8.8
2023	2.8	–4.2	1.9	2.5	–3.5	4.6	3.3	–2.4	–3.5	–1.4	8.8	4.8	13.7
2024	1.2	2.2	2.1	–5.0	2.3	1.1	4.4	1.8	1.8	–1.3	7.5	–5.3	12.9
2025	4.7	–1.6	–4.2	–3.2	3.9	4.3	0.1	3.2	1.9	2.5	0.3	0.7	13.0
2026	1.7	0.2	–5.4	7.1									
TOTALS	**75.3**	**4.5**	**62.9**	**142.0**	**2.1**	**–8.0**	**105.1**	**–4.1**	**–59.9**	**57.1**	**144.1**	**110.6**	
AVG.	**1.0**	**0.1**	**0.8**	**1.8**	**0.03**	**–0.1**	**1.4**	**–0.1**	**–0.8**	**0.8**	**1.9**	**1.5**	
# Up	**49**	**45**	**49**	**52**	**42**	**37**	**51**	**43**	**31**	**45**	**53**	**53**	
# Down	**28**	**32**	**28**	**25**	**34**	**39**	**25**	**33**	**45**	**31**	**23**	**23**	

DOW JONES INDUSTRIALS MONTHLY POINT CHANGES SINCE 1950

	Jan	Feb	Mar	Apr	May	Jun	Jul	Aug	Sep	Oct	Nov	Dec	Year
1950	1.66	1.65	2.61	8.28	9.09	–14.31	0.29	7.47	9.49	–1.35	2.59	7.81	235.41
1951	13.42	3.22	–4.11	11.19	–9.48	–7.01	15.22	12.39	0.91	–8.81	–1.08	7.96	269.23
1952	1.46	–10.61	9.38	–11.83	5.31	11.32	5.30	–4.52	–4.43	–1.38	14.43	8.24	291.90
1953	–2.13	–5.50	–4.40	–5.12	–2.47	–4.02	7.12	–14.16	2.82	11.77	5.56	–0.47	280.90
1954	11.49	2.15	8.97	15.82	8.16	6.04	14.39	–12.12	24.66	–8.32	34.63	17.62	404.39
1955	4.44	3.04	–2.17	15.95	–0.79	26.52	14.47	2.33	–1.56	–11.75	28.39	5.14	488.40
1956	–17.66	12.91	28.14	4.33	–38.07	14.73	25.03	–15.77	–26.79	4.60	–7.07	26.69	499.47
1957	–20.31	–14.54	10.19	19.55	10.57	–1.64	5.23	–24.17	–28.05	–15.26	8.83	–14.18	435.69
1958	14.33	–10.10	6.84	9.10	6.84	15.48	24.81	5.64	23.46	11.13	14.24	26.19	583.65
1959	10.31	9.54	–1.79	22.04	20.04	–0.19	31.28	–10.47	–32.73	14.92	12.58	20.18	679.36
1960	–56.74	7.50	–13.53	–14.89	23.80	15.12	–23.89	9.26	–45.85	0.22	16.86	18.67	615.89
1961	32.31	13.88	14.55	2.08	18.01	–12.76	21.41	14.57	–18.73	2.71	17.68	9.54	731.14
1962	–31.14	8.05	–1.10	–41.62	–51.97	–52.08	36.65	11.25	–30.20	10.79	59.53	2.80	652.10
1963	30.75	–19.91	19.58	35.18	9.26	–20.08	–11.45	33.89	3.47	22.44	–4.71	12.43	762.95
1964	22.39	14.80	13.15	–2.52	9.79	10.94	9.60	–2.62	36.89	–2.29	2.35	–1.30	874.13
1965	28.73	0.62	–14.43	33.26	–4.27	–50.01	13.71	11.36	37.48	30.24	–14.11	22.55	969.26
1966	14.25	–31.62	–27.12	8.91	–49.61	–13.97	–22.72	–58.97	–14.19	32.85	–15.48	–5.90	785.69
1967	64.20	–10.52	26.61	31.07	–44.49	7.70	43.98	–2.95	25.37	–46.92	–3.93	29.30	905.11
1968	–49.64	–14.97	0.17	71.55	–13.22	–1.20	–14.80	13.01	39.78	16.60	32.69	–41.33	943.75
1969	2.30	–40.84	30.27	14.70	–12.62	–64.37	–57.72	21.25	–23.63	42.90	–43.69	–11.94	800.36
1970	–56.30	33.53	7.98	–49.50	–35.63	–16.91	50.59	30.46	–3.90	–5.07	38.48	44.83	838.92
1971	29.58	10.33	25.54	37.38	–33.94	–16.67	–32.71	39.64	–10.88	–48.19	–7.66	58.86	890.20
1972	11.97	25.96	12.57	13.47	6.55	–31.69	–4.29	38.99	–10.46	2.25	62.69	1.81	1020.02
1973	–21.00	–43.95	–4.06	–29.58	–20.02	–9.70	34.69	–38.83	59.53	9.48	–134.33	28.61	850.86
1974	4.69	4.98	–13.85	–9.93	–34.58	0.24	–44.98	–78.85	–70.71	57.65	–46.86	–2.42	616.24
1975	87.45	35.36	29.10	53.19	10.95	46.70	–47.48	3.83	–41.46	42.16	24.63	–8.26	852.41
1976	122.87	–2.67	26.84	–2.60	–21.62	27.55	–18.14	–10.90	16.45	–25.26	–17.71	57.43	1004.65
1977	–50.28	–17.95	–17.29	7.77	–28.24	17.64	–26.23	–28.58	–14.38	–28.76	11.35	1.47	831.17
1978	–61.25	–27.80	15.24	79.96	3.29	–21.66	43.32	14.55	–11.00	–73.37	6.58	5.98	805.01
1979	34.21	–30.40	53.36	–7.28	–32.57	19.65	4.44	41.21	–9.05	–62.88	6.65	16.39	838.74
1980	37.11	–12.71	–77.39	31.31	33.79	17.07	67.40	–2.73	–0.17	–7.93	68.85	–29.35	963.99
1981	–16.72	27.31	29.29	–6.12	–6.00	–14.87	–24.54	–70.87	–31.49	2.57	36.43	–13.98	875.00
1982	–3.90	–46.71	–1.62	25.59	–28.82	–7.61	–3.33	92.71	–5.06	95.47	47.56	7.26	1046.54
1983	29.16	36.92	17.41	96.17	–26.22	21.98	–22.74	16.94	16.97	–7.93	50.82	–17.38	1258.64
1984	–38.06	–65.95	10.26	5.86	–65.90	27.55	–17.12	109.10	–17.67	0.67	–18.44	22.63	1211.57
1985	75.20	–2.76	–17.23	–8.72	57.35	20.05	11.99	–13.44	–5.38	45.68	97.82	74.54	1546.67
1986	24.32	138.07	109.55	–34.63	92.73	16.01	–117.41	123.03	–130.76	110.23	36.42	–18.28	1895.95
1987	262.09	65.95	80.70	–18.33	5.21	126.96	153.54	90.88	–66.67	–602.75	–159.98	105.28	1938.83
1988	19.39	113.40	–83.56	44.27	–1.21	110.59	–12.98	–97.08	81.26	35.74	–34.14	54.06	2168.57

continued

DOW JONES INDUSTRIALS MONTHLY POINT CHANGES SINCE 1950 (continued)

	Jan	Feb	Mar	Apr	May	Jun	Jul	Aug	Sep	Oct	Nov	Dec	Year
1989	173.75	–83.93	35.23	125.18	61.35	–40.09	220.60	76.61	–44.45	–47.74	61.19	46.93	2753.20
1990	–162.66	36.71	79.96	–50.45	219.90	4.03	24.51	–290.84	–161.88	–10.15	117.32	74.01	2633.66
1991	102.73	145.79	31.68	–25.99	139.63	–120.75	118.07	18.78	–26.83	52.33	–174.42	274.15	3168.83
1992	54.56	44.28	–32.20	123.65	37.76	–78.36	75.26	–136.43	14.31	–45.38	78.88	–4.05	3301.11
1993	8.92	60.78	64.30	–7.56	99.88	–11.35	23.39	111.78	–96.13	125.47	3.36	70.14	3754.09
1994	224.27	–146.34	–196.06	45.73	76.68	–133.41	139.54	148.92	–70.23	64.93	–168.89	95.21	3834.44
1995	9.42	167.19	146.64	163.58	143.87	90.96	152.37	–97.91	178.52	–33.60	319.01	42.63	5117.12
1996	278.18	90.32	101.52	–18.06	74.10	11.45	–125.72	87.30	265.96	147.21	492.32	–73.43	6448.27
1997	364.82	64.65	–294.26	425.51	322.05	341.75	549.82	–600.19	322.84	–503.18	381.05	85.12	7908.25
1998	–1.75	639.22	254.09	263.56	–163.42	52.07	–68.73	–1344.22	303.55	749.48	524.45	64.88	9181.43
1999	177.40	–52.25	479.58	1002.88	–229.30	411.06	–315.65	174.13	–492.33	392.91	147.95	619.31	11497.12
2000	–556.59	–812.22	793.61	–188.01	–211.58	–74.44	74.09	693.12	–564.18	320.22	–556.65	372.36	10786.85
2001	100.51	–392.08	–616.50	856.19	176.97	–409.54	20.41	–573.06	–1102.19	227.58	776.42	169.94	10021.50
2002	–101.50	186.13	297.81	–457.72	–20.97	–681.99	–506.67	–73.09	–1071.57	805.10	499.06	–554.46	8341.63
2003	–287.82	–162.73	101.05	487.96	370.17	135.18	248.36	182.02	–140.76	526.06	–18.66	671.46	10453.92
2004	34.15	95.85	–226.22	–132.13	–37.12	247.03	–295.77	34.21	–93.65	–52.80	400.55	354.99	10783.01
2005	–293.07	276.29	–262.47	–311.25	274.97	–192.51	365.94	–159.31	87.10	–128.63	365.80	–88.37	10717.50
2006	147.36	128.55	115.91	257.82	–198.83	–18.09	35.46	195.47	297.92	401.66	141.20	241.22	12463.15
2007	158.54	–353.06	85.72	708.56	564.73	–219.02	–196.63	145.75	537.89	34.38	–558.29	–106.90	13264.82
2008	–614.46	–383.97	–3.50	557.24	–181.81	–1288.31	28.01	165.53	–692.89	–1525.65	–495.97	–52.65	8776.39
2009	–775.53	–937.93	545.99	559.20	332.21	–53.33	724.61	324.67	216.00	0.45	632.11	83.21	10428.05
2010	–360.72	257.93	531.37	151.98	–871.98	–362.61	691.92	–451.22	773.33	330.44	–112.47	571.49	11577.51
2011	314.42	334.41	93.39	490.81	–240.75	–155.45	–271.10	–529.71	–700.15	1041.63	90.67	171.88	12217.56
2012	415.35	319.16	259.97	1.59	–820.18	486.64	128.59	82.16	346.29	–340.67	–70.88	78.56	13104.14
2013	756.44	193.91	524.05	261.26	275.77	–205.97	589.94	–689.23	319.36	416.08	540.66	490.25	16576.66
2014	–877.81	622.86	135.95	123.18	136.33	109.43	–263.30	535.15	–55.55	347.62	437.72	–5.17	17823.07
2015	–658.12	967.75	–356.58	64.40	170.16	–391.17	70.35	–1161.83	–244.03	1379.54	56.38	–294.89	17425.03
2016	–958.73	50.20	1168.59	88.55	13.56	142.79	502.25	–31.36	–92.73	–165.73	981.16	639.02	19762.60
2017	101.49	948.15	–149.02	277.29	68.14	340.98	541.49	56.98	456.99	972.15	895.11	446.87	24719.22
2018	1430.17	–1120.19	–926.09	60.04	252.69	–144.43	1143.78	549.63	493.49	–1342.55	422.70	–2211.00	23327.46
2019	1672.21	916.33	12.68	664.23	–1777.87	1784.92	264.31	–460.99	513.55	129.40	1005.18	487.03	28538.44
2020	–282.41	–2846.67	–3492.20	2428.56	1037.39	429.77	615.44	2001.73	–648.35	–1280.10	3137.04	967.84	30606.48
2021	– 623.86	949.75	2049.18	893.30	654.60	–26.94	432.96	425.26	–1516.81	1975.64	–1335.84	1854.58	36338.30
2022	–1206.44	–1239.26	785.75	–1701.14	12.91	–2214.69	2069.70	–1334.70	–2784.92	4007.44	1856.82	–1442.52	33147.25
2023	938.79	–1429.34	617.45	824.01	–1189.89	1499.33	1151.93	–837.62	–1214.41	–454.63	2898.02	1738.65	37689.54
2024	460.76	846.09	810.98	–1991.45	870.40	432.54	1723.93	720.29	767.07	–566.69	3147.19	–2366.43	42544.22
2025	2000.44	–703.75	–1839.15	–1332.40	1600.71	1824.70	36.21	1413.90	853.01	1164.98	153.55	346.87	48063.29
2026	829.18	85.45	–2636.41	3310.63									
TOTALS	**3557.34**	**–2076.31**	**–603.56**	**9456.04**	**1812.23**	**1721.27**	**10851.60**	**–371.59**	**–5343.52**	**8760.05**	**17300.25**	**4388.21**	
# Up	**49**	**45**	**49**	**52**	**42**	**37**	**51**	**43**	**31**	**45**	**53**	**53**	
# Down	**28**	**32**	**28**	**25**	**34**	**39**	**25**	**33**	**45**	**31**	**23**	**23**	

DOW JONES INDUSTRIALS MONTHLY CLOSING PRICES SINCE 1950

	Jan	Feb	Mar	Apr	May	Jun	Jul	Aug	Sep	Oct	Nov	Dec
1950	201.79	203.44	206.05	214.33	223.42	209.11	209.40	216.87	226.36	225.01	227.60	235.41
1951	248.83	252.05	247.94	259.13	249.65	242.64	257.86	270.25	271.16	262.35	261.27	269.23
1952	270.69	260.08	269.46	257.63	262.94	274.26	279.56	275.04	270.61	269.23	283.66	291.90
1953	289.77	284.27	279.87	274.75	272.28	268.26	275.38	261.22	264.04	275.81	281.37	280.90
1954	292.39	294.54	303.51	319.33	327.49	333.53	347.92	335.80	360.46	352.14	386.77	404.39
1955	408.83	411.87	409.70	425.65	424.86	451.38	465.85	468.18	466.62	454.87	483.26	488.40
1956	470.74	483.65	511.79	516.12	478.05	492.78	517.81	502.04	475.25	479.85	472.78	499.47
1957	479.16	464.62	474.81	494.36	504.93	503.29	508.52	484.35	456.30	441.04	449.87	435.69
1958	450.02	439.92	446.76	455.86	462.70	478.18	502.99	508.63	532.09	543.22	557.46	583.65
1959	593.96	603.50	601.71	623.75	643.79	643.60	674.88	664.41	631.68	646.60	659.18	679.36
1960	622.62	630.12	616.59	601.70	625.50	640.62	616.73	625.99	580.14	580.36	597.22	615.89
1961	648.20	662.08	676.63	678.71	696.72	683.96	705.37	719.94	701.21	703.92	721.60	731.14
1962	700.00	708.05	706.95	665.33	613.36	561.28	597.93	609.18	578.98	589.77	649.30	652.10
1963	682.85	662.94	682.52	717.70	726.96	706.88	695.43	729.32	732.79	755.23	750.52	762.95
1964	785.34	800.14	813.29	810.77	820.56	831.50	841.10	838.48	875.37	873.08	875.43	874.13
1965	902.86	903.48	889.05	922.31	918.04	868.03	881.74	893.10	930.58	960.82	946.71	969.26
1966	983.51	951.89	924.77	933.68	884.07	870.10	847.38	788.41	774.22	807.07	791.59	785.69
1967	849.89	839.37	865.98	897.05	852.56	860.26	904.24	901.29	926.66	879.74	875.81	905.11
1968	855.47	840.50	840.67	912.22	899.00	897.80	883.00	896.01	935.79	952.39	985.08	943.75
1969	946.05	905.21	935.48	950.18	937.56	873.19	815.47	836.72	813.09	855.99	812.30	800.36
1970	744.06	777.59	785.57	736.07	700.44	683.53	734.12	764.58	760.68	755.61	794.09	838.92
1971	868.50	878.83	904.37	941.75	907.81	891.14	858.43	898.07	887.19	839.00	831.34	890.20
1972	902.17	928.13	940.70	954.17	960.72	929.03	924.74	963.73	953.27	955.52	1018.21	1020.02
1973	999.02	955.07	951.01	921.43	901.41	891.71	926.40	887.57	947.10	956.58	822.25	850.86
1974	855.55	860.53	846.68	836.75	802.17	802.41	757.43	678.58	607.87	665.52	618.66	616.24
1975	703.69	739.05	768.15	821.34	832.29	878.99	831.51	835.34	793.88	836.04	860.67	852.41
1976	975.28	972.61	999.45	996.85	975.23	1002.78	984.64	973.74	990.19	964.93	947.22	1004.65
1977	954.37	936.42	919.13	926.90	898.66	916.30	890.07	861.49	847.11	818.35	829.70	831.17
1978	769.92	742.12	757.36	837.32	840.61	818.95	862.27	876.82	865.82	792.45	799.03	805.01
1979	839.22	808.82	862.18	854.90	822.33	841.98	846.42	887.63	878.58	815.70	822.35	838.74
1980	875.85	863.14	785.75	817.06	850.85	867.92	935.32	932.59	932.42	924.49	993.34	963.99
1981	947.27	974.58	1003.87	997.75	991.75	976.88	952.34	881.47	849.98	852.55	888.98	875.00
1982	871.10	824.39	822.77	848.36	819.54	811.93	808.60	901.31	896.25	991.72	1039.28	1046.54
1983	1075.70	1112.62	1130.03	1226.20	1199.98	1221.96	1199.22	1216.16	1233.13	1225.20	1276.02	1258.64
1984	1220.58	1154.63	1164.89	1170.75	1104.85	1132.40	1115.28	1224.38	1206.71	1207.38	1188.94	1211.57
1985	1286.77	1284.01	1266.78	1258.06	1315.41	1335.46	1347.45	1334.01	1328.63	1374.31	1472.13	1546.67
1986	1570.99	1709.06	1818.61	1783.98	1876.71	1892.72	1775.31	1898.34	1767.58	1877.81	1914.23	1895.95
1987	2158.04	2223.99	2304.69	2286.36	2291.57	2418.53	2572.07	2662.95	2596.28	1993.53	1833.55	1938.83

continued

DOW JONES INDUSTRIALS MONTHLY CLOSING PRICES SINCE 1950 (continued)

	Jan	Feb	Mar	Apr	May	Jun	Jul	Aug	Sep	Oct	Nov	Dec
1988	1958.22	2071.62	1988.06	2032.33	2031.12	2141.71	2128.73	2031.65	2112.91	2148.65	2114.51	2168.5
1989	2342.32	2258.39	2293.62	2418.80	2480.15	2440.06	2660.66	2737.27	2692.82	2645.08	2706.27	2753.20
1990	2590.54	2627.25	2707.21	2656.76	2876.66	2880.69	2905.20	2614.36	2452.48	2442.33	2559.65	2633.66
1991	2736.39	2882.18	2913.86	2887.87	3027.50	2906.75	3024.82	3043.60	3016.77	3069.10	2894.68	3168.83
1992	3223.39	3267.67	3235.47	3359.12	3396.88	3318.52	3393.78	3257.35	3271.66	3226.28	3305.16	3301.11
1993	3310.03	3370.81	3435.11	3427.55	3527.43	3516.08	3539.47	3651.25	3555.12	3680.59	3683.95	3754.09
1994	3978.36	3832.02	3635.96	3681.69	3758.37	3624.96	3764.50	3913.42	3843.19	3908.12	3739.23	3834.44
1995	3843.86	4011.05	4157.69	4321.27	4465.14	4556.10	4708.47	4610.56	4789.08	4755.48	5074.49	5117.12
1996	5395.30	5485.62	5587.14	5569.08	5643.18	5654.63	5528.91	5616.21	5882.17	6029.38	6521.70	6448.27
1997	6813.09	6877.74	6583.48	7008.99	7331.04	7672.79	8222.61	7622.42	7945.26	7442.08	7823.13	7908.25
1998	7906.50	8545.72	8799.81	9063.37	8899.95	8952.02	8883.29	7539.07	7842.62	8592.10	9116.55	9181.43
1999	9358.83	9306.58	9786.16	10789.04	10559.74	10970.80	10655.15	10829.28	10336.95	10729.86	10877.81	11497.12
2000	10940.53	10128.31	10921.92	10733.91	10522.33	10447.89	10521.98	11215.10	10650.92	10971.14	10414.49	10786.85
2001	10887.36	10495.28	9878.78	10734.97	10911.94	10502.40	10522.81	9949.75	8847.56	9075.14	9851.56	10021.50
2002	9920.00	10106.13	10403.94	9946.22	9925.25	9243.26	8736.59	8663.50	7591.93	8397.03	8896.09	8341.63
2003	8053.81	7891.08	7992.13	8480.09	8850.26	8985.44	9233.80	9415.82	9275.06	9801.12	9782.46	10453.92
2004	10488.07	10583.92	10357.70	10225.57	10188.45	10435.48	10139.71	10173.92	10080.27	10027.47	10428.02	10783.01
2005	10489.94	10766.23	10503.76	10192.51	10467.48	10274.97	10640.91	10481.60	10568.70	10440.07	10805.87	10717.50
2006	10864.86	10993.41	11109.32	11367.14	11168.31	11150.22	11185.68	11381.15	11679.07	12080.73	12221.93	12463.15
2007	12621.69	12268.63	12354.35	13062.91	13627.64	13408.62	13211.99	13357.74	13895.63	13930.01	13371.72	13264.82
2008	12650.36	12266.39	12262.89	12820.13	12638.32	11350.01	11378.02	11543.55	10850.66	9325.01	8829.04	8776.39
2009	8000.86	7062.93	7608.92	8168.12	8500.33	8447.00	9171.61	9496.28	9712.28	9712.73	10344.84	10428.05
2010	10067.33	10325.26	10856.63	11008.61	10136.63	9774.02	10465.94	10014.72	10788.05	11118.49	11006.02	11577.51
2011	11891.93	12226.34	12319.73	12810.54	12569.79	12414.34	12143.24	11613.53	10913.38	11955.01	12045.68	12217.56
2012	12632.91	12952.07	13212.04	13213.63	12393.45	12880.09	13008.68	13090.84	13437.13	13096.46	13025.58	13104.14
2013	13860.58	14054.49	14578.54	14839.80	15115.57	14909.60	15499.54	14810.31	15129.67	15545.75	16086.41	16576.66
2014	15698.85	16321.71	16457.66	16580.84	16717.17	16826.60	16563.30	17098.45	17042.90	17390.52	17828.24	17823.07
2015	17164.95	18132.70	17776.12	17840.52	18010.68	17619.51	17689.86	16528.03	16284.00	17663.54	17719.92	17425.03
2016	16466.30	16516.50	17685.09	17773.64	17787.20	17929.99	18432.24	18400.88	18308.15	18142.42	19123.58	19762.60
2017	19864.09	20812.24	20663.22	20940.51	21008.65	21349.63	21891.12	21948.10	22405.09	23377.24	24272.35	24719.22
2018	26149.39	25029.20	24103.11	24163.15	24415.84	24271.41	25415.19	25964.82	26458.31	25115.76	25538.46	23327.46
2019	24999.67	25916.00	25928.68	26592.91	24815.04	26599.96	26864.27	26403.28	26916.83	27046.23	28051.41	28538.44
2020	28256.03	25409.36	21917.16	24345.72	25383.11	25812.88	26428.32	28430.05	27781.70	26501.60	29638.64	30606.48
2021	29982.62	30932.37	32981.55	33874.85	34529.45	34502.51	34935.47	35360.73	33843.92	35819.56	34483.72	36338.30
2022	35131.86	33892.60	34678.35	32977.21	32990.12	30775.43	32845.13	31510.43	28725.51	32732.95	34589.77	33147.25
2023	34086.04	32656.70	33274.15	34098.16	32908.27	34407.60	35559.53	34721.91	33507.50	33052.87	35950.89	37689.54
2024	38150.30	38996.39	39807.37	37815.92	38686.32	39118.86	40842.79	41563.08	42330.15	41763.46	44910.65	42544.22
2025	44544.66	43840.91	42001.76	40669.36	42270.07	44094.77	44130.98	45544.88	46397.89	47562.87	47716.42	48063.29
2026	48892.47	48977.92	46341.51	49652.14								

STANDARD & POOR'S 500 MONTHLY PERCENT CHANGES SINCE 1950

	Jan	Feb	Mar	Apr	May	Jun	Jul	Aug	Sep	Oct	Nov	Dec	Year
1950	1.7	1.0	0.4	4.5	3.9	–5.8	0.8	3.3	5.6	0.4	–0.1	4.6	21.8
1951	6.1	0.6	–1.8	4.8	–4.1	–2.6	6.9	3.9	–0.1	–1.4	–0.3	3.9	16.5
1952	1.6	–3.6	4.8	–4.3	2.3	4.6	1.8	–1.5	–2.0	–0.1	4.6	3.5	11.8
1953	–0.7	–1.8	–2.4	–2.6	–0.3	–1.6	2.5	–5.8	0.1	5.1	0.9	0.2	–6.6
1954	5.1	0.3	3.0	4.9	3.3	0.1	5.7	–3.4	8.3	–1.9	8.1	5.1	45.0
1955	1.8	0.4	–0.5	3.8	–0.1	8.2	6.1	–0.8	1.1	–3.0	7.5	–0.1	26.4
1956	–3.6	3.5	6.9	–0.2	–6.6	3.9	5.2	–3.8	–4.5	0.5	–1.1	3.5	2.6
1957	–4.2	–3.3	2.0	3.7	3.7	–0.1	1.1	–5.6	–6.2	–3.2	1.6	–4.1	–14.3
1958	4.3	–2.1	3.1	3.2	1.5	2.6	4.3	1.2	4.8	2.5	2.2	5.2	38.1
1959	0.4	–0.02	0.1	3.9	1.9	–0.4	3.5	–1.5	–4.6	1.1	1.3	2.8	8.5
1960	–7.1	0.9	–1.4	–1.8	2.7	2.0	–2.5	2.6	–6.0	–0.2	4.0	4.6	–3.0
1961	6.3	2.7	2.6	0.4	1.9	–2.9	3.3	2.0	–2.0	2.8	3.9	0.3	23.1
1962	–3.8	1.6	–0.6	–6.2	–8.6	–8.2	6.4	1.5	–4.8	0.4	10.2	1.3	–11.8
1963	4.9	–2.9	3.5	4.9	1.4	–2.0	–0.3	4.9	–1.1	3.2	–1.1	2.4	18.9
1964	2.7	1.0	1.5	0.6	1.1	1.6	1.8	–1.6	2.9	0.8	–0.5	0.4	13.0
1965	3.3	–0.1	–1.5	3.4	–0.8	–4.9	1.3	2.3	3.2	2.7	–0.9	0.9	9.1
1966	0.5	–1.8	–2.2	2.1	–5.4	–1.6	–1.3	–7.8	–0.7	4.8	0.3	–0.1	–13.1
1967	7.8	0.2	3.9	4.2	–5.2	1.8	4.5	–1.2	3.3	–2.9	0.1	2.6	20.1
1968	–4.4	–3.1	0.9	8.2	1.1	0.9	–1.8	1.1	3.9	0.7	4.8	–4.2	7.7
1969	–0.8	–4.7	3.4	2.1	–0.2	–5.6	–6.0	4.0	–2.5	4.4	–3.5	–1.9	–11.4
1970	–7.6	5.3	0.1	–9.0	–6.1	–5.0	7.3	4.4	3.3	–1.1	4.7	5.7	0.1
1971	4.0	0.9	3.7	3.6	–4.2	0.1	–4.1	3.6	–0.7	–4.2	–0.3	8.6	10.8
1972	1.8	2.5	0.6	0.4	1.7	–2.2	0.2	3.4	–0.5	0.9	4.6	1.2	15.6
1973	–1.7	–3.7	–0.1	–4.1	–1.9	–0.7	3.8	–3.7	4.0	–0.1	–11.4	1.7	–17.4
1974	–1.0	–0.4	–2.3	–3.9	–3.4	–1.5	–7.8	–9.0	–11.9	16.3	–5.3	–2.0	–29.7
1975	12.3	6.0	2.2	4.7	4.4	4.4	–6.8	–2.1	–3.5	6.2	2.5	–1.2	31.5
1976	11.8	–1.1	3.1	–1.1	–1.4	4.1	–0.8	–0.5	2.3	–2.2	–0.8	5.2	19.1
1977	–5.1	–2.2	–1.4	0.02	–2.4	4.5	–1.6	–2.1	–0.2	–4.3	2.7	0.3	–11.5
1978	–6.2	–2.5	2.5	8.5	0.4	–1.8	5.4	2.6	–0.7	–9.2	1.7	1.5	1.1
1979	4.0	–3.7	5.5	0.2	–2.6	3.9	0.9	5.3	N/C	–6.9	4.3	1.7	12.3
1980	5.8	–0.4	–10.2	4.1	4.7	2.7	6.5	0.6	2.5	1.6	10.2	–3.4	25.8
1981	–4.6	1.3	3.6	–2.3	–0.2	–1.0	–0.2	–6.2	–5.4	4.9	3.7	–3.0	–9.7
1982	–1.8	–6.1	–1.0	4.0	–3.9	–2.0	–2.3	11.6	0.8	11.0	3.6	1.5	14.8
1983	3.3	1.9	3.3	7.5	–1.2	3.5	–3.3	1.1	1.0	–1.5	1.7	–0.9	17.3
1984	–0.9	–3.9	1.3	0.5	–5.9	1.7	–1.6	10.6	–0.3	–0.01	–1.5	2.2	1.4
1985	7.4	0.9	–0.3	–0.5	5.4	1.2	–0.5	–1.2	–3.5	4.3	6.5	4.5	26.3
1986	0.2	7.1	5.3	–1.4	5.0	1.4	–5.9	7.1	–8.5	5.5	2.1	–2.8	14.6
1987	13.2	3.7	2.6	–1.1	0.6	4.8	4.8	3.5	–2.4	–21.8	–8.5	7.3	2.0
1988	4.0	4.2	–3.3	0.9	0.3	4.3	–0.5	–3.9	4.0	2.6	–1.9	1.5	12.4
1989	7.1	–2.9	2.1	5.0	3.5	–0.8	8.8	1.6	–0.7	–2.5	1.7	2.1	27.3

continued

STANDARD & POOR'S 500 MONTHLY PERCENT CHANGES SINCE 1950 (continued)

	Jan	Feb	Mar	Apr	May	Jun	Jul	Aug	Sep	Oct	Nov	Dec	Year
1990	–6.9	0.9	2.4	–2.7	9.2	–0.9	–0.5	–9.4	–5.1	–0.7	6.0	2.5	–6.6
1991	4.2	6.7	2.2	0.03	3.9	–4.8	4.5	2.0	–1.9	1.2	–4.4	11.2	26.3
1992	–2.0	1.0	–2.2	2.8	0.1	–1.7	3.9	–2.4	0.9	0.2	3.0	1.0	4.5
1993	0.7	1.0	1.9	–2.5	2.3	0.1	–0.5	3.4	–1.0	1.9	–1.3	1.0	7.1
1994	3.3	–3.0	–4.6	1.2	1.2	–2.7	3.1	3.8	–2.7	2.1	–4.0	1.2	–1.5
1995	2.4	3.6	2.7	2.8	3.6	2.1	3.2	–0.03	4.0	–0.5	4.1	1.7	34.1
1996	3.3	0.7	0.8	1.3	2.3	0.2	–4.6	1.9	5.4	2.6	7.3	–2.2	20.3
1997	6.1	0.6	–4.3	5.8	5.9	4.3	7.8	–5.7	5.3	–3.4	4.5	1.6	31.0
1998	1.0	7.0	5.0	0.9	–1.9	3.9	–1.2	–14.6	6.2	8.0	5.9	5.6	26.7
1999	4.1	–3.2	3.9	3.8	–2.5	5.4	–3.2	–0.6	–2.9	6.3	1.9	5.8	19.5
2000	–5.1	–2.0	9.7	–3.1	–2.2	2.4	–1.6	6.1	–5.3	–0.5	–8.0	0.4	–10.1
2001	3.5	–9.2	–6.4	7.7	0.5	–2.5	–1.1	–6.4	–8.2	1.8	7.5	0.8	–13.0
2002	–1.6	–2.1	3.7	–6.1	–0.9	–7.2	–7.9	0.5	–11.0	8.6	5.7	–6.0	–23.4
2003	–2.7	–1.7	1.0	8.0	5.1	1.1	1.6	1.8	–1.2	5.5	0.7	5.1	26.4
2004	1.7	1.2	–1.6	–1.7	1.2	1.8	–3.4	0.2	0.9	1.4	3.9	3.2	9.0
2005	–2.5	1.9	–1.9	–2.0	3.0	–0.01	3.6	–1.1	0.7	–1.8	3.5	–0.1	3.0
2006	2.5	0.05	1.1	1.2	–3.1	0.01	0.5	2.1	2.5	3.2	1.6	1.3	13.6
2007	1.4	–2.2	1.0	4.3	3.3	–1.8	–3.2	1.3	3.6	1.5	–4.4	–0.9	3.5
2008	–6.1	–3.5	–0.6	4.8	1.1	–8.6	–1.0	1.2	–9.1	–16.9	–7.5	0.8	–38.5
2009	–8.6	–11.0	8.5	9.4	5.3	0.02	7.4	3.4	3.6	–2.0	5.7	1.8	23.5
2010	–3.7	2.9	5.9	1.5	–8.2	–5.4	6.9	–4.7	8.8	3.7	–0.2	6.5	12.8
2011	2.3	3.2	–0.1	2.8	–1.4	–1.8	–2.1	–5.7	–7.2	10.8	–0.5	0.9	–0.003
2012	4.4	4.1	3.1	–0.7	–6.3	4.0	1.3	2.0	2.4	–2.0	0.3	0.7	13.4
2013	5.0	1.1	3.6	1.8	2.1	–1.5	4.9	–3.1	3.0	4.5	2.8	2.4	29.6
2014	–3.6	4.3	0.7	0.6	2.1	1.9	–1.5	3.8	–1.6	2.3	2.5	–0.4	11.4
2015	–3.1	5.5	–1.7	0.9	1.0	–2.1	2.0	–6.3	–2.6	8.3	0.1	–1.8	–0.7
2016	–5.1	–0.4	6.6	0.3	1.5	0.1	3.6	–0.1	–0.1	–1.9	3.4	1.8	9.5
2017	1.8	3.7	–0.04	0.9	1.2	0.5	1.9	0.1	1.9	2.2	2.8	1.0	19.4
2018	5.6	–3.9	–2.7	0.3	2.2	0.5	3.6	3.0	0.4	–6.9	1.8	–9.2	–6.2
2019	7.9	3.0	1.8	3.9	–6.6	6.9	1.3	–1.8	1.7	2.0	3.4	2.9	28.9
2020	–0.2	–8.4	–12.5	12.7	4.5	1.8	5.5	7.0	–3.9	–2.8	10.8	3.7	16.3
2021	–1.1	2.6	4.2	5.2	0.5	2.2	2.3	2.9	–4.8	6.9	–0.8	4.4	26.9
2022	–5.3	–3.1	3.6	–8.8	0.01	–8.4	9.1	–4.2	–9.3	8.0	5.4	–5.9	–19.4
2023	6.2	–2.6	3.5	1.5	0.2	6.5	3.1	–1.8	–4.9	–2.2	8.9	4.4	24.2
2024	1.6	5.2	3.1	–4.2	4.8	3.5	1.1	2.3	2.0	–1.0	5.7	–2.5	23.3
2025	2.7	–1.4	–5.8	–0.8	6.2	5.0	2.2	1.9	3.5	2.3	0.1	–0.1	16.4
2026	1.4	–0.9	–5.1	10.4									
TOTALS	**83.4**	**–2.7**	**73.5**	**119.9**	**27.5**	**16.4**	**98.2**	**3.3**	**–47.7**	**68.9**	**140.5**	**107.2**	
AVG.	**1.1**	**–0.03**	**1.0**	**1.6**	**0.4**	**0.2**	**1.3**	**0.04**	**–0.6**	**0.9**	**1.8**	**1.4**	
# Up	**47**	**41**	**49**	**54**	**47**	**43**	**46**	**42**	**34**	**45**	**53**	**55**	
# Down	**30**	**36**	**28**	**23**	**29**	**33**	**30**	**34**	**41**	**31**	**23**	**21**	

STANDARD & POOR'S 500 MONTHLY CLOSING PRICES SINCE 1950

	Jan	Feb	Mar	Apr	May	Jun	Jul	Aug	Sep	Oct	Nov	Dec
1950	17.05	17.22	17.29	18.07	18.78	17.69	17.84	18.42	19.45	19.53	19.51	20.41
1951	21.66	21.80	21.40	22.43	21.52	20.96	22.40	23.28	23.26	22.94	22.88	23.77
1952	24.14	23.26	24.37	23.32	23.86	24.96	25.40	25.03	24.54	24.52	25.66	26.57
1953	26.38	25.90	25.29	24.62	24.54	24.14	24.75	23.32	23.35	24.54	24.76	24.81
1954	26.08	26.15	26.94	28.26	29.19	29.21	30.88	29.83	32.31	31.68	34.24	35.98
1955	36.63	36.76	36.58	37.96	37.91	41.03	43.52	43.18	43.67	42.34	45.51	45.48
1956	43.82	45.34	48.48	48.38	45.20	46.97	49.39	47.51	45.35	45.58	45.08	46.67
1957	44.72	43.26	44.11	45.74	47.43	47.37	47.91	45.22	42.42	41.06	41.72	39.99
1958	41.70	40.84	42.10	43.44	44.09	45.24	47.19	47.75	50.06	51.33	52.48	55.21
1959	55.42	55.41	55.44	57.59	58.68	58.47	60.51	59.60	56.88	57.52	58.28	59.89
1960	55.61	56.12	55.34	54.37	55.83	56.92	55.51	56.96	53.52	53.39	55.54	58.11
1961	61.78	63.44	65.06	65.31	66.56	64.64	66.76	68.07	66.73	68.62	71.32	71.55
1962	68.84	69.96	69.55	65.24	59.63	54.75	58.23	59.12	56.27	56.52	62.26	63.10
1963	66.20	64.29	66.57	69.80	70.80	69.37	69.13	72.50	71.70	74.01	73.23	75.02
1964	77.04	77.80	78.98	79.46	80.37	81.69	83.18	81.83	84.18	84.86	84.42	84.75
1965	87.56	87.43	86.16	89.11	88.42	84.12	85.25	87.17	89.96	92.42	91.61	92.43
1966	92.88	91.22	89.23	91.06	86.13	84.74	83.60	77.10	76.56	80.20	80.45	80.33
1967	86.61	86.78	90.20	94.01	89.08	90.64	94.75	93.64	96.71	93.90	94.00	96.47
1968	92.24	89.36	90.20	97.59	98.68	99.58	97.74	98.86	102.67	103.41	108.37	103.86
1969	103.01	98.13	101.51	103.69	103.46	97.71	91.83	95.51	93.12	97.24	93.81	92.06
1970	85.02	89.50	89.63	81.52	76.55	72.72	78.05	81.52	84.21	83.25	87.20	92.15
1971	95.88	96.75	100.31	103.95	99.63	99.70	95.58	99.03	98.34	94.23	93.99	102.09
1972	103.94	106.57	107.20	107.67	109.53	107.14	107.39	111.09	110.55	111.58	116.67	118.05
1973	116.03	111.68	111.52	106.97	104.95	104.26	108.22	104.25	108.43	108.29	95.96	97.55
1974	96.57	96.22	93.98	90.31	87.28	86.00	79.31	72.15	63.54	73.90	69.97	68.56
1975	76.98	81.59	83.36	87.30	91.15	95.19	88.75	86.88	83.87	89.04	91.24	90.19
1976	100.86	99.71	102.77	101.64	100.18	104.28	103.44	102.91	105.24	102.90	102.10	107.46
1977	102.03	99.82	98.42	98.44	96.12	100.48	98.85	96.77	96.53	92.34	94.83	95.10
1978	89.25	87.04	89.21	96.83	97.24	95.53	100.68	103.29	102.54	93.15	94.70	96.11
1979	99.93	96.28	101.59	101.76	99.08	102.91	103.81	109.32	109.32	101.82	106.16	107.94
1980	114.16	113.66	102.09	106.29	111.24	114.24	121.67	122.38	125.46	127.47	140.52	135.76
1981	129.55	131.27	136.00	132.81	132.59	131.21	130.92	122.79	116.18	121.89	126.35	122.55
1982	120.40	113.11	111.96	116.44	111.88	109.61	107.09	119.51	120.42	133.71	138.54	140.64
1983	145.30	148.06	152.96	164.42	162.39	168.11	162.56	164.40	166.07	163.55	166.40	164.93
1984	163.41	157.06	159.18	160.05	150.55	153.18	150.66	166.68	166.10	166.09	163.58	167.24
1985	179.63	181.18	180.66	179.83	189.55	191.85	190.92	188.63	182.08	189.82	202.17	211.28
1986	211.78	226.92	238.90	235.52	247.35	250.84	236.12	252.93	231.32	243.98	249.22	242.17
1987	274.08	284.20	291.70	288.36	290.10	304.00	318.66	329.80	321.83	251.79	230.30	247.08

continued

STANDARD & POOR'S 500 MONTHLY CLOSING PRICES SINCE 1950 (continued)

	Jan	Feb	Mar	Apr	May	Jun	Jul	Aug	Sep	Oct	Nov	Dec
1988	257.07	267.82	258.89	261.33	262.16	273.50	272.02	261.52	271.91	278.97	273.70	277.72
1989	297.47	288.86	294.87	309.64	320.52	317.98	346.08	351.45	349.15	340.36	345.99	353.40
1990	329.08	331.89	339.94	330.80	361.23	358.02	356.15	322.56	306.05	304.00	322.22	330.22
1991	343.93	367.07	375.22	375.35	389.83	371.16	387.81	395.43	387.86	392.46	375.22	417.09
1992	408.79	412.70	403.69	414.95	415.35	408.14	424.21	414.03	417.80	418.68	431.35	435.71
1993	438.78	443.38	451.67	440.19	450.19	450.53	448.13	463.56	458.93	467.83	461.79	466.45
1994	481.61	467.14	445.77	450.91	456.50	444.27	458.26	475.49	462.69	472.35	453.69	459.27
1995	470.42	487.39	500.71	514.71	533.40	544.75	562.06	561.88	584.41	581.50	605.37	615.93
1996	636.02	640.43	645.50	654.17	669.12	670.63	639.95	651.99	687.31	705.27	757.02	740.74
1997	786.16	790.82	757.12	801.34	848.28	885.14	954.29	899.47	947.28	914.62	955.40	970.43
1998	980.28	1049.34	1101.75	1111.75	1090.82	1133.84	1120.67	957.28	1017.01	1098.67	1163.63	1229.23
1999	1279.64	1238.33	1286.37	1335.18	1301.84	1372.71	1328.72	1320.41	1282.71	1362.93	1388.91	1469.25
2000	1394.46	1366.42	1498.58	1452.43	1420.60	1454.60	1430.83	1517.68	1436.51	1429.40	1314.95	1320.28
2001	1366.01	1239.94	1160.33	1249.46	1255.82	1224.42	1211.23	1133.58	1040.94	1059.78	1139.45	1148.08
2002	1130.20	1106.73	1147.39	1076.92	1067.14	989.82	911.62	916.07	815.28	885.76	936.31	879.82
2003	855.70	841.15	849.18	916.92	963.59	974.50	990.31	1008.01	995.97	1050.71	1058.20	1111.92
2004	1131.13	1144.94	1126.21	1107.30	1120.68	1140.84	1101.72	1104.24	1114.58	1130.20	1173.82	1211.92
2005	1181.27	1203.60	1180.59	1156.85	1191.50	1191.33	1234.18	1220.33	1228.81	1207.01	1249.48	1248.29
2006	1280.08	1280.66	1294.83	1310.61	1270.09	1270.20	1276.66	1303.82	1335.85	1377.94	1400.63	1418.30
2007	1438.24	1406.82	1420.86	1482.37	1530.62	1503.35	1455.27	1473.99	1526.75	1549.38	1481.14	1468.36
2008	1378.55	1330.63	1322.70	1385.59	1400.38	1280.00	1267.38	1282.83	1166.36	968.75	896.24	903.25
2009	825.88	735.09	797.87	872.81	919.14	919.32	987.48	1020.62	1057.08	1036.19	1095.63	1115.10
2010	1073.87	1104.49	1169.43	1186.69	1089.41	1030.71	1101.60	1049.33	1141.20	1183.26	1180.55	1257.64
2011	1286.12	1327.22	1325.83	1363.61	1345.20	1320.64	1292.28	1218.89	1131.42	1253.30	1246.96	1257.60
2012	1312.41	1365.68	1408.47	1397.91	1310.33	1362.16	1379.32	1406.58	1440.67	1412.16	1416.18	1426.19
2013	1498.11	1514.68	1569.19	1597.57	1630.74	1606.28	1685.73	1632.97	1681.55	1756.54	1805.81	1848.36
2014	1782.59	1859.45	1872.34	1883.95	1923.57	1960.23	1930.67	2003.37	1972.29	2018.05	2067.56	2058.90
2015	1994.99	2104.50	2067.89	2085.51	2107.39	2063.11	2103.84	1972.18	1920.03	2079.36	2080.41	2043.94
2016	1940.24	1932.23	2059.74	2065.30	2096.96	2098.86	2173.60	2170.95	2168.27	2126.15	2198.81	2238.83
2017	2278.87	2363.64	2362.72	2384.20	2411.80	2423.41	2470.30	2471.65	2519.36	2575.26	2647.58	2673.61
2018	2823.81	2713.83	2640.87	2648.05	2705.27	2718.37	2816.29	2901.52	2913.98	2711.74	2760.16	2506.85
2019	2704.10	2784.49	2834.40	2945.83	2752.06	2941.76	2980.38	2926.46	2976.74	3037.56	3140.98	3230.78
2020	3225.52	2954.22	2584.59	2912.43	3044.31	3100.29	3271.12	3500.31	3363.00	3269.96	3621.63	3756.07
2021	3714.24	3811.15	3972.89	4181.17	4204.11	4297.50	4395.26	4522.68	4307.54	4605.38	4567.00	4766.18
2022	4515.55	4373.94	4530.41	4131.93	4132.15	3785.38	4130.29	3955.00	3585.62	3871.98	4080.11	3839.50
2023	4076.60	3970.15	4109.31	4169.48	4179.83	4450.38	4588.96	4507.66	4288.05	4193.80	4567.80	4769.83
2024	4845.65	5096.27	5254.35	5035.69	5277.51	5460.48	5522.30	5648.40	5762.48	5705.45	6032.38	5881.63
2025	6040.53	5954.50	5611.85	5569.06	5911.69	6204.95	6339.39	6460.26	6688.46	6840.20	6849.09	6845.50
2026	6939.03	6878.88	6528.52	7209.01								

NASDAQ COMPOSITE MONTHLY PERCENT CHANGES SINCE 1971

	Jan	Feb	Mar	Apr	May	Jun	Jul	Aug	Sep	Oct	Nov	Dec	Year
1971	10.2	2.6	4.6	6.0	–3.6	–0.4	–2.3	3.0	0.6	–3.6	–1.1	9.8	27.4
1972	4.2	5.5	2.2	2.5	0.9	–1.8	–1.8	1.7	–0.3	0.5	2.1	0.6	17.2
1973	–4.0	–6.2	–2.4	–8.2	–4.8	–1.6	7.6	–3.5	6.0	–0.9	–15.1	–1.4	–31.1
1974	3.0	–0.6	–2.2	–5.9	–7.7	–5.3	–7.9	–10.9	–10.7	17.2	–3.5	–5.0	–35.1
1975	16.6	4.6	3.6	3.8	5.8	4.7	–4.4	–5.0	–5.9	3.6	2.4	–1.5	29.8
1976	12.1	3.7	0.4	–0.6	–2.3	2.6	1.1	–1.7	1.7	–1.0	0.9	7.4	26.1
1977	–2.4	–1.0	–0.5	1.4	0.1	4.3	0.9	–0.5	0.7	–3.3	5.8	1.8	7.3
1978	–4.0	0.6	4.7	8.5	4.4	0.05	5.0	6.9	–1.6	–16.4	3.2	2.9	12.3
1979	6.6	–2.6	7.5	1.6	–1.8	5.1	2.3	6.4	–0.3	–9.6	6.4	4.8	28.1
1980	7.0	–2.3	–17.1	6.9	7.5	4.9	8.9	5.7	3.4	2.7	8.0	–2.8	33.9
1981	–2.2	0.1	6.1	3.1	3.1	–3.5	–1.9	–7.5	–8.0	8.4	3.1	–2.7	–3.2
1982	–3.8	–4.8	–2.1	5.2	–3.3	–4.1	–2.3	6.2	5.6	13.3	9.3	0.04	18.7
1983	6.9	5.0	3.9	8.2	5.3	3.2	–4.6	–3.8	1.4	–7.4	4.1	–2.5	19.9
1984	–3.7	–5.9	–0.7	–1.3	–5.9	2.9	–4.2	10.9	–1.8	–1.2	–1.8	2.0	–11.2
1985	12.7	2.0	–1.7	0.5	3.6	1.9	1.7	–1.2	–5.8	4.4	7.3	3.5	31.4
1986	3.3	7.1	4.2	2.3	4.4	1.3	–8.4	3.1	–8.4	2.9	–0.3	–2.8	7.5
1987	12.2	8.4	1.2	–2.8	–0.3	2.0	2.4	4.6	–2.3	–27.2	–5.6	8.3	–5.4
1988	4.3	6.5	2.1	1.2	–2.3	6.6	–1.9	–2.8	3.0	–1.4	–2.9	2.7	15.4
1989	5.2	–0.4	1.8	5.1	4.4	–2.4	4.3	3.4	0.8	–3.7	0.1	–0.3	19.3
1990	–8.6	2.4	2.3	–3.6	9.3	0.7	–5.2	–13.0	–9.6	–4.3	8.9	4.1	–17.8
1991	10.8	9.4	6.5	0.5	4.4	–6.0	5.5	4.7	0.2	3.1	–3.5	11.9	56.8
1992	5.8	2.1	–4.7	–4.2	1.1	–3.7	3.1	–3.0	3.6	3.8	7.9	3.7	15.5
1993	2.9	–3.7	2.9	–4.2	5.9	0.5	0.1	5.4	2.7	2.2	–3.2	3.0	14.7
1994	3.0	–1.0	–6.2	–1.3	0.2	–4.0	2.3	6.0	–0.2	1.7	–3.5	0.2	–3.2
1995	0.4	5.1	3.0	3.3	2.4	8.0	7.3	1.9	2.3	–0.7	2.2	–0.7	39.9
1996	0.7	3.8	0.1	8.1	4.4	–4.7	–8.8	5.6	7.5	–0.4	5.8	–0.1	22.7
1997	6.9	–5.1	–6.7	3.2	11.1	3.0	10.5	–0.4	6.2	–5.5	0.4	–1.9	21.6
1998	3.1	9.3	3.7	1.8	–4.8	6.5	–1.2	–19.9	13.0	4.6	10.1	12.5	39.6
1999	14.3	–8.7	7.6	3.3	–2.8	8.7	–1.8	3.8	0.2	8.0	12.5	22.0	85.6

continued

Based on NASDAQ composite, prior to Feb. 5, 1971, based on National Quotation Bureau indices

NASDAQ COMPOSITE MONTHLY PERCENT CHANGES SINCE 1971 (continued)

	Jan	Feb	Mar	Apr	May	Jun	Jul	Aug	Sep	Oct	Nov	Dec	Year
2000	−3.2	19.2	−2.6	−15.6	−11.9	16.6	−5.0	11.7	−12.7	−8.3	−22.9	−4.9	−39.3
2001	12.2	−22.4	−14.5	15.0	−0.3	2.4	−6.2	−10.9	−17.0	12.8	14.2	1.0	−21.1
2002	−0.8	−10.5	6.6	−8.5	−4.3	−9.4	−9.2	−1.0	−10.9	13.5	11.2	−9.7	−31.5
2003	−1.1	1.3	0.3	9.2	9.0	1.7	6.9	4.3	−1.3	8.1	1.5	2.2	50.0
2004	3.1	−1.8	−1.8	−3.7	3.5	3.1	−7.8	−2.6	3.2	4.1	6.2	3.7	8.6
2005	−5.2	−0.5	−2.6	−3.9	7.6	−0.5	6.2	−1.5	−0.02	−1.5	5.3	−1.2	1.4
2006	4.6	−1.1	2.6	−0.7	−6.2	−0.3	−3.7	4.4	3.4	4.8	2.7	−0.7	9.5
2007	2.0	−1.9	0.2	4.3	3.1	−0.05	−2.2	2.0	4.0	5.8	−6.9	−0.3	9.8
2008	−9.9	−5.0	0.3	5.9	4.6	−9.1	1.4	1.8	−11.6	−17.7	−10.8	2.7	−40.5
2009	−6.4	−6.7	10.9	12.3	3.3	3.4	7.8	1.5	5.6	−3.6	4.9	5.8	43.9
2010	−5.4	4.2	7.1	2.6	−8.3	−6.5	6.9	−6.2	12.0	5.9	−0.4	6.2	16.9
2011	1.8	3.0	−0.04	3.3	−1.3	−2.2	−0.6	−6.4	−6.4	11.1	−2.4	−0.6	−1.8
2012	8.0	5.4	4.2	−1.5	−7.2	3.8	0.2	4.3	1.6	−4.5	1.1	0.3	15.9
2013	4.1	0.6	3.4	1.9	3.8	−1.5	6.6	−1.0	5.1	3.9	3.6	2.9	38.3
2014	−1.7	5.0	−2.5	−2.0	3.1	3.9	−0.9	4.8	−1.9	3.1	3.5	−1.2	13.4
2015	−2.1	7.1	−1.3	0.8	2.6	−1.6	2.8	−6.9	−3.3	9.4	1.1	−2.0	5.7
2016	−7.9	−1.2	6.8	−1.9	3.6	−2.1	6.6	1.0	1.9	−2.3	2.6	1.1	7.5
2017	4.3	3.8	1.5	2.3	2.5	−0.9	3.4	1.3	1.0	3.6	2.2	0.4	28.2
2018	7.4	−1.9	−2.9	0.04	5.3	0.9	2.2	5.7	−0.8	−9.2	0.3	−9.5	−3.9
2019	9.7	3.4	2.6	4.7	−7.9	7.4	2.1	−2.6	0.5	3.7	4.5	3.5	35.2
2020	2.0	−6.4	−10.1	15.4	6.8	6.0	6.8	9.6	−5.2	−2.3	11.8	5.7	43.6
2021	1.4	0.9	0.4	5.4	−1.5	5.5	1.2	4.0	−5.3	7.3	0.3	0.7	21.4
2022	−9.0	−3.4	3.4	−13.3	−2.1	−8.7	12.3	−4.6	−10.5	3.9	4.4	−8.7	−33.1
2023	10.7	−1.1	6.7	0.04	5.8	6.6	4.0	−2.2	−5.8	−2.8	10.7	5.5	43.4
2024	1.0	6.1	1.8	−4.4	6.9	6.0	−0.8	0.6	2.7	−0.5	6.2	0.5	28.6
2025	1.6	−4.0	−8.2	0.9	9.6	6.6	3.7	1.6	5.6	4.7	−1.5	−0.5	20.4
2026	0.9	−3.4	−4.8	15.3									
TOTALS	**145.6**	**24.6**	**31.6**	**88.3**	**68.8**	**60.5**	**51.0**	**18.8**	**−42.1**	**42.8**	**113.4**	**82.4**	
AVG.	**2.6**	**0.4**	**0.6**	**1.6**	**1.3**	**1.1**	**0.9**	**0.3**	**−0.8**	**0.8**	**2.1**	**1.5**	
# Up	**38**	**29**	**35**	**37**	**34**	**32**	**32**	**31**	**29**	**30**	**39**	**33**	
# Down	**18**	**27**	**21**	**19**	**21**	**23**	**23**	**24**	**26**	**25**	**16**	**22**	

Based on NASDAQ composite, prior to Feb. 5, 1971, based on National Quotation Bureau indices

NASDAQ COMPOSITE MONTHLY CLOSING PRICES SINCE 1971

	Jan	Feb	Mar	Apr	May	Jun	Jul	Aug	Sep	Oct	Nov	Dec
1971	98.77	101.34	105.97	112.30	108.25	107.80	105.27	108.42	109.03	105.10	103.97	114.12
1972	118.87	125.38	128.14	131.33	132.53	130.08	127.75	129.95	129.61	130.24	132.96	133.73
1973	128.40	120.41	117.46	107.85	102.64	100.98	108.64	104.87	111.20	110.17	93.51	92.19
1974	94.93	94.35	92.27	86.86	80.20	75.96	69.99	62.37	55.67	65.23	62.95	59.82
1975	69.78	73.00	75.66	78.54	83.10	87.02	83.19	79.01	74.33	76.99	78.80	77.62
1976	87.05	90.26	90.62	90.08	88.04	90.32	91.29	89.70	91.26	90.35	91.12	97.88
1977	95.54	94.57	94.13	95.48	95.59	99.73	100.65	100.10	100.85	97.52	103.15	105.05
1978	100.84	101.47	106.20	115.18	120.24	120.30	126.32	135.01	132.89	111.12	114.69	117.98
1979	125.82	122.56	131.76	133.82	131.42	138.13	141.33	150.44	149.98	135.53	144.26	151.14
1980	161.75	158.03	131.00	139.99	150.45	157.78	171.81	181.52	187.76	192.78	208.15	202.34
1981	197.81	198.01	210.18	216.74	223.47	215.75	211.63	195.75	180.03	195.24	201.37	195.84
1982	188.39	179.43	175.65	184.70	178.54	171.30	167.35	177.71	187.65	212.63	232.31	232.41
1983	248.35	260.67	270.80	293.06	308.73	318.70	303.96	292.42	296.65	274.55	285.67	278.60
1984	268.43	252.57	250.78	247.44	232.82	239.65	229.70	254.64	249.94	247.03	242.53	247.35
1985	278.70	284.17	279.20	280.56	290.80	296.20	301.29	297.71	280.33	292.54	313.95	324.93
1986	335.77	359.53	374.72	383.24	400.16	405.51	371.37	382.86	350.67	360.77	359.57	349.33
1987	392.06	424.97	430.05	417.81	416.54	424.67	434.93	454.97	444.29	323.30	305.16	330.47
1988	344.66	366.95	374.64	379.23	370.34	394.66	387.33	376.55	387.71	382.46	371.45	381.38
1989	401.30	399.71	406.73	427.55	446.17	435.29	453.84	469.33	472.92	455.63	456.09	454.82
1990	415.81	425.83	435.54	420.07	458.97	462.29	438.24	381.21	344.51	329.84	359.06	373.84
1991	414.20	453.05	482.30	484.72	506.11	475.92	502.04	525.68	526.88	542.98	523.90	586.34
1992	620.21	633.47	603.77	578.68	585.31	563.60	580.83	563.12	583.27	605.17	652.73	676.95
1993	696.34	670.77	690.13	661.42	700.53	703.95	704.70	742.84	762.78	779.26	754.39	776.80
1994	800.47	792.50	743.46	733.84	735.19	705.96	722.16	765.62	764.29	777.49	750.32	751.96
1995	755.20	793.73	817.21	843.98	864.58	933.45	1001.21	1020.11	1043.54	1036.06	1059.20	1052.13
1996	1059.79	1100.05	1101.40	1190.52	1243.43	1185.02	1080.59	1141.50	1226.92	1221.51	1292.61	1291.03
1997	1379.85	1309.00	1221.70	1260.76	1400.32	1442.07	1593.81	1587.32	1685.69	1593.61	1600.55	1570.35

continued

Based on NASDAQ composite, prior to Feb. 5, 1971, based on National Quotation Bureau indices

NASDAQ COMPOSITE MONTHLY CLOSING PRICES SINCE 1971 (continued)

	Jan	Feb	Mar	Apr	May	Jun	Jul	Aug	Sep	Oct	Nov	Dec
1998	1619.36	1770.51	1835.68	1868.41	1778.87	1894.74	1872.39	1499.25	1693.84	1771.39	1949.54	2192.69
1999	2505.89	2288.03	2461.40	2542.85	2470.52	2686.12	2638.49	2739.35	2746.16	2966.43	3336.16	4069.31
2000	3940.35	4696.69	4572.83	3860.66	3400.91	3966.11	3766.99	4206.35	3672.82	3369.63	2597.93	2470.52
2001	2772.73	2151.83	1840.26	2116.24	2110.49	2160.54	2027.13	1805.43	1498.80	1690.20	1930.58	1950.40
2002	1934.03	1731.49	1845.35	1688.23	1615.73	1463.21	1328.26	1314.85	1172.06	1329.75	1478.78	1335.51
2003	1320.91	1337.52	1341.17	1464.31	1595.91	1622.80	1735.02	1810.45	1786.94	1932.21	1960.26	2003.37
2004	2066.15	2029.82	1994.22	1920.15	1986.74	2047.79	1887.36	1838.10	1896.84	1974.99	2096.81	2175.44
2005	2062.41	2051.72	1999.23	1921.65	2068.22	2056.96	2184.83	2152.09	2151.69	2120.30	2232.82	2205.32
2006	2305.82	2281.39	2339.79	2322.57	2178.88	2172.09	2091.47	2183.75	2258.43	2366.71	2431.77	2415.29
2007	2463.93	2416.15	2421.64	2525.09	2604.52	2603.23	2545.57	2596.36	2701.50	2859.12	2660.96	2652.28
2008	2389.86	2271.48	2279.10	2412.80	2522.66	2292.98	2325.55	2367.52	2091.88	1720.95	1535.57	1577.03
2009	1476.42	1377.84	1528.59	1717.30	1774.33	1835.04	1978.50	2009.06	2122.42	2045.11	2144.60	2269.15
2010	2147.35	2238.26	2397.96	2461.19	2257.04	2109.24	2254.70	2114.03	2368.62	2507.41	2498.23	2652.87
2011	2700.08	2782.27	2781.07	2873.54	2835.30	2773.52	2756.38	2579.46	2415.40	2684.41	2620.34	2605.15
2012	2813.84	2966.89	3091.57	3046.36	2827.34	2935.05	2939.52	3066.96	3116.23	2977.23	3010.24	3019.51
2013	3142.13	3160.19	3267.52	3328.79	3455.91	3403.25	3626.37	3589.87	3771.48	3919.71	4059.89	4176.59
2014	4103.88	4308.12	4198.99	4114.56	4242.62	4408.18	4369.77	4580.27	4493.39	4630.74	4791.63	4736.05
2015	4635.24	4963.53	4900.88	4941.42	5070.03	4986.87	5128.28	4776.51	4620.16	5053.75	5108.67	5007.41
2016	4613.95	4557.95	4869.85	4775.36	4948.05	4842.67	5162.13	5213.22	5312.00	5189.13	5323.68	5383.12
2017	5614.79	5825.44	5911.74	6047.61	6198.52	6140.42	6348.12	6428.66	6495.96	6727.67	6873.97	6903.39
2018	7411.48	7273.01	7063.44	7066.27	7442.12	7510.30	7671.79	8109.54	8046.35	7305.90	7330.54	6635.28
2019	7281.74	7532.53	7729.32	8095.39	7453.15	8006.24	8175.42	7962.88	7999.34	8292.36	8665.47	8972.60
2020	9150.94	8567.37	7700.10	8889.55	9489.87	10058.77	10745.27	11775.46	11167.51	10911.59	12198.74	12888.28
2021	13070.69	13192.35	13246.87	13962.68	13748.74	14503.95	14672.68	15259.24	14448.58	15498.39	15537.69	15644.97
2022	14239.88	13751.40	14220.52	12334.64	12081.39	11028.74	12390.69	11816.20	10575.62	10988.15	11468.00	10466.48
2023	11584.55	11455.54	12221.91	12226.58	12935.29	13787.92	14346.02	14034.97	13219.32	12851.24	14226.22	15011.35
2024	15164.01	16091.92	16379.46	15657.82	16735.02	17732.60	17599.40	17713.62	18189.17	18095.15	19218.17	19310.79
2025	19627.44	18847.28	17299.29	17446.34	19113.77	20369.73	21122.45	21455.55	22660.01	23724.96	23365.69	23241.99
2026	23461.82	22668.21	21590.63	24892.31								

Based on NASDAQ composite, prior to Feb. 5, 1971, based on National Quotation Bureau indices

RUSSELL 1000 INDEX MONTHLY PERCENT CHANGES SINCE 1979

	Jan	Feb	Mar	Apr	May	Jun	Jul	Aug	Sep	Oct	Nov	Dec	Year
1979	4.2	–3.5	6.0	0.3	–2.2	4.3	1.1	5.6	0.02	–7.1	5.1	2.1	16.1
1980	5.9	–0.5	–11.5	4.6	5.0	3.2	6.4	1.1	2.6	1.8	10.1	–3.9	25.6
1981	–4.6	1.0	3.8	–1.9	0.2	–1.2	–0.1	–6.2	–6.4	5.4	4.0	–3.3	–9.7
1982	–2.7	–5.9	–1.3	3.9	–3.6	–2.6	–2.3	11.3	1.2	11.3	4.0	1.3	13.7
1983	3.2	2.1	3.2	7.1	–0.2	3.7	–3.2	0.5	1.3	–2.4	2.0	–1.2	17.0
1984	–1.9	–4.4	1.1	0.3	–5.9	2.1	–1.8	10.8	–0.2	–0.1	–1.4	2.2	–0.1
1985	7.8	1.1	–0.4	–0.3	5.4	1.6	–0.8	–1.0	–3.9	4.5	6.5	4.1	26.7
1986	0.9	7.2	5.1	–1.3	5.0	1.4	–5.9	6.8	–8.5	5.1	1.4	–3.0	13.6
1987	12.7	4.0	1.9	–1.8	0.4	4.5	4.2	3.8	–2.4	–21.9	–8.0	7.2	0.02
1988	4.3	4.4	–2.9	0.7	0.2	4.8	–0.9	–3.3	3.9	2.0	–2.0	1.7	13.1
1989	6.8	–2.5	2.0	4.9	3.8	–0.8	8.2	1.7	–0.5	–2.8	1.5	1.8	25.9
1990	–7.4	1.2	2.2	–2.8	8.9	–0.7	–1.1	–9.6	–5.3	–0.8	6.4	2.7	–7.5
1991	4.5	6.9	2.5	–0.1	3.8	–4.7	4.6	2.2	–1.5	1.4	–4.1	11.2	28.8
1992	–1.4	0.9	–2.4	2.3	0.3	–1.9	4.1	–2.5	1.0	0.7	3.5	1.4	5.9
1993	0.7	0.6	2.2	–2.8	2.4	0.4	–0.4	3.5	–0.5	1.2	–1.7	1.6	7.3
1994	2.9	–2.9	–4.5	1.1	1.0	–2.9	3.1	3.9	–2.6	1.7	–3.9	1.2	–2.4
1995	2.4	3.8	2.3	2.5	3.5	2.4	3.7	0.5	3.9	–0.6	4.2	1.4	34.4
1996	3.1	1.1	0.7	1.4	2.1	–0.1	–4.9	2.5	5.5	2.1	7.1	–1.8	19.7
1997	5.8	0.2	–4.6	5.3	6.2	4.0	8.0	–4.9	5.4	–3.4	4.2	1.9	30.5
1998	0.6	7.0	4.9	0.9	–2.3	3.6	–1.3	–15.1	6.5	7.8	6.1	6.2	25.1
1999	3.5	–3.3	3.7	4.2	–2.3	5.1	–3.2	–1.0	–2.8	6.5	2.5	6.0	19.5
2000	–4.2	–0.4	8.9	–3.3	–2.7	2.5	–1.8	7.4	–4.8	–1.2	–9.3	1.1	–8.8
2001	3.2	–9.5	–6.7	8.0	0.5	–2.4	–1.4	–6.2	–8.6	2.0	7.5	0.9	–13.6
2002	–1.4	–2.1	4.0	–5.8	–1.0	–7.5	–7.5	0.3	–10.9	8.1	5.7	–5.8	–22.9
2003	–2.5	–1.7	0.9	7.9	5.5	1.2	1.8	1.9	–1.2	5.7	1.0	4.6	27.5
2004	1.8	1.2	–1.5	–1.9	1.3	1.7	–3.6	0.3	1.1	1.5	4.1	3.5	9.5
2005	–2.6	2.0	–1.7	–2.0	3.4	0.3	3.8	–1.1	0.8	–1.9	3.5	0.01	4.4
2006	2.7	0.01	1.3	1.1	–3.2	0.003	0.1	2.2	2.3	3.3	1.9	1.1	13.3
2007	1.8	–1.9	0.9	4.1	3.4	–2.0	–3.2	1.2	3.7	1.6	–4.5	–0.8	3.9
2008	–6.1	–3.3	–0.8	5.0	1.6	–8.5	–1.3	1.2	–9.7	–17.6	–7.9	1.3	–39.0
2009	–8.3	–10.7	8.5	10.0	5.3	0.1	7.5	3.4	3.9	–2.3	5.6	2.3	25.5
2010	–3.7	3.1	6.0	1.8	–8.1	–5.7	6.8	–4.7	9.0	3.8	0.1	6.5	13.9
2011	2.3	3.3	0.1	2.9	–1.3	–1.9	–2.3	–6.0	–7.6	11.1	–0.5	0.7	–0.5
2012	4.8	4.1	3.0	–0.7	–6.4	3.7	1.1	2.2	2.4	–1.8	0.5	0.8	13.9
2013	5.3	1.1	3.7	1.7	2.0	–1.5	5.2	–3.0	3.3	4.3	2.6	2.5	30.4
2014	–3.3	4.5	0.5	0.4	2.1	2.1	–1.7	3.9	–1.9	2.3	2.4	–0.4	11.1
2015	–2.8	5.5	–1.4	0.6	1.1	–2.0	1.8	–6.2	–2.9	8.0	0.1	–2.0	–1.1
2016	–5.5	–0.3	6.8	0.4	1.5	0.1	3.7	–0.1	–0.1	–2.1	3.7	1.7	9.7
2017	1.9	3.6	–0.1	0.9	1.0	0.5	1.9	0.1	2.0	2.2	2.8	1.0	19.3
2018	5.4	–3.9	–2.4	0.2	2.3	0.5	3.3	3.2	0.2	–7.2	1.8	–9.3	–6.6
2019	8.2	3.2	1.6	3.9	–6.6	6.9	1.4	–2.0	1.6	2.0	3.6	2.7	28.9
2020	–0.01	–8.3	–13.4	13.1	5.1	2.1	5.7	7.2	–3.8	–2.5	11.6	4.1	18.9
2021	–0.9	2.8	3.7	5.3	0.3	2.4	2.0	2.8	–4.7	6.9	–1.5	3.9	24.8
2022	–5.7	–2.9	3.2	–9.0	–0.3	–8.5	9.2	–4.0	–9.4	7.9	5.2	–5.9	–20.4
2023	6.6	–2.5	3.0	1.1	0.3	6.6	3.3	–1.9	–4.8	–2.5	9.1	4.8	24.5
2024	1.3	5.2	3.1	–4.3	4.6	3.2	1.4	2.2	2.0	–0.8	6.3	–2.9	22.8
2025	3.1	–1.9	–5.9	–0.7	6.2	4.9	2.1	2.0	3.3	2.1	0.1	–0.1	15.9
2026	1.3	–0.6	–5.1	10.0									
TOTALS	**54.0**	**8.1**	**34.2**	**79.2**	**49.6**	**25.0**	**56.8**	**16.9**	**–38.1**	**45.3**	**103.0**	**57.1**	
AVG.	**1.1**	**0.2**	**0.7**	**1.7**	**1.1**	**0.5**	**1.2**	**0.4**	**–0.8**	**1.0**	**2.2**	**1.2**	
# Up	**30**	**27**	**31**	**33**	**33**	**30**	**27**	**29**	**23**	**29**	**36**	**34**	
# Down	**18**	**21**	**17**	**15**	**14**	**17**	**20**	**18**	**24**	**18**	**11**	**13**	

RUSSELL 1000 INDEX MONTHLY CLOSING PRICES SINCE 1979

	Jan	Feb	Mar	Apr	May	Jun	Jul	Aug	Sep	Oct	Nov	Dec
1979	53.76	51.88	54.97	55.15	53.92	56.25	56.86	60.04	60.05	55.78	58.65	59.87
1980	63.40	63.07	55.79	58.38	61.31	63.27	67.30	68.05	69.84	71.08	78.26	75.20
1981	71.75	72.49	75.21	73.77	73.90	73.01	72.92	68.42	64.06	67.54	70.23	67.93
1982	66.12	62.21	61.43	63.85	61.53	59.92	58.54	65.14	65.89	73.34	76.28	77.24
1983	79.75	81.45	84.06	90.04	89.89	93.18	90.18	90.65	91.85	89.69	91.50	90.38
1984	88.69	84.76	85.73	86.00	80.94	82.61	81.13	89.87	89.67	89.62	88.36	90.31
1985	97.31	98.38	98.03	97.72	103.02	104.65	103.78	102.76	98.75	103.16	109.91	114.39
1986	115.39	123.71	130.07	128.44	134.82	136.75	128.74	137.43	125.70	132.11	133.97	130.00
1987	146.48	152.29	155.20	152.39	152.94	159.84	166.57	172.95	168.83	131.89	121.28	130.02
1988	135.55	141.54	137.45	138.37	138.66	145.31	143.99	139.26	144.68	147.55	144.59	146.99
1989	156.93	152.98	155.99	163.63	169.85	168.49	182.27	185.33	184.40	179.17	181.85	185.11
1990	171.44	173.43	177.28	172.32	187.66	186.29	184.32	166.69	157.83	156.62	166.69	171.22
1991	179.00	191.34	196.15	195.94	203.32	193.78	202.67	207.18	204.02	206.96	198.46	220.61
1992	217.52	219.50	214.29	219.13	219.71	215.60	224.37	218.86	221.15	222.65	230.44	233.59
1993	235.25	236.67	241.80	235.13	240.80	241.78	240.78	249.20	247.95	250.97	246.70	250.71
1994	258.08	250.52	239.19	241.71	244.13	237.11	244.44	254.04	247.49	251.62	241.82	244.65
1995	250.52	260.08	266.11	272.81	282.48	289.29	299.98	301.40	313.28	311.37	324.36	328.89
1996	338.97	342.56	345.01	349.84	357.35	357.10	339.44	347.79	366.77	374.38	401.05	393.75
1997	416.77	417.46	398.19	419.15	445.06	462.95	499.89	475.33	500.78	483.86	504.25	513.79
1998	517.02	553.14	580.31	585.46	572.16	592.57	584.97	496.66	529.11	570.63	605.31	642.87
1999	665.64	643.67	667.49	695.25	679.10	713.61	690.51	683.27	663.83	707.19	724.66	767.97
2000	736.08	733.04	797.99	771.58	750.98	769.68	755.57	811.17	772.60	763.06	692.40	700.09
2001	722.55	654.25	610.36	658.90	662.39	646.64	637.43	597.67	546.46	557.29	599.32	604.94
2002	596.66	583.88	607.35	572.04	566.18	523.72	484.39	486.08	433.22	468.51	495.00	466.18
2003	454.30	446.37	450.35	486.09	512.92	518.94	528.53	538.40	532.15	562.51	568.32	594.56
2004	605.21	612.58	603.42	591.83	599.40	609.31	587.21	589.09	595.66	604.51	629.26	650.99
2005	633.99	646.93	635.78	623.32	644.28	645.92	670.26	663.13	668.53	656.09	679.35	679.42
2006	697.79	697.83	706.74	714.37	691.78	691.80	692.59	707.55	723.48	747.30	761.43	770.08
2007	784.11	768.92	775.97	807.82	835.14	818.17	792.11	801.22	830.59	844.20	806.44	799.82
2008	750.97	726.42	720.32	756.03	768.28	703.22	694.07	702.17	634.08	522.47	481.43	487.77
2009	447.32	399.61	433.67	476.84	501.95	502.27	539.88	558.21	579.97	566.50	598.41	612.01
2010	589.41	607.45	643.79	655.06	601.79	567.37	606.09	577.68	629.78	653.57	654.24	696.90
2011	712.97	736.24	737.07	758.45	748.75	734.48	717.77	674.79	623.45	692.41	688.77	693.36
2012	726.33	756.42	778.92	773.50	724.12	750.61	758.60	775.07	793.74	779.35	783.37	789.90
2013	831.74	840.97	872.11	886.89	904.44	890.67	937.16	909.28	939.50	979.68	1004.97	1030.36
2014	996.48	1041.36	1046.42	1050.20	1071.96	1094.59	1075.60	1117.71	1096.43	1121.98	1148.90	1144.37
2015	1111.85	1173.46	1156.95	1164.03	1176.67	1152.64	1173.55	1100.51	1068.46	1153.55	1154.66	1131.88
2016	1069.78	1066.58	1138.84	1143.76	1160.95	1161.57	1204.43	1203.05	1202.25	1177.22	1220.68	1241.66
2017	1265.35	1311.34	1310.06	1322.44	1336.18	1343.52	1368.57	1369.61	1396.90	1427.43	1467.42	1481.81
2018	1561.66	1501.23	1464.87	1468.28	1502.31	1509.96	1560.36	1610.70	1614.54	1498.65	1525.56	1384.26
2019	1498.36	1545.73	1570.23	1631.87	1524.42	1629.02	1652.40	1618.61	1644.18	1677.08	1736.85	1784.21
2020	1784.03	1635.21	1416.49	1601.82	1682.75	1717.47	1815.99	1946.15	1872.70	1825.67	2037.36	2120.87
2021	2101.36	2159.32	2238.17	2356.67	2364.53	2421.14	2469.17	2537.31	2418.16	2583.83	2545.78	2645.91
2022	2494.64	2422.79	2501.29	2276.45	2269.07	2075.96	2267.10	2176.45	1972.29	2128.36	2239.12	2105.90
2023	2244.91	2187.75	2253.36	2279.16	2285.65	2436.93	2518.42	2470.02	2351.35	2292.38	2501.69	2622.14
2024	2656.44	2795.56	2881.91	2757.14	2882.75	2974.64	3015.48	3082.73	3145.06	3120.81	3317.38	3221.05
2025	3320.99	3259.07	3066.42	3045.67	3235.83	3395.61	3468.53	3537.39	3655.86	3732.15	3736.93	3732.87
2026	3781.24	3756.96	3565.72	3923.58								

RUSSELL 2000 INDEX MONTHLY PERCENT CHANGES SINCE 1979

	Jan	Feb	Mar	Apr	May	Jun	Jul	Aug	Sep	Oct	Nov	Dec	Year
1979	9.0	–3.2	9.7	2.3	–1.8	5.3	2.9	7.8	–0.7	–11.3	8.1	6.6	38.0
1980	8.2	–2.1	–18.5	6.0	8.0	4.0	11.0	6.5	2.9	3.9	7.0	–3.7	33.8
1981	–0.6	0.3	7.7	2.5	3.0	–2.5	–2.6	–8.0	–8.6	8.2	2.8	–2.0	–1.5
1982	–3.7	–5.3	–1.5	5.1	–3.2	–4.0	–1.7	7.5	3.6	14.1	8.8	1.1	20.7
1983	7.5	6.0	2.5	7.2	7.0	4.4	–3.0	–4.0	1.6	–7.0	5.0	–2.1	26.3
1984	–1.8	–5.9	0.4	–0.7	–5.4	2.6	–5.0	11.5	–1.0	–2.0	–2.9	1.4	–9.6
1985	13.1	2.4	–2.2	–1.4	3.4	1.0	2.7	–1.2	–6.2	3.6	6.8	4.2	28.0
1986	1.5	7.0	4.7	1.4	3.3	–0.2	–9.5	3.0	–6.3	3.9	–0.5	–3.1	4.0
1987	11.5	8.2	2.4	–3.0	–0.5	2.3	2.8	2.9	–2.0	–30.8	–5.5	7.8	–10.8
1988	4.0	8.7	4.4	2.0	–2.5	7.0	–0.9	–2.8	2.3	–1.2	–3.6	3.8	22.4
1989	4.4	0.5	2.2	4.3	4.2	–2.4	4.2	2.1	0.01	–6.0	0.4	0.1	14.2
1990	–8.9	2.9	3.7	–3.4	6.8	0.1	–4.5	–13.6	–9.2	–6.2	7.3	3.7	–21.5
1991	9.1	11.0	6.9	–0.2	4.5	–6.0	3.1	3.7	0.6	2.7	–4.7	7.7	43.7
1992	8.0	2.9	–3.5	–3.7	1.2	–5.0	3.2	3.1	2.2	3.1	7.5	3.4	16.4
1993	3.2	–2.5	3.1	–2.8	4.3	0.5	1.3	4.1	2.7	2.5	–3.4	3.3	17.0
1994	3.1	–0.4	–5.4	0.6	–1.3	–3.6	1.6	5.4	–0.5	–0.4	–4.2	2.5	–3.2
1995	–1.4	3.9	1.6	2.1	1.5	5.0	5.7	1.9	1.7	–4.6	4.2	2.4	26.2
1996	–0.2	3.0	1.8	5.3	3.9	–4.2	–8.8	5.7	3.7	–1.7	4.0	2.4	14.8
1997	1.9	–2.5	–4.9	0.1	11.0	4.1	4.6	2.2	7.2	–4.5	–0.8	1.7	20.5
1998	–1.6	7.4	4.1	0.5	–5.4	0.2	–8.2	–19.5	7.6	4.0	5.2	6.1	–3.4
1999	1.2	–8.2	1.4	8.8	1.4	4.3	–2.8	–3.8	–0.1	0.3	5.9	11.2	19.6
2000	–1.7	16.4	–6.7	–6.1	–5.9	8.6	–3.2	7.4	–3.1	–4.5	–10.4	8.4	–4.2
2001	5.1	–6.7	–5.0	7.7	2.3	3.3	–5.4	–3.3	–13.6	5.8	7.6	6.0	1.0
2002	–1.1	–2.8	7.9	0.8	–4.5	–5.1	–15.2	–0.4	–7.3	3.1	8.8	–5.7	–21.6
2003	–2.9	–3.1	1.1	9.4	10.6	1.7	6.2	4.5	–2.0	8.3	3.5	1.9	45.4
2004	4.3	0.8	0.8	–5.2	1.5	4.1	–6.8	–0.6	4.6	1.9	8.6	2.8	17.0
2005	–4.2	1.6	–3.0	–5.8	6.4	3.7	6.3	–1.9	0.2	–3.2	4.7	–0.6	3.3
2006	8.9	–0.3	4.7	–0.1	–5.7	0.5	–3.3	2.9	0.7	5.7	2.5	0.2	17.0
2007	1.6	–0.9	0.9	1.7	4.0	–1.6	–6.9	2.2	1.6	2.8	–7.3	–0.2	–2.7
2008	–6.9	–3.8	0.3	4.1	4.5	–7.8	3.6	3.5	–8.1	–20.9	–12.0	5.6	–34.8
2009	–11.2	–12.3	8.7	15.3	2.9	1.3	9.5	2.8	5.6	–6.9	3.0	7.9	25.2
2010	–3.7	4.4	8.0	5.6	–7.7	–7.9	6.8	–7.5	12.3	4.0	3.4	7.8	25.3
2011	–0.3	5.4	2.4	2.6	–2.0	–2.5	–3.7	–8.8	–11.4	15.0	–0.5	0.5	–5.5
2012	7.0	2.3	2.4	–1.6	–6.7	4.8	–1.4	3.2	3.1	–2.2	0.4	3.3	14.6
2013	6.2	1.0	4.4	–0.4	3.9	–0.7	6.9	–3.3	6.2	2.5	3.9	1.8	37.0
2014	–2.8	4.6	–0.8	–3.9	0.7	5.2	–6.1	4.8	–6.2	6.5	–0.02	2.7	3.5
2015	–3.3	5.8	1.6	–2.6	2.2	0.6	–1.2	–6.4	–5.1	5.6	3.1	–5.2	–5.7
2016	–8.8	–0.1	7.8	1.5	2.1	–0.2	5.9	1.6	0.9	–4.8	11.0	2.6	19.5
2017	0.3	1.8	–0.1	1.0	–2.2	3.3	0.7	–1.4	6.1	0.8	2.8	–0.6	13.1
2018	2.6	–4.0	1.1	0.8	5.9	0.6	1.7	4.2	–2.5	–10.9	1.4	–12.0	–12.2
2019	11.2	5.1	–2.3	3.3	–7.9	6.9	0.5	–5.1	1.9	2.6	4.0	2.7	23.7
2020	–3.3	–8.5	–21.9	13.7	6.4	3.4	2.7	5.5	–3.5	2.0	18.3	8.5	18.4
2021	5.0	6.1	0.9	2.1	0.1	1.8	–3.6	2.1	–3.1	4.2	–4.3	2.1	13.7
2022	–9.7	1.0	1.1	–10.0	–0.003	–8.4	10.4	–2.2	–9.7	10.9	2.2	–6.6	–21.6
2023	9.7	–1.8	–5.0	–1.9	–1.1	7.9	6.1	–5.2	–6.0	–6.9	8.8	12.1	15.1
2024	–3.9	5.5	3.4	–7.1	4.9	–1.1	10.1	–1.6	0.6	–1.5	10.8	–8.4	10.0
2025	2.6	–5.4	–7.0	–2.4	5.2	5.3	1.7	7.0	3.0	1.8	0.8	–0.7	11.3
2026	5.3	0.7	–5.2	12.2									
TOTALS	**73.5**	**46.9**	**21.1**	**67.7**	**63.3**	**40.6**	**18.4**	**12.3**	**–33.3**	**–7.7**	**122.5**	**95.4**	
AVG.	**1.5**	**1.0**	**0.4**	**1.4**	**1.3**	**0.9**	**0.4**	**0.3**	**–0.7**	**–0.2**	**2.6**	**2.0**	
# Up	**27**	**28**	**32**	**29**	**30**	**30**	**26**	**26**	**25**	**27**	**33**	**34**	
# Down	**21**	**20**	**16**	**19**	**17**	**17**	**21**	**21**	**22**	**20**	**14**	**13**	

RUSSELL 2000 INDEX MONTHLY CLOSING PRICES SINCE 1979

	Jan	Feb	Mar	Apr	May	Jun	Jul	Aug	Sep	Oct	Nov	Dec
1979	44.18	42.78	46.94	48.00	47.13	49.62	51.08	55.05	54.68	48.51	52.43	55.91
1980	60.50	59.22	48.27	51.18	55.26	57.47	63.81	67.97	69.94	72.64	77.70	74.80
1981	74.33	74.52	80.25	82.25	84.72	82.56	80.41	73.94	67.55	73.06	75.14	73.67
1982	70.96	67.21	66.21	69.59	67.39	64.67	63.59	68.38	70.84	80.86	87.96	88.90
1983	95.53	101.23	103.77	111.20	118.94	124.17	120.43	115.60	117.43	109.17	114.66	112.27
1984	110.21	103.72	104.10	103.34	97.75	100.30	95.25	106.21	105.17	103.07	100.11	101.49
1985	114.77	117.54	114.92	113.35	117.26	118.38	121.56	120.10	112.65	116.73	124.62	129.87
1986	131.78	141.00	147.63	149.66	154.61	154.23	139.65	143.83	134.73	139.95	139.26	135.00
1987	150.48	162.84	166.79	161.82	161.02	164.75	169.42	174.25	170.81	118.26	111.70	120.42
1988	125.24	136.10	142.15	145.01	141.37	151.30	149.89	145.74	149.08	147.25	142.01	147.37
1989	153.84	154.56	157.89	164.68	171.53	167.42	174.50	178.20	178.21	167.47	168.17	168.30
1990	153.27	157.72	163.63	158.09	168.91	169.04	161.51	139.52	126.70	118.83	127.50	132.16
1991	144.17	160.00	171.01	170.61	178.34	167.61	172.76	179.11	180.16	185.00	176.37	189.94
1992	205.16	211.15	203.69	196.25	198.52	188.64	194.74	188.79	192.92	198.90	213.81	221.01
1993	228.10	222.41	229.21	222.68	232.19	233.35	236.46	246.19	252.95	259.18	250.41	258.59
1994	266.52	265.53	251.06	252.55	249.28	240.29	244.06	257.32	256.12	255.02	244.25	250.36
1995	246.85	256.57	260.77	266.17	270.25	283.63	299.72	305.31	310.38	296.25	308.58	315.97
1996	315.38	324.93	330.77	348.28	361.85	346.61	316.00	333.88	346.39	340.57	354.11	362.61
1997	369.45	360.05	342.56	343.00	380.76	396.37	414.48	423.43	453.82	433.26	429.92	437.02
1998	430.05	461.83	480.68	482.89	456.62	457.39	419.75	337.95	363.59	378.16	397.75	421.96
1999	427.22	392.26	397.63	432.81	438.68	457.68	444.77	427.83	427.30	428.64	454.08	504.75
2000	496.23	577.71	539.09	506.25	476.18	517.23	500.64	537.89	521.37	497.68	445.94	483.53
2001	508.34	474.37	450.53	485.32	496.50	512.64	484.78	468.56	404.87	428.17	460.78	488.50
2002	483.10	469.36	506.46	510.67	487.47	462.64	392.42	390.96	362.27	373.50	406.35	383.09
2003	372.17	360.52	364.54	398.68	441.00	448.37	476.02	497.42	487.68	528.22	546.51	556.91
2004	580.76	585.56	590.31	559.80	568.28	591.52	551.29	547.93	572.94	583.79	633.77	651.57
2005	624.02	634.06	615.07	579.38	616.71	639.66	679.75	666.51	667.80	646.61	677.29	673.22
2006	733.20	730.64	765.14	764.54	721.01	724.67	700.56	720.53	725.59	766.84	786.12	787.66
2007	800.34	793.30	800.71	814.57	847.19	833.69	776.13	792.86	805.45	828.02	767.77	766.03
2008	713.30	686.18	687.97	716.18	748.28	689.66	714.52	739.50	679.58	537.52	473.14	499.45
2009	443.53	389.02	422.75	487.56	501.58	508.28	556.71	572.07	604.28	562.77	579.73	625.39
2010	602.04	628.56	678.64	716.60	661.61	609.49	650.89	602.06	676.14	703.35	727.01	783.65
2011	781.25	823.45	843.55	865.29	848.30	827.43	797.03	726.81	644.16	741.06	737.42	740.92
2012	792.82	810.94	830.30	816.88	761.82	798.49	786.94	812.09	837.45	818.73	821.92	849.35
2013	902.09	911.11	951.54	947.46	984.14	977.48	1045.26	1010.90	1073.79	1100.15	1142.89	1163.64
2014	1130.88	1183.03	1173.04	1126.86	1134.50	1192.96	1120.07	1174.35	1101.68	1173.51	1173.23	1204.70
2015	1165.39	1233.37	1252.77	1220.13	1246.53	1253.95	1238.68	1159.45	1100.69	1161.86	1198.11	1135.89
2016	1035.38	1033.90	1114.03	1130.84	1154.79	1151.92	1219.94	1239.91	1251.65	1191.39	1322.34	1357.13
2017	1361.82	1386.68	1385.92	1400.43	1370.21	1415.36	1425.14	1405.28	1490.86	1502.77	1544.14	1535.51
2018	1574.98	1512.45	1529.43	1541.88	1633.61	1643.07	1670.80	1740.75	1696.57	1511.41	1533.27	1348.56
2019	1499.42	1575.55	1539.74	1591.21	1465.49	1566.57	1574.61	1494.84	1523.37	1562.45	1624.50	1668.47
2020	1614.06	1476.43	1153.10	1310.66	1394.04	1441.37	1480.43	1561.88	1507.69	1538.48	1819.82	1974.86
2021	2073.64	2201.05	2220.52	2266.45	2268.97	2310.55	2226.25	2273.77	2204.37	2297.19	2198.91	2245.31
2022	2028.45	2048.09	2070.13	1864.10	1864.04	1707.99	1885.23	1844.12	1664.72	1846.86	1886.58	1761.25
2023	1931.95	1896.99	1802.48	1768.99	1749.65	1888.73	2003.18	1899.68	1785.10	1662.28	1809.02	2027.07
2024	1947.34	2054.84	2124.55	1973.91	2070.13	2047.69	2254.48	2217.63	2229.97	2196.65	2434.73	2230.16
2025	2287.69	2163.07	2011.91	1964.12	2066.29	2175.04	2211.65	2366.42	2436.48	2479.38	2500.43	2481.91
2026	2613.74	2632.36	2496.37	2799.91								

10 BEST DAYS BY PERCENT AND POINT

BY PERCENT CHANGE				BY POINT CHANGE			
DAY	CLOSE	PNT CHANGE	% CHANGE	DAY	CLOSE	PNT CHANGE	% CHANGE
DJIA 1901 to 1949							
3/15/33	62.10	8.26	15.3	10/30/29	258.47	28.40	12.3
10/6/31	99.34	12.86	14.9	11/14/29	217.28	18.59	9.4
10/30/29	258.47	28.40	12.3	10/5/29	341.36	16.19	5.0
9/21/32	75.16	7.67	11.4	10/31/29	273.51	15.04	5.8
8/3/32	58.22	5.06	9.5	10/6/31	99.34	12.86	14.9
2/11/32	78.60	6.80	9.5	11/15/29	228.73	11.45	5.3
11/14/29	217.28	18.59	9.4	6/19/30	228.97	10.13	4.6
12/18/31	80.69	6.90	9.4	9/5/39	148.12	10.03	7.3
2/13/32	85.82	7.22	9.2	11/22/28	290.34	9.81	3.5
5/6/32	59.01	4.91	9.1	10/1/30	214.14	9.24	4.5
DJIA 1950 to MAY 1, 2026							
3/24/2020	20704.91	2112.98	11.4	4/9/2025	40608.45	2962.86	7.9
10/13/2008	9387.61	936.42	11.1	3/24/2020	20704.91	2112.98	11.4
10/28/2008	9065.12	889.35	10.9	3/13/2020	23185.62	1985.00	9.4
10/21/1987	2027.85	186.84	10.2	4/6/2020	22679.99	1627.46	7.7
3/13/2020	23185.62	1985.00	9.4	11/6/2024	43729.93	1508.05	3.6
4/9/2025	40608.45	2962.86	7.9	3/26/2020	22552.17	1351.62	6.4
4/6/2020	22679.99	1627.46	7.7	4/8/2026	47909.92	1325.46	2.9
3/23/2009	7775.86	497.48	6.8	3/2/2020	26703.32	1293.96	5.1
11/13/2008	8835.25	552.59	6.7	2/6/2026	50115.67	1206.95	2.5
11/21/2008	8046.42	494.13	6.5	11/10/2022	33715.37	1201.43	3.7
S&P 500 1930 to MAY 1, 2026							
3/15/1933	6.81	0.97	16.6	4/9/2025	5456.90	474.13	9.5
10/6/1931	9.91	1.09	12.4	3/13/2020	2711.02	230.38	9.3
9/21/1932	8.52	0.90	11.8	3/24/2020	2447.33	209.93	9.4
10/13/2008	1003.35	104.13	11.6	11/10/2022	3956.37	207.80	5.5
10/28/2008	940.51	91.59	10.8	3/31/2026	6528.52	184.80	2.9
2/16/1935	10.00	0.94	10.4	5/12/2025	5844.19	184.28	3.3
8/17/1935	11.70	1.08	10.2	4/6/2020	2663.68	175.03	7.0
3/16/1935	9.05	0.82	10.0	4/8/2026	6782.81	165.96	2.5
9/12/1938	12.06	1.06	9.6	3/26/2020	2630.07	154.51	6.2
9/5/1939	12.64	1.11	9.6	11/6/2024	5929.04	146.28	2.5
NASDAQ 1971 to MAY 1, 2026							
1/3/2001	2616.69	324.83	14.2	4/9/2025	17124.97	1857.06	12.2
4/9/2025	17124.97	1857.06	12.2	3/31/2026	21590.63	795.99	3.8
10/13/2008	1844.25	194.74	11.8	5/12/2025	18708.34	779.42	4.4
12/5/2000	2889.80	274.05	10.5	11/10/2022	11114.15	760.98	7.4
10/28/2008	1649.47	143.57	9.5	3/13/2020	7874.88	673.08	9.4
3/13/2020	7874.88	673.08	9.4	4/8/2026	22635.00	617.15	2.8
4/5/2001	1785.00	146.20	8.9	11/24/2025	22872.01	598.93	2.7
4/18/2001	2079.44	156.22	8.1	3/24/2020	7417.86	557.19	8.1
3/24/2020	7417.86	557.19	8.1	11/6/2024	18983.47	544.30	3.0
5/30/2000	3459.48	254.37	7.9	4/6/2020	7913.24	540.16	7.3
RUSSELL 1000 1979 to MAY 1, 2026							
10/13/2008	542.98	56.75	11.7	4/9/2025	2980.19	260.20	9.6
10/28/2008	503.74	47.68	10.5	3/13/2020	1488.04	123.38	9.0
4/9/2025	2980.19	260.20	9.6	11/10/2022	2173.72	117.45	5.7
3/24/2020	1340.32	115.87	9.5	3/24/2020	1340.32	115.87	9.5
3/13/2020	1488.04	123.38	9.0	5/12/2025	3201.93	101.31	3.3
10/21/1987	135.85	11.15	8.9	3/31/2026	3565.72	101.22	2.9
4/6/2020	1455.56	96.55	7.1	4/6/2020	1455.56	96.55	7.1
3/23/2009	446.90	29.36	7.0	4/8/2026	3702.84	89.88	2.5
11/13/2008	489.83	31.99	7.0	11/6/2024	3248.37	83.93	2.7
11/24/2008	456.14	28.26	6.6	3/26/2020	1442.70	83.87	6.2
RUSSELL 2000 1979 to MAY 1, 2026							
3/24/2020	1096.54	94.14	9.4	4/9/2025	1913.16	152.45	8.7
10/13/2008	570.89	48.41	9.3	11/6/2024	2392.92	132.08	5.8
4/9/2025	1913.16	152.45	8.7	11/10/2022	1867.93	107.53	6.1
11/13/2008	491.23	38.43	8.5	3/24/2020	1096.54	94.14	9.4
3/23/2009	433.72	33.61	8.4	11/14/2023	1798.32	92.82	5.4
4/6/2020	1138.78	86.73	8.2	2/6/2026	2670.34	92.69	3.6
3/13/2020	1210.13	87.20	7.8	8/22/2025	2361.95	87.85	3.9
10/21/1987	130.65	9.26	7.6	3/13/2020	1210.13	87.20	7.8
10/28/2008	482.55	34.15	7.6	4/6/2020	1138.78	86.73	8.2
11/24/2008	436.80	30.26	7.4	3/31/2026	2496.37	82.36	3.4

10 WORST DAYS BY PERCENT AND POINT

BY PERCENT CHANGE				BY POINT CHANGE			
DAY	CLOSE	PNT CHANGE	% CHANGE	DAY	CLOSE	PNT CHANGE	% CHANGE

DJIA 1901 to 1949

DAY	CLOSE	PNT CHANGE	% CHANGE	DAY	CLOSE	PNT CHANGE	% CHANGE
10/28/1929	260.64	–38.33	–12.8	10/28/1929	260.64	–38.33	–12.8
10/29/1929	230.07	–30.57	–11.7	10/29/1929	230.07	–30.57	–11.7
11/6/1929	232.13	–25.55	–9.9	11/6/1929	232.13	–25.55	–9.9
8/12/1932	63.11	–5.79	–8.4	10/23/1929	305.85	–20.66	–6.3
3/14/1907	55.84	–5.05	–8.3	11/11/1929	220.39	–16.14	–6.8
7/21/1933	88.71	–7.55	–7.8	11/4/1929	257.68	–15.83	–5.8
10/18/1937	125.73	–10.57	–7.8	12/12/1929	243.14	–15.30	–5.9
2/1/1917	88.52	–6.91	–7.2	10/3/1929	329.95	–14.55	–4.2
10/5/1932	66.07	–5.09	–7.2	6/16/1930	230.05	–14.20	–5.8
9/24/1931	107.79	–8.20	–7.1	8/9/1929	337.99	–14.11	–4.0

DJIA 1950 to MAY 1, 2026

DAY	CLOSE	PNT CHANGE	% CHANGE	DAY	CLOSE	PNT CHANGE	% CHANGE
10/19/1987	1738.74	–508.00	–22.6	3/16/2020	20188.52	–2997.10	–12.9
3/16/2020	20188.52	–2997.10	–12.9	3/12/2020	21200.62	–2352.60	–10.0
3/12/2020	21200.62	–2352.60	–10.0	4/4/2025	38314.86	–2231.07	–5.5
10/26/1987	1793.93	–156.83	–8.0	3/9/2020	23851.02	–2013.76	–7.8
10/15/2008	8577.91	–733.08	–7.9	6/11/2020	25128.17	–1861.82	–6.9
3/9/2020	23851.02	–2013.76	–7.8	4/3/2025	40545.93	–1679.39	–4.0
12/1/2008	8149.09	–679.95	–7.7	3/11/2020	23553.22	–1464.94	–5.9
10/9/2008	8579.19	–678.91	–7.3	3/18/2020	19898.92	–1338.46	–6.3
10/27/1997	7161.15	–554.26	–7.2	9/13/2022	31104.97	–1276.37	–3.9
9/17/2001	8920.70	–684.81	–7.1	2/27/2020	25766.64	–1190.95	–4.4

S&P 500 1930 to MAY 1, 2026

DAY	CLOSE	PNT CHANGE	% CHANGE	DAY	CLOSE	PNT CHANGE	% CHANGE
10/19/1987	224.84	–57.86	–20.5	3/16/2020	2386.13	–324.89	–12.0
3/16/2020	2386.13	–324.89	–12.0	4/4/2025	5074.08	–322.44	–6.0
3/18/1935	8.14	–0.91	–10.1	4/3/2025	5396.52	–274.45	–4.8
4/16/1935	8.22	–0.91	–10.0	3/12/2020	2480.64	–260.74	–9.5
9/3/1946	15.00	–1.65	–9.9	3/9/2020	2746.56	–225.81	–7.6
3/12/2020	2480.64	–260.74	–9.5	4/10/2025	5268.05	–188.85	–3.5
10/18/1937	10.76	–1.10	–9.3	6/11/2020	3002.10	–188.04	–5.9
10/15/2008	907.84	–90.17	–9.0	10/10/2025	6552.51	–182.60	–2.7
12/1/2008	816.21	–80.03	–8.9	12/18/2024	5872.16	–178.45	–3.0
7/20/1933	10.57	–1.03	–8.9	9/13/2022	3932.69	–177.72	–4.3

NASDAQ 1971 to MAY 1, 2026

DAY	CLOSE	PNT CHANGE	% CHANGE	DAY	CLOSE	PNT CHANGE	% CHANGE
3/16/2020	6904.59	–970.29	–12.3	4/3/2025	16550.61	–1050.44	–6.0
10/19/1987	360.21	–46.12	–11.4	3/16/2020	6904.59	–970.29	–12.3
4/14/2000	3321.29	–355.49	–9.7	4/4/2025	15587.79	–962.82	–5.8
3/12/2020	7201.80	–750.25	–9.4	10/10/2025	22204.43	–820.20	–3.6
9/29/2008	1983.73	–199.61	–9.1	3/12/2020	7201.80	–750.25	–9.4
10/26/1987	298.90	–29.55	–9.0	4/10/2025	16387.31	–737.66	–4.3
10/20/1987	327.79	–32.42	–9.0	3/10/2025	17468.32	–727.90	–4.0
12/1/2008	1398.07	–137.50	–9.0	12/18/2024	19392.69	–716.37	–3.6
8/31/1998	1499.25	–140.43	–8.6	7/24/2024	17342.41	–654.94	–3.6
10/15/2008	1628.33	–150.68	–8.5	5/5/2022	12317.69	–647.17	–5.0

RUSSELL 1000 1979 to MAY 1, 2026

DAY	CLOSE	PNT CHANGE	% CHANGE	DAY	CLOSE	PNT CHANGE	% CHANGE
10/19/1987	121.04	–28.40	–19.0	3/16/2020	1306.51	–181.53	–12.2
3/16/2020	1306.51	–181.53	–12.2	4/4/2025	2772.12	–175.69	–6.0
3/12/2020	1364.66	–144.34	–9.6	4/3/2025	2947.81	–154.68	–5.0
10/15/2008	489.71	–49.11	–9.1	3/12/2020	1364.66	–144.34	–9.6
12/1/2008	437.75	–43.68	–9.1	3/9/2020	1514.77	–127.21	–7.8
9/29/2008	602.34	–57.35	–8.7	4/10/2025	2875.07	–105.12	–3.5
10/26/1987	119.45	–10.74	–8.3	6/11/2020	1660.70	–104.50	–5.9
3/9/2020	1514.77	–127.21	–7.8	12/18/2024	3217.90	–102.73	–3.1
10/9/2008	492.13	–40.05	–7.5	10/10/2025	3580.79	–99.74	–2.7
8/8/2011	617.28	–45.56	–6.9	9/13/2022	2167.18	–97.21	–4.3

RUSSELL 2000 1979 to MAY 1, 2026

DAY	CLOSE	PNT CHANGE	% CHANGE	DAY	CLOSE	PNT CHANGE	% CHANGE
3/16/2020	1037.42	–172.71	–14.3	3/16/2020	1037.42	–172.71	–14.3
10/19/1987	133.60	–19.14	–12.5	3/12/2020	1122.93	–141.37	–11.2
12/1/2008	417.07	–56.07	–11.9	3/9/2020	1313.44	–135.78	–9.4
3/12/2020	1122.93	–141.37	–11.2	4/3/2025	1910.55	–134.81	–6.6
3/18/2020	991.16	–115.35	–10.4	3/18/2020	991.16	–115.35	–10.4
10/15/2008	502.11	–52.54	–9.5	6/11/2020	1356.22	–111.17	–7.6
3/9/2020	1313.44	–135.78	–9.4	12/18/2024	2231.51	–102.57	–4.4
10/26/1987	110.33	–11.26	–9.3	3/11/2020	1264.30	–86.60	–6.4
10/20/1987	121.39	–12.21	–9.1	6/13/2022	1714.60	–85.68	–4.8
8/8/2011	650.96	–63.67	–8.9	11/26/2021	2245.94	–85.52	–3.7

10 BEST WEEKS BY PERCENT AND POINT

BY PERCENT CHANGE				BY POINT CHANGE			
WEEK ENDS	CLOSE	PNT CHANGE	% CHANGE	WEEK ENDS	CLOSE	PNT CHANGE	% CHANGE
DJIA 1901 to 1949							
8/6/1932	66.56	12.30	22.7	12/7/1929	263.46	24.51	10.3
6/25/1938	131.94	18.71	16.5	6/25/1938	131.94	18.71	16.5
2/13/1932	85.82	11.37	15.3	6/27/1931	156.93	17.97	12.9
4/22/1933	72.24	9.36	14.9	11/22/1929	245.74	17.01	7.4
10/10/1931	105.61	12.84	13.8	8/17/1929	360.70	15.86	4.6
7/30/1932	54.26	6.42	13.4	12/22/1928	285.94	15.22	5.6
6/27/1931	156.93	17.97	12.9	8/24/1929	375.44	14.74	4.1
9/24/1932	74.83	8.39	12.6	2/21/1929	310.06	14.21	4.8
8/27/1932	75.61	8.43	12.6	5/10/1930	272.01	13.70	5.3
3/18/1933	60.56	6.72	12.5	11/15/1930	186.68	13.54	7.8
DJIA 1950 to MAY 1, 2026							
3/27/2020	21636.78	2462.80	12.8	4/9/2020	23719.37	2666.84	12.7
4/9/2020	23719.37	2666.84	12.7	3/27/2020	21636.78	2462.80	12.8
10/11/1974	658.17	73.61	12.6	5/27/2022	33212.96	1951.06	6.2
10/31/2008	9325.01	946.06	11.3	11/8/2024	43988.99	1936.80	4.6
8/20/1982	869.29	81.24	10.3	4/11/2025	40212.71	1897.85	5.0
11/28/2008	8829.04	782.62	9.7	11/6/2020	28323.40	1821.80	6.9
3/13/2009	7223.98	597.04	9.0	3/18/2022	34754.93	1810.74	5.5
10/8/1982	986.85	79.11	8.7	10/28/2022	32861.80	1779.24	5.7
3/21/2003	8521.97	662.26	8.4	6/5/2020	27110.98	1727.87	6.8
8/3/1984	1202.08	87.46	7.9	11/3/2023	34061.32	1643.73	5.1
S&P 500 1930 to MAY 1, 2026							
8/6/1932	7.22	1.12	18.4	4/17/2026	7126.06	309.17	4.5
6/25/1938	11.39	1.72	17.8	4/9/2020	2789.82	301.17	12.1
7/30/1932	6.10	0.89	17.1	5/16/2025	5958.38	298.47	5.3
4/22/1933	7.75	1.09	16.4	4/11/2025	5363.36	289.28	5.7
10/11/1974	71.14	8.80	14.1	11/8/2024	5995.54	266.74	4.7
2/13/1932	8.80	1.08	14.0	3/18/2022	4463.12	258.81	6.2
9/24/1932	8.52	1.02	13.6	5/27/2022	4158.24	256.88	6.6
10/10/1931	10.64	1.27	13.6	11/28/2025	6849.09	246.10	3.7
8/27/1932	8.57	1.01	13.4	4/25/2025	5525.21	242.51	4.6
3/18/1933	6.61	0.77	13.2	11/3/2023	4358.34	240.97	5.9
NASDAQ 1971 to MAY 1, 2026							
6/2/2000	3813.38	608.27	19.0	4/17/2026	24468.48	1565.59	6.8
4/12/2001	1961.43	241.07	14.0	5/16/2025	19211.10	1282.18	7.2
11/28/2008	1535.57	151.22	10.9	4/11/2025	16724.46	1136.67	7.3
10/31/2008	1720.95	168.92	10.9	4/25/2025	17382.94	1096.49	6.7
3/13/2009	1431.50	137.65	10.6	11/28/2025	23365.69	1092.61	4.9
4/9/2020	8153.58	780.50	10.6	3/18/2022	13893.84	1050.03	8.2
4/20/2001	2163.41	201.98	10.3	11/8/2024	19286.78	1046.86	5.7
12/8/2000	2917.43	272.14	10.3	4/10/2026	22902.89	1023.71	4.7
4/20/2000	3643.88	322.59	9.7	9/13/2024	17683.98	993.15	6.0
10/11/1974	60.42	5.26	9.5	11/6/2020	11895.23	983.64	9.0
RUSSELL 1000 1979 to MAY 1, 2026							
4/9/2020	1530.05	171.04	12.6	4/9/2020	1530.05	171.04	12.6
11/28/2008	481.43	53.55	12.5	4/17/2026	3886.69	169.75	4.6
10/31/2008	522.47	50.94	10.8	5/16/2025	3263.57	162.95	5.3
3/13/2009	411.10	39.88	10.7	4/11/2025	2926.05	153.93	5.6
3/27/2020	1394.65	133.96	10.6	11/8/2024	3285.81	152.93	4.9
8/20/1982	61.51	4.83	8.5	3/18/2022	2466.14	146.57	6.3
6/2/2000	785.02	57.93	8.0	5/27/2022	2285.42	140.71	6.6
9/28/2001	546.46	38.48	7.6	11/28/2025	3736.93	137.45	3.8
10/16/1998	546.09	38.45	7.6	11/6/2020	1962.60	136.93	7.5
8/3/1984	87.43	6.13	7.5	3/27/2020	1394.65	133.96	10.6
RUSSELL 2000 1979 to MAY 1, 2026							
4/9/2020	1246.73	194.68	18.5	4/9/2020	1246.73	194.68	18.5
11/28/2008	473.14	66.60	16.4	11/8/2024	2399.64	189.51	8.6
10/31/2008	537.52	66.40	14.1	3/12/2021	2352.79	160.58	7.3
6/2/2000	513.03	55.66	12.2	2/5/2021	2233.33	159.69	7.7
3/13/2009	393.09	42.04	12.0	4/17/2026	2776.90	146.31	5.6
3/27/2020	1131.99	118.10	11.7	11/5/2021	2437.08	139.89	6.1
12/2/2011	735.02	68.86	10.3	11/28/2025	2500.43	130.84	5.5
11/11/2016	1282.38	118.94	10.2	11/3/2023	1760.70	123.76	7.6
10/14/2011	712.46	56.25	8.6	7/12/2024	2148.27	121.54	6.0
11/8/2024	2399.64	189.51	8.6	11/11/2016	1282.38	118.94	10.2

10 WORST WEEKS BY PERCENT AND POINT

BY PERCENT CHANGE WEEK ENDS	CLOSE	PNT CHANGE	% CHANGE	BY POINT CHANGE WEEK ENDS	CLOSE	PNT CHANGE	% CHANGE
DJIA 1901 to 1949							
7/22/1933	88.42	–17.68	–16.7	11/8/1929	236.53	–36.98	–13.5
5/18/1940	122.43	–22.42	–15.5	12/8/1928	257.33	–33.47	–11.5
10/8/1932	61.17	–10.92	–15.2	6/21/1930	215.30	–28.95	–11.9
10/3/1931	92.77	–14.59	–13.6	10/19/1929	323.87	–28.82	–8.2
11/8/1929	236.53	–36.98	–13.5	5/3/1930	258.31	–27.15	–9.5
9/17/1932	66.44	–10.10	–13.2	10/31/1929	273.51	–25.46	–8.5
10/21/1933	83.64	–11.95	–12.5	10/26/1929	298.97	–24.90	–7.7
12/12/1931	78.93	–11.21	–12.4	5/18/1940	122.43	–22.42	–15.5
5/8/1915	62.77	–8.74	–12.2	2/8/1929	301.53	–18.23	–5.7
6/21/1930	215.30	–28.95	–11.9	10/11/1930	193.05	–18.05	–8.6
DJIA 1950 to MAY 1, 2026							
10/10/2008	8451.19	–1874.19	–18.2	3/20/2020	19173.98	–4011.64	–17.3
3/20/2020	19173.98	–4011.64	–17.3	2/28/2020	25409.36	–3583.05	–12.4
9/21/2001	8235.81	–1369.70	–14.3	4/4/2025	38314.86	–3269.04	–7.9
10/23/1987	1950.76	–295.98	–13.2	3/13/2020	23185.62	–2679.16	–10.4
2/28/2020	25409.36	–3583.05	–12.4	10/10/2008	8451.19	–1874.19	–18.2
3/13/2020	23185.62	–2679.16	–10.4	10/30/2020	26501.60	–1833.97	–6.5
10/16/1987	2246.74	–235.47	–9.5	12/21/2018	22445.37	–1655.14	–6.9
4/4/2025	38314.86	–3269.04	–7.9	1/21/2022	34265.37	–1646.44	–4.6
10/13/1989	2569.26	–216.26	–7.8	6/10/2022	31392.79	–1506.91	–4.6
3/16/2001	9823.41	–821.21	–7.7	6/12/2020	25605.54	–1505.44	–5.6
S&P 500 1930 to MAY 1, 2026							
7/22/1933	9.71	–2.20	–18.5	4/4/2025	5074.08	–506.86	–9.1
10/10/2008	899.22	–200.01	–18.2	3/20/2020	2304.92	–406.10	–15.0
5/18/1940	9.75	–2.05	–17.4	2/28/2020	2954.22	–383.53	–11.5
10/8/1932	6.77	–1.38	–16.9	1/21/2022	4397.94	–264.91	–5.7
3/20/2020	2304.92	–406.10	–15.0	3/13/2020	2711.02	–261.35	–8.8
9/17/1932	7.50	–1.28	–14.6	9/6/2024	5408.42	–239.98	–4.3
10/21/1933	8.57	–1.31	–13.3	6/17/2022	3674.84	–226.02	–5.8
10/3/1931	9.37	–1.36	–12.7	6/10/2022	3900.86	–207.68	–5.1
10/23/1987	248.22	–34.48	–12.2	10/10/2008	899.22	–200.01	–18.2
12/12/1931	8.20	–1.13	–12.1	10/30/2020	3269.96	–195.43	–5.6
NASDAQ 1971 to MAY 1, 2026							
4/14/2000	3321.29	–1125.16	–25.3	4/4/2025	15587.79	–1735.20	–10.0
10/23/1987	328.45	–77.88	–19.2	4/14/2000	3321.29	–1125.16	–25.3
9/21/2001	1423.19	–272.19	–16.1	1/21/2022	13768.92	–1124.83	–7.6
10/10/2008	1649.51	–297.88	–15.3	9/6/2024	16690.83	–1022.79	–5.8
3/20/2020	6879.52	–995.36	–12.6	2/28/2020	8567.37	–1009.22	–10.5
11/10/2000	3028.99	–422.59	–12.2	3/20/2020	6879.52	–995.36	–12.6
10/3/2008	1947.39	–235.95	–10.8	4/19/2024	15282.01	–893.08	–5.5
7/28/2000	3663.00	–431.45	–10.5	11/7/2025	23004.54	–720.42	–3.0
2/28/2020	8567.37	–1009.22	–10.5	1/7/2022	14935.90	–709.07	–4.5
4/4/2025	15587.79	–1735.20	–10.0	3/13/2020	7874.88	–700.74	–8.2
RUSSELL 1000 1979 to MAY 1, 2026							
10/10/2008	486.23	–108.31	–18.2	4/4/2025	2772.12	–279.44	–9.2
3/20/2020	1260.69	–227.35	–15.3	3/20/2020	1260.69	–227.35	–15.3
10/23/1987	130.19	–19.25	–12.9	2/28/2020	1635.21	–214.22	–11.6
9/21/2001	507.98	–67.59	–11.7	3/13/2020	1488.04	–153.94	–9.4
2/28/2020	1635.21	–214.22	–11.6	1/21/2022	2427.56	–149.96	–5.8
4/14/2000	715.20	–90.39	–11.2	9/6/2024	2950.08	–132.65	–4.3
10/3/2008	594.54	–65.15	–9.9	6/17/2022	2017.35	–126.66	–5.9
3/13/2020	1488.04	–153.94	–9.4	6/10/2022	2144.01	–114.51	–5.1
4/4/2025	2772.12	–279.44	–9.2	10/30/2020	1825.67	–110.60	–5.7
10/16/1987	149.44	–14.42	–8.8	3/10/2023	2120.53	–109.44	–4.9
RUSSELL 2000 1979 to MAY 1, 2026							
10/23/1987	121.59	–31.15	–20.4	3/13/2020	1210.13	–239.09	–16.5
3/13/2020	1210.13	–239.09	–16.5	2/28/2020	1476.43	–202.18	–12.0
4/14/2000	453.72	–89.27	–16.4	3/20/2020	1013.89	–196.24	–16.2
3/20/2020	1013.89	–196.24	–16.2	4/4/2025	1827.03	–196.24	–9.7
10/10/2008	522.48	–96.92	–15.7	1/21/2022	1987.92	–174.54	–8.1
9/21/2001	378.89	–61.84	–14.0	3/10/2023	1772.70	–155.56	–8.1
10/3/2008	619.40	–85.39	–12.1	8/2/2024	2109.31	–150.76	–6.7
2/28/2020	1476.43	–202.18	–12.0	6/17/2022	1665.69	–134.59	–7.5
11/21/2008	406.54	–49.98	–11.0	9/6/2024	2091.41	–126.22	–5.7
10/24/2008	471.12	–55.31	–10.5	6/12/2020	1387.68	–119.47	–7.9

10 BEST MONTHS BY PERCENT AND POINT

BY PERCENT CHANGE				BY POINT CHANGE			
MONTH	CLOSE	PNT CHANGE	% CHANGE	MONTH	CLOSE	PNT CHANGE	% CHANGE
DJIA 1901 to 1949							
Apr-1933	77.66	22.26	40.2	Nov-1928	293.38	41.22	16.3
Aug-1932	73.16	18.90	34.8	Jun-1929	333.79	36.38	12.2
Jul-1932	54.26	11.42	26.7	Aug-1929	380.33	32.63	9.4
Jun-1938	133.88	26.14	24.3	Jun-1938	133.88	26.14	24.3
Apr-1915	71.78	10.95	18.0	Aug-1928	240.41	24.41	11.3
Jun-1931	150.18	21.72	16.9	Apr-1933	77.66	22.26	40.2
Nov-1928	293.38	41.22	16.3	Feb-1931	189.66	22.11	13.2
Nov-1904	52.76	6.59	14.3	Jun-1931	150.18	21.72	16.9
May-1919	105.50	12.62	13.6	Aug-1932	73.16	18.90	34.8
Sep-1939	152.54	18.13	13.5	Jan-1930	267.14	18.66	7.5
DJIA 1950 to APRIL 2026							
Jan-1976	975.28	122.87	14.4	Oct-2022	32732.95	4007.44	14.0
Jan-1975	703.69	87.45	14.2	Apr-2026	49652.14	3310.63	7.1
Oct-2022	32732.95	4007.44	14.0	Nov-2024	44910.65	3147.19	7.5
Jan-1987	2158.04	262.09	13.8	Nov-2020	29638.64	3137.04	11.8
Nov-2020	29638.64	3137.04	11.8	Nov-2023	35950.89	2898.02	8.8
Aug-1982	901.31	92.71	11.5	Apr-2020	24345.72	2428.56	11.1
Apr-2020	24345.72	2428.56	11.1	Jul-2022	32845.13	2069.70	6.7
Oct-1982	991.72	95.47	10.7	Mar-2021	32981.55	2049.18	6.6
Oct-2002	8397.03	805.10	10.6	Aug-2020	28430.05	2001.73	7.6
Apr-1978	837.32	79.96	10.6	Jan-2025	44544.66	2000.44	4.7
S&P 500 1930 to APRIL 2026							
Apr-1933	8.32	2.47	42.2	Apr-2026	7209.01	680.49	10.4
Jul-1932	6.10	1.67	37.7	Nov-2023	4567.80	374.00	8.9
Aug-1932	8.39	2.29	37.5	Nov-2020	3621.63	351.67	10.8
Jun-1938	11.56	2.29	24.7	Jul-2022	4130.29	344.91	9.1
Sep-1939	13.02	1.84	16.5	May-2025	5911.69	342.63	6.2
Oct-1974	73.90	10.36	16.3	Apr-2020	2912.43	327.84	12.7
May-1933	9.64	1.32	15.9	Nov-2024	6032.38	326.93	5.7
Apr-1938	9.70	1.20	14.1	Oct-2021	4605.38	297.84	6.9
Jun-1931	14.83	1.81	13.9	Jun-2025	6204.95	293.26	5.0
Jan-1987	274.08	31.91	13.2	Oct-2022	3871.98	286.36	8.0
NASDAQ 1971 to APRIL 2026							
Dec-1999	4069.31	733.15	22.0	Apr-2026	24892.31	3301.68	15.3
Feb-2000	4696.69	756.34	19.2	May-2025	19113.77	1667.43	9.6
Oct-1974	65.23	9.56	17.2	Nov-2023	14226.22	1374.98	10.7
Jan-1975	69.78	9.96	16.7	Jul-2022	12390.69	1361.95	12.4
Jun-2000	3966.11	565.20	16.6	Nov-2020	12198.74	1287.15	11.8
Apr-2020	8889.55	1189.45	15.5	Jun-2025	20369.73	1255.96	6.6
Apr-2026	24892.31	3301.68	15.3	Sep-2025	22660.01	1204.46	5.6
Apr-2001	2116.24	275.98	15.0	Apr-2020	8889.55	1189.45	15.5
Jan-1999	2505.89	313.20	14.3	Nov-2024	19218.17	1123.02	6.2
Nov-2001	1930.58	240.38	14.2	Jan-2023	11584.55	1118.07	10.7
RUSSELL 1000 1979 to APRIL 2026							
AApr-2020	1601.82	185.33	13.1	Apr-2026	3923.58	357.86	10.0
Jan-1987	146.48	16.48	12.7	Nov-2020	2037.36	211.69	11.6
Nov-2020	2037.36	211.69	11.6	Nov-2023	2501.69	209.31	9.1
Oct-1982	73.34	7.45	11.3	Nov-2024	3317.38	196.57	6.3
Aug-1982	65.14	6.60	11.3	Jul-2022	2267.10	191.14	9.2
Dec-1991	220.61	22.15	11.2	May-2025	3235.83	190.16	6.2
Oct-2011	692.41	68.96	11.1	Apr-2020	1601.82	185.33	13.1
Aug-1984	89.87	8.74	10.8	Oct-2021	2583.83	165.67	6.9
Nov-1980	78.26	7.18	10.1	Jun-2025	3395.61	159.78	4.9
Apr-2026	3923.58	357.86	10.0	Oct-2022	2128.36	156.07	7.9
RUSSELL 2000 1979 to APRIL 2026							
Nov-2020	1819.82	281.34	18.3	Apr-2026	2799.91	303.54	12.2
Feb-2000	577.71	81.48	16.4	Nov-2020	1819.82	281.34	18.3
Apr-2009	487.56	64.81	15.3	Nov-2024	2434.73	238.08	10.8
Oct-2011	741.06	96.90	15.0	Dec-2023	2027.07	218.05	12.1
Oct-1982	80.86	10.02	14.1	Jul-2024	2254.48	206.79	10.1
Apr-2020	1310.66	157.56	13.7	Oct-2022	1846.86	182.14	10.9
Jan-1985	114.77	13.28	13.1	Jul-2022	1885.23	177.24	10.4
Sep-2010	676.14	74.08	12.3	Jan-2023	1931.95	170.70	9.7
Apr-2026	2799.91	303.54	12.2	Apr-2020	1310.66	157.56	13.7
Dec-2023	2027.07	218.05	12.1	Dec-2020	1974.86	155.04	8.5

10 WORST MONTHS BY PERCENT AND POINT

BY PERCENT CHANGE				BY POINT CHANGE			
MONTH	CLOSE	PNT CHANGE	% CHANGE	MONTH	CLOSE	PNT CHANGE	% CHANGE
DJIA 1901 to 1949							
Sep-1931	96.61	−42.80	−30.7	Oct-1929	273.51	−69.94	−20.4
Mar-1938	98.95	−30.69	−23.7	Jun-1930	226.34	−48.73	−17.7
Apr-1932	56.11	−17.17	−23.4	Sep-1931	96.61	−42.80	−30.7
May-1940	116.22	−32.21	−21.7	Sep-1929	343.45	−36.88	−9.7
Oct-1929	273.51	−69.94	−20.4	Sep-1930	204.90	−35.52	−14.8
May-1932	44.74	−11.37	−20.3	Nov-1929	238.95	−34.56	−12.6
Jun-1930	226.34	−48.73	−17.7	May-1940	116.22	−32.21	−21.7
Dec-1931	77.90	−15.97	−17.0	Mar-1938	98.95	−30.69	−23.7
Feb-1933	51.39	−9.51	−15.6	Sep-1937	154.57	−22.84	−12.9
May-1931	128.46	−22.73	−15.0	May-1931	128.46	−22.73	−15.0
DJIA 1950 to APRIL 2026							
Oct-1987	1993.53	−602.75	−23.2	Mar-2020	21917.16	−3492.20	−13.7
Aug-1998	7539.07	−1344.22	−15.1	Feb-2020	25409.36	−2846.67	−10.1
Oct-2008	9325.01	−1525.65	−14.1	Sep-2022	28725.51	−2784.92	−8.8
Nov-1973	822.25	−134.33	−14.0	Mar-2026	46341.51	−2636.41	−5.4
Mar-2020	21917.16	−3492.20	−13.7	Dec-2024	42544.22	−2366.43	−5.3
Sep-2002	7591.93	−1071.57	−12.4	Jun-2022	30775.43	−2214.69	−6.7
Feb-2009	7062.93	−937.93	−11.7	Dec-2018	23327.46	−2211.00	−8.7
Sep-2001	8847.56	−1102.19	−11.1	Apr-2024	37815.92	−1991.45	−5.0
Sep-1974	607.87	−70.71	−10.4	Mar-2025	42001.76	−1839.15	−4.2
Aug-1974	678.58	−78.85	−10.4	May-2019	24815.04	−1777.87	−6.7
S&P 500 1930 to APRIL 2026							
Sep-1931	9.71	−4.15	−29.9	Apr-2022	4131.93	−398.48	−8.8
Mar-1938	8.50	−2.84	−25.0	Mar-2020	2584.59	−369.63	−12.5
May-1940	9.27	−2.92	−24.0	Sep-2022	3585.62	−369.38	−9.3
May-1932	4.47	−1.36	−23.3	Mar-2026	6528.52	−350.36	−5.1
Oct-1987	251.79	−70.04	−21.8	Jun-2022	3785.38	−346.77	−8.4
Apr-1932	5.83	−1.48	−20.2	Mar-2025	5611.85	−342.65	−5.8
Feb-1933	5.66	−1.28	−18.4	Feb-2020	2954.22	−271.30	−8.4
Oct-2008	968.75	−197.61	−16.9	Dec-2018	2506.85	−253.31	−9.2
Jun-1930	20.46	−4.03	−16.5	Jan-2022	4515.55	−250.63	−5.3
Aug-1998	957.28	−163.39	−14.6	Dec-2022	3839.50	−240.61	−5.9
NASDAQ 1971 to APRIL 2026							
Oct-1987	323.30	−120.99	−27.2	Apr-2022	12334.64	−1885.88	−13.3
Nov-2000	2597.93	−771.70	−22.9	Mar-2025	17299.29	−1547.99	−8.2
Feb-2001	2151.83	−620.90	−22.4	Jan-2022	14239.88	−1405.09	−9.0
Aug-1998	1499.25	−373.14	−19.9	Sep-2022	10575.62	−1240.58	−10.5
Oct-2008	1720.95	−370.93	−17.7	Mar-2026	21590.63	−1077.58	−4.8
Mar-1980	131.00	−27.03	−17.1	Jun-2022	11028.74	−1052.65	−8.7
Sep-2001	1498.80	−306.63	−17.0	Dec-2022	10466.48	−1001.52	−8.7
Oct-1978	111.12	−21.77	−16.4	Mar-2020	7700.10	−867.27	−10.1
Apr-2000	3860.66	−712.17	−15.6	Sep-2023	13219.32	−815.65	−5.8
Nov-1973	93.51	−16.66	−15.1	Sep-2021	14448.58	−810.66	−5.3
RUSSELL 1000 1979 to APRIL 2026							
Oct-1987	131.89	−36.94	−21.9	Apr-2022	2276.45	−224.84	−9.0
Oct-2008	522.47	−111.61	−17.6	Mar-2020	1416.49	−218.72	−13.4
Aug-1998	496.66	−88.31	−15.1	Sep-2022	1972.29	−204.16	−9.4
Mar-2020	1416.49	−218.72	−13.4	Jun-2022	2075.96	−193.11	−8.5
Mar-1980	55.79	−7.28	−11.5	Mar-2025	3066.42	−192.65	−5.9
Sep-2002	433.22	−52.86	−10.9	Mar-2026	3565.72	−191.24	−5.1
Feb-2009	399.61	−47.71	−10.7	Jan-2022	2494.64	−151.27	−5.7
Sep-2008	634.08	−68.09	−9.7	Feb-2020	1635.21	−148.82	−8.3
Aug-1990	166.69	−17.63	−9.6	Dec-2018	1384.26	−141.30	−9.3
Feb-2001	654.25	−68.30	−9.5	Dec-2022	2105.90	−133.22	−5.9
RUSSELL 2000 1979 to APRIL 2026							
Oct-1987	118.26	−52.55	−30.8	Mar-2020	1153.10	−323.33	−21.9
Mar-2020	1153.10	−323.33	−21.9	Jan-2022	2028.45	−216.86	−9.7
Oct-2008	537.52	−142.06	−20.9	Apr-2022	1864.10	−206.03	−10.0
Aug-1998	337.95	−81.80	−19.5	Dec-2024	2230.16	−204.57	−8.4
Mar-1980	48.27	−10.95	−18.5	Oct-2018	1511.41	−185.16	−10.9
Jul-2002	392.42	−70.22	−15.2	Dec-2018	1348.56	−184.71	−12.0
Aug-1990	139.52	−21.99	−13.6	Sep-2022	1664.72	−179.40	−9.7
Sep-2001	404.87	−63.69	−13.6	Jun-2022	1707.99	−156.05	−8.4
Feb-2009	389.02	−54.51	−12.3	Mar-2025	2011.91	−151.16	−7.0
Dec-2018	1348.56	−184.71	−12.0	Apr-2024	1973.91	−150.64	−7.1

10 BEST QUARTERS BY PERCENT AND POINT

BY PERCENT CHANGE				BY POINT CHANGE			
QUARTER	CLOSE	PNT CHANGE	% CHANGE	QUARTER	CLOSE	PNT CHANGE	% CHANGE
DJIA 1901 to 1949							
Jun-1933	98.14	42.74	77.1	Dec-1928	300.00	60.57	25.3
Sep-1932	71.56	28.72	67.0	Jun-1933	98.14	42.74	77.1
Jun-1938	133.88	34.93	35.3	Mar-1930	286.10	37.62	15.1
Sep-1915	90.58	20.52	29.3	Jun-1938	133.88	34.93	35.3
Dec-1928	300.00	60.57	25.3	Sep-1927	197.59	31.36	18.9
Dec-1904	50.99	8.80	20.9	Sep-1928	239.43	28.88	13.7
Jun-1919	106.98	18.13	20.4	Sep-1932	71.56	28.72	67.0
Sep-1927	197.59	31.36	18.9	Jun-1929	333.79	24.94	8.1
Dec-1905	70.47	10.47	17.4	Sep-1939	152.54	21.91	16.8
Jun-1935	118.21	17.40	17.3	Sep-1915	90.58	20.52	29.3
DJIA 1950 to MARCH 2026							
Mar-1975	768.15	151.91	24.7	Dec-2022	33147.25	4421.74	15.4
Mar-1987	2304.69	408.74	21.6	Dec-2023	37689.54	4182.04	12.5
Jun-2020	25812.88	3895.72	17.8	Jun-2020	25812.88	3895.72	17.8
Mar-1986	1818.61	271.94	17.6	Sep-2024	42330.15	3211.29	8.2
Mar-1976	999.45	147.04	17.3	Dec-2020	30606.48	2824.78	10.2
Dec-1998	9181.43	1338.81	17.1	Mar-2019	25928.68	2601.22	11.2
Dec-1982	1046.54	150.29	16.8	Dec-2021	36338.30	2494.38	7.4
Jun-1997	7672.79	1089.31	16.6	Mar-2021	32981.55	2375.07	7.8
Dec-1985	1546.67	218.04	16.4	Dec-2017	24719.22	2314.13	10.3
Dec-2022	33147.25	4421.74	15.4	Sep-2025	46397.89	2303.12	5.2
S&P 500 1930 to MARCH 2026							
Jun-1933	10.91	5.06	86.5	Jun-2025	6204.95	593.10	10.6
Sep-1932	8.08	3.65	82.4	Jun-2020	3100.29	515.70	20.0
Jun-1938	11.56	3.06	36.0	Mar-2024	5254.35	484.52	10.2
Mar-1975	83.36	14.80	21.6	Sep-2025	6688.46	483.51	7.8
Dec-1998	1229.23	212.22	20.9	Dec-2023	4769.83	481.78	11.2
Jun-1935	10.23	1.76	20.8	Dec-2021	4766.18	458.64	10.7
Mar-1987	291.70	49.53	20.5	Dec-2020	3756.07	393.07	11.7
Jun-2020	3100.29	515.70	20.0	Jun-2023	4450.38	341.07	8.3
Sep-1939	13.02	2.16	19.9	Mar-2019	2834.40	327.55	13.1
Mar-1943	11.58	1.81	18.5	Jun-2021	4297.50	324.61	8.2
NASDAQ 1971 to MARCH 2026							
Dec-1999	4069.31	1323.15	48.2	Jun-2025	20369.73	3070.44	17.8
Jun-2020	10058.77	2358.67	30.6	Jun-2020	10058.77	2358.67	30.6
Dec-2001	1950.40	451.60	30.1	Sep-2025	22660.01	2290.28	11.2
Dec-1998	2192.69	498.85	29.5	Dec-2023	15011.35	1792.03	13.6
Mar-1991	482.30	108.46	29.0	Mar-2023	12221.91	1755.43	16.8
Mar-1975	75.66	15.84	26.5	Dec-2020	12888.28	1720.77	15.4
Dec-1982	232.41	44.76	23.9	Jun-2023	13787.92	1566.01	12.8
Mar-1987	430.05	80.72	23.1	Mar-2024	16379.46	1368.11	9.1
Jun-2003	1622.80	281.63	21.0	Jun-2024	17732.60	1353.14	8.3
Jun-1980	157.78	26.78	20.4	Dec-1999	4069.31	1323.15	48.2
RUSSELL 1000 1979 to MARCH 2026							
Dec-1998	642.87	113.76	21.5	Jun-2025	3395.61	329.19	10.7
Jun-2020	1717.47	300.98	21.3	Jun-2020	1717.47	300.98	21.3
Mar-1987	155.20	25.20	19.4	Dec-2023	2622.14	270.79	11.5
Dec-1982	77.24	11.35	17.2	Sep-2025	3655.86	260.25	7.7
Jun-1997	462.95	64.76	16.3	Mar-2024	2881.91	259.77	9.9
Dec-1985	114.39	15.64	15.8	Dec-2020	2120.87	248.17	13.3
Jun-2009	502.27	68.60	15.8	Dec-2021	2645.91	227.75	9.4
Dec-1999	767.97	104.14	15.7	Mar-2019	1570.23	185.97	13.4
Sep-2009	579.97	77.70	15.5	Jun-2023	2436.93	183.57	8.2
Jun-2003	518.94	68.59	15.2	Jun-2021	2421.14	182.97	8.2
RUSSELL 2000 1979 to MARCH 2026							
Dec-2020	1974.86	467.17	31.0	Dec-2020	1974.86	467.17	31.0
Mar-1991	171.01	38.85	29.4	Jun-2020	1441.37	288.27	25.0
Dec-1982	88.90	18.06	25.5	Sep-2025	2436.48	261.44	12.0
Jun-2020	1441.37	288.27	25.0	Mar-2021	2220.52	245.66	12.4
Mar-1987	166.79	31.79	23.6	Dec-2023	2027.07	241.97	13.6
Jun-2003	448.37	83.83	23.0	Mar-2019	1539.74	191.18	14.2
Sep-1980	69.94	12.47	21.7	Sep-2024	2229.97	182.28	8.9
Dec-2001	488.50	83.63	20.7	Jun-2025	2175.04	163.13	8.1
Jun-2009	508.28	85.53	20.2	Dec-2019	1668.47	145.10	9.5
Jun-1983	124.17	20.40	19.7	Jun-2018	1643.07	113.64	7.4

10 WORST QUARTERS BY PERCENT AND POINT

BY PERCENT CHANGE				BY POINT CHANGE			
QUARTER	CLOSE	PNT CHANGE	% CHANGE	QUARTER	CLOSE	PNT CHANGE	% CHANGE
DJIA 1901 to 1949							
Jun-1932	42.84	–30.44	–41.5	Dec-1929	248.48	–94.97	–27.7
Sep-1931	96.61	–53.57	–35.7	Jun-1930	226.34	–59.76	–20.9
Dec-1929	248.48	–94.97	–27.7	Sep-1931	96.61	–53.57	–35.7
Sep-1903	33.55	–9.73	–22.5	Dec-1930	164.58	–40.32	–19.7
Dec-1937	120.85	–33.72	–21.8	Dec-1937	120.85	–33.72	–21.8
Jun-1930	226.34	–59.76	–20.9	Sep-1946	172.42	–33.20	–16.1
Dec-1930	164.58	–40.32	–19.7	Jun-1932	42.84	–30.44	–41.5
Dec-1931	77.90	–18.71	–19.4	Jun-1940	121.87	–26.08	–17.6
Mar-1938	98.95	–21.90	–18.1	Mar-1939	131.84	–22.92	–14.8
Jun-1940	121.87	–26.08	–17.6	Jun-1931	150.18	–22.18	–12.9
DJIA 1950 to MARCH 2026							
Dec-1987	1938.83	–657.45	–25.3	Mar-2020	21917.16	–6621.28	–23.2
Sep-1974	607.87	–194.54	–24.2	Jun-2022	30775.43	–3902.92	–11.3
Mar-2020	21917.16	–6621.28	–23.2	Dec-2018	23327.46	–3130.85	–11.8
Jun-1962	561.28	–145.67	–20.6	Dec-2008	8776.39	–2074.27	–19.1
Dec-2008	8776.39	–2074.27	–19.1	Sep-2022	28725.51	–2049.92	–6.7
Sep-2002	7591.93	–1651.33	–17.9	Mar-2026	46341.51	–1721.78	–3.6
Sep-2001	8847.56	–1654.84	–15.8	Mar-2022	34678.35	–1659.95	–4.6
Sep-1990	2452.48	–428.21	–14.9	Sep-2001	8847.56	–1654.84	–15.8
Mar-2009	7608.92	–1167.47	–13.3	Sep-2002	7591.93	–1651.33	–17.9
Sep-1981	849.98	–126.90	–13.0	Sep-2011	10913.38	–1500.96	–12.1
S&P 500 1930 to MARCH 2026							
Jun-1932	4.43	–2.88	–39.4	Jun-2022	3785.38	–745.03	–16.4
Sep-1931	9.71	–5.12	–34.5	Mar-2020	2584.59	–646.19	–20.0
Sep-1974	63.54	–22.46	–26.1	Dec-2018	2506.85	–407.13	–14.0
Dec-1937	10.55	–3.21	–23.3	Mar-2026	6528.52	–316.98	–4.6
Dec-1987	247.08	–74.75	–23.2	Mar-2025	5611.85	–269.78	–4.6
Dec-2008	903.25	–263.11	–22.6	Dec-2008	903.25	–263.11	–22.6
Jun-1962	54.75	–14.80	–21.3	Mar-2022	4530.41	–235.77	–4.9
Mar-2020	2584.59	–646.19	–20.0	Sep-2022	3585.62	–199.76	–5.3
Mar-1938	8.50	–2.05	–19.4	Sep-2011	1131.42	–189.22	–14.3
Jun-1970	72.72	–16.91	–18.9	Sep-2001	1040.94	–183.48	–15.0
NASDAQ 1971 to MARCH 2026							
Dec-2000	2470.52	–1202.30	–32.7	Jun-2022	11028.74	–3191.78	–22.4
Sep-2001	1498.80	–661.74	–30.6	Mar-2025	17299.29	–2011.50	–10.4
Sep-1974	55.67	–20.29	–26.7	Mar-2026	21590.63	–1651.36	–7.1
Dec-1987	330.47	–113.82	–25.6	Mar-2022	14220.52	–1424.45	–9.1
Mar-2001	1840.26	–630.26	–25.5	Dec-2018	6635.28	–1411.07	–17.5
Sep-1990	344.51	–117.78	–25.5	Mar-2020	7700.10	–1272.50	–14.2
Dec-2008	1577.03	–514.85	–24.6	Dec-2000	2470.52	–1202.30	–32.7
Jun-2022	11028.74	–3191.78	–22.4	Sep-2001	1498.80	–661.74	–30.6
Jun-2002	1463.21	–382.14	–20.7	Mar-2001	1840.26	–630.26	–25.5
Sep-2002	1172.06	–291.15	–19.9	Jun-2000	3966.11	–606.72	–13.3
RUSSELL 1000 1979 to MARCH 2026							
Dec-2008	487.77	–146.31	–23.1	Jun-2022	2075.96	–425.33	–17.0
Dec-1987	130.02	–38.81	–23.0	Mar-2020	1416.49	–367.72	–20.6
Mar-2020	1416.49	–367.72	–20.6	Dec-2018	1384.26	–230.28	–14.3
Sep-2002	433.22	–90.50	–17.3	Mar-2026	3565.72	–167.15	–4.5
Jun-2022	2075.96	–425.33	–17.0	Mar-2025	3066.42	–154.63	–4.8
Sep-2001	546.46	–100.18	–15.5	Dec-2008	487.77	–146.31	–23.1
Sep-1990	157.83	–28.46	–15.3	Mar-2022	2501.29	–144.62	–5.5
Sep-2011	623.45	–111.03	–15.1	Sep-2011	623.45	–111.03	–15.1
Dec-2018	1384.26	–230.28	–14.3	Sep-2022	1972.29	–103.67	–5.0
Jun-2002	523.72	–83.63	–13.8	Sep-2001	546.46	–100.18	–15.5
RUSSELL 2000 1979 to MARCH 2026							
Mar-2020	1153.10	–515.37	–30.9	Mar-2020	1153.10	–515.37	–30.9
Dec-1987	120.42	–50.39	–29.5	Jun-2022	1707.99	–362.14	–17.5
Dec-2008	499.45	–180.13	–26.5	Dec-2018	1348.56	–348.01	–20.5
Sep-1990	126.70	–42.34	–25.0	Mar-2025	2011.91	–218.25	–9.8
Sep-2011	644.16	–183.27	–22.1	Sep-2011	644.16	–183.27	–22.1
Sep-2002	362.27	–100.37	–21.7	Dec-2008	499.45	–180.13	–26.5
Sep-2001	404.87	–107.77	–21.0	Mar-2022	2070.13	–175.18	–7.8
Dec-2018	1348.56	–348.01	–20.5	Sep-2015	1100.69	–153.26	–12.2
Sep-1998	363.59	–93.80	–20.5	Sep-2001	404.87	–107.77	–21.0
Sep-1981	67.55	–15.01	–18.2	Sep-2021	2204.37	–106.18	–4.6

10 BEST YEARS BY PERCENT AND POINT

BY PERCENT CHANGE				BY POINT CHANGE			
YEAR	CLOSE	PNT CHANGE	% CHANGE	YEAR	CLOSE	PNT CHANGE	% CHANGE
DJIA 1901 to 1949							
1915	99.15	44.57	81.7	1928	300.00	97.60	48.2
1933	99.90	39.97	66.7	1927	202.40	45.20	28.8
1928	300.00	97.60	48.2	1915	99.15	44.57	81.7
1908	63.11	20.07	46.6	1945	192.91	40.59	26.6
1904	50.99	15.01	41.7	1935	144.13	40.09	38.5
1935	144.13	40.09	38.5	1933	99.90	39.97	66.7
1905	70.47	19.48	38.2	1925	156.66	36.15	30.0
1919	107.23	25.03	30.5	1936	179.90	35.77	24.8
1925	156.66	36.15	30.0	1938	154.76	33.91	28.1
1927	202.40	45.20	28.8	1919	107.23	25.03	30.5
DJIA 1950 to 2025							
1954	404.39	123.49	44.0	2021	36338.30	5731.82	18.7
1975	852.41	236.17	38.3	2025	48063.29	5519.07	13.0
1958	583.65	147.96	34.0	2019	28538.44	5210.98	22.3
1995	5117.12	1282.68	33.5	2017	24719.22	4956.62	25.1
1985	1546.67	335.10	27.7	2024	42544.22	4854.68	12.9
1989	2753.20	584.63	27.0	2023	37689.54	4542.29	13.7
2013	16576.66	3472.52	26.5	2013	16576.66	3472.52	26.5
1996	6448.27	1331.15	26.0	2016	19762.60	2337.57	13.4
2003	10453.92	2112.29	25.3	1999	11497.12	2315.69	25.2
1999	11497.12	2315.69	25.2	2003	10453.92	2112.29	25.3
S&P 500 1930 to 2025							
1933	10.10	3.21	46.6	2024	5881.63	1111.80	23.3
1954	35.98	1.17	45.0	2021	4766.18	1010.11	26.9
1935	13.43	3.93	41.4	2025	6845.50	963.87	16.4
1958	55.21	15.22	38.1	2023	4769.83	930.33	24.2
1995	615.93	156.66	34.1	2019	3230.78	723.93	28.9
1975	90.19	21.63	31.5	2020	3756.07	525.29	16.3
1997	970.43	229.69	31.0	2017	2673.61	434.78	19.4
1945	17.36	4.08	30.7	2013	1848.36	422.17	29.6
2013	1848.36	422.17	29.6	1998	1229.23	258.80	26.7
2019	3230.78	723.93	28.9	1999	1469.25	240.02	19.5
NASDAQ 1971 to 2025							
1999	4069.31	1876.62	85.6	2023	15011.35	4544.87	43.4
1991	586.34	212.50	56.8	2024	19310.79	4299.44	28.6
2003	2003.37	667.86	50.0	2025	23241.99	3931.20	20.4
2009	2269.15	692.12	43.9	2020	12888.28	3915.68	43.6
2020	12888.28	3915.68	43.6	2021	15644.97	2756.69	21.4
2023	15011.35	4544.87	43.4	2019	8972.60	2337.32	35.2
1995	1052.13	300.17	39.9	1999	4069.31	1876.62	85.6
1998	2192.69	622.34	39.6	2017	6903.39	1520.27	28.2
2013	4176.59	1157.08	38.3	2013	4176.59	1157.08	38.3
2019	8972.60	2337.32	35.2	2009	2269.15	692.12	43.9
RUSSELL 1000 1979 to 2025							
1995	328.89	84.24	34.4	2024	3221.05	598.91	22.8
1997	513.79	120.04	30.5	2021	2645.91	525.04	24.8
2013	1030.36	240.46	30.4	2023	2622.14	516.24	24.5
2019	1784.21	399.95	28.9	2025	3732.87	511.82	15.9
1991	220.61	49.39	28.9	2019	1784.21	399.95	28.9
2003	594.56	128.38	27.5	2020	2120.87	336.66	18.9
1985	114.39	24.08	26.7	2013	1030.36	240.46	30.4
1989	185.11	38.12	25.9	2017	1481.81	240.15	19.3
1980	75.20	15.33	25.6	1998	642.87	129.08	25.1
2009	612.01	124.24	25.5	2003	594.56	128.38	27.5
RUSSELL 2000 1979 to 2025							
2003	556.91	173.82	45.4	2019	1668.47	319.91	23.7
1991	189.94	57.78	43.7	2013	1163.64	314.29	37.0
1979	55.91	15.39	38.0	2020	1974.86	306.39	18.4
2013	1163.64	314.29	37.0	2021	2245.31	270.45	13.7
1980	74.80	18.89	33.8	2023	2027.07	265.82	15.1
1985	129.87	28.38	28.0	2025	2481.91	251.75	11.3
1983	112.27	23.37	26.3	2016	1357.13	221.24	19.5
1995	315.97	65.61	26.2	2024	2230.16	203.09	10.0
2010	783.65	158.26	25.3	2017	1535.51	178.38	13.1
2009	625.39	125.94	25.2	2003	556.91	173.82	45.4

10 WORST YEARS BY PERCENT AND POINT

BY PERCENT CHANGE				BY POINT CHANGE			
YEAR	CLOSE	PNT CHANGE	% CHANGE	YEAR	CLOSE	PNT CHANGE	% CHANGE
DJIA 1901 to 1949							
1931	77.90	−86.68	−52.7	1931	77.90	−86.68	−52.7
1907	43.04	−26.08	−37.7	1930	164.58	−83.90	−33.8
1930	164.58	−83.90	−33.8	1937	120.85	−59.05	−32.8
1920	71.95	−35.28	−32.9	1929	248.48	−51.52	−17.2
1937	120.85	−59.05	−32.8	1920	71.95	−35.28	−32.9
1903	35.98	−11.12	−23.6	1907	43.04	−26.08	−37.7
1932	59.93	−17.97	−23.1	1917	74.38	−20.62	−21.7
1917	74.38	−20.62	−21.7	1941	110.96	−20.17	−15.4
1910	59.60	−12.96	−17.9	1940	131.13	−19.11	−12.7
1929	248.48	−51.52	−17.2	1932	59.93	−17.97	−23.1
DJIA 1950 to 2025							
2008	8776.39	−4488.43	−33.8	2008	8776.39	−4488.43	−33.8
1974	616.24	−234.62	−27.6	2022	33147.25	−3191.05	−8.8
1966	785.69	−183.57	−18.9	2002	8341.63	−1679.87	−16.8
1977	831.17	−173.48	−17.3	2018	23327.46	−1391.76	−5.6
2002	8341.63	−1679.87	−16.8	2001	10021.50	−765.35	−7.1
1973	850.86	−169.16	−16.6	2000	10786.85	−710.27	−6.2
1969	800.36	−143.39	−15.2	2015	17425.03	−398.04	−2.2
1957	435.69	−63.78	−12.8	1974	616.24	−234.62	−27.6
1962	652.10	−79.04	−10.8	1966	785.69	−183.57	−18.9
1960	615.89	−63.47	−9.3	1977	831.17	−173.48	−17.3
S&P 500 1930 to 2025							
1931	8.12	−7.22	−47.1	2022	3839.50	−926.68	−19.4
1937	10.55	−6.63	−38.6	2008	903.25	−565.11	−38.5
2008	903.25	−565.11	−38.5	2002	879.82	−268.26	−23.4
1974	68.56	−28.99	−29.7	2001	1148.08	−172.20	−13.0
1930	15.34	−6.11	−28.5	2018	2506.85	−166.76	−6.2
2002	879.82	−268.26	−23.4	2000	1320.28	−148.97	−10.1
2022	3839.50	−926.68	−19.4	1974	68.56	−28.99	−29.7
1941	8.69	−1.89	−17.9	1990	330.22	−23.18	−6.6
1973	97.55	−20.50	−17.4	1973	97.55	−20.50	−17.4
1940	10.58	−1.91	−15.3	2015	2043.94	−14.96	−0.7
NASDAQ 1971 to 2025							
2008	1577.03	−1075.25	−40.5	2022	10466.48	−5178.49	−33.1
2000	2470.52	−1598.79	−39.3	2000	2470.52	−1598.79	−39.3
1974	59.82	−32.37	−35.1	2008	1577.03	−1075.25	−40.5
2022	10466.48	−5178.49	−33.1	2002	1335.51	−614.89	−31.5
2002	1335.51	−614.89	−31.5	2001	1950.40	−520.12	−21.1
1973	92.19	−41.54	−31.1	2018	6635.28	−268.11	−3.9
2001	1950.40	−520.12	−21.1	1990	373.84	−80.98	−17.8
1990	373.84	−80.98	−17.8	2011	2605.15	−47.72	−1.8
1984	247.35	−31.25	−11.2	1973	92.19	−41.54	−31.1
1987	330.47	−18.86	−5.4	1974	59.82	−32.37	−35.1
RUSSELL 1000 1979 to 2025							
2008	487.77	−312.05	−39.0	2022	2105.90	−540.01	−20.4
2002	466.18	−138.76	−22.9	2008	487.77	−312.05	−39.0
2022	2105.90	−540.01	−20.4	2002	466.18	−138.76	−22.9
2001	604.94	−95.15	−13.6	2018	1384.26	−97.55	−6.6
1981	67.93	−7.27	−9.7	2001	604.94	−95.15	−13.6
2000	700.09	−67.88	−8.8	2000	700.09	−67.88	−8.8
1990	171.22	−13.89	−7.5	1990	171.22	−13.89	−7.5
2018	1384.26	−97.55	−6.6	2015	1131.88	−12.49	−1.1
1994	244.65	−6.06	−2.4	1981	67.93	−7.27	−9.7
2015	1131.88	−12.49	−1.1	1994	244.65	−6.06	−2.4
RUSSELL 2000 1979 to 2025							
2008	499.45	−266.58	−34.8	2022	1761.25	−484.06	−21.6
2002	383.09	−105.41	−21.6	2008	499.45	−266.58	−34.8
2022	1761.25	−484.06	−21.6	2018	1348.56	−186.95	−12.2
1990	132.16	−36.14	−21.5	2002	383.09	−105.41	−21.6
2018	1348.56	−186.95	−12.2	2015	1135.89	−68.81	−5.7
1987	120.42	−14.58	−10.8	2011	740.92	−42.73	−5.5
1984	101.49	−10.78	−9.6	1990	132.16	−36.14	−21.5
2015	1135.89	−68.81	−5.7	2007	766.03	−21.63	−2.7
2011	740.92	−42.73	−5.5	2000	483.53	−21.22	−4.2
2000	483.53	−21.22	−4.2	1998	421.96	−15.06	−3.4

STRATEGY PLANNING AND RECORD SECTION

CONTENTS

These forms are available at our website, www.stocktradersalmanac.com under "Forms" located at the bottom of the homepage.

PORTFOLIO AT START OF 2027

DATE ACQUIRED	NO. OF SHARES	SECURITY	PRICE	TOTAL COST	PAPER PROFITS	PAPER LOSSES

ADDITIONAL PURCHASES

DATE ACQUIRED	NO. OF SHARES	SECURITY	PRICE	TOTAL COST	REASON FOR PURCHASE PRIME OBJECTIVE, ETC.

ADDITIONAL PURCHASES

DATE ACQUIRED	NO. OF SHARES	SECURITY	PRICE	TOTAL COST	REASON FOR PURCHASE PRIME OBJECTIVE, ETC.

SHORT-TERM TRANSACTIONS

Pages 188–191 can accompany next year's income tax return (Schedule D). Enter transactions as completed to avoid last-minute pressures.

NO. OF SHARES	SECURITY	DATE ACQUIRED	DATE SOLD	SALE PRICE	COST	LOSS	GAIN
					TOTALS: Carry over to next page		

SHORT-TERM TRANSACTIONS *(continued)*

NO. OF SHARES	SECURITY	DATE ACQUIRED	DATE SOLD	SALE PRICE	COST	LOSS	GAIN
					TOTALS:		

LONG-TERM TRANSACTIONS

Pages 188–191 can accompany next year's income tax return (Schedule D). Enter transactions as completed to avoid last-minute pressures.

NO. OF SHARES	SECURITY	DATE ACQUIRED	DATE SOLD	SALE PRICE	COST	LOSS	GAIN
					TOTALS: Carry over to next page		

LONG-TERM TRANSACTIONS *(continued)*

NO. OF SHARES	SECURITY	DATE ACQUIRED	DATE SOLD	SALE PRICE	COST	LOSS	GAIN
					TOTALS:		

INTEREST/DIVIDENDS RECEIVED DURING 2027

SHARES	STOCK/BOND	FIRST QUARTER		SECOND QUARTER		THIRD QUARTER		FOURTH QUARTER	
		$		$		$		$	

BROKERAGE ACCOUNT DATA 2027

	MARGIN INTEREST	TRANSFER TAXES	CAPITAL ADDED	CAPITAL WITHDRAWN
JAN				
FEB				
MAR				
APR				
MAY				
JUN				
JUL				
AUG				
SEP				
OCT				
NOV				
DEC				

WEEKLY PORTFOLIO PRICE RECORD 2027 (FIRST HALF)

Place purchase price above stock name and weekly closes below.

	Week Ending	1	2	3	4	5	6	7	8	9	10
	STOCKS										
JANUARY	1										
	8										
	15										
	22										
	29										
FEBRUARY	5										
	12										
	19										
	26										
MARCH	5										
	12										
	19										
	26										
APRIL	2										
	9										
	16										
	23										
	30										
MAY	7										
	14										
	21										
	28										
JUNE	4										
	11										
	18										
	25										

WEEKLY PORTFOLIO PRICE RECORD 2027 (SECOND HALF)

Place purchase price above stock name and weekly closes below.

	STOCKS										
	Week Ending	1	2	3	4	5	6	7	8	9	10
JULY	2										
	9										
	16										
	23										
	30										
AUGUST	6										
	13										
	20										
	27										
SEPTEMBER	3										
	10										
	17										
	24										
OCTOBER	1										
	8										
	15										
	22										
	29										
NOVEMBER	5										
	12										
	19										
	26										
DECEMBER	3										
	10										
	17										
	24										
	31										

WEEKLY INDICATOR DATA 2027 (FIRST HALF)

	Week Ending	Dow Jones Industrial Average	Net Change for Week	Net Change on Friday	Net Change Next Monday	S&P or NASDAQ	NYSE Ad-vances	NYSE De-clines	New Highs	New Lows	CBOE Put/Call Ratio	90-Day Treas. Rate	Moody's AAA Rate
JANUARY	1												
	8												
	15												
	22												
	29												
FEBRUARY	5												
	12												
	19												
	26												
MARCH	5												
	12												
	19												
	26												
APRIL	2												
	9												
	16												
	23												
	30												
MAY	7												
	14												
	21												
	28												
JUNE	4												
	11												
	18												
	25												

WEEKLY INDICATOR DATA 2027 (SECOND HALF)

Month	Week Ending	Dow Jones Industrial Average	Net Change for Week	Net Change on Friday	Net Change Next Monday	S&P or NASDAQ	NYSE Ad-vances	NYSE De-clines	New Highs	New Lows	CBOE Put/Call Ratio	90-Day Treas. Rate	Moody's AAA Rate
JULY	2												
	9												
	16												
	23												
	30												
AUGUST	6												
	13												
	20												
	27												
SEPTEMBER	3												
	10												
	17												
	24												
OCTOBER	1												
	8												
	15												
	22												
	29												
NOVEMBER	5												
	12												
	19												
	26												
DECEMBER	3												
	10												
	17												
	24												
	31												

MONTHLY INDICATOR DATA 2027

	DJIA% Last 3 + 1st 2 Days	DJIA% 9th to 11th Trading Days	DJIA% Change Rest of Month	DJIA% Change Whole Month	% Change Your Stocks	Gross Domestic Product	Prime Rate	Trade Deficit $ Billion	CPI % Change	% Unemployment Rate
JAN										
FEB										
MAR										
APR										
MAY										
JUN										
JUL										
AUG										
SEP										
OCT										
NOV										
DEC										

INSTRUCTIONS:

Weekly Indicator Data (pages 195–196). Keeping data on several indicators may give you a better feel of the market. In addition to the closing Dow and its net change for the week, post the net change for Friday's Dow and also the following Monday's. A series of "down Fridays" followed by "down Mondays" often precedes a downswing (see page 78). Tracking either the S&P or NASDAQ composite, and advances and declines, will help prevent the Dow from misleading you. New highs and lows and put/call ratios (www.cboe.com) are also useful indicators. Many of these weekly figures appear in weekend papers or *Barron's* (https://www.barrons.com/market-data/market-lab). Data for the 90-day Treasury Rate and 30-year Treasury Rate are quite important for tracking short- and long-term interest rates. These figures are available from:

https://fred.stlouisfed.org/

Monthly Indicator Data. The purpose of the first three columns is to enable you to track the market's bullish bias near the end, beginning and middle of the month, which has been shifting lately (see pages 72, 147, and 148). Market direction, performance of your stocks, gross domestic product, prime rate, trade deficit, Consumer Price Index, and unemployment rate are worthwhile indicators to follow. Or, readers may wish to gauge other data.

PORTFOLIO AT END OF 2027

DATE ACQUIRED	NO. OF SHARES	SECURITY	PRICE	TOTAL COST	PAPER PROFITS	PAPER LOSSES

IF YOU DON'T PROFIT FROM YOUR INVESTMENT MISTAKES, SOMEONE ELSE WILL

No matter how much we may deny it, almost every successful person on Wall Street pays a great deal of attention to trading suggestions—especially when they come from "the right sources."

One of the hardest things to learn is to distinguish between good tips and bad ones. Usually, the best tips have a logical reason behind them, which accompanies the tip. Poor tips usually have no reason to support them.

The important thing to remember is that the market discounts. It does not review, it does not reflect. The Street's real interest in "tips," inside information, buying and selling suggestions, and everything else of this kind emanates from a desire to find out just what the market has on hand to discount. The process of finding out involves separating the wheat from the chaff—and there is plenty of chaff.

HOW TO MAKE USE OF STOCK "TIPS"

- The source should be **reliable**. (By listing all "tips" and suggestions on a Performance Record of Recommendations, such as the form below, and then periodically evaluating the outcomes, you will soon know the "batting average" of your sources.)
- The story should make sense. Would the merger violate antitrust laws? Are the presented Total Addressable Market (TAM), Serviceable Available Market (SAM), Serviceable Obtainable Market (SOM) numbers reasonable? How many years will it take to become profitable?
- The stock should not have had a recent sharp run-up. Otherwise, the story may already be discounted, and confirmation or denial in the press would most likely be accompanied by a sell-off in the stock.

PERFORMANCE RECORD OF RECOMMENDATIONS

STOCK RECOMMENDED	BY WHOM	DATE	PRICE	REASON FOR RECOMMENDATION	SUBSEQUENT ACTION OF STOCK

INDIVIDUAL RETIREMENT ACCOUNTS: MOST AWESOME INVESTMENT INCENTIVE EVER DEVISED

MAX IRA INVESTMENTS OF $7,500* A YEAR COMPOUNDED AT VARIOUS INTEREST RATES OF RETURN FOR DIFFERENT PERIODS

Annual Rate	5 Yrs	10 Yrs	15 Yrs	20 Yrs	25 Yrs	30 Yrs	35 Yrs	40 Yrs	45 Yrs	50 Yrs
1%	$38,640	$79,251	$121,934	$166,794	$213,942	$263,496	$315,577	$370,314	$427,844	$488,309
2%	39,811	83,765	132,295	185,875	245,032	310,346	382,458	462,075	549,979	647,032
3%	41,013	88,558	143,677	207,574	281,648	367,520	467,070	582,475	716,261	871,356
4%	42,247	93,648	156,184	232,269	324,838	437,463	574,487	741,199	944,029	1,190,803
5%	43,514	99,051	169,931	260,394	375,851	523,206	711,272	951,298	1,257,639	1,648,615
6%	44,815	104,787	185,044	292,445	436,173	628,513	885,906	1,230,358	1,691,311	2,308,170
7%	46,150	110,877	201,660	328,989	507,574	758,048	1,109,351	1,602,072	2,293,138	3,262,395
8%	47,519	117,341	219,932	370,672	592,158	917,594	1,395,766	2,098,358	3,130,696	4,647,538
9%	48,925	124,202	240,025	418,234	692,430	1,114,314	1,763,435	2,762,189	4,298,895	6,663,308
10%	50,367	131,484	262,123	472,519	811,363	1,357,076	2,235,951	3,651,389	5,930,965	9,602,245
11%	51,846	139,211	286,425	534,489	952,491	1,656,849	2,843,733	4,843,702	8,213,766	13,892,520
12%	53,364	147,409	313,150	605,241	1,120,005	2,027,195	3,625,973	6,443,568	11,409,132	20,160,153
13%	54,920	156,107	342,538	686,024	1,318,876	2,484,863	4,633,120	8,591,143	15,883,545	29,319,323
14%	56,516	165,334	374,853	778,263	1,554,996	3,050,528	5,930,047	11,474,315	22,149,329	42,703,158
15%	58,153	175,120	410,381	883,576	1,835,340	3,749,677	7,600,093	15,344,654	30,921,733	62,252,803
16%	59,831	185,497	449,438	1,003,804	2,168,162	4,613,712	9,750,203	20,538,588	43,197,883	90,790,144
17%	61,551	196,500	492,366	1,141,039	2,563,220	5,681,278	12,517,459	27,505,429	60,365,775	132,410,377
18%	63,315	208,164	539,543	1,297,658	3,032,041	6,999,890	16,077,367	36,844,435	84,354,457	193,045,879
19%	65,122	220,527	591,377	1,476,356	3,588,229	8,627,906	20,654,357	49,353,724	117,840,561	281,274,377
20%	66,974	233,628	648,316	1,680,192	4,247,830	10,636,934	26,535,070	66,094,721	164,531,789	409,474,717

** At Press Time - 2027 Contribution Limit will be indexed to inflation*

G. M. LOEB'S "BATTLE PLAN" FOR INVESTMENT SURVIVAL

LIFE IS CHANGE: Nothing can ever be the same a minute from now as it was a minute ago. Everything you own is changing in price and value. You can find that last price of an active security on the stock ticker, but you cannot find the next price anywhere. The value of your money is changing. Even the value of your home is changing, though no one walks in front of it with a sandwich board consistently posting the changes.

RECOGNIZE CHANGE: Your basic objective should be to profit from change. The art of investing is being able to recognize change and to adjust investment goals accordingly.

WRITE THINGS DOWN: You will score more investment success and avoid more investment failures if you write things down. Very few investors have the drive and inclination to do this.

KEEP A CHECKLIST: If you aim to improve your investment results, get into the habit of keeping a checklist on every issue you consider buying. Before making a commitment, it will pay you to write down the answers to at least some of the basic questions—How much am I investing in this company? How much do I think I can make? How much do I have to risk? How long do I expect to take to reach my goal?

HAVE A SINGLE RULING REASON: Above all, writing things down is the best way to find "the ruling reason." When all is said and done, there is invariably a single reason that stands out above all others, why a particular security transaction can be expected to show a profit. All too often, many relatively unimportant statistics are allowed to obscure this single important point.

Any one of a dozen factors may be the point of a particular purchase or sale. It could be a technical reason—an increase in earnings or dividend not yet discounted in the market price—a change of management—a promising new product—an expected improvement in the market's valuation of earnings—or many others. But, in any given case, one of these factors will almost certainly be more important than all the rest put together.

CLOSING OUT A COMMITMENT: If you have a loss, the solution is automatic, provided you decide what to do at the time you buy. Otherwise, the question divides itself into two parts. Are we in a bull or bear market? Few of us really know until it is too late. For the sake of the record, if you think it is a bear market, just put that consideration first and sell as much as your conviction suggests and your nature allows.

If you think it is a bull market, or at least a market where some stocks move up, some mark time and only a few decline, do not sell unless:

- ✓ You see a bear market ahead.
- ✓ You see trouble for a particular company in which you own shares.
- ✓ Time and circumstances have turned up a new and seemingly far better buy than the issue you like least in your list.
- ✓ Your shares stop going up and start going down.

A subsidiary question is, which stock to sell first? Two further observations may help:

- ✓ Do not sell solely because you think a stock is "overvalued."
- ✓ If you want to sell some of your stocks and not all, in most cases it is better to go against your emotional inclinations and sell first the issues with losses, small profits or none at all, the weakest, the most disappointing, and so on.

Mr. Loeb is the author of *The Battle for Investment Survival*, John Wiley & Sons.

G. M. LOEB'S INVESTMENT SURVIVAL CHECKLIST

OBJECTIVES AND RISKS				
Security		Price	Shares	Date
"Ruling reason" for commitment			Amount of commitment $________	
			% of my investment capital ________%	
Price objective	Est. time to achieve it	I will risk ________ points	Which would be $________	

TECHNICAL POSITION		
Price action of stock:		Dow Jones Industrial Average
❑ Hitting new highs	❑ In a trading range	
❑ Pausing in an uptrend	❑ Moving up from low ground	Trend of market
❑ Acting stronger than market	❑ ________	

SELECTED YARDSTICKS				
	Price Range		Earnings Per Share Actual or Projected	Price/Earnings Ratio Actual or Projected
	High	Low		
Current year				
Previous year				
Merger possibilities				Years for earnings to double in past
Comment on future				Years for market price to double in past

PERIODIC RECHECKS				
Date	Stock Price	DJIA	Comment	Action taken, if any

COMPLETED TRANSACTIONS		
Date closed	Period of time held	Profit or loss
Reason for profit or loss		

NOTES

NOTES